Batsford Chess Library

Beating the Sicilian 3

John Nunn and Joe Gallagher

An Owl Book
Henry Holt and Company
New York

Henry Holt and Company, Inc.
Publishers since 1866
115 West 18th Street
New York, New York 10011

Henry Holt® is a registered
trademark of Henry Holt and Company, Inc.

Published in Canada by Fitzhenry & Whiteside Ltd.,
195 Allstate Parkway, Markham, Ontario L3R 4T8.
First published in the United States in 1995 by
Henry Holt and Company, Inc.
Originally published in Great Britain in 1995 by
B. T. Batsford Ltd.

Library of Congress Catalog Card Number: 95-79226
ISBN 0-8050-4227-X (An Owl Book: pbk.)

First American Edition—1995

Printed in the United Kingdom
All first editions are printed on acid-free paper.∞

10   9   8   7   6   5   4   3   2   1

Editorial Panel: Mark Dvoretsky, John Nunn, Jon Speelman
General Adviser: Raymond Keene OBE
Managing Editor: Graham Burgess

Contents

Symbols

+	Check
++	Double check
#	Checkmate
$\pm$ ($\mp$)	Slight advantage to White (Black)
$\pm$ ($\mp$)	Clear advantage to White (Black)
+– (–+)	Winning advantage to White (Black)
=	Level position
∞	Unclear position
!	Good move
?	Bad move
!!	Outstanding move
??	Blunder
!?	Interesting move
?!	Dubious move
Ch	Championship
Cht	Team championship
tt	Team tournament
jr	Junior Event
wom	Women's event
rpd	Rapidplay
Wch	World Championship
Z	Zonal
IZ	Interzonal
Ct	Candidates
OL	Olympiad
Corr	Postal game
(D)	Diagram follows

Introduction

This third edition of *Beating the Sicilian* (BTS) does not need a lengthy introduction, since repertoire books are now a familiar concept. No one will be surprised to learn that the aim of this book is to provide a complete repertoire for White against the Sicilian, sufficiently detailed for most players to meet any line of the Sicilian with confidence.

As in *BTS2*, the lines we recommend are well-established main variations. Too many opening books advocate one or another sideline, claiming it to be no worse than the usual variations, and offering analysis which appears convincing – until you actually play the line over-the-board. Main lines of the type analysed in this book cannot be refuted, although the whims of fashion may lead to them becoming more or less popular as the years go by. The lines we recommend should remain valid for years to come (until *Beating the Sicilian 4?*) and readers may be confident that the effort put into studying them will earn a long-term reward.

We would like to use the rest of this introduction to describe the changes in the proposed repertoire.

The lines given against the Najdorf, Scheveningen, Classical and Pelikan variations are broadly the same as in *BTS2*, although all have been thoroughly updated to reflect both developments in the pre-existing theory and new ideas for Black which have arisen in the intervening years. Retaining the original recommendations was not done to minimise the authors' efforts, but because most players do not have the time to change their repertoires completely overnight. Even grandmasters normally change their openings incrementally, because of the considerable study required to grasp both the ideas behind openings and the concrete variations embodying those ideas.

The repertoire against the Dragon has substantially changed. The main line of the Yugoslav Attack has become just too vast for most players to study in depth, and anyone intending to venture into such tricky waters needs to have an intimate knowledge of all the hidden reefs. Therefore, we have switched from 9 ♗c4 to 9 0-0-0 d5 10 ♕e1, a promising but relatively undeveloped line.

The Kan and Maroczy Bind chapters include many new finesses, but the broad outline remains little changed.

Against the Taimanov, we have abandoned *BTS2's* 5 ♘b5, both because recent practical results have been disappointing for White, and because the stodgy positions which result don't fit in very well with the style of the rest of the repertoire. The current recommendation of 5 ♘c3 ♕c7 6 f4 has had a knock-on effect, in that lines also need to be provided against 5...d6 and 5...a6. This new material is also covered in Chapter 8, and those who have earlier editions of *BTS* are recommended to study this chapter carefully, in order not to be left stranded high and dry if Black does not play 5...♕c7.

The Sicilian Four Knights experienced a bit of a revival a few years ago, which resulted in some new developments. Although it has now faded again into semi-obscurity, readers should be aware that this chapter has altered substantially.

Perhaps the greatest change since BTS2 has been the rise of the Kalashnikov variation, the only really new Black system to have been developed in the Sicilian for the past 15 years. It may be that the popularity of this line has now passed its peak, but it is still relatively common and deserves careful attention. Chapter 10 has the details.

The remaining chapters constitute the Odds and Ends of the Sicilian. Maybe they are not really so bad, but the tide of fashion has turned firmly against them and new ideas are few and far between. Perhaps the one exception is the line 1 e4 c5 2 ♘f3 g6, covered in Chapter 14, which is often used for transpositional purposes; although still a little unusual, it appears to be increasing in popularity.

John Nunn
London
Joe Gallagher
Neuchâtel

1 Najdorf Variation

Of all the lines in the Sicilian which Black can adopt, the Najdorf has developed the largest body of theory. Whole books have been written on mere sub-variations of the Najdorf, for example the Polugaevsky Variation and the infamous Poisoned Pawn. The Najdorf starts with the moves 1 e4 c5 2 ♘f3 d6 3 d4 cxd4 4 ♘xd4 ♘f6 5 ♘c3 a6. Black's first aim is to play ...e5 without allowing the reply ♗b5+, while the secondary point is to prepare queenside expansion by ...b5. Some of White's systems against the Najdorf are specifically aimed at preventing ...e5, while others allow Black to play this move in the hope of exploiting the backward d-pawn later. Devising a counter which is viable in tournament play, while at the same time necessitating relatively slight book knowledge, has proved especially hard. These days the five major systems against the Najdorf, 6 ♗g5, 6 ♗e2, 6 ♗c4, 6 ♗e3 and 6 f4 seem to occur with about equal frequency. As in *BTS2* we have opted for 6 f4, a system which offers good attacking chances while retaining an element of solidity. Another advantage of 6 f4 is that as it has not been popular for as long as some of the other moves there is not quite as much to learn. In Games 1 to 4 we investigate the replies most commonly encountered in practice. The main division is between those lines involving an early ...e5 and those in which Black delays this move or omits it entirely. We will postpone consideration of the former lines until Games 3 and 4, and concentrate first on the alternatives to ...e5.

Game 1
J. Polgar – Pliester
Aruba 1992

1	e4	c5
2	♘f3	d6
3	d4	cxd4
4	♘xd4	♘f6
5	♘c3	a6
6	f4 *(D)*	

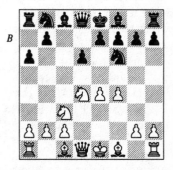

6 f4 is a flexible move; White gives little away regarding his piece deployment, and waits for Black's

reply before deciding where to put his bishops.

6 ...　　　　　　♘bd7

This move is designed to reserve the option of playing ...e5 under more favourable circumstances if White should develop his pieces to unsuitable squares. **6...♕c7** is covered in Game 2, but there are other playable moves:

1) **6...♘c6** 7 ♘xc6 bxc6 8 e5 ♘d7 (8...dxe5 9 ♕xd8+ ♔xd8 10 fxe5 ♘d5 11 ♗d2 is good for White) 9 ♗c4!? dxe5 10 0-0 e6 11 f5 ♗c5+ 12 ♔h1 and White has good attacking chances.

2) **6...g6** 7 ♗d3 and after a subsequent ...♕c7 or ...♘bd7 there will probably be a transposition into lines considered in Game 2.

3) **6...e6** (after this White may transpose into various lines of the Scheveningen, but since these lines do not form part of the repertoire recommended in this book, we suggest an independent alternative which promises good chances for White) **7 ♕f3** (White's advantage over similar lines is that his bishops are not committed, so he can force through g4-g5 very quickly) and now:

3a) **7...♘bd7 8 g4 h6** (8...e5 9 ♘f5!? and now 9...exf4?! 10 ♗xf4 ♘e5 11 ♗xe5 dxe5 12 g5 ♘d7 13 ♗c4 gives White a tremendous attack, whilst 9...g6 10 g5 gxf5 11 exf5 leaves Black under heavy pressure) **9 h4** (9 ♗e2 ♕b6 10 ♘b3 ♕c7 11 ♕g2 ♖b8 12 ♗e3 b5 13 g5 hxg5 14 fxg5 ♘h5 15 g6 ♘e5 was distinctly unclear in Short-Kasparov, Belgrade

1989) **9...e5 10 ♘b3 exf4 11 ♗xf4 ♘e5 12 ♗xe5 dxe5** and now:

3a1) **13 g5** hxg5 14 hxg5 ♖xh1 15 ♕xh1 ♘g4 16 ♘d5 is given as unclear by Kasparov.

3a2) **13 ♗h3** looks more testing to me. Now 13...g5 loses to 14 ♖f1 ♗e7 15 ♘d5 and 13...♗e6 14 g5 is at least slightly better for White. 13...h5 should be met by 14 ♖d1! (14 g5 ♗xh3 15 gxf6 ♗g4 16 fxg7 ♗xg7 17 ♕g3 0-0 is OK for Black) followed by g5. This leaves the critical line as **13...♗b4 14 g5** *(D)* and now:

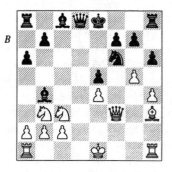

3a21) **14...♗xc3+** (14...♗xh3 is met by 15 gxf6!) 15 ♕xc3 (15 bxc3 ♘g8 looks OK for Black) 15...♘xe4 (15...hxg5 16 ♖d1! is very strong) 16 ♕xe5+ ♕e7 and the big question is whether White can get away with the cheeky 17 ♕xg7. I believe he can, although strong nerves are required. Here is a sample variation: 17...♘g3+ (17...♖f8 18 ♗xc8 favours White after 18...♖xc8 19 0-0-0 or 18...♘g3+ 19 ♔f2 ♘e4+ 20 ♔f3! ♖xc8 21 ♖he1) 18 ♔d2 ♕e2+ 19 ♔c3! ♕e3+ (19...♘e4+ 20 ♔d4!)

20 ♔b4 ♕b6+ (20...a5+ 21 ♔b5
♕e2+ 22 c4) 21 ♔a3 ♕d6+ 22 ♘c5!
♕xc5+ 23 b4 ♕e3+ 24 ♔b2 and the
checks have run out and although
Black is a piece up he is in trouble as
White threatens both ♕xh8 and ♖e1.
3a22) **14...hxg5 15 ♖d1!** (after
15 hxg5 ♗xc3+! both 16 ♕xc3
♘g4! and 16 bxc3 ♖xh3! 17 ♖xh3
♗xh3 18 gxf6 ♗e6 19 fxg7 ♕g5!
are OK for Black) **15...♕c7 16 hxg5**
and now:
3a221) **16...♗g4** 17 gxf6! is winning for White.
3a222) **16...♘h7** 17 ♗xc8 ♖xc8
18 ♖d2! and Black is caught in a fatal pin on the h-file.
3a223) **16...♘g4** and now the reply 17 ♗xg4 is not so good on account of 17...♗xc3+ 18 bxc3 ♖xh1+
19 ♕xh1 ♕xc3+ 20 ♖d2 ♗xg4!
with a winning attack for Black.
However, White does have the very
surprising **17 ♔e2!** (17 ♔d2 ♕d8+!
is unclear) which seems to win
material. A possible continuation is
17...♗xc3+ 18 bxc3 ♖h4 19 ♕g3
♕c4+ 20 ♔d2 ♖xh3 (20...♕xe4 21
♗g2!) 21 ♖xh3 ♕xe4 22 ♖h8+ ♔e7
23 ♖e1 (safest) 23...♕f5 24 ♔c1!
♕xg5+ 25 ♔b2 when the dominant
factor in assessing this position is the
safety of the respective kings.
3b) **7...♕c7 8 g4 b5** (8...♘c6 9
♘b3 b5 10 g5 ♘d7 11 ♗e3 b4 12
♘a4 ♗b7 13 ♕f2 g6 14 ♘b6 ♘xb6
15 ♗xb6 ♕e7 16 0-0-0 was pleasant
for White in Zso.Polgar-Pliester,
Aruba 1992, whilst 9 ♘xc6 bxc6 10
g5 ♘d7 11 b3!? also comes into consideration) **9 g5** and now:

3b1) **9...♘fd7** 10 a3 ♗b7 11 ♗e3
(11 ♗g2 g6 12 ♕f2 ♘c6 13 ♘de2 h6
14 f5 was also promising in Smys-
lov-Kamsky, New York Open 1989)
11...♘c6 12 ♗h3 b4 13 axb4 ♘xb4
14 0-0 ♘c5 15 ♖ad1 g6 16 ♖d2 ♗e7
17 ♖df2 with advantage to White,
Timman-Hjartarson, Belfort World
Cup 1988.
3b2) **9...b4** 10 ♘cb5 axb5 11
gxf6 gxf6 12 f5 (12 ♗xb5+ ♗d7 13
♗d3 is also quite good) 12...exf5?!
(12...e5 13 ♘xb5 ♕c6 14 c4 is given
as ± by Rogers) 13 ♗xb5+ ♗d7 14
♕xf5 ♘c6 (14...♖a5 15 ♕xf6 ♖g8
16 ♘e6! ♕b6 17 ♖f1 is winning) 15
♗xc6! ♗xc6, Rogers-Ehlvest, Biel
IZ 1993, and now Rogers gives 16
♖g1! ♗e7 17 ♘xc6 ♕xc6 18 ♗d2 or
18 ♗e3 as clearly better for White.
3c) **7...♕b6** is the main line, after
which White has:
3c1) **8 a3**, with the blunt point
8...♕xd4?? 9 ♗e3, was very fash-
ionable for a few years, but the
most recent evidence suggests that
Black has managed to overcome his
initial difficulties. For example, Al-
masi-Kasparov, Lyon 1994 continued **8...♘c6!** (8...♘bd7 9 ♗e2 g6 10
♗e3! is good for White as 10...♕xb2
loses to 11 ♔d2!) 9 ♘xc6 (9 ♘b3 is
quite often played, and may in fact
be better than 9 ♘xc6, but if you're
going to play this it seems more
logical to play 8 ♘b3; I can't believe, as some people do, that the
inclusion of a3 and ...♘c6 is in
White's favour) 9...bxc6 10 b3 ♗b7
11 ♗b2 d5! 12 0-0-0 ♕a5! 13 e5
♘d7 14 ♘a4 ♕c7 15 ♖e1? (15 c4 d4

16 ♗d3 c5 17 ♗e4 is given as unclear by Kasparov) 15...g6 16 g4 c5 17 ♗g2 ♖b8 18 ♕d1 c4 and Black was clearly on top.

3c2) **8 ♘b3 ♕c7 9 g4 b5 10 ♗d3** (10 g5 b4 is less good for White than the similar line above as his knight is now more passively placed on b3) **10...♗b7** (after 10...h6 11 h4, both 11...h5 12 g5 ♘g4 13 g6! ♗b7 14 gxf7+ ♕xf7 15 ♗d2 and 11...b4 12 ♘e2 h5 13 g5 ♘g4, Yudasin-Dorfman, USSR 1981, 14 ♗d2! ♕b6 15 g6! fxg6 16 e5 ♗b7 17 ♗xg6+ ♔d7 18 ♗e4 ♗xe4 19 ♕xe4 ♕f2+ 20 ♔d1 are good for White) **11 g5 ♘fd7 12 ♕h3** (perhaps the most accurate move order as Black has been doing OK after 12 ♗e3 ♘c5) **12...g6** *(D)* (White was threatening ...g6) and now there are a couple of ways for White to handle the position:

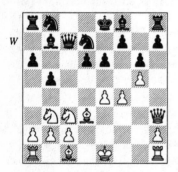

3c21) **13 ♖f1!?** occurred in the game Ulybin-Khurtsidze, Oakham 1992. White, who is a leading specialist in this variation, decided to develop his kingside initiative before turning his attention to the mundane matter of king safety. Play continued

13...b4 14 ♘e2 ♘c6 15 f5 gxf5 16 exf5 e5 17 f6 0-0-0 18 ♕h5 ♘b6 19 ♗e3 d5 20 ♗f5+ ♔b8 21 ♗xb6 ♕xb6 22 0-0-0 a5 23 ♔b1 and then **23...♗a6** 24 ♘bc1 ♕b7 25 g6 fxg6 26 ♗xg6 ♗c5 27 ♗d3 with an indisputable advantage for White, although his means of achieving this advantage were not totally convincing. For example, **23...a4** 24 ♘bc1 a3 looks very unclear to me. It will be interesting to see whether Ulybin repeats 13 ♖f1 in his next outing with this line.

3c22) **13 ♗e3 b4** (13...♘c5 is not so good now on account of 14 ♗d4 and after 13...♘c6 White has the option of 14 f5) **14 ♘e2** (14 ♘d5 exd5 15 ♗d4 dxe4 16 ♗e2 ♘e5 is good for Black) **14...♘c6 15 0-0-0 ♗g7 16 ♖hf1!** (more accurate than 16 ♔b1, which gave Black adequate counterplay in Nijboer-Van Wely, Dutch Ch 1993 after 16...0-0! 17 f5 exf5 18 exf5 ♖fe8 19 ♖hf1 ♘ce5 as 20 ♖f4 is met by 20...♖ac8) **16...0-0-0** (now 16...0-0 17 f5 exf5 18 exf5 ♖fe8 19 ♖f4 is more dangerous for Black) **17 f5 ♘ce5 18 ♔b1** with a slight advantage for White, Ulybin-Magerramov, Uzhgorod 1988.

7 ♗e2 *(D)*

This position frequently arises via the move order 6 ♗e2 ♘bd7 (instead of the more common 6...e5) 7 f4.

7 ...   e5

This move is most common, the following lines being somewhat unpleasant for Black:

1) **7...g6** (an attempt to reach positions akin to the Dragon, but here

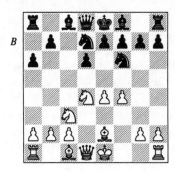

White can exploit an interesting tactical resource) **8 g4 ♘c5** (8...h6 9 f5 ♘c5 10 ♗f3 e5 11 ♘b3 gxf5 12 exf5 e4 13 ♗g2 ♘xb3 14 axb3 ♖g8 15 h3 ♗xf5 16 ♕d4 ♗e6 was unclear in Beliavsky-Ljubojević, Bugojno 1984, but this line is certainly risky for Black) **9 ♘b3! ♘xb3** (9...♘fxe4? loses to 10 ♘xe4 ♘xe4 11 ♕d4 ♘f6 12 g5, and after 9...b6 10 g5 ♘fd7, Arnason-Tringov, Plovdiv 1986, White should play 11 ♗f3 ♗b7 12 ♕e2 supporting e4 and preparing ♗d2 and 0-0-0 with a promising position) **9...♘xb3 10 axb3 ♗g7** and now:

1a) **11 g5 ♘d7 12 ♗e3** is given as a clear plus for White in *BTS2*. Perhaps this is true, but the continuation of the game Langumina-Gallagher, Forli 1992, shows that Black is not without counterchances: 12...b6! 13 ♕d2 ♗b7 14 ♗f3?! (14 0-0-0 b5 15 ♔b1) 14...b5 15 h4 b4 16 ♘a4 ♕a5 17 h5 ♖g8 18 hxg6 hxg6 and now my opponent played 19 ♗g4?, falling straight into my trap: 19...♗xb2! 20 ♗xd7+ (20 ♖b1 ♕xa4!) 20...♔xd7 21 ♘c5+ ♕xc5! 22 ♗xc5 ♗c3 23 ♗xb4 ♗xd2+ 24 ♔xd2 ♗xe4 and

the extra pawn was soon converted into victory.

1b) I think the best way for White to proceed in this line is **11 ♗f3!**, preventing ...b6 and providing the option of ♕e2. In that case White could claim a sizeable advantage.

2) **7...♘c5 8 ♗f3 ♕b6 9 ♘b3** (once again this move, putting the question to the c5-knight, gives White the advantage) 9...♘xb3 10 axb3 g6 11 e5 dxe5 12 fxe5 ♘d7 13 ♘d5 ♕d8 14 ♗g5, Gipslis-Quinteros, Olot 1973 and White stands very well since 14...♘xe5? loses to 15 ♘f6+ exf6 16 ♕xd8+ ♔xd8 17 ♗xf6+.

3) **7...♕b6 8 ♘b3 g6 9 ♕d3** (preparing ♗e3, when Black is driven back in confusion) 9...♕c7 10 g4 ♘c5 11 ♘xc5 ♕xc5 12 ♗e3 ♕a5 13 b4! with advantage to White, Torre-Quinteros, Leningrad IZ 1973.

4) **7...b5** (I {JN} suggested this move in 1982 but a few months later found a good reply) **8 ♘d5! ♗b7** (9 ♘c6 was the threat and 8...♘xd5 9 exd5 gives White a superb outpost at c6) 9 ♘xf6+ ♘xf6 (or else White has a positional advantage) 10 e5 dxe5 11 fxe5 followed by e6, when Black has problems developing his kingside pieces.

8 fxe5

Inexperienced players sometimes try **8 ♘b3** but after the reply 8...b5 White should be thinking about equalising! Natural moves like 8 ♘b3 quite often turn out badly in the Najdorf, which is one reason why it is so popular.

BTS2 recommended **8 ♘f5**, but currently the immediate exchange on e5 is creating more trouble for Black. The problem with 8 ♘f5 is that after 8...♘c5 9 ♘g3 ♛b6 10 ♖b1 ♗d7 11 fxe5 dxe5 12 ♗e3 ♛c6 13 0-0, Black can actually take the pawn on e4. After 13...♘cxe4 14 ♘cxe4 ♘xe4 15 ♗f3 (15 ♘xe4 was played in Short-Gelfand, Tilburg 1990 but White never had enough for the pawn) 15...♗c5! 16 ♘xe4 ♗xe3+ 17 ♔h1 0-0 18 ♘c3 ♛e6! (*BTS2* only took 18...♛c8? into account) 19 ♘d5 e4! White may win some material but Black is going to obtain a lot of compensation.

8 ...   ♘xe5

This has been played most often in practice, but perhaps the alternative recapture, **8...dxe5**, is better. After **9 ♘f5** (D) Black has played:

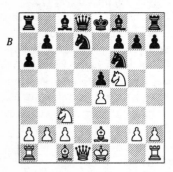

1) **9...♛c7** 10 0-0 ♘c5 11 ♘g3 ♗e6 12 ♗g5 ♘cd7, Wahls-Gelfand, Munich 1991, and now Gelfand gives 13 ♔h1! as good for White. For example, 13...h6 (13...♖d8 14 ♘d5!) 14 ♗xf6 ♘xf6 15 ♘d5 ♘xd5 16 exd5 0-0-0 17 c4 ±.

2) **9...♛b6**, aiming to interfere with White's smooth development, is the most recent try. Kasparov-Gelfand, Horgen 1994 now continued **10 ♘d5 ♘xd5 11 ♛xd5 ♛c5!** 12 ♛b3 ♘f6 13 ♗c4 ♛b4+ 14 ♛xb4 ♗xb4+ 15 c3 ♗f8 16 ♗d3! with a roughly level game. In his notes, though, Kasparov criticises his 10th move, giving instead **10 ♗f3 ♘c5** 11 ♘e3 ♗e6 12 0-0 ♖d8 13 ♛e1 as ±. This remains to be tested although it's hard to see what Black can do against the logical follow-up, 14 ♔h1 and 15 ♘ed5.

9 ♗g5   ♗e7
10 ♛d2   0-0

The bishop on g5 exerts a lot of pressure on Black's position, which no doubt explains the urge to drive it away with 10...h6, as was played in the game J.Polgar-I.Gurevich, Hastings 1992/3. After **11 ♗f4 ♗e6** 12 ♘f5 ♗xf5 13 exf5 ♖c8 14 0-0-0 ♛a5 15 ♔b1 ♛c5 16 ♖he1 0-0 17 ♗f1 White's position was preferable.

11 0-0   h6?!

Once Black has castled he should leave this pawn well alone. **11...♗e6** is more solid, although in J.Polgar-Gelfand, Munich 1991 White still obtained an edge after 12 ♘f5 ♗xf5 13 ♖xf5 ♖c8 (13...♛d7? 14 ♗xf6! ♗xf6 15 ♖xf6 gxf6 16 ♘d5 ♛e6 17 ♛h6 ♘d7 18 ♖f1 is a typical sacrifice in this variation, and one which Black should usually take care not to allow) 14 ♔h1 ♛b6 15 ♖b1 ♘ed7 16 ♗d3 ♖fe8 17 ♗e3 ♛d8 18 ♖bf1.

12 ♗e3   ♗e6

13 ⚔h1

White plans ♘f5 but must first take this precautionary measure as after **13 ♘f5 ♗xf5 14 ♖xf5 ♘fg4 15 ♗d4 ♗g5** with ...♗e3 or ...♘e3 to follow, Black has clearly overcome his opening difficulties.

13 ... ♖c8
14 ♘f5 ♗xf5
15 ♖xf5 ♖e8

It is easy to be wise after the event and criticise this move for weakening f7, but the alternatives are also not so palatable. **15...♘fg4 16 ♗g1 ♗g5 17 ♕d4** now gets nowhere as Black can't infiltrate on e3 and after **15...♕d7 16 ♖af1** White enjoys a considerable kingside space advantage and will be able to start thinking about punishing Black for his 11th move.

16 ♖af1 ♘h7?

Black wants to exchange the dark-squared bishops but this is a hopelessly optimistic plan.

17 ♕d5!

Thanks to Black's last move the white queen is able to take up a menacing position, creating threats on both the kingside and queenside.

17 ... ♖c6

17...b5 is well met by 18 ♕b7!.

18 ♕b3 b5
19 ♘d5 ♕a8 *(D)*

Black neutralises the threat of ♘b4, but allows something much more devastating.

20 ♖xf7!! ♘xf7
21 ♖xf7 ♔xf7

21...♗d8 is no help at all: 22 ♖a7! ♕xa7 23 ♘e7+ and 24 ♘g6#.

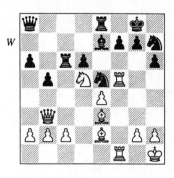

22 ♘b6+ ♔g6

Or **22...♔f8 23 ♘d7** and **22...♔f6 23 ♘d7+! ♔g6 24 ♗h5+!**, which is similar to the game.

23 ♗h5+! ♔xh5
24 ♕f7+ 1-0

24...♔h4 25 g3+ is instant mate.

Game 2
Nunn – Grünfeld
England-Israel Telex Match 1981

1 e4 c5
2 ♘f3 d6
3 d4 cxd4
4 ♘xd4 ♘f6
5 ♘c3 a6
6 f4 ♕c7

If Black wishes to delay ...e5 (or even dispense with it altogether) then this is probably the most reliable way to go about it. Black avoids the tactical problems resulting from a quick e5 by White and can continue his development by ...g6, ...♗g7, ...♘bd7 and maybe ...b5 and ...0-0 as well.

7 ♘f3 *(D)*

This is more accurate than **7 ♗d3**, when 7...e5 8 ♘f3 b5 transposes into a relatively comfortable line for Black.

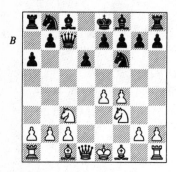

7 ... ᗡbd7

After this we reach a standard position which can arise by a wide range of move-orders. The main question is whether Black can exploit White's early ᗡf3 by playing 7...e6. The analysis runs **7...e6 8 ᗺd3** and now:

1) **8...b5** (this is thought to be very risky, but it was recently tried by Kasparov) 9 e5! (in Renet-Kasparov, French League 1993 White played the less critical move 9 ₩e2) 9...dxe5 (9...b4 10 ᗡe4 ᗡxe4 11 ᗺxe4 d5 12 ᗺd3 is slightly better for White, while Sax-Guerra, Dubai OL 1986 continued 9...ᗡfd7 10 0-0 ᗡc6 11 ᗝh1 ᗺe7 12 ₩e1 0-0 13 ₩g3 f5 14 exf6 ᗡxf6 15 ᗺd2 with some advantage to White) 10 fxe5 ᗡfd7 (10...ᗡg4 11 ₩e2 ᗺb7 12 ᗺe4 also gives White an edge) 11 0-0 ᗡc6 12 ᗺf4 ᗺb7 13 ᗝh1 ᗡc5 14 ᗡe4 ᗡxe4 15 ᗺxe4 ᗡb4, Reeh-Schulz, West German Ch 1987, and now 16 ᗡg5!? gives White dangerous attacking chances.

2) **8...ᗡc6 9 0-0** and now:

2a) **9...ᗺe7 10 ₩e1** and Black has a range of possibilities.

2a1) **10...ᗡd7** (passive) 11 ₩g3 0-0 12 ᗝh1 ᗤe8?! 13 e5! ᗡb4 14 f5! with a strong attack for White, Hazai-Karolyi, Hungary Ch 1986.

2a2) **10...0-0** 11 e5 ᗡd7 (the line 11...dxe5 12 fxe5 ᗡd7 13 ᗺf4 ᗡc5 14 ₩g3 ᗡxd3 15 cxd3 ᗝh8 16 ᗡe4 is better for White, according to Sax and Hazai) 12 ᗡg5 ᗺxg5 13 exd6 ₩xd6 14 fxg5 ᗡc5 15 ᗺe4 e5 16 ᗺxc6 bxc6 17 ᗺe3 gave White an edge in Kindermann-Schlosser, Altensteig 1992.

2a3) **10...ᗡb4** (perhaps the best) 11 e5 ᗡxd3 12 cxd3 ᗡd5 13 ᗡxd5 exd5 14 ₩g3 0-0 15 ᗝh1 dxe5 16 fxe5 ᗺf5 17 ᗡd4 ᗺg6 18 ᗺd2 with a level position in Sax-De Firmian, New York Open 1987, although nobody has since cared to repeat this with Black.

2b) **9...b5** 10 ₩e1 ᗺb7 11 ᗝh1 ᗺe7 12 e5! dxe5 13 fxe5 ᗡd7 14 ᗺf4 ᗡc5 15 ᗡe4! (just as in line '1' above, except for the additional moves ₩e1 and ...ᗺe7) 15...ᗡxe4 (15...ᗡxd3 16 cxd3 0-0 17 ₩g3 ᗝh8 18 ᗡf6! ₩d8 19 ᗡg5 is very good for White) 16 ᗺxe4 h6?! (16...ᗡb4 17 ᗺxb7 ₩xb7 18 ₩g3 g6 may be better, although 19 ᗺh6 cuts Black off from the kingside), Sax-A.Sokolov, Reykjavik 1988, and now 17 a4 b4 18 ₩f2 gives White good attacking prospects.

3) **8...ᗡbd7 9 0-0** and now:

3a) **9...b5** may be met by the simple 10 ₩e1, or even by 10 e5!? dxe5

11 fxe5 ♘xe5 12 ♘xe5 ♕xe5 13 ♕f3 and now 13...♖b8?! 14 ♗f4 ♕c5+ 15 ♔h1 ♗b7 16 ♗e4! ♘xe4 17 ♗xb8 f5 18 ♖ae1 was favourable for White in Ničevski-Markiewicz, Dembica 1987, so Black should have continued 13...♖a7 14 ♗f4 ♕h5 15 ♕g3 with an unclear position; it is worth noting that the natural continuation 15...♗c5+ 16 ♔h1 0-0 loses material to 17 ♗b8!, with a double attack on the rook at a7 and the knight on f6.

3b) 9...♗e7 10 ♕e1 0-0 11 e5! ♘e8 12 ♕g3 ♘c5 13 ♗e3 ♗d7?! 14 ♗xh7+! ♔xh7 15 ♘g5+ ♔g8 (after 15...♗xg5, 16 fxg5 ♖h8 17 ♖xf7 is unpleasant) 16 ♕h4 ♗xg5 17 fxg5 ♗c6, Wedberg-Ionescu, Berlin 1988, and after 18 exd6 ♘xd6 (but not 18...♕xd6 19 ♖ad1 ♕e7 20 ♕b4) 19 ♗xc5 ♘f5 Black does not have enough for the pawn.

8 ♗d3   g6

8...e5 9 a4 transposes to Game 3, while 8...e6 is line '3' in the above analysis.

9 0-0

White's strategy in this line is rather crude. He intends a straightforward attacking build-up on the kingside by ♕e1-h4, f5, ♗h6, and ♘g5. Of course Black is also playing moves while all this is going on but if he continues naively with his development without taking specific countermeasures he can easily fall victim to White's attack.

9 ...   ♗g7
10 ♕e1 (D)
10 ...   0-0

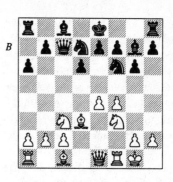

This move is probably already an inaccuracy. The alternatives are:

1) **10...e5** and after 11 a4 we have transposed to Game 3.

2) **10...♘c5** 11 e5 dxe5 12 fxe5 ♘fd7 13 ♗f4 ♘e6 14 ♗g3 ♘b6 (after 14...0-0 15 ♔h1 Black has to find an answer to ♘d5) 15 a4 ♗d7 16 a5 ♘c8 17 ♘e4 and White's initiative proved decisive in Sax-Minić, Rovinj-Zagreb 1975.

3) **10...b5** (probably the best move, aiming to complete Black's development before he gives White a target to attack by castling) 11 e5 (attacking moves like ♕h4 serve no function while Black's king is still in the centre) 11...dxe5 12 fxe5 ♘g4 13 e6 fxe6 14 ♕h4 with an unclear position. For the pawn White has some initiative and Black has problems finding a refuge for his king. White also has the option of opening lines on the queenside by a timely a4, and in practice Black will not have an easy defensive task ahead of him.

The above paragraph remains unchanged from *BTS2* as this pawn sacrifice has still not been seriously tested, mainly because 10...b5 is believed to be too risky. However, Daniel King, in *Winning with the Najdorf* (Batsford 1993), examines this line in some detail and concludes that White has insufficient compensation for the material. I think, though, that he is overestimating Black's chances. For example, he gives 14...♘de5 (after 14 ♕h4) 15 ♘xe5 ♘xe5 and then **16 ♗h6 ♗xh6 17 ♕xh6 ♗b7** followed by ...0-0-0 as very good for Black; but after 18 ♖ae1 0-0-0 19 ♕e3 ♘xd3 20 ♕xe6+, Svendsen-Gallagher, Lenk 1995, the position is about equal. Moreover, at the board I was more concerned about **16 ♗e4 ♗b7** (otherwise Black loses his right to castle long) 17 ♗xb7 ♕xb7 18 ♗h6 ♗xh6 19 ♕xh6 0-0-0 20 ♖ae1 when the assessment from the above paragraph sums up this position perfectly.

11 ♕h4   b5
12 f5

At one time White invariably played ♔h1 before proceeding with his attack. This type of consolidating move is often a symptom of chess laziness, in that White does not want to be bothered with calculating the consequences of Black's queen check in every variation and so simply rules it out, even though it may cost him a vital tempo.

12 ...   ♗b7?

Black continues to play normal Sicilian moves without realising how critical his position has become. The point is that after White's fxg6 Black does not want to play ...hxg6 when ♘g5 gives White a permanent

mating threat on h7. However, the recapture ...fxg6 invites White's knight to come in at e6 and Black's ...♗b7 removes a vital defence from this square. **12...♘c5** was essential, when 13 ♗h6 b4 may enable Black to defend.

13 fxg6

In a game Velikov-Valenti, Pernik 1979, White played **13 ♗e3** (laziness again) when Black missed his second chance to play ...♘c5 and lost after 13...b4? 14 ♘d5! ♗xd5 15 exd5 ♘xd5 16 fxg6 hxg6 17 ♘g5 ♘5f6 18 ♖f3 with a crushing attack.

13 ...   fxg6

After **13...hxg6** 14 ♘g5 Black cannot move either knight since ...♘h5 is met by g4. White can just build up by ♖f3 and ♖af1 to eliminate the defensive knights at f6.

14 ♘g5   ♘c5 *(D)*

Too late! **14...♕b6+** (14...♘h5 15 ♗e3 is good for White) 15 ♔h1 ♘h5 was best, but even then 16 ♗d2 threatening both ♘e6 and ♘d5 gives White a promising attack.

15 ♖xf6!   ♖xf6
16 ♕xh7+   ♔f8

17 ♗e3

White's material investment is very slight for such a strong attack. The main threat is 18 ♘d5 ♗xd5 19 exd5 attacking g6 and preparing b4 followed by the occupation of e6 by White's knight.

17 ...   ♘xd3

17...e5 18 ♘d5 ♗xd5 19 exd5 e4 20 ♗e2 ♖e8 21 b4 followed by ♘e6+ is also winning.

18 cxd5   ♕d7

Black cannot meet the threat of ♘d5 by **18...e6** since 19 ♘xe6+! ♖xe6 20 ♖f1+ ♔e8 (20...♖f6 21 ♖xf6+ wins the queen) 21 ♕g8+ is decisive.

19	**♘d5**	**♗xd5**
20	**exd5**	**♕f5**
21	**♘e6+**	**♖xe6**
22	**dxe6**	**♕xe6**
23	**♗h6**	**1-0**

23...♗xh6 24 ♕h8+ ♔f7 25 ♖f1+ wins everything.

Game 3
Nunn – Cserna
Lugano 1984

1	**e4**	**c5**
2	**♘f3**	**d6**
3	**d4**	**cxd4**
4	**♘xd4**	**♘f6**
5	**♘c3**	**a6**
6	**f4**	**e5**

Black's most popular move. After all, ...a6 was designed to prepare ...e5 and the determined Najdorf player will generally play ...e5 unless it is absolutely impossible.

7 ♘f3   ♕c7

At one time it was held that Black should prevent the active development of White's bishop at c4 and so this move was almost universal. But more recently **7...♘bd7** has become the most popular move. We consider this in Game 4.

8 a4

The alternative is 8 ♗d3. The continuations after 8 a4 and 8 ♗d3 are rather similar, but there are some important differences. Firstly 8 a4 expends a tempo, but this is not especially serious since White can often omit ♔h1 (after 8 ♗d3 b5 White usually has to play ♔h1 since Black's check on b6 gives him extra defensive possibilities). More significantly, a4 reserves the c4-square for White's use (by ♕e2 and ♗c4 or ♘d2 and ♗c4) and in some lines the added pressure White can exert on f7 by these manoeuvres improves his chances considerably.

8 ...   ♘bd7

9 ♗d3 *(D)*

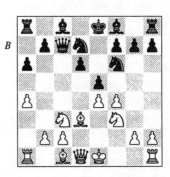

9 ...   g6

Black's main decision is whether the f8-bishop should go to e7 or g7.

There are two other lines, one in which Black commits himself to ...♗e7 at once and one in which he postpones the decision:

1) **9...♗e7 10 0-0 0-0 11 ♘h4!?** (White can also play 11 ♔h1 and after 11...♘c5 we have transposed to Game 4) when Black has played:

1a) **11...♗d8?!** 12 ♘f5 g6 13 ♘h6+ ♔g7 14 f5 b6 15 g4 with a dangerous attack for White, Sax-Bukić, Vrbas 1980.

1b) **11...g6** (the usual response to ♘h4) **12 f5 d5!? 13 exd5** with a further branch:

1b1) **13...♘xd5?** 14 ♘xd5 ♕c5+ 15 ♗e3 ♕xd5 16 fxg6 hxg6, Cramling-Gallagher, Oakham 1984, and now instead of 17 ♘xg6? fxg6 18 ♕g4 ♖xf1+ 19 ♖xf1 ♘f8! when Black was able to repulse the attack, White could have won by **17 ♕g4!**, e.g. 17...♘f6 18 ♘xg6 ♗xg4 19 ♘xe7+ ♔h8 20 ♘xd5 ♘xd5 21 ♗h6, 17...♗c5 18 ♘xg6 ♗xe3+ 19 ♔h1 ♕e6 20 ♗f5, 17...♘b6 18 ♕g3 and White has threats at b6 and g6, or finally 17...♗xh4 18 ♕xh4 followed by ♗c4 and ♗h6, and in every case White has a winning position.

1b2) **13...e4** 14 ♗e2 ♗d6 15 g3 b6, Sax-Andersson, London 1980, and now 16 ♘g2 is best, followed by ♗h6 and ♘e3 supporting the pawns at d5 and f5, when White should have the advantage.

1c) **11...d5!?** 12 ♘f5 (12 exd5 e4! 13 ♗e2 ♕c5+ 14 ♔h1 ♘b6 is fine for Black) 12...♗c5+ 13 ♔h1 dxe4 14 ♗xe4 ♗b4 15 fxe5 ♗xc3 (15...♘xe5 16 ♘d5 ♘xd5 17 ♕xd5

appears to be a little better for White, whilst the hackers can investigate 16 ♘xg7!?) 16 exf6 ♘xf6 17 ♗d3 ♗e5 18 ♗g5 with some pressure for White, Mortensen-Zso.Polgar, Hastings 1992/3.

2) **9...b6** (the problem with this delaying move is that Black may have trouble getting castled) 10 0-0 ♗b7 11 ♕e1 g6 (11...♗e7 12 ♔h1 0-0 13 ♘h4 g6 14 fxe5 dxe5 15 ♗h6 ♖e8 16 ♘f5! ♗f8 17 ♗xf8 ♖xf8 18 ♘e3 is slightly better for White, Sznapik-Ostermeyer, Oslo 1983) 12 fxe5 dxe5 13 ♕h4 ♗e7 (13...♗g7 14 ♗h6 0-0 transposes into the main line) 14 ♗g5 h6 15 ♔h1 (15 ♘d2? ♗c5+ and 16...♘h5) 15...♔f8 (or 15...0-0-0 16 ♗e3 and White has an automatic attack against Black's weakened queenside) 16 ♘d2! ♔g7 17 ♗e3 ♘c5 18 ♗c4 ♖af8 19 ♕f2 ♗d8 20 ♗xc5 ♕xc5 21 ♕xc5 bxc5 22 a5 ½-½ Rantanen-Nunn, Helsinki 1981, although White is distinctly better. This is an example of the advantage of having c4 available for the bishop.

10	0-0	♗g7
11	♕e1	0-0
12	fxe5	dxe5
13	♕h4	b6
14	♗h6	♗b7
15	♘g5 *(D)*	

This position is the natural result of White's blunt play. Although its evaluation has fluctuated over the years, the scales have recently tipped in White's favour. It is very rarely seen today because Black players steer well clear of it.

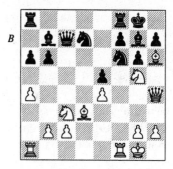

15 ... **♖fc8**

The two lines **15...♘h5?** 16 ♗xg7 ♔xg7 17 ♖xf7+ and **15...♖ae8** 16 g4! are best avoided, while **15...♖fe8** 16 ♗xg7 ♔xg7 17 ♘xf7! ♔xf7 18 ♕xh7+ ♔e6 19 ♖xf6+! ♔xf6 20 ♖f1+ ♔e6 21 ♗c4+ ♔d6 22 ♖d1+ ♔c6 23 ♗d5+ ♔c5 24 ♗xb7 1-0 Rantanen-Morris, Gausdal 1978, was a devastating win for White.

The only other reasonable move is **15...♕d6**, but 16 ♖ad1 causes serious problems. After 16...♘h5 White plays 17 ♗xg7 ♔xg7 18 ♗e2 ♕c5+ 19 ♔h1, when 19...♘hf6 loses to 20 ♖xd7 and 19...♘df6 loses to 20 ♗xh5 ♘xh5 22 ♖xf7+. Other 16th moves are almost as bad.

16 ♔h1

Black intended to meet moves such as 16 g4 and 16 ♖ad1 with ...♕c5+ and ...♕f8 whereafter, with the rook on c8 preventing ♗c4, he should be able to defend his kingside. Unfortunately White has a tactical idea which cuts across Black's plan to bring his queen to f8.

16 ... **♕d6**
17 ♗xg7 **♔xg7**
18 ♘xf7!

This hardly counts as a sacrifice, since White immediately gains three pawns for the piece, while Black's king is left floating around in the middle of the board.

18 ... **♔xf7**
19 ♕xh7+ **♔e6**
20 ♕xg6 *(D)*

There was even a second good line in **20 ♖xf6+ ♘xf6 21 ♕xb7** since the attempt to liquidate by 21...♕c7 allows 22 ♗xa6.

20 ... **♕e7**
21 ♖ad1

As is so often the case, it is better to spend time cutting off the king's escape route than to give pointless checks which only serve to drive the king into safety.

21 ... **♕h7**
22 ♕g3 **♔e7**

Black cannot play **22...♖g8** because of the check at c4.

23 ♘d5+ **♗xd5**
24 exd5 **♕h6?**

This error allows White to force the king onto the back rank, cutting off both black rooks from the kingside. However even the best line

24...e4 is very good for White after 25 Ⓡde1 Ⓡg8 26 ⓦc7! ⓦg6 27 g3 Ⓡac8 28 d6+ ♔e6 29 ⓦb7, and with the fall of the e4-pawn White's rooks can at last get to grips with the black king.

25	d6+	♔d8
26	♗f5!	Ⓡa7

It is hardly surprising that Black has no reasonable move. The immediate threat is 27 ♗xd7 ♔xd7 28 ⓦxe5.

27	♗xd7	Ⓡxd7
28	Ⓡxf6	1-0

Game 4
Nunn – King
Bundesliga 1986/7

1	e4	c5
2	♘f3	d6
3	d4	cxd4
4	♘xd4	♘f6
5	♘c3	a6
6	f4	e5
7	♘f3	♘bd7

In my (JN) view this is Black's best reply to 6 f4. Although White's bishop can now be developed more actively at c4, Black saves a vital tempo by missing out ...ⓦc7 and this gives him good chances to equalise. In fact current theory suggests that White's best plan is to ignore the option to play ♗c4, and to proceed with his normal development by ♗d3. Admittedly Black benefits from missing out ...ⓦc7, but it is not clear that the alternatives to ...ⓦc7 fully equalise.

8   a4

White cannot do without this as **8 ♗c4** allows 8...b5 9 ♗d5 Ⓡb8 10 ♘g5 (after 10 fxe5 dxe5 11 ♗g5 ♗b4 Black was slightly better in Hort-Andersson, Wijk aan Zee 1979) 10...♘xd5 11 ⓦxd5 ⓦe7 12 0-0 h6 with equality, Korchnoi-Hort, Zurich 1984, while **8 ♗d3** allows 8...b5, just the line White is trying to avoid.

8   ...   ♗e7

If Black relents by **8...ⓦc7**, we reach Game 3.

8...d5 enjoyed a brief spell of popularity a few years ago but has now virtually disappeared from practice. The best line for White seems to be **9 exd5 e4 10 ♘e5 ♗b4** (10...♗c5 11 ♘c4 followed by ♗e3 is good for White) **11 ♗c4** when Black has:

1) **11...♘b6** 12 ♗b3 when both **12...♘bxd5** 13 0-0 ♗xc3 14 bxc3 0-0 15 ⓦd4 and **12...♘fxd5** 13 a5 ♘xc3 14 ⓦxd8+ ♔xd8 15 ♘xf7+ ♔e7 18 bxc3 ♗xc3+ 17 ♔f2 are good for White.

2) **11...0-0** 12 0-0 ⓦc7 13 ♔h1! ♘xe5 14 fxe5 ♗xc3 15 bxc3 ⓦxe5 16 ⓦd4! ⓦxd4 17 cxd4 with a better ending for White, Reeh-Gallagher, Kecskemet 1990.

3) **11...♘xe5** 12 fxe5 ⓦc7 13 0-0! ⓦxc4 (13...♗g4 14 ♗e2 ♗xe2 15 ⓦxe2 ⓦxe5 16 ♗f4 is good for White) 14 exf6 gxf6 15 Ⓡxf6 ♗xc3 16 bxc3 ⓦxc3 17 ♗g5 and White was clearly better in Adams-Van der Wiel, Wijk aan Zee 1991.

9	♗d3	0-0
10	0-0 *(D)*	

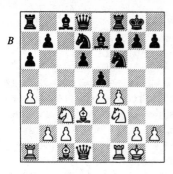

10 ...   ♘c5

Grabbing a pawn with **10...exf4 11 ♗xf4 ♕b6+ 12 ♔h1 ♕xb2** is a risky business, but that hasn't prevented it becoming a more and more frequent visitor to the tournament hall over the last few years:

1) *BTS2* recommended **13 ♕e1** (still the main line) after which Black has:

1a) **13...♘c5** 14 ♖b1 ♘xd3 15 cxd3 ♕c2 16 d4 ♖e8 17 ♖f2! ♕d3 18 ♖c1 ♗f8 19 ♖e2 with advantage to White, Ciocaltea-Danner, Timisoara 1982.

1b) **13...♕b4** 14 ♖b1 ♕c5 15 ♘d5 ♘xd5 16 exd5 ♗f6 (16...♗d8 17 c4 ♘f6 18 ♗e3 ♕c7 19 ♗d4 gave White a dangerous attack in Ledermann-Lau, Ramat-Hasharon 1982) 17 c4 ♕c7 18 ♕g3! ♘e5 19 ♗g5 ♗xg5 20 ♗xh7+! ♔xh7 21 ♘xg5+ ♔h6 (21...♔g8 22 ♕h4 ♖e8 23 ♖be1 also gives White a winning attack) 22 ♕h4+ ♔g6 23 ♖b3 f5 24 ♖g3 ♘g4 25 ♖xg4 fxg4 26 ♖xf8 ♕e7 27 ♖f7 ♕e8 28 ♕h7+ ♔xg5 29 ♖xg7+ ♔f6 30 ♕h6+ ♔f5 31 ♕g5+ ♔e4 32 ♖e7+ 1-0 Vogt-Womacka, E.Germany 1989.

1c) **13...♕b6** (thought to be best) and now:

1c1) **14 ♗g5!?** is the latest try:

1c11) **14...♕d8?!** 15 ♕h4 ♖e8 16 e5! dxe5 17 ♗xf6 ♘xf6 18 ♘xe5 ♗e6 19 ♖ae1 ♕a5 20 ♘e4 and now **20...h6?** 21 ♘xf6+ ♗xf6 22 ♖xf6! gxf6 23 ♖e3! ♕xe5 24 ♖xe5 fxe5 25 ♕xh6 left White close to victory in the game Kveinys-Van Wely, Moscow OL 1994. However, it's doubtful whether White would have been able to claim any advantage after **20...♘d5!**.

1c12) Van Wely suggests the alternative **14...♘c5!**, intending ...♗e6 and providing the option of ...♘xd3.

1c2) **14 ♘d5 ♘xd5** 15 exd5 ♕d8 16 c4 ♘c5 17 ♗c2 ♗g4 18 ♕g3 ♗xf3 19 ♖xf3 ♗h4 20 ♕h3 g6 and now the best continuation, according to Am. Rodriguez, is 21 ♗h6 ♗f6 22 ♖af1 ♗g7 23 g4! (Jepson-Am.Rodriguez, Mondariz Balneario 1994) 23...♕e7! 24 ♖e3! ♗e5 25 ♗xf8 ♖xf8 when Black has compensation for the exchange.

2) **13 ♘d5!?** ♘xd5 14 exd5 ♕b6 15 ♕e2! (15 ♕e1 ♕d8 transposes to '1c2', whilst now 15...♕d8 is met by 16 ♖ae1 as 16...♖e8 allows 17 ♗xd6) 15...♗f6 16 ♖ab1 ♕c5 17 c4 ♕c7 18 ♗g5 ♕d8 19 ♕e4! g6 20 ♕h4 h5 21 ♗xf6 ♕xf6 22 ♘g5 ♕e7 23 ♖be1 ♘e5 24 c5! with very dangerous pressure for the pawn, Kindermann-Ftačnik, Pardubice 1994.

11 ♔h1

This is not the only reasonable move, but judging by recent results it is the most dangerous for Black.

11 ... d5

This is the tactical justification of Black's play, but there are quieter alternatives:

1) **11...♘xd3** 12 cxd3 ♕a5 13 ♕e1 exf4 14 ♘d5 ♕d8 15 ♘xf4 ♗d7 16 ♗d2 was good for White in Mateo-Byrne, New York 1986.

2) **11...♕c7 12 ♕e1** *(D)* (threatening 13 fxe5 dxe5 14 ♕g3, when Black has no natural way to defend the e5-pawn) and now:

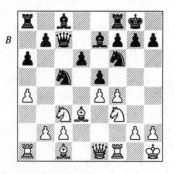

2a) **12...♗d7** 13 fxe5 dxe5 14 ♕g3 ♖ae8 15 ♕xe5 ♗d6 16 ♕d4, with inadequate compensation in view of White's control of d5.

2b) **12...♖e8** 13 fxe5 dxe5 14 ♕g3 ♗d8 15 ♘h4 ♔h8 16 ♘f5 ♗xf5 17 ♖xf5 ♘xd3?! (17...♕c6 18 ♗e3 ♘xd3 19 cxd3 ♕d7 20 ♗g5 ♘g8 ± is a more accurate continuation) 18 cxd3 ♕d7, Almasi-Novikov, Cattolica 1993, and now instead of 19 ♗g5 ♘g8!, transposing to the note just above, White could have gained a more serious advantage with **19 ♕f3!** followed by ♗g5.

2c) **12...♗e6 13 f5 ♗d7 14 g4!?** (14 ♗g5 ♗c6 15 ♗xf6 ♗xf6 16 g4

is also slightly better for White) **14...♗c6** (14...♘xg4 loses after 15 ♘d5 ♕d8 16 ♖g1 ♘f6 17 ♗h6 ♘e8 18 ♖xg7+ ♘xg7 19 ♕g3 ♗f6 20 ♖g1 with a winning attack) **15 g5 ♘h5** (retreating to d7 gives White a completely free hand on the kingside, e.g. 15...♘fd7 16 f6 ♗d8 17 ♕h4 ♘e6 18 ♘d5 and wins) **16 f6 ♗d8** (not 16...gxf6? 17 ♕h4 winning) **17 ♕h4 g6 18 ♗e3**. White's kingside attack has come to a temporary halt, so the time has come to bring the remaining pieces into play. There is a positional threat of 19 ♗xc5 dxc5 20 ♗c4, followed by the occupation of d5. Thus the c5-knight must move.

2c1) However, **18...♘e6** 19 ♘d5 ♗xd5 20 exd5 ♘f4 21 ♗xf4 exf4 22 ♗f5! followed by ♗g4 is good for White.

2c2) **18...♘xd3** 19 cxd3 ♔h8 20 ♘e2 and now:

2c21) **20...♗d7**, planning ...♕c2, is refuted by 21 ♖fc1 when 21...♕a5 surprisingly loses to 22 ♖c4! and Black has no defence to 23 b4.

2c22) **20...♕d7!** is the best defence, aiming for counterplay by attacking a4, when White should continue 21 ♘g3 ♗xa4 22 ♘xh5 gxh5 23 ♕xh5 ♗b5 24 ♖a3 and Black still has to find a defence to the threat of ♖g1-g4-h4.

2c23) **20...d5?** (a natural move aiming to weaken e4 and activate the c6-bishop against the white king, but it also weakens the important e5-pawn and this turns out to balance White's weak spot at e4) 21 ♘g3 dxe4 (Black cannot play 21...♕d6 due to 22 d4!, when both 22...dxe4 23 ♘xe5 and 22...exd4 23 e5 followed by ♗xd4 leave the c6-h1 diagonal blocked by a black pawn) 22 dxe4 ♕d6 23 ♖ad1! ♕b4 (23...♕e6 24 ♗c5 ♖g8 25 ♗d6 leads to the loss of e5) 24 ♘xe5 ♘xg3+ 25 hxg3 ♕xe4+ (after 25...♗xe4+ 26 ♔g1 ♗b6 27 ♗xb6 ♕xb6+ 28 ♖f2 Black cannot meet the threats of ♕xe4 and ♕h6) 26 ♕xe4 ♗xe4+ 27 ♔h2 (the immediate threat is 28 ♗c5; both 27...♖c8 28 ♖d7 ♔g8 29 ♘g4! heading for h6 and 27...♔g8 28 ♗c5 ♖e8 29 ♘xf7! ♔xf7 30 ♖d7+ ♔e6 31 f7 ♖f8 32 ♖d4 ♖xf7 33 ♖d6+ win for White) 27...♗c7 28 ♗c5 ♗xe5 29 ♗xf8 ♖xf8 30 ♖fe1 ♗c2 31 ♖d2 ♗xa4 (Black cannot get two pawns for the exchange since 31...♗xg3+ 32 ♔xg3 ♗xa4 33 ♖e7 threatens both ♖xb7 and ♖xf7) 32 ♖xe5 h6 33 gxh6 ♔h7 34 g4 ♔xh6 35 g5+ ♔h7 36 ♖e4 ♗c6 37 ♖h4+ ♔g8 38 ♔g3 1-0 Nunn-Portisch, Brussels 1986.

2d) **12...exf4 13 ♗xf4 ♖e8** (after 13...♗e6 14 ♘d4 ♕b6 15 ♗e3 ♘g4 16 ♗g1 ♘e5 17 ♘f5 ♗xf5 18 ♘d5 ♕d8 19 exf5 ♗f6 20 ♗e2 ♘ed7 21 ♘xf6+ ♘xf6 22 ♗f3 White's two bishops gave him the advantage in Short-Gallagher, British Ch 1987) 14 ♘d4 ♗d7 15 ♗g5 ♕d8, Hazai-Novikov, Camaguey 1987, and now White should have taken the chance to activate his bishop by 16 ♗c4!, pointing it at the sensitive square f7. The key tactical line 16...♘xa4 17 ♖xa4 ♗xa4 (17...b5 18 ♘cxb5 axb5 19 ♖xa8 ♕xa8 20 ♗xb5 is good for White) 18 ♘xa4 b5 19 ♘c6 ♕c7 20 ♘xe7+ ♕xe7 21 ♗xf6 gxf6 22 ♘b6 bxc4 23 ♘d5 ♕e5 24 ♘xf6+ ♔g7 25 ♕h4 h6 (25...♖h8 26 ♕g4+) 26 ♖f5! turns out well for White since 26...♕xb2 loses to 27 ♖g5+!.

3) **11...exf4 12 ♗xf4** (D) with two main possibilities:

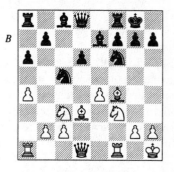

3a) **12...♗d7 13 ♕e2 ♖c8 14 a5 ♖e8 15 ♗e3 ♗f8** (perhaps 15...♘g4 is better, although there was no need for White to agree a draw after 16 ♗d4 ♗f6 17 ♕d2, as he did in Kindermann-Brunner, Eurodata 1992) **16 ♗d4!** (intending ♘g5) with a total of five lines:

3a1) **16...♗e7** 17 b4 ♘e6 18 ♗b6 with a clear plus for White.

3a2) **16...h6** 17 ♘d2 ♘g4 18 ♗c4 ±.

3a3) **16...♘e6** 17 ♗b6 ♕e7 18 ♘h4 g6 19 ♖ae1 ±.

3a4) **16...♗g4** 17 ♕e3 ♗h5 18 ♗xf6 ♕xf6 19 ♘d5 ♕d8 20 ♘d4 ♗g6 21 ♘f5 ♖e5 22 b4! ♘xe4 23 ♗xe4 ♖c4 24 ♖ae1 ♖cxe4 25 ♕xe4 ♖xe4 26 ♖xe4 was very promising for White in Ulybin-Pigusov, Pavlodar 1987.

3a5) **16...♘fxe4** (Ulybin's recommendation in *Informator*, but it appears to have a tactical flaw) 17 ♘xe4 ♘xe4 18 ♗xe4 ♗b5 19 c4! (Ulybin only considered 19 ♕e3, which leads to a draw) 19...♖xc4 (or 19...♗xc4 20 ♕c2 ♗xf1 21 ♗xh7+ ♔h8 22 ♕f5 with a winning attack) 20 ♕d3 ♖c5 21 ♗xh7+ ♔h8 22 ♕b3 ♗xf1 23 ♗xc5 dxc5 24 ♖xf1 ♔xh7 25 ♕xf7 with a large advantage for White.

3b) **12...♗g4!**, with the idea of transferring the bishop to g6, from where it will exert pressure on e4 whilst still covering the important f5-square, makes it difficult for White to achieve any advantage. Perhaps the best try is **13 ♗e3!?** (the ideal square for this bishop is d4):

3b1) **13...♗h5?** is a serious error on account of 14 ♗xc5! dxc5 15 e5 ♘e8 16 ♕e1 ±.

3b2) Better is **13...♖c8** 14 ♕d2 and now **14...♗h5** 15 ♘d4 ♘g4 16 ♘d5 (thus far Svidler-Nebodora, Linares 1994) 16...♘xe3 17 ♕xe3 permits White a slight advantage, but **14...♘xd3!** 15 ♕xd3 (15 cxd3 d5 16 e5 ♗xf3 17 exf6 ♗xf6! 18 ♖xf3 d4 19 ♘e4 dxe3 20 ♘xf6+ ♕xf6! slightly better for Black) 15...♗e6 is given as = in *Informator*, although I believe White may have a faint edge after 16 ♘d5.

12 ♘xe5 (D)
12 ... ♘fxe4

Black has two important alternatives:

1) **12...♘cxe4 13 ♗xe4 dxe4 14 ♕e2** and now:

1a) **14...♗f5** 15 g4 ♗c8 16 ♖d1 ♕e8 17 g5 ♘d7 18 ♘c4 e3 (the lines 18...♘c5 19 b4 ♘e6 20 ♘d5 and 18...b6 19 ♗e3 ♗b7 20 ♘d5 are also good for White) and now there are two favourable variations for White, either **19 ♗xe3 b5** 20 axb5 ♗b7+ 21 ♔g1 axb5, Kengis-Loginov, Pavlodar 1987, and now 22 ♖xa8 ♗xa8 23 ♘xb5 ♕c8 24 ♘cd6 ♕c6 25 ♔f2 leaves Black with inadequate play for the two pawns, or the simple **19 ♕xe3**.

1b) **14...♕d4** 15 ♖d1 ♕b4 16 a5` ♗d8 17 ♖a4 ♕e7 is Loginov's suggestion in *Informator*, but now 18 b3! appears good for White.

2) **12...dxe4 13 ♗e2** (Black gains time, but the pawn on e4 obstructs Black's pieces) **13...♕c7** (13...♕xd1 14 ♖xd1 ♗e6 15 ♗e3 ♖fd8 16 g4 g6 17 g5 ♘d5 18 ♘xd5 ♗xd5 19 b3 ♘e6 20 ♘c4 ♗xc4 21 ♖xc4 ♗c5 22 ♗xc5 ♘xc5 23 ♔g2 ♖ac8 24 ♔f2 was marginally better for White in Kindermann-de Firmian, Biel 1986, but 19 b4 ♘e6 20 c4 ♗c6 21 ♘xc6 bxc6 22 ♖xd8 ♖xd8 23 c5 looks more dangerous) **14 ♗e3** (White may also play 14 ♕e1 first, so as to

meet 14...♘e6 by 15 ♗d1 attacking e4) **14...b6 15 ♕e1 ♗b7 16 ♕g3** and now:

2a) Beliavsky-Chandler, Vienna 1986 continued **16...♘e6?!** (intending to exchange bishops by ...♗c5, but this plan fails tactically) 17 ♖ad1 (not 17 f5 ♗d6!, but now f5 is a serious threat) 17...♗c5? (an error, but Black's position was uncomfortable in any case) 18 f5! ♗d6 (the point is that 18...♗xe3 19 fxe6 fxe6 loses to 20 ♖xf6! ♖xf6 21 ♖d7) 19 ♖xd6 ♕xd6 20 fxe6 and White won.

2b) Black tried **16...♖ad8** in Psakhis-Balashov, Irkutsk 1986, but after 17 ♖ad1 ♘cd7 18 ♗d4 ♘xe5 19 fxe5 ♘d7 20 b3! (20 ♗xa6! was even stronger) followed by ♗c4 White had a decisive attack. Black should have played for exchanges by **17...♖xd1** 18 ♖xd1 ♖d8, but White is still slightly better.

    13 ♗xe4   dxe4
    14 ♘d5! *(D)*

White played **14 ♗e3** in Beliavsky-Portisch, Tilburg 1986 (a couple of weeks after the main game), but then 14...f6 15 ♗xc5 ♗xc5 16 ♘xe4 ♕xd1 17 ♖axd1 fxe5 18 ♘xc5 ♗g4 19 ♖de1 exf4 led to equality. The idea of 14 ♘d5 is to eliminate the e7-bishop; Black's remaining bishop will be obstructed by the e4-pawn, while White's can become active along the b2-g7 diagonal.

    14 ...   ♗e6
Or:

1) **14...♗d6** 15 ♘c4! and Black has immediate difficulties since the natural developing move 15...♗e6

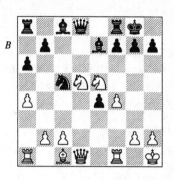

loses a piece to 16 ♘xd6. Otherwise White can proceed with ♘db6, or b4 followed by ♗b2.

2) **14...f5** 15 b4 ♘d7 was suggested by Busch and Olthof in *New in Chess*, but 16 ♗e3! is promising for White. Then both 16...♘f6 and 16...♘xe5 17 fxe5 ♗e6 lose material to ♘xe7+ and ♗c5.

3) **14...f6!** 15 ♘xe7+ ♕xe7 16 ♘c4 ♗e6 17 ♘e3 f5 leads to a structure similar to the game, except that Black has managed to play ...f5. White can continue with b3, ♗b2 and ♕e1, when his bishop is more effective than Black's. However, the opposite-coloured bishops will exert a drawish tendency, particularly if Black can exchange knights by means of ...♘d7-f6-d5.

    15 ♘xe7+   ♕xe7
    16 f5

This is the difference between 14...♗e6 and 14...f6!. Playing f4-f5 benefits White in three ways. First of all, it increases the scope of his bishop; secondly, it prevents Black supporting the e4-pawn with another pawn, and thirdly it gives White kingside attacking chances.

16 ...   **f6**
17 ♘g4
17 fxe6 fxe5 18 ♗e3 ♘xe6 19 ♕d5 may give White a minute advantage, but the move played is far more combative.

17 ...   **♗f7**
The reply **17...♗c4** is ineffective after 18 ♖f4, and the bishop will soon be driven away by b3.

18 ♕e1?!
I decided that it was time to start developing my queenside pieces, but I should have spent just one more tempo improving my position by 18 a5!. It looks strange to put a pawn on a dark square when White's plan is to block out Black's bishop using the pawns on c2, b3, a4, e4 and f5, but it is very useful to have the option of attacking the knight on c5. Not only may White push it away by b4 at a later stage, but by preventing ...b6 White can also set up an awkward pin by ♗a3. Moreover, the possible elimination of this knight gives White the option of playing for the win of the e4-pawn by ♕e1-h4, ♗a3 and ♖ae1.

18 ...   **a5!**
Black seizes on the mistake and permanently secures the c5-square for his knight.

19	b3	♖fd8
20	♗b2	♖d6
21	♕g3	♔h8
22	♖ae1	b6
23	♕h4	♖f8 *(D)*

I decided to make as much progress as I could without taking any risk, by trying to arrange a position

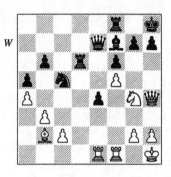

with ♗c3, ♘f2 and ♖e3. This controls the d-file entry squares, and the bishop is defended so Black has no tricks.

24 ♖e3?!
White tries a little trick; perhaps Black won't notice the threat of 25 ♖h3 ♗g8 26 ♘e5.

24 ...   **♕d8**
Unfortunately he does. Moreover, now it is hard to prevent a black rook invasion.

25 ♔g1
Avoiding immediate back-rank problems and future long-diagonal troubles after a possible g4. Note that Black cannot initiate counterplay by **25...♖d2** because of 26 ♘xf6 ♗g8 27 ♘h5!.

25 ...   **♗g8**
Now, however, 26...♖d2 is a threat.

26 ♗c3
White must prevent ...♖d2, even if he thereby allows the alternative penetration ...♖d1.

26 ...   **♖d1**
27 ♖ee1   **♖d6?!**
If correctly followed up, this is a perfectly reasonable defence, but the

alternative **27...♖xe1** 28 ♖xe1 ♕d6 29 ♘e3 ♕c6 is safer. Swapping a pair of rooks reduces White's attacking chances, and in this case Black would not have many problems drawing.

If White had played less carelessly at move 24 (e.g. by 24 ♗c3), then this possibility would not have existed.

28   ♘f2

Sometimes an oversight is the best chance to win! It seemed to me that this was the moment to set up a favourable position with ♘f2 and ♖e3, but this move should fail for tactical reasons.

28   ...   ♕c8!

Since Black obviously cannot play ...♕xf5 because of ♘e4, I decided to continue with my plan. There was nothing better in any case, since 29 ♕g3 ♖c6 is awkward.

29   ♖e3

After having made this move, I suddenly noticed that Black could play **29...♕xf5** 30 ♘xe4 ♕e6! with a certain draw, but perhaps the confident way I had made the move led my opponent to believe that the pawn was invulnerable.

29   ...   ♖d5? *(D)*

30   g4!

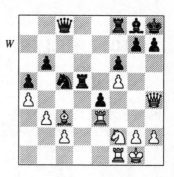

White not only achieves the position he has been aiming for, but in a very favourable form, since the rooks on d5 and f8 are both vulnerable to the manoeuvre ♘h3-f4-g6.

30   ...   ♕c7

Perhaps Black could have offered more resistance, but the twin possibilities of ♘h3-f4 and g5 make his position very unpleasant.

31	♘h3	♘d3
32	cxd3	♕xc3
33	♘f4	g5
34	♘xd5	♗xd5
35	♕e1	

Thanks to the earlier ♔g1, Black has no real counterplay and he is soon forced to give up.

35	...	♕d4
36	dxe4	♗xe4
37	♕c3	♕d5
38	♕c4	1-0

2 Scheveningen Variation

This line is popular with many of the world's leading players, including Kasparov, and so one would hardly expect there to be a clear way for White to obtain an advantage. The characteristic feature of the Scheveningen is Black's pawn centre at d6 and e6 covering all the central squares on Black's 4th rank. Thus Black avoids the slight weakness at d5 inherent in the Najdorf and Dragon systems. Behind the cover of his modest but solid pawn centre Black intends to complete his development in peace. The most common move order for Black to adopt if he is aiming for a Scheveningen is 1 e4 c5 2 ♘f3 e6 3 d4 cxd4 4 ♘xd4 ♘f6 5 ♘c3 d6, but Black can invert his second and fifth moves in this line.

The system we are recommending, the Keres Attack, is undoubtedly the line Scheveningen players fear most. In fact they fear it so much that many of them are now trying to reach their beloved Scheveningen via a Najdorf move order (i.e. 2...d6 and 5...a6 and against moves such as 6 f4, 6 ♗e2 or 6 ♗e3 they reply 6...e6, whereas real Najdorf players prefer ...e5). The Keres Attack starts 1 e4 c5 2 ♘f3 e6 3 d4 cxd4 4 ♘xd4 ♘f6 5 ♘c3 d6 6 g4. This kingside pawn push aims firstly to drive the knight from f6, thereby making it harder for Black to break open the centre by ...d5, and secondly to gain space on the kingside and dissuade Black from castling there. Although White usually obtains good attacking chances with this system he must not neglect his development since Black can often break the position open by ...d5 and even if this loses a pawn White can find his own king stuck in the centre. In other words, a balance must be struck between furthering White's own kingside ambitions and restraining Black in other sectors of the board.

There are two major options for Black after 6 g4. He may either prevent the further advance of the pawn by 6...h6, as covered in Games 5 and 6, or he may continue his own plans and allow the knight to be driven back to d7. In this case Black may choose 6...a6, 6...♗e7 or 6...♘c6. The specific choice of sixth move may not be very important because there are many transpositions. In Game 7 we deal with lines specific to 6...a6 (i.e. those involving an early ...b5), in Game 8 we deal with those specific to 6...♘c6 (i.e. those involving an early ...♕c7), and the other lines may be found in Game 9. Apart from these two major options, there is a third possibility for Black, namely to counterattack by 6...e5.

With this move Black loses a tempo, but he hopes to prove that White's g4 has only served to weaken his kingside. This is covered in Game 7.

Game 5
Nunn – Bischoff
Lugano 1986

1	e4	c5
2	♘f3	e6
3	d4	cxd4
4	♘xd4	♘f6
5	♘c3	d6
6	g4	h6 (D)

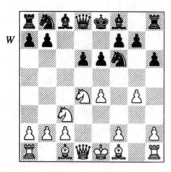

Black avoids having his knight driven away from f6. For a long time White almost always played 7 g5 hxg5 8 ♗xg5, Anatoly Karpov being one supporter of White's point of view. Although this continuation gives White a lead in development it has defects, not the least being that Black's rook on h8 is activated and presses down on White's weak h-pawn. Now 7 h4 is considered to give White better chances than 7 g5 and is currently the most popular line. White wants to continue with

♖g1 and g5, driving away the knight after all.

7 h4 a6!?

Although this is a natural move, it only became popular in the 1980s. The main variation is 7...♘c6, and this will be examined in Game 6, but there is one other important possibility, namely 7...♗e7 (7...e5 8 ♘f5! ♗e6 9 g5 ♘xe4 10 ♘xg7+ ♗xg7 11 ♘xe4 d5 12 gxh6 ♗xh6 13 ♗xh6 ♖xh6 14 ♕d2 ♖xh4 15 ♗b5+ ♘c6 16 0-0-0 was very good for White in Stanciu-Vegh, Ulan Bator 1986) **8 ♕f3 (D)** and now:

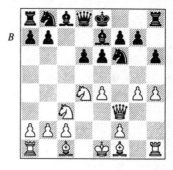

1) **8...♘c6?!** 9 ♗b5 ♗d7 10 ♗xc6 bxc6 (10...♗xc6 11 g5 is also good for White) 11 g5 hxg5 12 hxg5 ♖xh1 13 ♕xh1 ♘g8 14 ♕h7 ♔f8 15 f4, with advantage to White, Howell-Taher, Dublin 1991.

2) **8...♘fd7** 9 ♕g3 ♘c6 10 ♗e3 a6 11 0-0-0 ♕c7, Ljubojević-Timman, Brussels SWIFT 1986, and now Ljubojević recommends 12 ♗e2 as slightly better for White.

3) **8...g6!?** 9 g5 hxg5 10 ♗xg5 a6 11 0-0-0 e5 12 ♘de2 ♗g4 13 ♕g3 ♘bd7 and then **14 f3 ♗e6 15 ♗h3**

♗xh3 16 ♖xh3 ♖c8 17 f4 was unclear in the game De Wit-Oll, Groningen 1984/5. This interesting idea does not seem to have been repeated. Perhaps **14 f4** is better, hoping to prove that the exposed position of the g4-bishop is a liability.

4) **8...h5 9 gxh5** and now:

4a) **9...♘c6** 10 ♗b5 (an attempt to exploit Black's move-order; 10 ♘xc6 bxc6 11 ♗g5 may be better, when Black has to prove that he has something better than 11...♘xh5 transposing to line '4b') 10...♗d7 11 ♗xc6 bxc6 12 e5 ♘d5?! (12...dxe5 13 ♘xc6 ♗xc6 14 ♕xc6+ ♔f8 15 h6 gxh6 16 ♗d2 ♖b8 17 0-0-0 ♕b6 18 ♕xb6 ♖xb6 is equal according to Ljubojević) 13 exd6 ♗xd6 14 ♗g5 ♕b6 15 0-0-0 ♗e5 16 ♘xd5 cxd5 17 c3 with an edge for White, Ljubojević-Timman, Bugojno 1986.

4b) **9...♘xh5** 10 ♗g5 (10 ♗e3!? is an interesting untested idea, offering the h-pawn in return for a quick attack with 0-0-0) 10...♘c6 11 ♘xc6!? bxc6 12 0-0-0 ♗xg5+?! (accepting the sacrifice turns out to be too risky; Black should develop by 12...♖b8) 13 hxg5 ♕xg5+ 14 ♔b1 ♔e7 (not 14...d5? 15 exd5 cxd5 16 ♘xd5 exd5 17 ♖xd5 nor 14...♕c5? 15 e5! and White wins in both cases, while 14...♕e5 15 ♗e2 g6 16 ♕e3 intending f4 gives White a dangerous initiative) 15 ♗e2 g6 16 ♖xd6! ♔xd6 17 ♕xf7! (somewhat surprisingly Black has no defence) 17...a5 18 ♖d1+ ♔e5 19 ♗xh5 ♖xh5 20 f4+ ♕xf4 21 ♕g7+ 1-0 Sobura-Pieniazek, Poland 1988.

8 ♗g2 *(D)*

White abandons his plan to play ♖g1 and g5 because after **8 ♖g1** d5 9 exd5 ♘xd5 10 ♘xd5 ♕xd5 11 ♗g2 ♕c4 12 c3 ♗e7 13 g5 ♘d7 14 ♕e2 ♕xe2+ 15 ♔xe2 ♘b6 White had no advantage in Karpov-Kindermann, Vienna 1986.

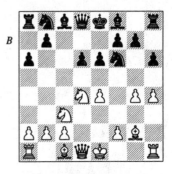

8 ... ♘c6

Or:

1) **8...g6** 9 g5 hxg5 10 ♗xg5 ♗e7 11 ♕d2 e5 12 ♘de2 ♗e6 13 0-0-0 ♘bd7 14 f4 ♕a5 (14...♕c7?! is inferior after 15 fxe5! dxe5 16 ♘d5 ♗xd5 17 exd5 ♖c8 18 ♖hf1! with some advantage for White, Ghinda-Bönsch, Halle 1987) 15 ♔b1 ♖c8 (15...♘b6 16 b3 ± Gufeld-Georgadze, USSR 1981) 16 ♖hf1 b5 17 b3 exf4 18 ♖xf4 ♘h5? (Timman considers that 18...♖h5 followed by an exchange sacrifice on g5 to be Black's best chance) 19 ♗xe7! ♘xf4 20 ♕xf4! ♔xe7 21 ♕xd6+ ♔e8 22 ♘d5 ♗xd5 23 ♗h3!! (Black has been convincingly punished for his optimistic 18th move) 23...♕c7 24 ♗xd7+ ♕xd7 25 ♕e5+ ♕e6 26 ♕xh8 ♔e7 27 ♕d4 with a winning

position for White, Ljubojević-Timman, Amsterdam 1986.

2) **8...d5** and then **9 exd5 ♘xd5 10 ♘xd5 exd5** is given as unclear by *ECO*. However, in distinction to 8 ♖g1 d5, White's rook is still defending the h-pawn, so White might consider **9 e5 ♘fd7 10 f4**, when 10...♗e7 11 h5 and 10...h5 11 gxh5 look good for White, so the critical reply is probably 10...♕b6. **9 g5** is also interesting.

9	**g5**	**hxg5**
10	**hxg5**	**♖xh1+**
11	**♗xh1**	**♘d7** *(D)*

If Black attacks the g5-pawn by **11...♘xd4 12 ♕xd4 ♘h7**, White continues **13 e5!** ♘xg5 (13...dxe5 14 ♕h4 traps the knight) **14 ♕a4+!** (14 exd6 is also promising) 14...♗d7 15 ♕g4 ♗e7 (15...♘h7 16 ♕h5 loses a piece while 15...f6 16 ♗xg5 fxg5 17 ♕h5 is disastrous) 16 exd6 ♗f6 17 ♗xb7 with a clear advantage.

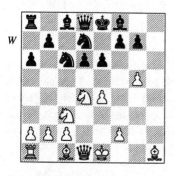

12 ♗g2

This move was the result of lengthy thought, but even so it wasn't the best. White has very few constructive moves apart from g6,

and the immediate **12 g6 ♘xd4 13 gxf7+ ♔xf7 14 ♕xd4 ♕h4 15 ♗g2 ♘e5** is obscure. White might be able to claim a slight plus after 16 ♗e3 ♕g4 17 ♔f1, but both kings are unhappily placed and I wanted to find something safer. When confronted with an unexpected move in the opening, players usually react by steering clear of very sharp lines which may have been well prepared by the opponent.

12 ♗e3 is bad due to 12...♘de5 threatening ...♘c4 (13 ♕e2 ♘xd4 loses a pawn).

Thus the only direct alternative to 12 g6 is 12 f4, but I was reluctant to create a huge empty space around my king. However, later analysis showed that Black has no way to exploit the temporary exposure of White's king, so in later games White preferred the more accurate **12 f4!**. Black has replied:

1) **12...♘xd4 13 ♕xd4 ♕b6 14 ♕xb6 ♘xb6 15 a4!? ♗d7 16 a5 ♘c8 17 ♗e3 ♗c6 18 0-0-0 ♔d7 19 ♗f3 ♘e7 20 ♗g4** with a clear plus for White, Ghinda-Vogt, Halle 1987.

2) **12...g6 13 ♗e3 ♕b6 14 a3 ♕c7 15 ♕e2 ♘a5 16 0-0-0 ♖b8 17 e5!?** (not strictly necessary, but very dangerous) dxe5 18 ♘xe6 fxe6 19 ♕d3 with a strong attack for the piece, Nunn-Suba, London (Lloyds Bank) 1990.

3) **12...♕b6 13 ♘de2 g6 14 b3** with a further branch:

3a) **14...♕c7 15 ♗b2 b5 16 ♕d2 ♖b8** (16...♗b7 17 ♘d1 0-0-0 18 ♘e3 ♗e7 19 0-0-0 ♘b6 20 ♔b1

♔b8 21 ♘c1 was also a little better for White in Grünfeld-Bischoff, Munich 1987) 17 ♗g2 (17 0-0-0 ♘b6 18 a3 ♗d7 19 ♗g2 b4 20 axb4 ♘xb4 was equal in Kir.Georgiev-Suba, Budapest Z 1993, but 18 ♖e1 b4 19 ♘d1 would have given White the edge, according to Stoica) 17...a5?! 18 ♘d1! a4 19 ♘e3 b4 20 0-0-0 ♗a6 21 ♔b1 axb3 22 axb3 was good for White in Watson-Suba, Kuala Lumpur 1992.

3b) **14...♕c5** 15 ♕d2 b5 16 ♗b2 ♗b7 17 0-0-0 0-0-0 18 ♔b1 ♕f2!? (or 18...♗e7 19 ♘c1! f6 20 gxf6 ♘xf6 21 ♘d3 with an edge) 19 a4 (19 ♖e1 ♗e7 20 ♘d1 ♕c5 21 ♘e3 gave White a small but lasting advantage, Short-Kindermann, Dortmund 1986) 19...♕b6 20 axb5 axb5 21 ♘c1 ♘c5 22 ♕h2! with a distinct plus for White, Anand-J.Polgar, Madrid 1993.

Although 12 ♗g2 is slightly inferior to 12 f4, it is still worth studying Nunn-Bischoff as the resulting positions are very similar.

| **12** | **...** | **g6!** |

The idea behind 12 ♗g2 was that White improves the position of his bishop (particularly in the g6 line given above, because ...♕h4 no longer gains a tempo), while Black has trouble finding useful moves. **12...♘de5** allows 13 f4 with gain of tempo (13...♘c4 14 b3 ♕b6 15 ♘ce2), **12...♕c7** (or ♗e7) allows 13 g6 and **12...♕b6** 13 ♘b3 loses time after a subsequent ♗e3. Black's reply is the best, cutting out g6 by White and again posing the question

as to how White can improve his position.

| **13** | **f4** *(D)* | |

Now the defect of 12 ♗g2 is revealed. In the analysis of 12 f4 we saw that Black generally plays ...g6 in any case, while White's ♗g2 is often not necessary. Therefore Black may gain a tempo, although in this position the extra move is not especially valuable. Now that e5 is denied to the black knights, White threatens simply ♗e3, so Black's reply is more or less forced.

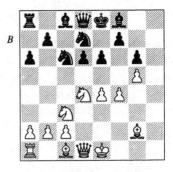

| **13** | **...** | **♕b6** |
| **14** | **♘de2** | |

Now White can only complete his development by ♕d2 (or ♕d3), b3, ♗b2 and 0-0-0, so before playing f4 I had to make sure that Black couldn't use the four(!) free tempi to harass White's centralised king.

| **14** | **...** | **♕c5** |

Black settles for finishing his own development by ...b5 and ...♗b7. This is clearly best, since **14...♕c7** allows 15 ♗e3 and **14...♘c5** is met by 15 b3 in any case.

| **15** | **♕d3** | |

15 ♕d2 would have been slightly better as the queen is exposed to possible knight attacks on d3. My idea was to leave open the possibility of ♗e3, but this is never feasible.

15 ... b5

16 b3

16 ♗e3 is effectively countered by 16...♘b4!.

16 ... ♗b7

17 ♗b2 ♖c8

A risky move; Black decides to leave his king in the centre in order to help his c-file counterplay. After **17...0-0-0** 18 0-0-0 White has a small space advantage, just as in the above analysis of 12 f4.

18 0-0-0 ♘b4

Thanks to Black's committal decision last move, he has to follow up with active play. If White is allowed to consolidate, then ♔b1, ♖f1 and ♘d1-e3-g4 will inevitably give White a strong attack against the centralised black king.

19 ♕d2 ♘xc2

20 ♔xc2 b4

21 ♔b1 ♕f2!

This is the point of Black's combination. The immediate **21...bxc3** 22 ♘xc3 leaves Black in a poor position, because his combination has failed to dent White's position, and the long-term prospects lie with White.

22 ♗h1 bxc3

At this stage Black surprisingly offered a draw, but although White must adopt the much less satisfactory recapture with the bishop, thus leaving e4 weak, I decided to play on. It goes without saying that allowing the queens to be exchanged would give White no advantage, because his main asset is the vulnerable position of Black's king, and this can only be exploited in the middlegame.

23 ♗xc3 *(D)*

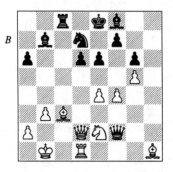

23 ... ♕a7?

A misjudgement. The main merit of Black's combination is that his queen has become a nuisance by taking up residence in the heart of White's position, the more so as White cannot contemplate a queen exchange. Bischoff retreats it to the passive square a8 in return for inconvenient but not really serious pressure against e4. He should have continued **23...♘c5** 24 ♗d4 ♕h2! (24...♘xe4 25 ♕d3! loses a piece, while 24...♕h4 25 ♘c3 e5 26 ♗e3 looks good for White) when White has problems with his e4-pawn. Then **25 ♕e3 e5** 26 ♗b2 ♗g7 creates a very awkward threat of ...exf4, so White would have to play **25 ♘c3** ♕xd2 26 ♖xd2 with equality.

24 ♗b2 ♕a8

25	♕e3	♘c5
26	♘c3	♗g7
27	♘d5! *(D)*	

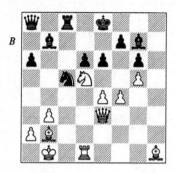

27 ...   ♗xb2

The most natural move. The alternatives are:

1) **27...♗xd5** 28 exd5 ♗xb2 29 dxe6!? (29 ♔xb2 gives White an edge) 29...♕a7 (preventing ♔xb2) 30 ♖xd6 ♔f8 (30...♗a3 31 exf7+ ♔f8 32 ♕c3 and 30...♗g7 31 ♗c6+ ♔f8 32 ♖d7 win for White) 31 ♖d7 ♕b6 32 e7+ ♔e8 33 ♖d8+ ♖xd8 34 exd8♕+ ♔xd8 35 ♕d2+ ♘d3 36 ♕xd3+ and the extra pawn gives White some winning chances in the ending.

2) **27...exd5** 28 ♗xg7 ♘xe4 (better than 28...dxe4 29 ♖xd6, as in this case the undefended c5-knight prevents 29...♖d8, while 29...♘d3 allows 30 ♖xd3) 29 ♗f3! is good for White. The threat is simply ♖h1-h8, and the bishop can move to g4 to cut off the escape of Black's king.

28	♘b6	♗xe4+
29	♔xb2	♕a7

The only defence. Now 30 ♘c4 d5 31 ♗xe4 is tempting, but Black

can reply 31...dxc4! 32 ♕d4 ♕c7, and it is doubtful if White has anything better than perpetual check.

30 ♖xd6   ♘d3+

Black's moves continue to be forced. **30...♗xh1** 31 ♕d4! (attacking the rook on c8 and threatening ♕h8+) 31...♖b8 (31...♖c7 32 ♕h8 and mate at d8) 32 ♕xc5 (threatening ♖d7) 32...♖d8 (32...♕e7 33 ♘c8 ♕b7 34 ♖xe6+ wins) 33 ♕e5 gives White a decisive attack, for example 33...♖xd6/♕e7/♕b8 34 ♕h8+ or 33...♖b8 34 ♖xe6+ fxe6 35 ♕h8+.

31 ♔a3   ♖c6!

I had overlooked this ingenious defence when I played 26 ♘c3. Alternatives lose quickly:

1) **31...♖c5** 32 ♖xd3 ♖a5+ (or 32...♕xb6 33 ♗xe4) 33 ♔b2 ♗xd3 (33...♗xh1 34 ♕d4) 34 ♗c6+ ♔d8 (otherwise a knight check wins the queen) 35 b4 ♖f5 36 ♕xd3+ ♔c7 37 ♕d7+ ♔xb6 38 ♕d4+ and Black loses his queen.

2) **31...♕c7** 32 ♖xd3 ♗xd3 33 ♘xc8 ♕xc8 34 ♕xd3 ♕c1+ 35 ♔b4 ♕xh1 36 ♕xa6 ♕e1+ 37 ♔b5 ♕e2+ 38 ♔b6 ♕f2+ 39 ♔b7 with a winning ending since 39...♕xf4 fails to 40 ♕a4+.

3) **31...♗xh1** 32 ♕h3 ♖b8 33 ♖xe6+ fxe6 34 ♕h8+ winning the queen.

32 ♖xc6

The best, since **32 ♘d5** ♕xe3 33 ♘f6+ is a draw by perpetual check and 32 ♖xd3 (32 ♕xd3 ♕xb6 is good for Black) 32...♗xh1 33 ♘c4 is roughly equal.

32 ...   ♕e7+ *(D)*

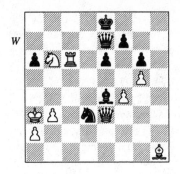

33 ♕c5!

33 ♖c5 ♗xh1 34 b4 ♘xc5 35 ♕xc5 is not so good since Black can avoid the exchange of queens by **35...♕d8**, when White's exposed king means an almost inevitable perpetual check. After the game Bischoff admitted that he had not foreseen this move in time.

33 ...   ♕xc5+

Or **33...♘xc5 34 ♖c8+ ♕d8 35 ♖xd8+ ♔xd8** transposing into the game, except for an unimportant change in the position of Black's king.

34 ♖xc5   ♘xc5
35 b4!

White is aiming for a good knight v bad bishop ending. He can also head for a knight v knight ending by **35 ♗xe4 (35 ♔b4 ♘d3+ 36 ♔c3 ♘f2!** leads to the same position) **35...♘xe4 36 ♔b4**, intending ♔a5, but although this is favourable for White, his advantage is less than in the game.

35 ...   ♗xh1
36 bxc5   ♗d5?

A blunder in severe time-trouble. He should have tried **36...♔e7** 37

♔b4 e5! 38 fxe5 ♔e6, but even here White wins by 39 ♘c4 ♗d5 40 a3! ♗xc4 41 ♔xc4 ♔xe5 42 ♔b4! ♔d5 43 a4 and Black is in a fatal zugzwang.

37 ♘xd5   exd5

White wins because Black's a-pawn has moved, while White's can still advance either one or two squares. This extra flexibility means that White can always arrange for the key reciprocal zugzwang position to arrive with Black to play.

38 ♔b4   ♔d7
39 ♔c3   1-0

Black lost on time, but in any case **39...♔c6** 40 ♔d4 a5 41 a4 and **39...♔c7** 40 ♔d4 ♔c6 41 a3 a5 42 a4 lead to the same position of reciprocal zugzwang.

Game 6
Nunn – Sax
Rotterdam 1989

1	e4	c5
2	♘f3	e6
3	d4	cxd4
4	♘xd4	♘f6
5	♘c3	d6
6	g4	h6
7	h4	♘c6
8	♖g1	h5

This is currently the most popular move. White's best reply is to take on h5 and since the recapture ...♘xh5 leaves the knight badly placed, Black normally returns it to f6. The net effect of this is to reach a position similar to that after 6 g4 h6 7 g5 hxg5 8 ♗xg5, but with White having the two extra tempi h4 and ⟂g1. This might seem to be a great improvement, but in fact the disadvantages almost balance the advantages. White has two problems; firstly the h-pawn can become weak without the defence of the rook and secondly Black's ...♕b6 effectively pins the f-pawn against the undefended g1-rook, so it is harder for White to play f4.

Apart from 8...h5, Black has:

1) **8...d5 9 ♗b5 ♗d7 10 exd5 ♘xd5** (10...♘xd4 11 ♗xd7+ ♕xd7 12 ♕xd4 ♘xd5 13 ♘xd5 ♕xd5 14 ♕xd5 exd5 15 ♗e3 gave White the better ending in Nikolenko-Zakharov, Smolensk 1991) **11 ♘xd5 exd5 12 ♗e3** *(D)* (this pawn sacrifice is more promising than 12 ♕e2+) and now:

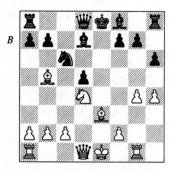

1a) The game Karpov-Spassky, Tilburg 1980 continued **12...♗e7 13 ♕d2 ♗xh4?!** (13...0-0 14 ♘f5 ♗xf5 15 gxf5 ♔h7 16 0-0-0 is also very good for White, but Black has better survival chances after 13...♘xd4 14 ♗xd7+ ♕xd7 15 ♕xd4 ♗f6 16 ♕b4 ♗e7, when he went on to draw in Marjanović-Cebalo, Yugoslav Ch 1982, although he needed to defend accurately until move 64 to achieve this) 14 0-0-0 ♗f6 (14...♘xd4 15 ♗xd7+ ♕xd7 16 ♗xd4 0-0 17 f4! followed by g5 and 14...0-0 15 g5! give White winning attacks) 15 ♘f5 ♗xf5 16 gxf5 a6 (Black could not castle without losing his vital h6-pawn, but now his king is permanently pinned down in the centre) 17 ♗xc6+ bxc6 18 ♗c5! (with White only needing to rip open the d-file by c4 to finish Black off, Spassky launches an ingenious counterattack which fails because of his inability to bring the h8-rook into the game) 18...♖b8 19 b4 ♖b5 (Black has to eliminate the deadly bishop) 20 ♖ge1+ ♔d7 21 c4 ♖xc5 22 bxc5 ♗g5 (after 22...♕b8 23 cxd5 ♗g5 24 ♖e3 ♗xe3 25 fxe3 ♕e5 26 dxc6+ ♔xc6 27 ♕d7+ White should win easily enough) 23 f4 ♕f6 24 cxd5! (not 24 fxg5 ♕a1+ 25 ♔c2 ♕xa2+ 26 ♔d3 ♕xc4+ 27 ♔e3 hxg5 when Black has four pawns and a tremendous attack for the rook) 24...♕a1+ 25 ♔c2 ♕xa2+ 26 ♔d3 ♕xd2+ (26...♕b3+ 27 ♕c3 also forces the queens off) 27 ♖xd2 ♗xf4 (although Black has two pawns for the exchange all White's pieces are very active and Black is unable to organise himself against the advance of the c-pawn) 28 ♖a2 cxd5 29 ♖xa6 h5 30 ♔d4 h4 31 ♔xd5 ♖b8 32 f6 gxf6 33 ♖xf6 ♗g3 34 ♖xf7+ ♔d8 35 ♖f8+ 1-0.

1b) **12...♕xh4** was recommended by Kasparov both in *ECO* and in his book with Nikitin on the Scheveningen, but of White's responses he only considers 13 ♕e2, which is curious as 13 ♕d2 was given in *Informator 30*:

1b1) **13 ♕e2 ♘xd4 14 ♗xd4+ ♕e7 15 ♗xd7+ ♔xd7 16 ♗e3 ♖d8 17 0-0-0 ♔c8** with an equal game according to Makarychev.

1b2) **13 ♕f3!? a6! 14 ♗xc6 bxc6 15 0-0-0 ♗d6 16 ♘f5 ♗xf5 17 gxf5 ♗e5 18 ♔b1 ♖b8 19 b3 ♕b4!** and though White still has compensation for his pawn, Black was able to hold the balance in Anand-Salov, Moscow Alekhine mem 1992.

1b3) **13 ♕d2!** (*BTS2*'s suggestion still seems to be best) and now **13...♗e7 14 0-0-0** followed by ♘f5 is dangerous for Black, whilst if he tries to follow the Salov plan with **13...a6 14 ♗xc6 bxc6 15 0-0-0 ♗d6 16 ♘f5 ♗xf5 17 gxf5 ♗e5**, then the fact that White has not blocked his f-pawn makes all the difference. After 18 f4! ♗f6 19 ♗c5 Black's queen is horribly out of the game and his king extremely exposed.

2) **8...♘d7 9 g5 hxg5** (D) and now:

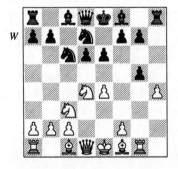

2a) **10 hxg5** g6 (10...♘de5 11 ♗e3 ♗d7 12 ♗e2 a6 13 f4 ± Matulović-Simić, Smederevo 1981) 11 ♗e3 a6 12 ♕e2 ♘a5 13 0-0-0 b5 14 f4 ♕c7?! (14...♘c4 is better) 15 ♔b1 ♘b6 16 ♘b3! ♘ac4 17 ♗d4 ♖g8? (17...♖h7) 18 ♕h2! ♗e7 19 ♕h7 ♖f8 20 f5 with a winning attack for White, Morović-J.Polgar, Las Palmas 1994.

2b) **10 ♗xg5 ♕b6 11 ♘b3 a6 12 h5 ♕c7 13 ♕e2 b5 14 0-0-0 b4** (Tseshkovsky-Zarubin, Sochi 1981) 15 ♘a4! a5 16 f4 with a good game for White, according to Tseshkovsky. My (JN) personal preference is for 10 ♗xg5, since Black's knight is badly placed at d7.

3) **8...g6 9 g5 hxg5 10 ♗xg5** (10 hxg5 ♘d7 transposes to line '2a') 10...♗e7 11 ♕d2 a6 12 0-0-0 ♕b6 13 ♘b3 ♕c7 14 f4 ♗d7 15 f5 0-0-0 16 ♗h3 was better for White in Sideif-Zade–Zarubin, USSR 1982.

9 gxh5 ♘xh5

Black has been known to try **9...♖xh5 10 ♗g5 ♖h8**, but this is quite pointless. Black reaches the same position as in the main line, but having forfeited the right to castle kingside.

10 ♗g5 (D)

10 ... ♘f6

The alternative is the immediate **10...♕b6**, which attempts to avoid the loss of time inherent in 10...♘f6. The problem is that the knight is genuinely badly placed at h5, so Black gains nothing by keeping it there. After **11 ♘b3 a6 12 ♗e2 g6** (12...♘f6 transposes to the analysis

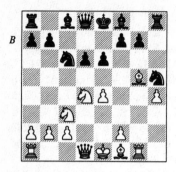

of 11...♕b6 in the main line) **13 ♕d2**
Black may play:

1) **13...♗d7 14 ♖g2!** (White is
not forced to sacrifice his f-pawn by
castling straight away) **14...♕c7 15
0-0-0 b5 16 a3** *(D)* and now:

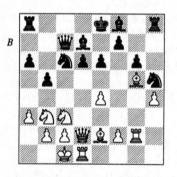

1a) **16...♘e5 17 ♕d4! ♖h7 18 f4
♘c4 19 ♗xh5 ♖xh5 20 ♖e1 ♗c6 21
♘d5 ♗xd5 22 exd5 e5 23 ♕d3 ♗e7
24 ♘d4!** and White stands well,
Motwani-Roca, Dubai OL 1986.

1b) **16...♖b8** (16...♖c8 should
also be met by 17 f4) **17 f4 b4 18
axb4 ♘xb4 19 f5!** (White must open
lines before Black can generate a
queenside attack) and now:

1b1) Gallagher-Chomet, Royan
1988 continued **19...exf5 20 exf5**

♗xf5 21 ♕e3+! ♗e7 (or 21...♗e6 22
♘d4 ♕d7 23 ♗g4 ♘g7 24 ♗f6 and
Black won't be able to tolerate the
pressure much longer) 22 ♘d4 f6
(not the most resilient but it was lost
anyway) 23 ♘xf5 fxg5 24 ♗xh5
gxh5 25 ♘xd6+ 1-0.

1b2) During the game I felt that
19...a5 was Black's only chance, but
after 20 fxg6 fxg6 21 ♖f1! White's
attack is much quicker, e.g. 21...a4
(if 21...♗g7, then 22 ♗xh5 and 23
♗f6 is very strong and on 21...♗c6,
22 ♘d4 looks good) 22 ♗xh5 gxh5
23 ♕f4 ♗c8 (23...♗c6 24 ♕f6 and
23...♗b5 24 ♘xb5 ♘d3+ 25 ♔b1
are no better) 24 ♕f6 ♖g8 25 ♗e3!
♘a2+ (25...♕h7 26 ♘xa4 is sufficient) 26 ♘xa2 axb3 27 ♘b4!! (27
♘c3 ♕h7 is good for White but far
less clear than the text) 27...♖xb4
(27...♕h7 28 ♘c6) 28 c3! ♕h7 29
♖xg8 ♕xg8 30 ♗g5! and it's time to
resign.

2) **13...♗e7 14 ♖g2! ♗d7 15 0-0-0
♖c8 16 ♔b1 ♕c7 17 a3 b5 18 ♗xb5
axb5 19 ♘xb5 ♕b8 20 ♗xe7 ♕xb5
21 ♗xd6** with a clear advantage for
White, Lobron-Marjanović, Reggio
Emilia 1985/6.

3) **13...♕c7** (this is even worse
than the lines above because White
need not spend time on ♖g2) **14
0-0-0 b5 15 a3 ♗d7 16 ♗xb5!** axb5
**17 ♘xb5 ♕b8 18 ♘xd6+ ♗xd6 19
♕xd6 ♕xd6 20 ♖xd6** with advantage to White, Govedarica-Mokry,
Trnava 1987.

11 ♗e2 *(D)*

This flexible move, which prepares a possible h5, has gained in

popularity, even though White sometimes has to sacrifice his f2-pawn after ♕d2 and 0-0-0. In reply the immediate ...♕b6 turns out badly because h5-h6 becomes strong, so Black normally bides his time with ...a6.

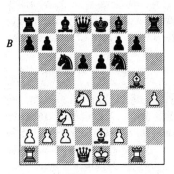

11 ...   a6

Or:

1) **11...♗e7 12 ♕d2 ♘xd4 13 ♕xd4 ♕b6 14 ♗b5+ ♔f8** (14...♗d7 15 ♗xd7+ ♔xd7 16 ♕d2 is good for White) **15 ♕xb6 axb6 16 0-0-0 e5** was unclear in Ljubojević-Adorjan, Linares 1985, but it is hard to believe that there is no way White can exploit the weak b-pawns. Perhaps **16 ♘a4!?** is best.

2) **11...♕b6 12 ♘b3 a6 13 h5 ♕c7** (or 13...♗d7 14 h6 ♖h7 15 ♕d2 ♘g8 16 ♗e3 ♕c7 17 hxg7 ♖xg7 18 0-0-0 with a plus for White, Alzate-Frias, Dubai OL 1986) **14 h6 ♘d7 15 hxg7 ♗xg7 16 ♕d2 ♗f8 17 0-0-0 b5 18 a3 ♗b7 19 ♖h1 ♖xh1 20 ♖xh1 ♘ce5**, Hellers-Sax, New York Open 1987, and now 21 ♖h8! ♘g6 22 ♖h7 would have given White a very dangerous attack.

3) **11...♗d7 12 h5** (on 12 ♕d2, 12...♘xd4 13 ♕xd4 ♕b6 is interesting, whilst 12 ♘db5 ♕b8 is not dangerous for Black) **12...a6 13 ♕d2** and now:

3a) **13...♕b6** transposes to '2' in the note to Black's 12th move.

3b) **13...♗e7 14 0-0-0 ♕c7? 15 h6! gxh6 16 ♗xf6 ♗xf6 17 ♘f5!! ♗e7** (the brilliant point is 17...exf5 18 ♘d5 ♕d8 19 ♕xh6!) **18 ♘xe7 ♔xe7** (18...♘xe7 was the lesser evil) **19 ♖g3! b5 20 ♕f4 ♖ad8 21 ♕h4+ ♔e8 22 ♗xb5!** with a winning position for White, Anand-Ye Jiangchuan, Kuala Lumpur 1989.

3c) **13...b5 14 a3 ♗e7 15 ♗e3!?** (15 0-0-0) **15...♘xh5 16 0-0-0 ♘f6** (it seems a strange decision to give the pawn back at once, even if after 16...g6 17 f4 ♘f6 18 ♖h1 ♖g8 19 ♗f3 White has good compensation according to Kasparov) **17 ♖xg7 ♕b8 18 ♘xc6! ♖xc6 19 ♕d4** with advantage to White, Kasparov-Sax, Tilburg 1989.

12 ♕d2   ♗d7

Playing for ...b5 is a relatively new idea, but the critical continuation is probably the older **12...♕b6 13 ♘b3** (D) and now:

1) **13...♕c7** with a couple of possibilities:

1a) **14 h5** (the most common continuation but I (JG) am not totally convinced) 14...b5 15 a3 ♘xh5 16 ♖h1 g6 17 ♗xh5 gxh5 (17...♘e5 18 ♕e2 gxh5 19 ♖xh5 ♖xh5 20 ♕xh5 ♗b7 21 0-0-0 was also unclear in the game Brunner-Adorjan, Altensteig 1989) 18 ♕e2 b4 19 axb4 (19 ♘d5 is

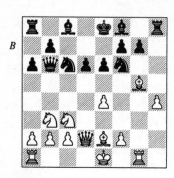

extremely speculative) 19...♘xb4 20 0-0-0 ♗g7 and I don't believe that Black has much to worry about. A possible continuation: 21 ♖xh5 (21 ♔b1 is probably the critical line) 21...♗xc3 22 bxc3 ♖xh5 23 ♕xh5 ♕xc3 24 ♖d2 (White now has the surprisingly awkward threat of ♕h7-g8 but Black has a spectacular defence) 24...♗b7! 25 ♕h7 ♘a2+! 26 ♔b1 (26 ♔d1 ♕f3+) 26...♕xb3+!! 27 cxb3 ♗xe4+ 28 ♔xa2! ♗xh7 29 ♖xd6 and a draw is inevitable.

1b) **14 0-0-0** and now:

1b1) The game Gallagher-Maxion, Bad Wörishofen 1991 didn't last vary long: **14...♗d7** 15 h5 ♗e7 16 ♗f4! ♘xh5?! 17 ♗xh5 ♖xh5 18 ♖xg7 ♘e5 19 ♖g8+ ♗f8 20 ♗xe5 ♖xe5 (or 20...dxe5 21 ♕xd7+ ♕xd7 22 ♖xf8+) 21 ♕h6 ♔e7 22 ♕h4+ 1-0.

1b2) **14...b5** is more active. After 15 a3 ♗b7 (15...♖b8 can also be met by 16 h5) 16 h5 ♘xh5 (16...b4 17 axb4 ♘xb4 18 ♕d4 d5 19 h6! ♖xh6 20 ♗xh6 e5 21 ♗f4! won for White in Luther-Bönsch, East German Ch 1989) 17 ♖h1 g6, White can transpose into Brunner-Adorjan with **18**

♗xh5 gxh5 19 ♕e2 ♘e5 20 ♖xh5 ♖xh5 21 ♕xh5, but he can also try **18 f4**, which seems to give him good compensation for the pawn. **18...b4** 19 axb4 ♘xb4 20 ♕d4 is not possible for Black, so he would most likely play **18...♖c8** when White can has the safe 19 ♔b1 followed by f5, or the sharper possibility 19 f5 b4 20 axb4 ♘xb4 21 fxe6 (21 ♕d4 ♘a2+!) 21...fxe6 22 ♗g4.

2) **13...♗d7 14 h5 ♘xh5** (Black should take everything on offer; the passive 14...0-0-0 15 h6 ♖h7 16 0-0-0! ♗e7 17 ♗e3 ♕c7 18 ♖xg7 ♖xg7 19 hxg7 ♖g8 20 ♖g1 ♘e5 21 ♗d4 ♘g6 22 ♕h6 ♗c6 23 ♗d3 was very good for White in Korolev-Agzamov, USSR 1983) **15 ♖h1 g6 16 0-0-0 ♕xf2** (once again the crucial move; 16...♕c7 17 ♗xh5 gxh5 18 ♕e2! ♗e7 19 ♗xe7 ♘xe7 20 ♖xh5 ♖xh5 21 ♕xh5 ♘g6 was played in Tseshkovsky-Mokry, Trnava 1986, and now 22 ♕h2! was promising for White) **17 e5! ♕f5!** *(D)* (17...♘xe5 18 ♘e4 ♕f5 19 ♕e3! ♗c6 20 ♘bd2! gives White a crushing attack) and the evaluation of the whole line depends critically on this position.

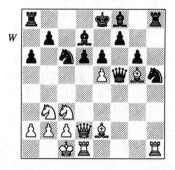

White has tried:

2a) **18 ♗xh5 ♖xh5 19 ♖xh5 gxh5 20 exd6 ♘e5 21 ♘d4 ♕g4 22 ♗e7 ♘c4 23 ♕d3 ♘e5 24 ♕e3 ♘c4 25 ♕d3 ♘e5** and there was only a draw by repetition, Chandler-Hellers, Thessaloniki OL 1988.

2b) White played **18 exd6 ♕g5 19 ♕xg5 ♗h6 20 ♕xh6 ♖xh6 21 ♘c5 ♘e5! 22 ♘3e4 0-0-0 23 ♘xd7! ♔xd7 24 ♖h3 ♖e8** in A.Rodriguez-Grooten, Dieren 1987, and although Rodriguez gives 25 b4! as unclear, this line is not convincing. It seems to me (JN) that it would have been more promising for White to play **21 ♘e4!**, intending a combination of ♘f6 and ♘bc5, while 21...0-0-0 22 ♘f6 ♖dh8 23 ♘xd7 ♔xd7 24 ♘c5+ ♔c8 25 ♗f3 gives White dangerous threats.

2c) **18 ♔b1!?** is the latest try, which rules out the queen exchange at the cost of another pawn. Lau-Lesiège, Eurodata 1992, continued 18...d5 (18...♕xe5 19 ♗xh5 ♖xh5 20 ♖xh5 gxh5 21 ♖e1 ♕f5 22 ♘d5 is good for White) 19 ♖df1!? (19 ♖de1 d4? 20 ♘xd4! ♘xd4 21 ♕xd4 ♕xg5 22 ♘e4 ♕d8 23 ♗xh5 ♗g7 24 ♗xg6 ♖xh1 25 ♖xh1 fxg6 26 ♘d6+ won for White in Hector-Mortensen, Græsted 1990, but Hector points out that 19...♗e7 would have been a much tougher defence) 19...♕xe5 (19...♘g3 20 ♖xh8 ♘xf1 21 ♕f4! ♕xf4 22 ♗xf4 g5 23 ♗xg5 ♘g3 24 ♗h6! ♔e7 25 ♗g5+ ♔e8 26 ♗d3 with excellent compensation for the pawn; an important point is that 26...♘xe5 fails to 27 ♗f4 ♘xd3

28 ♗d6! as 28...0-0-0 is now illegal) 19...♕xe5 20 ♗xh5 ♖xh5 21 ♖xh5 gxh5 22 ♖e1 ♕d6 23 ♘xd5 ♗e7! 24 ♘f6+ ♔d8 25 ♕f2 and White had compensation for the pawns but perhaps only enough for an equal game.

13 0-0-0 b5
14 ♘xc6!

The immediate **14 ♕e3** is met by 14...♕b6.

14 ... ♗xc6
15 ♕e3 *(D)*

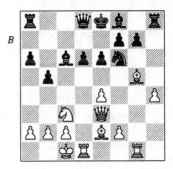

White has the unpleasant threats of 16 e5 and 16 ♘d5, while after **15...♕a5** White can afford to take time out for 16 ♔b1 because 16...b4 may be met by 17 ♘d5 ♘xd5 18 exd5 ♗xd5 19 ♖xd5 ♕xd5 20 ♗f3. Black is therefore forced into the unpalatable 15...♕c7.

15 ... ♕c7
16 ♘d5 ♗xd5
17 exd5 e5

After **17...♖c8** White replies 18 c3, and Black has achieved nothing positive, while he has forfeited the right to castle queenside. 17...e5 is better, but even so White's lead in development and Black's exposed king give him dangerous attacking chances.

18 ⊈b1?!

Chess laziness. Of course ⊈b1 is a desirable move, but by giving Black a free tempo White's attack loses much of its momentum. The immediate **18 f4!** was correct, when White has a clear advantage. Now by accurate defence Black survives the immediate crisis.

18 ... ♘h7

Eliminating the g5-bishop makes it easier to flee with the king, should that prove necessary, and ultimately the opposite-coloured bishops might provide a drawing mechanism.

19 f4 ♘xg5

Not **19...f6** 20 fxe5 dxe5 21 ♗h5+ ⊈d8 22 d6 ♗xd6 23 ♖xd6+ ♕xd6 24 ♖d1 ♕xd1+ 25 ♗xd1 fxg5 26 ♕xe5 with an excellent position for White.

20 ♖xg5

A difficult choice, as although White may win a pawn by **20 fxe5** (20 hxg5 g6 21 f5!? is probably also slightly better for White) 20...dxe5 21 ♖xg5 0-0-0! 22 ♖xe5 ♗d6, Black completes his development and the opposite-coloured bishops become an important factor.

20 ... ♖c8

Now **20...0-0-0** is bad because of 21 a4!, so Black must adopt a different defensive plan.

21 c3 ♕c5

Of course this is only possible when White has not exchanged on e5. Black gains time to reorganise his defences.

22 ♕g3 exf4
23 ♕xf4 ♖c7! *(D)*

An excellent move. Black's rook covers the vulnerable square f7 and when it arrives at e7 the attack on the bishop will gain more time for Black.

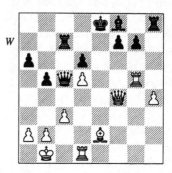

24 a4!

White's only chance to make something of his waning initiative is to create a new target on the queenside.

24 ... ♖e7
25 ♗d3 g6
26 axb5 axb5

Not **26...♗h6?** 27 ♕f6.

27 ♕d4

The ending now represents the best winning chance for White. Although White's gain of a pawn is only temporary, the passed b-pawn combined with an exposed Black king gives White a nagging advantage.

27 ... ♕xd4
28 ♗xb5+ ⊈d8
29 ♖xd4 ♖e1+
30 ⊈a2 ♗e7
31 ♖gg4 ♖h1

The h-pawn is doomed, so White switches to harassing Black's king. In this the opposite-coloured bishops prove a big help.

32	♖a4	♖8xh4
33	♖xh4	♖xh4 *(D)*

33...♗xh4 34 ♖a7 is worse, since White threatens the f-pawn directly and the d-pawn indirectly via ♖d7+.

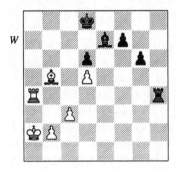

34 ♖a8+?

A careless check driving Black's king to a better square. White should have cut the king off by **34 ♖a7!** (threatening ♖d7+) 34...♗e4 (34...g5 35 ♖d7+ ♔e8 36 ♖xd6+ ♔f8 37 ♖c6 and the d-pawn becomes dangerous) 35 ♗c6! with winning chances because Black cannot challenge White to a pawn race (35...g5 36 b4 g4 37 b5 g3 38 b6 wins because the mate threat gains a tempo).

34	...	♔c7
35	♗c6	

35 ♖a7+ ♔b6 36 ♖xe7 ♔xb5 37 ♖xf7 ♔c5 is an easy draw.

| 35 | ... | ♖e4! |

White is effectively a tempo down over the above line since after **36 ♖a7+ ♔b8** White must waste time

with his rook. This tempo makes all the difference and Black can now draw comfortably.

36	b4	♗f6
37	♖a7+	♔b8
38	♖xf7	♗xc3
39	b5	♖b4
40	♔a3	♖b1
41	♖b7+	♔c8
42	b6	♗d4
43 ·	♖c7+	♔b8
44	♖b7+	

½-½

Game 7
Kotronias – Kr. Georgiev
Karditsa 1994

1	e4	c5
2	♘f3	e6
3	d4	cxd4
4	♘xd4	♘f6
5	♘c3	d6
6	g4	a6

Of the sixth move alternatives we only consider 6...e5 here; the others may be found in Games 8 and 9.

6...e5 7 ♗b5+ ♗d7 8 ♗xd7+ ♕xd7 (8...♘bxd7 9 ♘f5 is awful for Black) **9 ♘f5 h5 10 gxh5** (*BTS2* proposed 10 f3, which is also quite a good move) **10...♘xh5** (10...♖xh5 11 ♘d5! and 10...♘xe4 11 ♘xg7+ ♗xg7 12 ♘xe4 d5 13 h6! are not playable for Black) **11 ♗h6!** (the shock effect of this move is the main reason we have switched systems) **11...♘c6** (11...gxh6 12 ♕xh5 is a disaster, whilst 11...g6 12 ♗xf8 gxf5 13 ♗xd6 is no fun either) **12 ♕xh5** *(D)* and now:

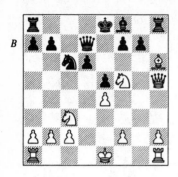

1) The game Shmuter-Obukhov, Russia 1993 continued **12...g6** 13 ♕g5 gxf5 14 ♗xf8 ♘d4 (14...♖xf8 15 ♘d5) 15 0-0-0 ♔xf8 16 ♖hg1 ♕e6 17 ♖xd4! (this ensures White a permanent attack for a minimal material investment) 17...exd4 18 ♕g7+ ♔e7 19 ♘d5+ ♔d7 20 ♕xd4 ♖hc8 (20...fxe4 21 ♕a4+ ♔c8 {21...♔d8 22 ♕a5+ b6 23 ♘xb6} 22 ♕c4+ ♔d8 23 ♕c7+ ♔e8 24 ♕xb7 and 20...♖ac8 21 ♖d1! fxe4 22 ♕xa7 ♖xh2 23 ♕xb7+ ♔d8 24 ♕b6+ ♔d7 25 ♕a7+ ♔d8 26 ♕a5+ ♔e8 27 ♘c7+ are good for White) 21 ♕b4! ♖ab8 22 ♕a4+ ♖c6 23 ♕xa7 ♕h6+ 24 ♔b1 ♕h8 25 ♘b4 ♖c7 26 e5! ♖a8 (26...b5 also meets a nice refutation: 27 e6+! fxe6 28 ♕xb8 ♕xb8 29 ♖g7+ ♔c8 30 ♖g8+ ♔b7 31 ♖xb8+ ♔xb8 32 ♘a6+ and White wins the resulting king and pawn ending) 27 e6+! ♔xe6 (27...fxe6 loses to 28 ♕xa8!) 28 ♕b6 ♖c5 29 ♘d3 ♕d4 30 ♕xb7 ♖h8 31 ♘xc5+ 1-0.

2) **12...♘e7** was not considered by Shmuter in his notes to the game, but this is probably Black's best defence. White now has two possible replies:

2a) **13 ♕g5 ♘xf5 14 exf5 ♖xh6** (White possesses a far superior minor piece but also a weakened kingside which is why Black is not without hope) 15 ♘d5 (15 0-0-0 f6 16 ♕g2 {16 ♕g4 g6!} 16...0-0-0 is unclear) 15...♕a4! (Black does best to mix it up as 15...♕c6 16 0-0-0 ♖c8 17 c3 ♕c4 18 f6! is good for White) 16 ♘c7+ (16 0-0-0 ♖c8 is awkward) 16...♔d7 17 ♘xa8 ♕e4+ 18 ♔d2 ♕d5+ 19 ♔e2 (19 ♔e3 ♖h3+) 19...♕c4+ 20 ♔f3 ♕c6+! and I can't see how White can escape the checks as 21 ♔g3 ♗e7! 22 f6 ♖xf6! appears bad for White.

2b) **13 ♕g4** (this seems to be the better choice as the queen controls the fourth rank) **13...♘xf5 14 exf5 ♖xh6 15 0-0-0** and Black has several possibilities which all seem insufficient to equalise:

2b1) **15...0-0-0** 16 f4! ±.

2b2) **15...♖g6** 16 ♕e4 ♖g5 17 ♘d5! ♖c8 (17...0-0-0 18 ♕e3) 18 ♘e3 ♕c6 19 ♖d5 is good for White.

2b3) **15...g6** 16 ♘d5! gxf5 17 ♕g5 ♖g6 (other moves are worse) 18 ♕xg6 fxg6 19 ♘f6+ ♔d8 20 ♘xd7 ♔xd7 21 h4! ♗h6+ 22 ♔b1 ♔e6 23 ♖hg1 ♖g8 24 c4 and White has some advantage. Black can try to break out with 24...b5, but after 25 cxb5 d5 26 ♖g3! followed by ♖a3 White may experience some nervous moments but should win in the end.

7	g5	♘fd7
8	h4	b5

8...♘c6 9 ♗e3 will transpose to either Game 8 or Game 9.

9	a3	

White should never play this move lightly in the Sicilian, especially when he plans to castle long. In this case, it is imperative that the knight on c3 has a stable base as it holds White's centre together whilst he goes mad on the kingside.

9 ... ♝b7

9...♘b6 is less accurate since after 10 h5 White may meet **10...♝e7** with the dangerous piece sacrifice 11 ♕g4 e5 12 ♘f5 g6 13 hxg6 fxg6 14 ♝e3! gxf5 15 exf5; in Nunn-Walden, Nottingham 1983, the continuation **10...♘8d7** 11 ♖h3 ♘c5 12 g6 f6 13 ♖g3 e5 14 ♘c6 ♕c7 15 ♘b4 was good for White.

10 ♝e3 *(D)*

10 h5 at once is not so good because 10...♝e7 awkwardly attacks the g5-pawn. 11 g6 doesn't work in this position since after 11...hxg6 12 hxg6 ♖xh1 13 gxf7+ ♚xf7 14 ♕f3+ ♝f6 15 ♕xh1, White's knight on d4 is hanging.

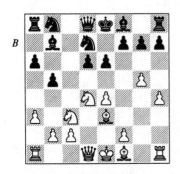

10 ... ♘b6

Or:

1) **10...♝e7 11 ♕d2** (11 ♕e2!?) and now:

1a) **11...♘c5** 12 f3 ♕c7 13 0-0-0 ♘c6 (13...♘bd7 14 ♝xb5 proved to be better for White in Fischer-Najdorf, Leipzig OL 1960) 14 ♘xc6 ♝xc6 and this position is assessed as slightly better for White by Kasparov in *ECO*.

1b) **11...♘b6?!** 12 ♘xe6! fxe6 13 ♕d4 ♘c4 14 ♕xg7 ♚d7 (14...♖f8 15 ♝xc4 bxc4 16 ♕xh7 is also good for White) 15 ♝xc4 bxc4 16 0-0-0 ♕f8?! (16...♕g8 would also be met by 17 ♖xd6+!, but the best try was 16...♘c6, although after 17 ♘a4 ♕f8 18 ♕c3 White has more than sufficient for a piece) 17 ♖xd6+! ♚xd6 18 ♕d4+ ♚c7 19 ♕b6+ ♚c8 20 ♕xe6+ ♘d7 (20...♚d8 21 ♖d1+ ♚e8 22 ♘d5 ♝xd5 23 ♕xd5 wins for White) 21 ♖d1 ♕d8 (21...♕e8 is slightly more resilient, but after 22 ♘a4! ♝d8 23 ♕xc4+ ♝c7 24 ♝f4 ♘e5 {24...♕d8 25 ♘b6+!}, White has at the very minimum 25 ♘b6+ ♚b8 26 ♝xe5! ♕c6 27 ♝xc7+ ♕xc7 28 ♕xc7+ ♚xc7 29 ♘xa8+ with no less than five pawns for the bishop) 22 ♘a4! and Black has no defence against ♖xd7, Karklins-Commons, USA 1972.

2) **10...♘c6** 11 ♕e2 ♘de5 12 0-0-0 ♘c4 13 ♘xc6 ♝xc6 14 f4 ♕a5?! 15 ♘d5! gave White a crushing attack in Alexander-Lundholm, Corr. 1970-1.

3) **10...♘c5** 11 ♕g4!? ♘bd7 12 0-0-0 ♘e5 13 ♕g2 ♘c4 14 ♝xc4 bxc4 15 h5 intending g6 is good for White according to Boudy.

11 h5 ♘8d7

12 g6! *(D)*

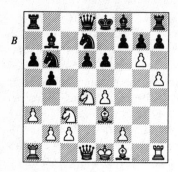

This discovery by Adams virtually refutes Black's whole set-up. Previously **12 ♖h3**, defending the rook in preparation for g6, had been played, but it turns out to be superfluous in this particular position as White can quite happily sacrifice a whole rook for a raging attack. Nevertheless, the idea behind ♖h1-h3 is an important one and has in fact led to a reassessment of many lines in the Keres Attack.

12 ... hxg6
13 hxg6 ♖xh1
14 gxf7+ ♔e7?

Black should settle for the bad position that arises after **14...♔xf7 15 ♕f3+ ♕f6 16 ♕xh1**, as he did in the prototype game, Adams-C.Hansen, Wijk aan Zee 1991. Play continued **16...♘e5** (Hansen prefers to sacrifice a pawn rather than allow White an excellent attacking position after something like 16...♘c4 17 ♗xc4 bxc4 18 0-0-0) **17 ♘xe6 ♕xe6** (17...♘f3+ fails to 18 ♕xf3! and 17...♔xe6 18 ♗xb6 ♘f3+ 19 ♔e2 is also no good for Black) **18 ♗xb6 d5 19 ♗d4 ♕c6!** (19...dxe4 20 ♕h5+ ♘g6 21 ♗h3 is crushing) **20 ♗h3**

♕e8 21 0-0-0 ♘xd4 22 ♖xd4 ♕e5 23 ♖d3 d4 24 ♘d5 ♗xd5 25 exd5 ♗d6 and now:

1) Adams continued to play for mate with **26 ♖f3+?** and was in fact lucky to win after 26...♔e7 27 ♖f5 ♕e2 28 ♕g1 ♗e5 29 f4 ♗f6 30 ♖xf6 gxf6 31 ♕g7+ ♔e8 32 ♕g8+ ♔e7 33 ♕h7+ ♔e8? (White has nothing after 33...♔f8 34 ♔b1 ♖e8 35 ♗e6 ♖xe6 36 dxe6 ♕e1+) 34 ♔b1 ♖d8? (Black would still have had some saving chances after 34...d3! 35 cxd3 ♕d1+ 36 ♔a2 b4 37 ♕b7 {37 ♗d7+ ♔d8 38 axb4 ♖a7!} 37...b3+) 35 ♗e6 1-0.

2) He should have headed for the ending with **26 ♗e6+ ♔e7 27 ♕h4+ ♕f6 28 ♕xf6+ ♔xf6 29 ♖xd4** when the technical difficulties are unlikely to prove insurmountable.

15 ♕g4! ♕c8

Forced; Black is unable to defend e6 (15...♘c5 16 ♗g5+) so he has to make some room for his king, and 15...♕b8 16 ♗g5+ ♘f6 17 ♕xe6+ ♔d8 18 ♕e8+ ♔c7 19 ♘e6 is mate.

16 ♕xe6+ ♔d8
17 ♕e8+ ♔c7
18 ♘e6+ ♔c6

Or 18...♔b8 19 ♘xf8 ♘xf8 20 ♗xb6 ♗c6 21 ♕e7 and Black is in a hopeless situation.

19 ♘d5!

The attack intensifies. 19...♕xe8 allows 20 ♘b4# and 19...♘xd5 20 exd5 ♔xd5 21 0-0-0 ♔c6 22 ♗g2+ is the end, so Black has to try...

19 ... ♖xf1+
20 ♔xf1 ♘xd5
21 exd5+ ♔xd5 *(D)*

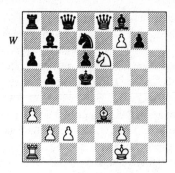

22 ♘xf8!

Up until this point Kotronias had simply been following Adams's analysis in *Informator* (Georgiev as well but I imagine unwittingly) but the text is clearly stronger than Adams's **22 ♘c7+ ♔c6 23 ♘xa8**, which, though strong, is not immediately decisive.

22 ... ♘e5

Useless, but so are **22...♘xf8 23 ♖d1+ ♔c4 24 ♖d4+ ♔c5 25 ♖h4+ ♔d5 26 ♕e4#, 22...♕xe8 23 fxe8♕ ♖xe8 24 ♘xd7 ♔c6 25 ♘b6 ♖xe3 26 fxe3 ♔xb6 27 ♖d1** and **22...♕c4+ 23 ♔e1**.

23 ♖d1+ ♔e4
24 ♖d4+ ♔f5
25 ♖f4+ 1-0

25...♔g5 26 ♕e7+ and mate next move.

Game 8
Karpov – Dorfman
USSR Ch 1976

1 e4 c5
2 ♘f3 e6
3 d4 cxd4
4 ♘xd4 ♘f6

5 ♘c3 d6
6 g4 ♘c6

I must confess to have taken some liberties with the move-order of Karpov-Dorfman, which actually continued 6...♗e7. We transpose back in a few moves, but this move-order makes it easier to explain the proposed repertoire.

7 g5 ♘d7
8 h4 (D)

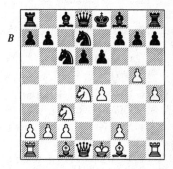

8 ... a6

8...♗e7 is the next game.

Here we examine a couple of rarer alternatives:

1) **8...♘xd4 9 ♕xd4 ♘e5 10 ♗e2 ♘c6 11 ♕d3 ♗e7** (or 11...a6 12 ♗f4 ♕c7 13 0-0-0 ♘e5 14 ♕d4 ♗d7 15 h5 with strong pressure for White, Lutikov-Malich, Leipzig 1977) 12 ♗f4 (were it not for this move, exposing the weakness of d6, Black's scheme would be viable – this is one of the few situations in the Sicilian where a direct attack on d6 works) 12...0-0 13 0-0-0 e5 14 ♗e3 ♗e6 15 ♘d5 ♕a5 16 a3 ♗xd5 17 ♕xd5 ♕xd5 18 ♖xd5 and Black has the type of ending Sicilian players

have bad dreams about, Nunn-Jansa, Dortmund 1979.

2) **8...♘b6 9 ♗e3** and now:

2a) **9...♘e5 10 f4 ♘bc4 11 ♗xc4 ♘xc4 12 ♕e2 ♘xe3 13 ♕xe3** followed by 0-0-0 and f5 with good attacking chances according to Glek.

2b) **9...♗e7 10 f4 d5** (10...h6 11 ♕f3 e5 12 ♘xc6 bxc6 13 0-0-0 is good for White) **11 ♗b5 ♗d7 12 exd5 exd5 13 ♕f3 ♗b4 14 0-0 ♗xc3 15 bxc3 ♘xd4 16 ♗xd7+ ♕xd7 17 ♗xd4 0-0 18 f5** with advantage to White, Mark Tseitlin-Lukin, USSR 1987.

2c) **9...d5 10 ♗b5 ♗d7 11 exd5 exd5 12 ♕e2 ♗e7 13 0-0-0 0-0 14 ♘b3 ♗e6 15 f4 ♖e8 16 h5 ♗b4 17 ♕d3! ♘c4** (17...♕c8 18 ♘d4+) **18 ♗c5! ♗xc5 19 ♘xc5** gave White a clear advantage in Glek-Dydyshko, USSR 1991 (in fact the game only lasted one more move: 19...♕d6?? 20 ♕xc4).

9 ♗e3   ♕c7 *(D)*

9...♗e7 is again the next game.

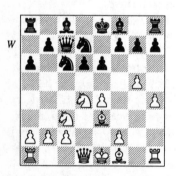

10 ♕e2

Karpov's move is very logical in that it prepares queenside castling as quickly as possible, while the f1-bishop and h1-rook are left at home because it is not yet clear which squares are best for these pieces. At e2 the queen sets up tactical chances down the e-file and avoids attack from a black knight arriving at c4. **10 ♕h5** can also be considered in this position, the one example I've seen being the quickplay game Khalifman-Machulsky, Moscow Tal mem 1992, which continued 10...♘xd4 11 ♗xd4 b5 12 0-0-0 ♗b7 (12...b4 looks like a more critical test) 13 ♗h3 ♘c5 14 ♖he1 b4 15 ♘d5 exd5 16 exd5+ ♔d8 17 ♗xc5 ♗c8 (or 17...dxc5 18 d6 ♗xd6 19 g6! with a dangerous attack) 18 ♗xc8 ♖xc8 19 ♖e2 dxc5 20 d6 ♕d7 21 g6 f6 22 gxh7 ♖c6 23 ♖e7 ♗xe7 24 dxe7+ ♔xe7 25 ♖xd7+ ♔xd7 26 ♕f7+ ♔d6 27 ♕xg7 with a won ending for White.

10 ...   ♗e7

This brings us back into Karpov-Dorfman, but Black has an interesting alternative in 10...b5. The idea is to exploit an obvious weakness of playing ♕e2, namely that the c3-knight has nowhere to go. The only real answer is to meet the advance of Black's b-pawn by ♘d5, but, provided Black avoids playing ...♗e7, the knight move creates no immediate threats and Black is not forced to capture it. After **10...b5 11 ♘xc6 ♕xc6 12 ♗d4** *(D)*:

1) Nunn-Howell, London 1990 continued **12...♗b7?** (stereotyped) **13 0-0-0 ♖c8 14 ♖h3! b4** (Black knows what's coming but has no

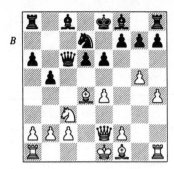

constructive way of avoiding it) 15 ♘d5 a5 (15...♕a4 16 ♘xb4! a5 17 ♖a3! ♕xb4 18 ♖b3 is very good for White) 16 c4! (cementing the knight in on d5 ensures White of long-term positional compensation when it is captured) 16...♔d8 17 ♔b1 ♘c5 (perhaps 17...exd5 would have been a better practical chance, although if White had found 18 exd5 ♕a6 19 ♖f3 ♘e5 20 ♖e3! he would have maintained a most promising position, e.g. 20...♖c7 21 f4 f6 22 ♕e1! is very unpleasant for Black and 20...f6 21 f4 ♘d7 22 ♕g4 ♕a8 23 ♗h3 ♖c7 24 ♕e6 is winning for White) 18 ♖f3 ♖c7 19 ♖e3 ♖d7 (now 19...exd5 loses at once as after 20 exd5 the black queen won't be able to stay protecting e8 for long) 20 ♗h3! (increasing the pressure) 20...h6 21 g6 fxg6 22 ♖g1? (this complicates the issue whereas the simple 22 ♗xc5! ♕xc5 23 ♘f4 would have soon led to the disintegration of Black's position) 22...g5! 23 hxg5 hxg5 24 ♖xg5 ♘xe4? (it was time to capture the knight: 24...exd5! 25 exd5 ♕a6 26 ♖e8+ ♔c7 27 ♗xd7 ♘xd7 28 ♗xg7 ♗xg7

29 ♖xg7 ♖xe8 30 ♕xe8 ♗c8 is still good for White but not so easy to win) 25 ♗b6+ ♔c8 26 ♖h5! (exchanging off Black's only active piece and exposing his back rank) 26...♖xh5 27 ♕xh5 ♔b8 (27...♘f6 28 ♖xe6!) 28 ♖xe4 exd5 (Black finally takes the knight which has been *en prise* for 13 moves) 29 ♖e8+ ♗c8 30 ♗xd7 ♕xd7 31 ♖xf8 ♕e7 32 ♕e8 1-0.

2) Black should have played **12...b4! 13 ♘d5 a5** when:

2a) **14 0-0-0?** ♗a6 15 ♕e1 ♖c8 16 ♖d2 ♗xf1 17 ♖xf1 ♕b5 probably threatens to take the knight and White can't retreat it to e3 in view of 18...e5 trapping the bishop.

2b) White should settle for the queenless middlegame that arises after **14 ♕b5!** ♕xb5 (14...♕xc2? 15 ♗d3) 15 ♘c7+ ♔d8 16 ♘xb5 ♗b7 17 ♗g2 where he can still claim an edge. If Black continues 17...♘c5, then 18 0-0-0! is good as 18...♘xe4 (18...♗xe4 19 ♗xe4 ♘xe4 20 ♖he1 d5 21 ♖xe4) 19 ♖he1 ♘c5 20 ♘xd6! gives White a clear plus.

11 0-0-0 b5

Tactical ideas for White are already in the air, for example 12 ♘f5 exf5 13 ♘d5 ♕d8 14 exf5, but although this is quite good for White Black can improve by 12 ♘f5 b4!.

11...♘xd4 doesn't look like an improvement as after 12 ♗xd4 0-0 13 f4 ♖e8 14 h5 b5 15 g6 White's attack is coming along nicely whilst Black's isn't even out of the starting blocks. Gufeld-Tilak, Calcutta 1992 concluded 15...fxg6 16 hxg6 hxg6

17 ♕h2 ♗f6 18 ♗xf6 ♘xf6 19 e5 dxe5 20 fxe5 b4 21 ♗d3! ♗b7 22 ♗xg6 1-0.

12	♘xc6	♕xc6
13	♗d4	b4 (D)

Black forces White to sacrifice on d5, but this move was itself virtually forced as **13...0-0** 14 ♖g1 gives White a crushing attack, e.g. 14...b4 15 ♘d5 exd5 16 exd5 ♕xd5 17 ♕xe7 ♕xa2 18 g6 hxg6 19 ♖xg6 and wins.

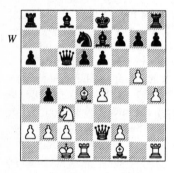

14	♘d5	exd5
15	♗xg7	♖g8
16	exd5	♕c7
17	♗f6	

The position of White's bishop at f1 is shown up as a defect since **17 ♖e1 ♘e5** 18 ♗xe5 dxe5 19 f4 exf4 achieves nothing when d6 is impossible. If the other rook could come to e1 Black would be finished.

17	...	♘e5
18	♗xe5	dxe5
19	f4	

Now White wins a third pawn for the piece since **19...e4** fails to 20 d6 ♗xd6 21 ♕xe4+. Black's king must remain stuck in the centre so one

must consider Karpov's sacrifice correct, although in the subsequent play Black's resourceful defence almost saves the game.

19	...	♗f5
20	♗h3	

White takes time out to neutralise Black's counterplay as **20 fxe5** at once allows the unclear 20...♖c8 21 ♖h2 ♕a5.

20	...	♗xh3
21	♖xh3	♖c8
22	fxe5	

After this Black activates his queen and Karpov is obliged to play with extreme accuracy to maintain his advantage. In his notes Karpov suggested **22 b3** to prevent the following manoeuvre.

22	...	♕c4!
23	♖dd3	♕f4+

23...♕xa2 24 d6 (the threat is simply d7+) 24...♖c4 (White meets 24...♖c5 by 25 ♕f2 and 26 dxe7) 25 dxe7 ♕a1+ 26 ♔d2 ♕xb2 27 ♖d8+ ♔xe7 28 ♖d7+ ♔xd7 29 ♕xc4 and **23...♖xg5** 24 hxg5 ♕xa2 25 d6 ♗xg5+ 26 ♖he3 ♖c4 27 ♕g2 are good for White.

24	♔b1	♖c4!

The rook follows the queen's path with the aim of causing White some problems on the back rank.

25	d6	♖e4
26	♖he3	♖xe3
27	♖xe3	♕xh4 (D)

If Black tries to save his bishop by **27...♗d8** (27...♗f8 28 ♕xa6 is even worse) he is crushed after 28 ♖f3 ♕g4 29 e6 fxe6 30 d7+ winning the queen, so he quite rightly decides to grab as many pawns as he can while White is taking his bishop.

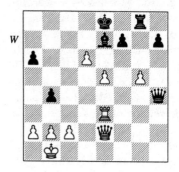

W

28 ♕f3!

Naturally not **28 dxe7** at once since Black exchanges queens by 28...♕h1+. White's advantage lies in the insecure black king, which causes trouble even when Black restores material equality.

28 ... ♕xg5

28...♗xg5 29 e6 fxe6 30 ♖xe6+ ♔d8 (30...♔d7 31 ♕f7+) 31 ♕c6! and **28...♖xg5** 29 ♕c6+ ♔f8 30 dxe7+ ♔xe7 31 a3 win for White.

29 ♖e1

29 ♕c6+ ♔f8 30 dxe7+ ♕xe7 31 ♕h6+ ♖g7 is a little better for White and this may in fact be his best line.

29 ... ♕g2?

29...♕g4 was better, when it is far from clear if White can do more than draw.

30	♕f5	♖g6
31	♖f1	♕d5
32	dxe7	♔xe7

Material equality is re-established but Black's king position makes his defensive task difficult. Detailed analysis of this position would take us too far afield, but Black does not seem to have any real improvements hereafter and the task of defending both his king and his pawns soon overstretches his forces.

33	♕f4	a5
34	♕h4+	♔e8
35	♕xh7	♕f3
36	♕h8+	♔e7
37	♕h4+	♔e8
38	♕c4	♕b7
39	b3	

One of the most impressive features of this game is the way Karpov managed to conduct all the tactical operations with a vulnerable back rank. Many players, through nervousness or laziness, would have wasted a tempo on b3 earlier, and this might well have cost the game (note that although b3 was a good idea at move 22, the point was to prevent the ...♕c4-f4 manoeuvre rather than to give the king air).

39 ... ♖e6 *(D)*

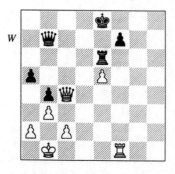

W

40 ♖g1?!

Perhaps Karpov assumed that the exposed king must succumb quickly to the combined attack of White's queen and rook, but the task is much more difficult than appears at first. I suspect that if Karpov had realised this he would not have been so hasty in giving back the pawn, because he could have waited for a more favourable moment.

40	...	♖xe5
41	♖g8+	♔e7
42	♕h4+	♔d7
43	♕f6!	♖e7
44	♕f5+	♔d6
45	♕xa5	♖e5

45...♕e4 would have held out longer, but the result is not in doubt.

46	♕d8+	♔e6
47	♔b2!	f6
48	♖f8	♕g7
49	♕c8+	♔d5
50	♕c4+	1-0

Game 9
Zakić – Cvetković
Aosta 1989

1	e4	c5
2	♘f3	d6
3	d4	cxd4
4	♘xd4	♘f6
5	♘c3	e6
6	g4	♗e7
7	g5	♘fd7
8	h4	♘c6
9	♗e3	0-0

If Black plays **9...a6** White may again reply 10 ♕h5 when Black has nothing better than 10...0-0 transposing back into the game.

10 ♕h5 (D)

BTS2 concentrated on the sideline **10 ♗c4**, but this has never really caught on, perhaps justifiably so. A possible line for Black is **10...♘b6** 11 ♗b3 d5 12 ♕e2 ♗b4 with unclear complications while **10...♘de5** is also interesting; Sznapik-Cvitan, Manila OL 1992 continued 11 ♗b3 ♘xd4 12 ♗xd4 ♗d7 13 ♕e2 ♘c6 14 0-0-0 (14 ♗e3 is more natural but after 14...♘a5 Black has a favourable version of the Velimirović Attack) 14...♘xd4 15 ♖xd4 b5 16 ♖hd1 a5 17 ♘xb5 ♗g5+ 18 hxg5 ♕xg5+ 19 f4 ♕xb5 with a good game for Black.

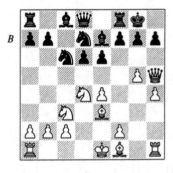

To select another line was not so easy as all three possible queen moves (10 ♕d2 and 10 ♕e2 are the other two) are quite dangerous for Black. I finally opted for 10 ♕h5, not so much because of its strength, but because it is the most overtly aggressive and should ensure the right frame of mind for playing the Keres Attack where the slightest dithering can turn out to be fatal. One point in favour of ♕h5 is that White is not committed to a pawn-storm and can sometimes carry out a successful attack with just pieces.

On the downside the h-pawn is blocked and occasionally the queen will have to retreat to make way for its advance.

10 ...   a6

It's rare that Black can get by without this move in the Sicilian. Examples here:

1) **10...d5?!**. A central strike is the recommended reaction to a wing attack, but here it just emphasises how active the white pieces are in comparison with their counterparts. Sax-Ehlvest, Reggio Emilia 1988, continued 11 0-0-0! dxe4 (11...♘xd4 12 ♖xd4 ♗c5 13 ♖d2 ♗xe3 14 fxe3 is ± according to Sax) 12 ♘xe4 ♕a5 13 ♘xc6 bxc6 14 ♗d4! (White goes straight for the jugular) 14...e5 (14...♕xa2? 15 ♘f6+! ♗xf6 16 gxf6 is winning for White) 15 ♗c3 ♕xa2 (Black may as well take the pawn as 15...♕c7 16 ♖xd7 ♗xd7 17 ♗d3 g6 18 ♕h6 allows White a winning attack) 16 ♖xd7!! (removing one of the defenders of f6) 16...♗xd7 17 ♘f6+! ♗xf6 (or 17...gxf6 18 gxf6 ♗xf6 19 ♖g1+ ♗g7 20 ♕h6) 18 gxf6 ♕a1+? (18...♖fd8 should be met by 19 ♗d3! as after 19 ♕g5? ♕a1+ 20 ♔d2 ♕d1+!! 21 ♔e3 ♕g4 Black has managed to defend himself; relatively best is 18...♕e6!, even though White is well on top after 19 ♗h3 ♕xf6 20 ♗xd7) 19 ♔d2 ♕a4 (Black's main idea is to transfer his queen to the kingside, but White's next move dashes all his hopes) 20 b4! ♖fd8 21 ♗d3 gxf6 22 ♖a1! (I bet you weren't expecting that one) 22...♕b5 23 ♕xh7+ ♔f8

24 ♕h6+ ♔e7 25 ♗xb5 cxb5 26 ♕e3 1-0.

2) **10...♖e8 11 0-0-0** and now 11...a6 transposes back into the main game, but Black has a couple of other tries:

2a) **11...♗f8** 12 ♘xc6 (12 f4?! ♘xd4 13 ♗xd4 e5) 12...bxc6 13 f4 d5 14 ♗d3 g6 15 ♕f3 with good attacking chances for White according to Sax.

2b) **11...♘xd4** 12 ♗xd4 ♗f8 13 ♗d3 a6 14 e5 g6 15 ♕g4 ♗g7 (15...dxe5 16 ♗e3 is dangerous for Black) 16 f4 dxe5 17 fxe5 ♗xe5 18 ♗xe5 ♘xe5 19 ♕e2 with a powerful attack to come.

11 0-0-0   ♖e8

The move ...♖e8 (which is usually followed by ...♗f8) is a common prophylactic measure against a white attack in the Sicilian. In this particular position, though, it has been more common for Black to immediately commence queenside operations with **11...♘xd4 12 ♗xd4 b5** after which White has chooses between 13 ♗d3 or 13 f4. I (JG) am, however, recommending a third possibility, **13 e5!?** *(D)*.

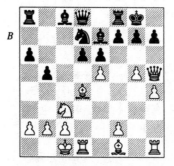

The idea is simple; to open as many lines as possible for White's aggressively placed pieces, especially the diagonals pointing towards the black king. As far as I know 13 e5 has only occurred in one fairly obscure game, which means that all the analysis given below is original and untested. After 13 e5 I have examined five possible replies, of which lines '4' and '5' appear to be the most critical:

1) **13...d5?!**. Closing the centre allows White to develop an attack free of charge. A possible continuation: 14 ♗d3 g6 15 ♕g4 ♘c5 16 ♗xc5!? ♗xc5 17 h5 ♗xf2 18 hxg6 fxg6 19 ♖xh7 ♗e3+ 20 ♔b1 ♕xg5 21 ♕h3 with advantage to White.

2) **13...b4?** 14 exd6 ♗xd6 15 ♗d3 g6 16 ♕h6 ♗f4+ (16...e5 17 h5! is crushing, e.g. 17...exd4 18 hxg6 ♗f4+ 19 ♔b1 ♘f6 20 g7! followed by mate) 17 ♔b1 e5 18 ♘e2 ♘f6 (18...exd4 19 ♘xf4 wins for White) 19 ♗c5! ♖e8 20 ♗xg6 fxg6 21 ♖xd8 ♖xd8 and now 22 f3!, avoiding 22...♘g4, wins for White.

3) **13...♗b7** (this also seems to lose, though the variations are much more complicated) **14 exd6** with the lines:

3a) **14...♗xh1** 15 ♗d3 g6 16 ♕h6 e5 17 ♖xh1 exd4 18 dxe7 ♕xe7 19 ♘d5 ♕e5 20 h5! ♕xd5 (20...♕g7 21 ♘e7+ ♔h8 22 hxg6 ♖xh6 23 ♖xh6 fxg6 24 ♘xg6+) 21 hxg6 ♕xh1+ (21...♖fe8 22 g7! – this g6-g7 move is an important point, which occurs in several variations) 22 ♕xh1 hxg6 23 ♗xg6! fxg6 24 ♕d5+ ♔g7 25

♕xd7+ ♔g8 26 ♕d5+ ♔h7 27 ♕xd4 and White has a material advantage which he should have no difficulty converting in view of the exposed black king.

3b) **14...♗xd6 15 ♗d3! g6 16 ♕h6** (D) and Black can play ...e5 with or without giving a bishop check:

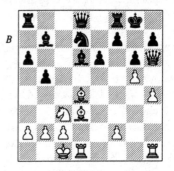

3b1) **16...e5 17 h5! ♕e7** (grabbing the material leads to a quick defeat, e.g. 17...♗xh1 18 ♖xh1 exd4 19 hxg6 ♗f4+ 20 ♔b1 ♘f6 21 g7!) **18 hxg6 fxg6 19 ♗xg6! ♗xh1** (or 19...hxg6 20 ♕h8+ ♔f7 21 ♖h7+ ♔e8 22 ♖xe7+ ♗xe7 23 ♕g7 winning for White) **20 ♖xh1 hxg6 21 ♕h8+ ♔f7 22 ♕h7+** (a simpler line is 22 ♖h7+ ♔e8 23 ♖xe7+ ♗xe7 24 ♕h1! with advantage to White, although perhaps less than after 22 ♕h7+) **22...♔e8 23 ♕xg6+** and now:

3b11) **23...♖f7** 24 ♘e4! ♔d8 (or 24...♗c7 25 ♖h8+ ♘f8 25 ♕c6+ +–) 25 ♘xd6 ♖g7 26 ♕e4 ♖b8 27 ♘f5 ♕xg5+ 28 f4 ♕g6 29 ♖h6! ♕g2 30 ♖h8+ and White wins.

3b12) **23...♔d8** 24 ♘d5 exd4 25 ♘xe7 ♗xe7 26 ♖h7 and White, with his passed pawns and ongoing attack should be winning.

3b13) **23...♕f7** 24 ♕xd6 exd4 25 ♘d5! wins.

3b2) **16...♗f4+** 17 ♔b1 e5 (the alternative 17...♘e5 18 ♗e4! is good for White) 18 ♗e3! (18 ♘e2 ♗xh1 19 ♖xh1 ♘f6! 20 f3 ♘h5! is much less clear) 18...♗xe3 19 fxe3 ♗xh1 20 ♖xh1 and I can't see how Black survives. As **20...♘c5** 21 h5 ♘xd3 22 hxg6 is all over, he must try **20...f5**, when 21 h5 gxh5 (21...♕e8 22 ♘d5! and 21...♕e7 22 hxg6 ♕g7 23 ♕xg7+ ♔xg7 24 ♖xh7+ ♔xg6 25 ♖xd7 are winning for White) 22 g6 ♘f6 23 ♗xf5 ♖a7 24 ♖g1 ♖e8 (24...♕e7 25 g7! wins for White) 25 ♘e4 ♘xe4 26 ♗e6+! ♖xe6 27 gxh7+ ♔h8 28 ♖g8+ ♕xg8 29 hxg8♕+ ♔xg8 30 ♕xe6+ and White is winning..

4) **13...g6** (one of the points behind ♕h5 in the Keres Attack is to tempt Black into playing this weakening move) **14 ♕e2** (it's not clear where the queen should retreat; 14 ♕g4 dxe5 15 ♗e3 looks quite promising and 14 ♕f3 also merits some attention as after 14...dxe5 15 ♗xe5 ♘xe5 16 ♕xa8 ♕a5 17 ♕e4 b4, White has the strong rejoinder 18 ♘d5!) **14...dxe5** (14...♗b7 15 ♖h3 b4 16 exd6 ♗xd6 17 ♘e4 is better for White) **15 ♗xe5** (D) and Black has several tries:

4a) **15...b4** 16 ♗g2! ♖a7 (after 16...bxc3 17 ♗xa8 cxb2+ 18 ♗xb2 White has the advantage) 17 ♘e4 (17 ♗b8!?) 17...♕a5 18 ♗d4 ♖c7 19 ♔b1 and White is much better.

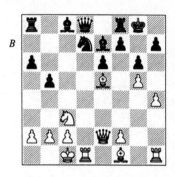

4b) **15...♕a5** 16 ♗d6! ♗xd6 (or 16...b4 17 ♗xe7 bxc3 18 ♗xf8 ♕xa2 19 bxc3 and White can follow up with ♕c4) 17 ♖xd6 b4 18 ♘e4! with a clear advantage for White.

4c) **15...♗b7** **16 ♖h3 b4 17 ♖hd3! ♗c6** and now:

4c1) **18 ♘e4 ♗d5!** (18...♗b5? 19 ♖xd7! ♗xd7 20 ♘f6+ ♗xf6 21 gxf6 and the threat of ♕d2-h6 is decisive) 19 ♖xd5 exd5 20 ♖xd5 is very unclear.

4c2) **18 ♖xd7 ♗xd7** 19 ♘e4 appears very dangerous for Black but I haven't found a way to make the white attack work.

4c3) **18 ♗g2! ♗xg5+** (18...♗xg2 19 ♖xd7 ♕e8 20 ♘e4 ♗xe4 21 ♕xe4 and 18...bxc3 19 ♗xc6 ♕b6 20 ♗xc3 are good for White) **19 ♔b1!** (D).

A most confusing position with five of the six minor pieces *en prise* and the other one caught in a fatal pin. I believe that White should emerge victorious from this chaos. For example:

4c31) **19...♕c8** 20 ♖xd7 ♗xd7 21 hxg5 bxc3 22 ♗xa8! ♗b5 23 ♕f3! ♕xa8 24 ♕f6 wins.

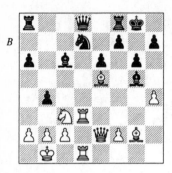

4c32) **19...♘xe5** 20 ♖xd8 ♗xd8 21 ♕xe5 ♗xg2 22 h5!! is very strong as after 22...bxc3 23 h6 f6 24 ♕xe6+ ♔h8 25 ♕d7 ♖g8 26 ♕f7! White threatens both ♖d7 and ♖xd8.

5) **13...dxe5 14 ♗xe5** and now:

5a) **14...g6** 15 ♕h6? (15 ♕e2 and 15 ♕f3 transpose into line '4') 15...♘xe5 16 ♖xd8 ♖xd8 17 ♗g2 ♖b8 and with ...♘g4 and ...♗f8 on the cards White is going to lose his queen and remain a rook behind.

5b) **14...♕b6** 15 ♖xd7! ♗xd7 16 ♗d3 g6 17 ♕h6 f6 18 ♗xg6! +–.

5c) **14...♗b7** 15 ♗xg7! ♔xg7 (15...♗xh1 16 ♗d3 f5 17 gxf6 ♘xf6 18 ♗xf6 ♖xf6 19 ♕xh7+ ♔f8 20 ♗g6 wins) 16 ♕h6+ ♔h8 (16...♔g8 17 ♗d3 f5 18 gxf6) 17 ♗d3 f5 18 g6! ♖f7 19 gxf7 ♗xh1 and now 20 ♕xe6! +– looks the strongest.

5d) **14...♕e8** (the toughest defence) **15 ♗g2!** (15 ♗d3 is met by 15...f5 whilst 15 ♗xg7 doesn't look quite good enough, e.g. 15...♔xg7 16 ♕h6+ ♔h8 17 ♖xd7 ♗xd7 18 ♗d3 f5 19 gxf6 ♖f7! 20 fxe7 ♕xe7 and White has some compensation for the exchange, but nothing more)

15...♘xe5 (15...♖a7 16 ♗d4 ♖c7 is possible, although White is well centralised after 17 ♖he1) **16 ♗xa8 b4** (16...♗d7 17 ♗e4 g6 18 ♕e2 b4 19 ♘b1 ♗b5 20 ♕e1 is good for White) **17 ♘e4!** *(D)* (cuts off the bishop's retreat, but the tactics seem to be working in White's favour) and now Black has:

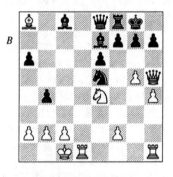

5d1) **17...♗d7** 18 ♖hg1! (suddenly White has kingside threats again) 18...♔h8 (18...♕xa8 19 ♘f6+ ♗xf6 20 gxf6 ♘g6 21 ♖xd7) 19 g6! ♘xg6 20 ♘g5 h6 (20...♗xg5+ 21 hxg5 is very good for White) 21 ♘xf7+! with a winning position for White.

5d2) **17...♕a4** and now White can play:

5d21) **18 ♔b1 ♗d7** 19 g6! ♘xg6 20 ♘g5 ♖xa8 (20...h6 21 ♘xf7! ♘f4 22 ♘xh6+ gxh6 23 ♖hg1+ wins for White) 21 ♕xh7+ ♔f8 22 h5 ♗xg5 23 hxg6 ♖c8 24 ♕h8+ ♔e7 25 ♕xg7 ♕xc2+ 26 ♔a1 ♕xg6 and now **27 ♕xg6** fxg6 28 ♖h7+ ♔f6 29 ♖hxd7 ♖c2 is probably only equal, but **27 ♕d4** gives White a strong attack.

5d22) **18 Ihg1!?** *(D)* with a further branch:

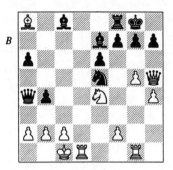

5d221) **18...♕xa2** 19 ♘f6+ ♗xf6 20 gxf6 ♘g6 (20...♕a1+ 21 ♔d2 Id8+ 22 ♔e2 Ixd1 23 Ixd1 ♕a5 24 ♕g5 leads to mate because after 24...♕b5+ 25 ♔e1 the bishop on a8 prevents Black's ...♘f3#) 21 fxg7 Ie8 (21...♕a1+ 22 ♔d2 Id8+ 23 ♔e3! and 21...♔xg7 22 ♕e5+ ♔g8 23 b3! are both winning for White) 22 ♕c5! ♕a1+ (22...♘f4 23 ♗c6 ♕a1+ 24 ♔d2 Id8+ 25 ♔e3! Ixd1 26 ♕f8#!) 23 ♔d2 ♕xb2 24 ♗c6 Id8+ 25 ♔e2 Ixd1 26 Ixd1 ♔xg7 27 h5 ♕e5+ (27...♘e5 28 f4! wins) 28 ♕xe5+ ♘xe5 29 Id8 ♘xc6 30 Ixc8 ♘d4+ 31 ♔d3 ♘f3 32 Ia8 and White should win the ending.

5d222) **18...♘g6** 19 ♔b1 ♗d7 20 ♗b7 ♕b5 21 ♕f3! Ib8 (this looks strong but White has a tactical way to solve his problems; 21...♘xh4 22 ♕d3! and 21...♘e5 22 ♕g3! are also good for White) 22 ♘f6+! ♗xf6 (22...gxf6 23 gxf6 ♕xb7 24 ♕xb7 Ixb7 25 fxe7 ♗e8 26 h5 +−) 23 gxf6 ♕xb7 24 ♕xb7 Ixb7 25 h5 gxf6 26 hxg6 hxg6 27 Id6 ♗b5 28

b3 and White has the edge in this ending as Black's queenside pawns are weak. For example, 28...♔f8 29 ♔b2 ♔e7 30 Igd1 f5 31 a4 bxa3+ 32 ♔xa3 with c4 to follow is good for White.

12 f4

The most natural, but **12 ♘xc6** bxc6 13 f4 is also interesting.

12 ... ♗f8 *(D)*

The main alternative is **12...♘xd4 13 ♗xd4 b5** (13...e5 14 fxe5 dxe5 15 ♗xe5 ♘xe5 16 Ixd8 ♗g4 17 Ixa8 Ixa8 18 ♗e2 ♗xh5 19 ♗xh5+) **14 f5 ♗f8** (14...b4 15 fxe6 fxe6 16 ♗c4 bxc3 17 ♗xe6+ ♔h8 18 ♗xg7+ ♔xg7 19 ♕h6+ ♔h8 20 g6 +− is a variation given by Polugaevsky) **15 ♗h3 b4 16 fxe6 fxe6 17 ♘d5!** (an improvement over the 17 g6 h6 18 ♘d5 of Sax-Polugaevsky, Haninge 1989 when Black was able to defend with 18...Ib8) and now:

1) **17...exd5** 18 g6 when White threatens both mate on h7 and ♕xd5+.

2) **17...Ib8** now fails to 18 ♘c7! g6 19 ♘xe8!, as in Hector-Ghitescu, Palma 1989.

3) **17...♗b7** is refuted by the sacrifice 18 ♘f6+! according to Sax, who no doubt had the following variation in mind: 18...gxf6 19 gxf6 ♘xf6 20 Ihg1+ ♗g7 (20...♔h8 21 ♕xe8 ♕xe8 22 ♗xf6+ ♗g7 23 Ixg7) 21 Ixg7+ ♔xg7 22 Ig1+ ♔h8 23 ♕xe8+! ♕xe8 24 ♗xf6#.

4) **17...g6** 18 ♕f3! exd5 19 e5! dxe5 (19...♗b7 20 e6 ♘e5 21 ♗xe5 dxe5 22 ♕f7+ ♔h8 23 ♕xb7 d4 24 ♕e4 is very good for White) 20

Wxd5+ ♔h8 21 ♗e3! and White has a clear advantage (Sax).

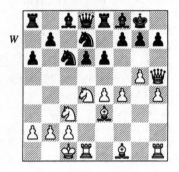

13 f5!?

This move is very hard to resist when you know what happens after 13...exf5. On the other hand it does concede control of e5 a little prematurely so White might prefer one of the alternatives:

1) **13 ♗d3 g6** (both 13...♘xd4 14 ♗xd4 e5 15 ♗c4! g6 16 ♗xf7+ and 13...♘c5 14 ♘xc6 ♘xd3+ 15 ♖xd3 bxc6 16 e5, with the idea of ♘e4-f6, are good for White) 14 ♕f3 ♘xd4 (14...♗g7 15 ♘de2 followed by h5 is also good for White) 15 ♗xd4 e5 16 ♗e3 exf4 (Landenbergue-Magerramov, Bad Wörishofen 1993) and now White should have played 17 Wxf4, as Black cannot then play 17...♘e5 in view of 18 ♘d5 ♗g7 19 ♗b6.

2) The Sax solution, **13 ♘xc6 bxc6 14 ♗d3**, was tried in Wegner-Bischoff, Bundesliga 1991. After **14...Wa5 15 e5 g6 16 Wf3** (16 Wg4) **16...dxe5:**

2a) White totally lost his way with 17 Wxc6 ♖b8 18 Wa4 Wxa4 19

♘xa4 exf4 when he couldn't even recapture in view of 20...♖b4!.

2b) Instead of grabbing a useless queenside pawn, he could have given Black a torrid time with **17 h5!**, for example 17...♗g7 (17...exf4 18 hxg6 hxg6 { 18...fxg6 19 ♖xh7!} 19 Wh3 ♗g7 20 ♗xf4 transposes) **18 hxg6** and now:

2b1) **18...fxg6** 19 ♖xh7! ♔xh7 20 Wh5+ ♔g8 21 ♗xg6 ♖e7 22 fxe5 and the opening of the f-file will prove fatal. On 22...♘xe5, 23 ♗c5! looks the clearest.

2b2) **18...hxg6** 19 Wh3 exf4 (or 19...♘f8 20 ♘e4!) 20 Wh7+ ♔f8 21 ♗xf4 e5 (21...♘e5 22 ♘e4! looks strong) 22 ♗e3 and it's hard to see Black surviving for long.

13 ... exf5? *(D)*

Black must have been counting upon 14 ♘xf5 ♘de5 when he has everything under control. Instead 13...♘de5 would have left the situation unclear.

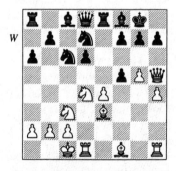

14 Wxf7+!!

This thunderbolt had obviously not been taken into account by Black.

| 14 ... | ♚xf7 |

14...♚h8 15 ♗c4 is completely hopeless.

| 15 ♗c4+ | ♜e6 |

Both 15...♚g6 and 15...♚e7 permit mate in one and the only other legal move, **15...d5**, leads to a lost position after 16 ♗xd5+ ♜e6 17 ♘xe6 ♕a5 18 ♘c7+ ♚e7 19 ♘xa8.

| 16 ♘xe6 | ♕a5 |

16...♕e7 17 ♘c7+ ♚g6 18 h5#.

17 ♘c7+	♚e7
18 ♘3d5+	♚d8
19 ♘e6+	

There is too much action in the centre to be distracted by a rook.

19 ...	♚e8
20 ♗d2!	♕a4
21 ♗b3	♕xe4
22 ♜he1 *(D)*	
22 ...	♜b8

As the queen can't go anywhere (22...♕xh4 fails to 23 ♘ec7++ ♚f7 24 ♘f4+ d5 25 ♗xd5#) Black decides to save his rook.

| 23 ♜xe4 | fxe4 |
| 24 ♜f1! | |

The attack is far from over.

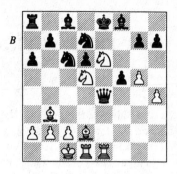

24 ...	♘ce5
25 ♗b4	♘f3
26 ♘dc7+	♚e7
27 ♜d1!	♘c5

Black could have resigned rather than play this move.

| 28 ♘xc5 | a5 |

28...dxc5 29 ♗xc5 is mate.

29 ♘5a6	axb4
30 ♘xb8	♘xh4
31 ♘b5	♗g4
32 ♜xd6	e3
33 ♜b6	e2
34 ♜xb7+	1-0

Finally the black king meets his fate; 34...♚e8 35 ♗f7+ ♚d8 36 ♘c6+ ♚c8 37 ♜c7 is mate.

3 Classical Variation

In the first edition of this book I (JN) christened the line 1 e4 c5 2 ♘f3 ♘c6 3 d4 cxd4 4 ♘xd4 ♘f6 5 ♘c3 d6, which can also occur with the move order 2...d6 and 5...♘c6, with the name 'Classical Variation'. This nomenclature seems to have caught on, so it has been maintained for subsequent editions.

The line we are recommending against the Classical is 6 ♗g5, generally called the Richter-Rauzer Attack even though the treatment used today doesn't seem to owe anything to Richter. This line is very common in practice, so there is a large body of theory. In general we will keep to the main lines in the proposed repertoire, but where there are interesting sidelines we will give them a brief mention.

The idea of 6 ♗g5 as it is played today is based on a quick ♕d2 and 0-0-0, exerting pressure down the d-file and restraining Black from active play in the centre.

Black's most solid reply is the natural 6...e6 7 ♕d2 ♗e7 8 0-0-0 0-0, but despite its solid appearance it can often lead to sharp tactical play. This is covered in Game 10.

Sometimes Black postpones ...0-0 so as to delay exposing the king to a possible pawn storm. The line 6...e6 7 ♕d2 a6 8 0-0-0 ♗d7 is the subject of Game 11 while 6...e6 7 ♕d2 a6 8 0-0-0 h6 appears in Game 12.

Finally, some players have experimented with the omission of 6...e6, not fearing the doubled pawns resulting from ♗xf6, and the most popular of these ideas, 6...♗d7, forms the basis of Game 13. Unusual lines involving ...e6 are dealt with in Game 10, while the others are in Game 13.

Game 10
Liss – Leko
Budapest 1993

1	e4	c5
2	♘f3	d6
3	d4	cxd4
4	♘xd4	♘f6
5	♘c3	♘c6
6	♗g5	e6

Other moves are considered in Game 13.

| 7 | ♕d2 (D) | |
| 7 | ... | ♗e7 |

7...a6 appears in Games 11 and 12.

There are two other alternatives for Black:

1) 7...h6 (7...♗d7? is just a mistake: 8 ♘db5) 8 ♗xf6 gxf6 (after 8...♕xf6 9 ♘db5 and 10 0-0-0 White wins the d6-pawn) 9 0-0-0 (playing for 0-0 is also slightly better for

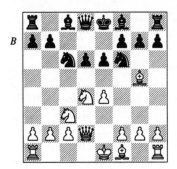

White, e.g. 9 ♖d1 a6 10 ♗e2 h5 11 0-0 ♗d7 12 ♘b3 ♕c7 13 ♔h1 0-0-0 14 f4, or 9 ♗e2 h5 10 0-0 a6 11 ♔h1! ♗d7 12 f4 ♕c7 13 ♖f3! ♘xd4 14 ♕xd4 ♗e7 15 ♖d1 h4 16 ♖fd3 ♖d8, Van der Wiel-J.Piket, Leiden 1986, and now 17 ♗f3 gives White an edge) 9...a6 10 f4 ♗d7 11 ♗e2 h5 (11...♕b6 12 ♗h5 {12 ♘b3 is also perfectly playable} 12...♕xd4 13 ♕xd4 ♘xd4 14 ♖xd4 ♖g8 15 g3 ♗e7 16 ♖f1 ♗c6 17 f5 ♖g5 18 ♗e2 with advantage, Bondarevsky-Botvinnik, USSR Ch 1951) 12 ♔b1 ♕c7 (or 12...♕b6 13 ♘b3 0-0-0 14 ♖hf1 ♔b8 15 ♖f3 ♗e7 16 ♖h3 h4 17 ♕e1 ♖hg8 18 ♗f3 again with a plus for White, Nunn-Čabrilo, Novi Sad OL 1990) 13 ♖hf1 0-0-0 (13...♗e7 14 ♖f3 ♘xd4 15 ♕xd4 ♕c5 16 ♕d2 ♗c6 17 ♖e3 ♕a5 18 a3 ♖d8 19 ♗c4 gives White an edge, Liberzon-Botvinnik, USSR 1967) 14 ♘b3 ♔b8 15 ♖f3 ♗e7 16 ♖h3 h4 17 ♕e1 and Black has not yet equalised, Vasiukov-Shamkovich, Dubna 1973. It would be fair to conclude that those who believe it is worth a tempo to encourage White to capture on f6 are members of a dying breed.

2) 7...♘xd4 8 ♕xd4 ♗d7 and now in the game Ivanchuk-Salov, Linares 1992, White produced the powerful novelty 9 ♘b5!. Play continued 9...♕b8 (9...♗c6 10 e5 dxe5 11 ♕xe5 is ± according to Salov) 10 0-0-0 (10 ♗xf6 gxf6 11 ♕xf6 ♖g8 is not as promising for White, but as Salov points out 10 ♖d1 might have been even stronger) 10...a6 11 ♘xd6+! (clearer than 11 ♗xf6 ♗xb5 when 12 ♗xg7 e5 13 ♗xe5 ♗h6+! 14 ♔b1 dxe5 15 ♗xb5+ axb5 16 ♕d7+ ♔f8 17 ♕xb5 is a mess) 11...♗xd6 12 ♗xf6 ♗f4+! 13 ♔b1 gxf6 14 ♕xd7+ ♔f8 15 g3 ♗c7. Salov considers this position to be only slightly better for White (which I find hard to believe).

2a) He now gives the solid variation 16 ♗c4 b5 17 ♗b3 (17 ♗xe6 fxe6 18 ♕xe6 ♕b6 is unclear) 17...♖a7 18 f4 ♗a5 19 ♕d6+ ♕xd6 20 ♖xd6 ♔e7 21 ♖hd1 as ±, when the presence of opposite-coloured bishops give Black good drawing chances.

2b) Ivanchuk preferred a more aggressive approach and played 16 ♗h3, telegraphing his intentions to sacrifice on e6. After 16...b5 17 ♕c6! ♖a7 18 ♗xe6 fxe6 19 ♕xe6 ♗d8 (now 19...♕b6 loses to 20 ♕c8+) 20 ♖d6! ♗e7 21 ♖hd1 ♖g8 he opted for 22 ♖xa6 ♖xa6 23 ♕xa6 ♔f7 when White had gained a fourth pawn but lost the initiative. Much better would have been 22 ♖b6! ♕e8 23 f4, maintaining his bind on the position.

8 0-0-0   0-0

Or **8...♘xd4 9 ♕xd4 0-0** and now
BTS2 recommended **10 e5 dxe5 11
♕xe5**, but current theory suggests
that Black can play 11...♗d7 12 h4
♖c8 13 ♖h3 ♕c7 14 ♕xc7 ♖xc7 15
♘b5 ♗xb5 16 ♗xb5 ♖fc8, with
what Kramnik told me (JN) was 'a
drawn ending'. So now we are recommending **10 f3** *(D)* with the possibilities:

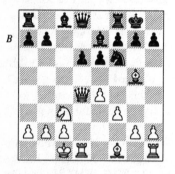

1) **10...♕a5** 11 ♕d2 ♖d8 12 ♔b1
♕c7 13 ♘b5 ♕d7 14 g4 a6 15 ♘d4
b5 16 h4 ♗b7 17 ♗e3 ♕e8 18 h5 e5
19 ♘f5 d5 20 ♘xg7! ♘xe4 (White
wins after 20...♔xg7 21 ♗h6+ ♔h8
22 ♕g5 ♕g8 23 ♕xe5 ♖e8 24 g5) 21
fxe4 ♔xg7 22 ♗h6+ ♔g8 23 ♕c3
and Black's exposed king gives
White an obvious advantage, J.Ben-
jamin-Kogan, US Ch 1984.

2) **10...e5** 11 ♕d2 ♗e6 12 ♔b1
♖c8 13 h4 ♖c5 14 a3 ♕b8 15 ♗e3
♖cc8 16 ♗d3 b5 17 ♘d5 ♗xd5 18
exd5 ♗d8 19 ♗f5 ♖c4 20 b3 ♖c7 21
g4 with a clear advantage for White,
Chandler-Lobron, Biel 1987.

3) **10...a6** was played in Kuzmin-
Oll, Lvov Z 1990, which continued
11 e5 dxe5 12 ♕xe5 ♕e8 13 ♗e2
♗d7 14 ♕g3 ♕c8 15 ♖d3 ♖d8 16
♕h4 with a satisfactory position for
Black. However, having rejected e5
at move 10 there doesn't seem to be
any special reason to play it at move
11. Starting kingside expansion by
11 h4 is more consistent with playing f3.

The position after 8...0-0 is one of
the most important in the whole Sicilian Defence and despite decades
of practical experience no definite
assessment can be given. Although 9
♘b3 was often played in late fifties
and early sixties, it fell into disuse
and 9 f4, which has always been regarded as the main line, became virtually universal. However, 9 ♘b3
has been regaining popularity and
now rivals 9 f4 for the distinction of
being considered the 'main line'.

9 ♘b3 *(D)*

Notice that **9 ♗xf6?** is bad since
Black can play 9...♗xf6 10 ♘xc6
bxc6 11 ♕xd6 ♕b6 when the threats
to b2 and f2 are more than enough
compensation for the pawn.

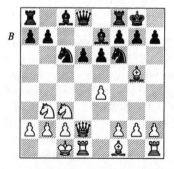

The main point of 9 ♘b3 is that
it unveils an attack against the pawn

on d6 and so prepares ♗xf6. Black has four main methods of countering White's plan:

The first is to sacrifice the d-pawn, for example by 9...h6 10 ♗xf6 ♗xf6, but a number of games prove that White can gain an advantage.

A second plan is to allow ♗xf6 and then recapture with the pawn. This leaves Black's king somewhat exposed, but White has no immediate method of launching an attack. More serious is that Black's central pawns are inflexible and White may have enough time to start a kingside pawn storm. The assessment of this line depends on the speed of the respective attacks.

Black's third plan is to counter White's pressure on d6 directly by playing 9...a5 10 a4 d5 (moreover the immediate 9...d5 is just about possible).

The final plan is to counterattack f2 by 9...♕b6, gaining enough time to defend d6 by ...♖d8.

With the exception of the first, all these lines are playable.

9 ... a6

Apart from the two major alternatives, there are a number of less common ideas:

1) **9...d5 10 ♗xf6 ♗xf6 11 exd5 ♗xc3** (11...♘b4 12 a3 ♘xd5 13 ♘xd5 exd5 14 ♕xd5 is slightly better for White since although Black has the two bishops it is not easy for him to avoid the exchange of queens) **12 ♕xc3 exd5** *(D)* and now:

1a) **13 g3 ♗g4 14 f3!** (a better choice than 14 ♖d2 d4! 15 ♕c5 {15

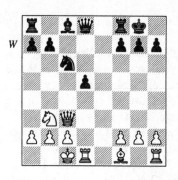

♘xd4 ♕d5!} 15...♗f3 16 ♖g1 ♖e8 17 ♗b5 ♖e5 18 ♕c4 ♕e7 19 ♕f1! which is unclear, Yudasin-Utemov, USSR 1989) 14...♕g5+ (14...♗e6 15 ♘d4 ♖c8 16 ♘xe6 fxe6 17 ♗h3! is better for White) 15 ♔b1 ♗f5 16 ♗d3 ♗g6? (16...♗xd3 17 ♖xd3 ±) 17 f4 ♕h5 18 g4! (the start of an elegant series of moves leading to victory) 18...♕xg4 19 f5 ♗h5 (19...d4 20 ♕d2 ♗xf5 21 ♖hg1 ♕h3 22 ♖g3 ♕h5 23 ♖g5 ♕f3 24 ♖f1 and the wriggling is at an end) 20 ♖dg1 d4 21 ♕d2 ♕f3 22 ♕g5 g6 23 ♘d2! (certainly not 23 ♕xh5? ♕xh1!) 23...♕d5 24 ♗e4 ♕a5 25 ♕xh5 ♘b4 26 a3 1-0 Van der Wiel-Mirallès, Cannes 1990.

1b) **13 ♘d4** should give White a small but safe advantage.

1c) **13 ♗b5!?** ♕g5+ and now both **14 ♕d2** ♕xg2 15 ♖hg1 and **14 ♔b1** d4 15 ♕c5 ♕xg2 give White an attack in return for the pawn.

2) **9...♘a5 10 ♔b1 ♘xb3 11 cxb3 a6 12 f4 b5 13 ♗xf6 gxf6 14 ♗d3 ♔h8 15 f5 b4 16 ♘e2 e5 17 ♗c4**, Anand-Mateo, Dubai OL 1986, is worth mentioning because it is a perfect example of what Black should

avoid. His king position has been weakened without any compensating queenside attack and Black has played ...e5 at a moment when White can reply ♗c4 to gain control of d5.

3) **9...h6** (it now seems firmly established that this line is good for White) **10 ♗xf6 ♗xf6 11 ♕xd6 ♗xc3** (11...♕b6 12 ♕c5 ♕c7 13 g3 ♗e7 14 ♕e3 a6 15 f4 b5 16 ♗g2 ♘e5 17 ♕e2 was also promising for White in Marjanović-Barlov, Yugoslav Ch 1985) **12 bxc3 ♕h4** *(D)* and now:

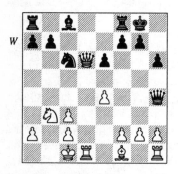

3a) **13 g3 ♕f6** (not 13...♕xe4? 14 ♗d3 and ♗h7+) 14 ♕c5 e5 15 ♗c4 ♗e6 (15...♗g4 16 ♖d6 ♕g5+ 17 ♔b2 ♗f3 18 ♖e1 ♖ac8 19 h4 ♕g4 20 ♕e3 ♖fd8 21 ♖xd8+ ♖xd8 22 ♗d5 ♗g2 23 ♖g1 ♕f3 24 g4 with advantage to White, Lobron-Kunsztowicz, Bad Neuenahr 1984) 16 ♗xe6 (16 ♗d5 ♖ac8 17 ♕e3 b6 18 ♔b2 ♕e7 19 ♖d3 ♖c7 20 ♖a1 ♖fc8 21 ♖b1 ♕a3 22 ♕c1 ♕a4 23 ♘d2 ♘a5, Gallagher-Van der Poel, San Bernardino 1994, and now instead of 24 ♕b2? ♘c4! with a roughly level game, White could have kept some

advantage with 24 ♖b4) 16...♕xe6 (16...fxe6!? was the reason I avoided the exchange on e6 in the above mentioned game; afterwards, I discovered that this had never been played although it does have the advantage of covering d5 and opening the f-file) 17 ♖d6 ♕h3 18 ♕e3 ♖fd8 19 ♖d5 and now both **19...♖dc8** 20 ♖hd1 ♖c7 21 f4 exf4 22 ♕xf4 ♖e7 23 ♘c5, as in Chandler-Torre, London 1984 and **19...♕g2** 20 ♖hd1 ♕xh2 21 ♘c5, Klovan-Tal, Jurmala 1983, were good for White.

3b) **13 f3!?** (this line is a little forgotten but it does seem very good for White) 13...♖d8 14 ♕c7! (maximising the queen's annoyance value) 14...♖xd1+ 15 ♔xd1 ♕f6 (15...e5 16 ♗c4+) 16 ♔c1 ♕xc3 17 ♗b5 e5 18 ♗xc6 ♗e6 (18...bxc6 gives White the option of 19 ♕d8+) 19 ♖d1 bxc6 20 ♖d3 ± Serper-Reznikov, USSR 1982.

We now move on to the major lines:

4) **9...a5** (quite popular in the 1980s, but it hasn't been seen so much of late) **10 a4 d5 11 ♗b5!** *(D)* (first appeared in the game Tal-Sisniega, although the idea belongs to Vitolinš) and now Black has:

4a) **11...♘xe4** 12 ♘xe4 dxe4 13 ♕xd8 ♗xd8 14 ♗xd8 ♘xd8 15 ♘c5 f5 (or 15...b6 16 ♘xe4 ♗b7 17 ♖he1 ♗d5 18 f3 ♖c8 19 ♘c3 ♗a8 20 ♗d7 ♖c7 21 ♘b5 ♖c5 22 ♖d6 ♘c6 23 ♘c3 with a slight plus for White, Rohde-Joshi, USA 1986) 16 ♖d6 ♔f7 17 ♖hd1 ♔e7 18 ♗d7 (Tal-Sisniega, Taxco IZ 1985) and now **18...♗xd7**

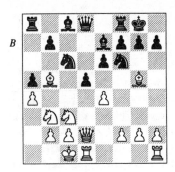

is just slightly better for White according to Tal. In the game **18...Rf7** 19 ②xe6 ♗xd7 20 ②c7 ♗xa4 21 ②xa8 led to a quick win for White.

4b) 11...dxe4 12 ♕xd8 ♗xd8 13 Rhe1 ②a7 (or 13...h6 14 ♗xf6 ♗xf6 15 ②xe4 with an edge for White) 14 ♗c4 h6 15 ♗xf6 gxf6 16 ②xe4 f5 17 ②d6 ♗c7 18 g3 b6? (18...Rd8 19 ②b5 ②xb5 20 ♗xb5 would have been slightly better for White according to Tal) 19 ②xf5! and White won in the famous game Tal-Korchnoi, Montpellier Ct 1985.

4c) 11...②a7 and now there are two tempting lines for White:

4c1) 12 ♗e2 ♗d7 (12...b5 13 exd5 bxa4 14 d6 axb3 15 dxe7 ♕xe7 16 cxb3 was unclear in Oll-Ryskin, USSR 1987, but 13 ♗xf6 ♗xf6 14 ②xb5 is better according to Oll) 13 ♗xf6 ♗xf6 14 exd5 ♗xc3 15 ♕xc3 ♗xa4 16 dxe6 ♕e7 17 exf7+ ♔h8 (Black has some initiative for the two pawns, but not nearly enough) 18 ♗c4 Rac8 19 Rhe1 ♕g5+ 20 ♕d2 ♕g6 21 ♗e6 Rc7 22 ♕d3 ♕xg2 23 ♕d6 and Black's counterattack has collapsed, Gelfand-Ryskin, Minsk 1986.

4c2) 12 ♗xf6 ♗xf6 13 exd5 ♗xc3 14 ♕xc3 ②xb5 15 axb5 a4?! (15...exd5 16 ②d4 ♕b6 is relatively best, but still good for White after 17 Rhe1) 16 dxe6! ♕g5+ (the point is that 16...axb3 17 Rxd8 Ra1+ 18 ♔d2 Rxd8+ 19 ♔e2 Rxh1 fails to 20 ♕c7 Rf8 21 e7 Re8 22 ♕d8) 17 ♕d2 ♕f6 18 ②d4 and Black has very little for his minus pawn, Hoffmann-Timoshchenko, Budapest 1989.

4d) 11...♗b4 (an untested suggestion by Tal) 12 exd5 exd5 13 ♕f4 with an edge for White.

4e) 11...②b4 *(D)* and White has a choice:

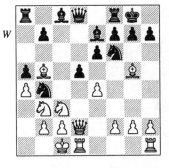

4e1) 12 e5 ②d7 13 ♗xe7 ♕xe7 14 f4 (in this French Defence type of position, the exchange of darksquared bishops theoretically favours White, but with the kings castled on opposite sides of the board the game is more likely to be decided by the speed of the respective attacks rather than by the endgame advantage of the better bishop) 14...②c5 (after 14...b6 15 Rhe1 ②c5 16 ②d4 ♗d7 17 ♔b1 Rac8? 18 g4 Rfd8 19 f5 ②e4 20 ②xe4 dxe4 21 c3

♘d3 22 ♗xd3 exd3 23 ♕f4! ♗xa4 24 ♖xd3 White had an excellent position in Balashov-Khalifman, Minsk 1986, but 17...♖fc8 intending ...♗xb5 was better) 15 ♘xc5 ♕xc5 16 h4 (the idea is to bring the rook to g3, not only helping the kingside attack, but also providing useful defence along the third rank) 16...b6 and now 17 h5 was unclear in Kindermann-Felsberger, Vienna 1986. Perhaps 17 ♖h3 was more accurate because in some lines the h-pawn plays no important role on h5, but in any case the position is very double-edged.

4e2) **12 ♖he1** *(D)* with a further branch:

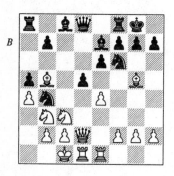

4e21) **12...h6** 13 exd5!? (or 13 ♗xf6 ♗xf6 14 exd5 exd5 15 ♘xd5 ♗g4 16 f3 ♗g5 17 ♘e7+! ♕xe7 18 ♖xe7 ♗xe7 19 ♕e2 ♗g5+ 20 ♔b1 ♗f5 21 ♘d4 ♗g6 22 ♔a1! and now White has excellent winning prospects, Oll-Khalifman, USSR 1987) 13...exd5 (13...hxg5 14 d6) 14 ♕e3 ♗e6 15 ♗f4 ♖c8 (Winsnes-Khalifman, Groningen 1985/6) and now 16 ♔b1 (intending ♘d4) 16...♘h5 17

♗e5 ♘c6 18 ♗xc6 bxc6 19 ♗d4 is good for White according to Donaldson.

4e22) **12...♗d7** (maybe the most solid move) 13 e5 (13 exd5 ♗xb5 14 d6 ♕xd6 15 ♕xd6 ♗xd6 16 ♖xd6 ♗c6 gives White an edge, as does 13 ♗xd7 ♕xd7 14 e5 ♘e8 15 ♗xe7 ♕xe7 16 f4 ♘c7 17 ♘d4 ♘c6 18 ♘db5 ♘xb5 19 ♘xb5 ♖ac8 even though a draw was agreed here in Rachels-D.Gurevich, Boston 1988) 13...♘e8 14 h4 ♘c7 15 ♘d4 ♘c6 16 ♗xe7 ♕xe7 17 ♕g5 and again White has a small advantage, Wang Zili-D.Gurevich, Belgrade 1988.

4e23) **12...dxe4** 13 ♕xd8 (White has a speculative alternative in 13 ♘xe4 ♘xe4 14 ♕xd8 ♗xg5+ 15 ♕xg5 ♘xg5 16 h4 e5 17 hxg5 ♗f5 18 ♖d2 ♖fc8 {18...f6 was a more cautious move} 19 c3 ♗e6 20 ♘a1 ♖c5 21 ♗d7! with some advantage to White, Vitolinš-Inkiov, Jurmala 1985) 13...♖xd8 (13...♗xd8 14 ♘xe4 is good for White after 14...♘xe4 15 ♗xd8 ♘xf2 16 ♖d2 or 14...♗e7 15 ♘xf6+ ♗xf6 16 ♗xf6 gxf6 17 ♖d6) 14 ♘xe4 ♘bd5 15 c4! ♘c7 (or 15...♘b4 16 ♖xd8+ ♗xd8 17 ♖d1 ♗e7 18 ♘d6 with a clear plus) 16 ♖xd8+ ♗xd8 17 ♖d1 ♗e7 18 ♘xf6+ gxf6 19 ♗e3 ♘xb5 20 axb5, Anand-Inkiov, Calcutta 1986, and the liquidation has left White with a clear advantage. Black still has problems developing his queenside pieces and White's queenside majority is ominously near to creating a passed pawn. True, Black has the two bishops, but White can always force an exchange (e.g. by ♗c5) if they show signs of becoming active. After the further moves 20...f5 21 ♘c5 e5 22 ♘d7 f4 23 ♗b6 f6 24 ♗c7 ♗xd7 25 ♖xd7 ♗c5 26 ♗d6 ♗xd6 27 ♖xd6 White had a winning rook ending.

5) 9...♛b6 (the counterattack against f2 nullifies White's threat to take on f6, so Black gets time to support his d-pawn by ...♖d8; White's usual reaction has been to start a kingside pawn storm, but he must be careful because too many pawn moves might encourage Black to open up the centre by ...d5) **10 f3** *(D)* and now:

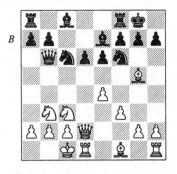

5a) 10...a6 11 h4! (this is the reply which has put 10...a6 out of favour) 11...♖d8 12 h5 ♛c7 (when the pawn reaches h5 Black faces a tricky problem – is he willing to let his dark squares be weakened by allowing h6, or should be play ...h6 himself, even though this makes the subsequent advance of White's g-pawn very strong? After 12...h6 13 ♗e3 ♛c7 14 ♛f2 ♘d7 15 g4 ♘ce5 16 ♖g1 b5 17 g5 White had developed

a very dangerous attack in Hellers-J.Piket, Amsterdam 1985) 13 g4 (or 13 h6 g6 14 ♛f4 ♘e8 15 ♗xe7 ♛xe7 16 ♛e3 b5 17 ♗e2 ♖b8, Martinović-Popović, Yugoslav Ch 1986, and now 18 ♖d2 followed by ♖hd1 is slightly better for White according to Martinović) 13...b5 14 ♗e3 ♘d7 15 g5 ♘ce5 16 g6! b4 (16...fxg6 17 f4! ♘c4 18 ♗xc4 bxc4 19 ♘d5! exd5 20 ♛xd5+ ♔h8 21 hxg6 ♘f6 22 ♖xh7+ ♘xh7 23 ♛h5 is mate) 17 gxf7+ ♔xf7 18 ♘d5! exd5 19 ♛xd5+ ♔f8 (19...♔e8 20 h6 g6 21 f4 ♘g4 22 ♗c4 is also good for White) 20 ♛xa8! ♗b7 21 ♛a7 with advantage to White as 21...♘c6 is met by 22 ♘d4, Serper-Brodsky, USSR 1986.

5b) 10...♖d8 11 ♔b1. A useful semi-waiting move; the reply 11...d5 is bad for tactical reasons, so Black plays either 11...a6, when White can switch to his kingside attack plan without allowing ...d5, or the immediate 11...♛c7 which has been quite popular recently:

5b1) 11...d5?! 12 ♗xf6 ♗xf6 (Black should not play 12...dxe4? because of the reply 13 ♗xe7! ♖xd2 14 ♘xd2! when 14...♘xe7 15 ♘c4 ♛c7 16 ♘b5 wins the queen; Anand-Benjamin, Wijk aan Zee 1989 continued 14...exf3 and now 15 ♘c4 fxg2 16 ♗xg2 ♛c7 17 ♗d6 ♛d8 18 ♗g3 ♛e7 19 ♖he1 is crushing for White) 13 exd5 ♗xc3 (13...a5 14 ♘a4 ♛a7 15 d6 b6 16 ♛e3! ♖b8 17 ♗b5 was very good for White in Mokry-Conquest, Gausdal 1989) 14 ♛xc3 exd5 (14...♘b4 is worse since

15 d6! ♖xd6 16 ♗c4 makes it hard for Black to complete his development) 15 ♕c5 followed by ♗b5, with advantage to White.

5b2) **11...a6** 12 ♗e3 ♕c7 13 ♕f2 (thanks to the threat of ♗b6 Black has no time for ...d5) 13...♘d7 14 h4 b5 with a position similar to line '5a' above. Admittedly White has spent a move on ♔b1, but this is certainly not a waste of tempo, and while White's chances are not quite as good as in line '5a' he has fair attacking prospects. For example, Timman-Salov, Linares 1991 continued **15 g4** ♖b8 16 g5 ♘b6 17 g6!? ♘a4 18 gxf7+ ♔xf7 19 ♘e2 ♗f6 20 ♘ed4 ♘xd4 21 ♖xd4 e5 22 ♗e3 ♔g8 23 ♗h3 with just an edge for White. Another possibility is **15 ♗g5!?**, when Govedarica-Thorsteins, Clermont-Ferrand 1989 continued 15...♗b7?! 16 ♘d5! exd5 17 exd5 ♗xg5 18 dxc6 with advantage to White.

5c) **11...♕c7** 12 ♗xf6!? (White parts company with his bishop in order to speed up the attack) 12...♗xf6 13 g4 g6 (Black wishes to keep his bishop on the long diagonal, even if this means allowing White to open the h-file; 13...a6 14 g5 ♗e7 15 f4 does look quite promising for White) **14 h4 a6 15 g5** (15 h5 g5!) **15...♗g7 16 h5 b5 17 hxg6 hxg6 18 f4!** (a strong move, threatening to play f5 and clearing the third rank so that the queen's rook has access to the h-file) **18...b4 19 ♘a4** (19 ♘e2 a5 would allow Black counterplay; although the knight can certainly get

into trouble on a4, White hopes that it will survive long enough for him to develop his attack) **19...♖b8 20 ♕h2** (20 ♗d3, aiming for f5, is well met by 20...♘e7!) **20...♗f8** (20...♗d7 21 ♖d3! ♘e7 runs into trouble: 22 ♖h3 ♔f8 23 ♖h7! ♘g8 24 ♖xg7 ♔xg7 25 ♕h8+ ♔f8 26 ♖h7 ♔e7 27 f5! with a crushing attack) **21 ♖d3!** *(D)* (preparing to triple) and now:

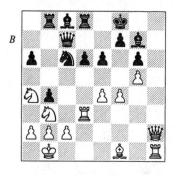

5c1) Benjamin-Anand, Groningen 1993 continued **21...e5 22 f5 gxf5 23 ♖h3! ♘e7!** (23...fxe4 24 ♖h7!) **24 ♖h8+ ♘g8** (24...♗xh8 25 ♕xh8+ ♘g8 26 ♖h7) **25 ♖xg8+ ♔xg8 26 ♕h7+ ♔f8 27 exf5 ♗xf5!** (27...♕e7 28 f6 ♗xf6 29 gxf6 ♕xf6 30 ♗d3 is better for White) **28 ♕xf5 ♕c6 29 g6 ♖b7 30 ♖h7 ♕xa4** *(D)* and now:

5c11) The game continued **31 ♕g5?!** ♕e8! 32 ♗xa6 (Anand's suggestion 32 ♗g2 is also insufficient; not because of 32...♖c7 or 32...e4, since both lose to 33 ♖xg7!, but 32...d5! when 33 ♘c5 can be met by 33...♕e7!) 32...♖e7! 33 ♗d3 e4! 34 ♗b5?! ♖e5! 35 gxf7 ♖xg5 36 fxe8♕+ ♖xe8 37 ♗xe8 ♖g1+ 38

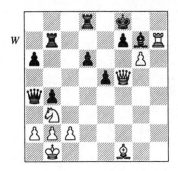

♘c1 ♔xe8 39 a4? (White had to try 39 c3 bxc3 40 bxc3 ♗xc3 41 ♔c2 ♗f6, although Black should still win) 39...bxa3 40 bxa3 ♗c3! 41 ♖h4 d5 0-1.

5c12) 31 ♖xg7 ♔xg7 32 gxf7 looks good enough for a draw, e.g. **32...♕d7** (certainly not 32...♖xf7? 33 ♕g5+ ♔h7 34 ♗d3+, nor 32...♖f8 33 ♕g4+ when White picks up the rook on b7 after both 33...♔h7 34 ♕h3+! and 35 ♕g2+ and 33...♔xf7 34 ♗c4+ ♔f6 35 ♕f3+) 33 ♕g5+ ♔xf7 34 ♘c5! dxc5 (34...♕e7 35 ♕h5+) 35 ♗c4+ and White has perpetual check, or **32...♔f8** 33 ♕g5 ♖bb8 (33...♕d7 34 ♗c4 d5 35 ♘c5 is OK for White) 34 ♗c4 d5 35 ♕g8+ ♔e7 36 ♕g5+ and after both **36...♔d6** 37 ♕f6+ and **36...♔xf7** 37 ♕f5+ White has at least a draw.

5c13) 31 ♗c4!? is an interesting winning attempt. **31...d5** can be met by 32 ♘c5 and **31...♕d7** by 32 ♕h5! when 32...fxg6? 33 ♖h8+! leads to mate. Black should probably respond with **31...♖dd7**, and in this critical position White has various ways to force perpetual check, and one way to continue the fight:

5c131) 32 ♕h5 fxg6 33 ♖h8+ ♗xh8 34 ♕xh8+ ♔e7 35 ♕h4+ is a draw by perpetual check.

5c132) 32 ♕h3 fxg6 33 ♕e6 (33 ♖h8+ is again a draw, while after 33 ♗d5 ♕b5! it is time for White to settle for the draw) 33...d5 34 ♗xd5 (34 ♘c5 dxc4 35 ♖h1 looks strong, but Black can reply 35...♖e7! 36 ♕d5 ♕e8) 34...♖xd5 35 ♕xd5 ♕d7 and Black has an extra pawn, but his king remains somewhat exposed.

5c133) 32 ♕f3!? is the move to play if White wants to win at all costs. It prevents 32...♕c6 and sets up the rather slow threat of ♕g2 followed by ♖xg7. Even if Black plays 32...♖dc7 33 ♕g2 ♕c6, White can still play 34 ♗d5 followed by ♖xg7. I (JN) don't believe that White can be worse in this position.

5c2) Benjamin believes **21...♗d7** to be the best defence. He gives **22 f5** exf5 23 ♘ac5 as unclear and I imagine this could easily end in a draw after 23...♗e5 24 ♕h6+ ♗g7 25 ♕h2 etc. After **22 ♖h3** he suggests 22...♔e7! so that **23 ♖h7** can be met by 23...♖h8!. However, I like the look of **23 ♕e2!** threatening to play f5. One line runs **23...♘a5** 24 f5 ♗xa4 25 ♖h7!? and now 25...♖g8 26 ♖xg7 and 25...♗e5 26 f6+ ♔e8 27 ♖g7! are winning for White. If Black tries **23...♔f8**, White plays 24 ♖h7 ♘e7 25 ♕h2! and Black has been tricked into the variation given in the notes to Black's 20th move. Perhaps the best is **23...e5** although after 24 ♖h7 I prefer White. Another advantage of the queen on e2 is that

White may be able to snatch the a6-pawn one day.

Now we return to the main line after 9...a6 (D).

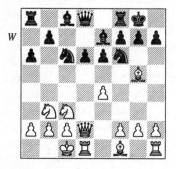

10 ♗xf6   gxf6

10...♗xf6 is dubious: 11 ♕xd6 ♗xc3 (or 11...♕b6 12 f4 ♗e7 13 ♕d2 a5 14 a4 ♖d8 15 ♗d3 with advantage to White, Shaposhnikov-Boleslavsky, USSR 1950; as usual 12...♗xc3 13 bxc3 ♕e3+ 14 ♔b2 ♕xe4 loses to 15 ♗d3 followed by 16 ♗xh7+) 12 bxc3 (the position is the same as after 9...h6, except that Black has played ...a6 instead; the verdict is unchanged) 12...♕f6 (12...♕h4 13 g3 {13 f3!?} 13...♕f6 14 ♕c5 e5 15 ♗c4 ♗g4 16 ♖d6 ♕g5+ 17 f4 and White was clearly better in Ivanović-Popović, Novi Sad 1984) 13 ♕g3 e5 14 ♗c4 ♗e6 15 ♗xe6 ♕xe6 16 ♖d5 and again White had won the opening battle, Benjamin-Christiansen, USA 1984.

11 ♕h6

White plans a general kingside pawn advance by g4, f4, h4 and g5, but first he transports his queen into the vicinity of the black king.

11 ...   ♔h8
12 ♕h5

Black is now virtually forced to lose time with his queen because he must free the f8-rook to defend h7 by ...♖g8-g7.

12 ...   ♕e8

12...♖g8?, Ernst-Chandler, London 1988, 13 ♕xf7! ♖g6 14 f4 ♗d7 15 ♖d3 e5 16 ♖g3! ♗e8 17 ♕d5 exf4 18 ♖xg6 hxg6 19 ♕d2 g5 20 ♘d4 ♘xd4 21 ♕xd4 is good for White.

13 f4   ♖g8

13...b5 14 ♗d3 ♖g8 would give White the chance to play 15 ♘d5!?. Tisdall points out that after **15...exd5** 16 exd5 ♖g7 17 dxc6 ♗g4 18 ♕d5 ♗xd1 19 ♖xd1 White has fantastic compensation for a slight material deficit; of course Black should play **15...♗b7** 16 ♘xe7 ♕xe7 and it is far from certain that the exchange of minor pieces favours White, especially as he has spent two tempi achieving it.

14 g4   b5
15 ♗d3   ♖g7

15...b4 16 e5 clears e4 for the knight with gain of tempo.

16 h4   b4
17 ♘e2 (D)
17 ...   e5

In view of the hard time Black received in this game perhaps his attention will once again turn towards **17...a5**. The analysis runs **18 g5** (18 ♘bd4!?) **18...a4 19 ♘bd4** and now:

1) **19...♘xd4** 20 ♘xd4 ♗d7 21 gxf6 ♗xf6 22 e5 dxe5 23 ♖hg1 ♕g8,

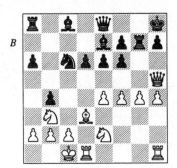

Arnason-Inkiov, Plovdiv 1986, and now Inkiov suggests 24 ♘f3! ♗e8 (24...exf4 25 ♖xg7 ♗xg7 26 ♘g5 wins) 25 ♗e4 (25 fxe5 also deserves attention, though perhaps Black can defend with 25...♖xg1 26 ♖xg1 ♗g7) as good for White.

2) **19...b3!?** 20 axb3 (or 20 cxb3 axb3 21 a3, after which 21...♘xd4 22 ♘xd4 ♕a4 is unclear) 20...axb3 21 ♘xb3 ♗b7 22 ♘c3 ♘b4 23 ♖hg1 ♕c6 24 ♖g3 ♕b6 25 ♕e2 d5 was played in Psakhis-Kotronias, Dortmund 1989, and now the best move is 26 ♕e3!, when Kotronias gives 26...♘xd3+ 27 ♖xd3 ♕xe3+ 28 ♖dxe3 ♗d6 29 e5 fxe5 30 fxe5 ♗e7 intending ...h6 as unclear. However after 31 ♘b5! I doubt that Black has enough for the pawn, e.g. 31...h6 32 gxh6 ♖xg3 33 ♖xg3 ♗xh4 34 ♖g7 intending ♘d6.

18 f5   a5
19 ♖dg1!

Previous games had seen **19 ♔b1** but it seems that White can do without this precautionary move, thus gaining an important tempo for the attack.

19 ...   ♗b7

19...a4 20 ♘d2 b3 is met by 21 a3! and after 21...bxc2 22 g5 White is miles ahead in the hunt for the opposing king.

20 g5   a4?!

This natural move is probably a mistake. Black has insufficient force in the vicinity of the white king to start an attack so there was little point in forcing the knight to a more active square. Leko gives the immediate **20...♘b8** as better, but he still doesn't like Black's position after **21 ♕h6!** ♘d7 22 gxf6 ♖xg1+ 23 ♖xg1 ♗xf6 24 ♘g3 ♕f8 25 ♕e3 a4 26 ♘d2 when White has a particularly menacing knight pair. It's worth pointing out that if White had continued as in the game, namely **21 gxf6** ♗xf6 22 ♖xg7 ♗xg7 23 f6 ♗xf6 24 ♖f1 ♕e7 25 ♘f4, then Black can defend with 25...♘d7 26 ♘d5 ♗xd5 27 exd5 ♘f8 as there is no ♘e4 to finish him off.

21 ♘d2   ♘b8

As **21...b3** 22 a3! achieves nothing, Black makes this defensive manoeuvre in order to shore up the critical f6-square.

22 gxf6

22 ♕h6 is possible but the text seems even stronger.

22 ...   ♗xf6
23 ♖xg7   ♗xg7

23...♔xg7 24 ♘f3! looks pretty nasty for Black.

24 f6!

White is willing to invest a fair amount of material to clear the b1-h7 diagonal for his bishop.

24 ...   ♗xf6

25 ♖f1   ♕e7 *(D)*

25...♘d7 26 ♗b5! +− is Leko's comment in *Informator*. True, but White has to take great care as after 26...♗g7 the seemingly crushing **27 ♖xf7** gives Black the chance to defend himself by **27...♗a6! 28 ♗xd7 ♗xe2!** and it's not even clear if White is better; **29 ♕f5 ♕g8!** with the idea of ...♖f8 looks OK for Black as does **29 ♘f3 ♕g8! 30 ♗e6 ♗xf3 31 ♖xf3 ♗h6+ 32 ♔d1 ♕g1+** with a likely draw. **27 ♗xd7 ♕xd7 28 ♖xf7 ♕c6** is very unclear, and **27 ♕xf7 ♕xf7 28 ♖xf7 ♘c5** is not recommended but White does have one very strong move though: **27 ♘g3!**. The knight heads for f5 and ♖xf7 is once again threatened. Black will be hard pressed to find any sort of defence, especially as 27...♘f6 fails to **28 ♗xe8! ♘xh5 29 ♘xh5 ♖xe8 30 ♖xf7.**

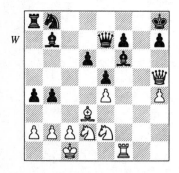

W

26 ♘f4!   exf4

There was no choice as 26...♘d7 27 ♘d5 ♗xd5 (27...♕d8 28 ♘xf6 ♘xf6 29 ♕xf7) 28 exd5 ♘f8 29 ♘e4 ♗g7 30 ♖xf7 is terminal.

27 e5   ♔g8

28 ♖g1+?

This only assists the black king to escape. Much stronger was **28 ♕xh7+ ♔f8 29 exf6 ♕xf6 30 ♘e4! ♕e5** (there is no relief for Black in 30...♕g7 31 ♕xg7+ ♔xg7 32 ♘xd6 followed by ♖xf4) **31 ♕h6+ ♔e7 32 ♖xf4 ♘d7 33 ♖xf7+! ♔xf7 34 ♘g5+ ♔e7 35 ♕h7+ ♔d8** (35...♔e8 36 ♗g6+) **36 ♘f7+.**

28 ...   ♔f8
29 ♕h6+   ♔e8
30 exf6   ♕e3!

Even if White's 28th move was an error it's still nothing short of miraculous that Black managed to save himself from this position.

31 ♕g7   ♗d5!

Covering f7. It's now quite hard for White to get at the black king.

32 ♔d1

How else can White increase the pressure?

32 ...   b3!!

Black finds an incredible saving resource.

33 ♖e1

White cannot be called a coward for avoiding **33 a3** bxc2+ 34 ♗xc2 ♕d4 35 ♖e1+ ♔d7 36 ♖e7+ ♔c6 when his own king is in at least as much danger as Black's.

33 ...   bxa2
34 ♖xe3+   fxe3
35 ♗b5+   ♔d8
36 ♕f8+   ♔c7
37 ♕e7+   ♔c8
38 ♕e8+   ♔c7
39 ♕e7+   ½-½

With no way to stop the a-pawn White must take the perpetual.

Game 11
Z. Almasi – Gabriel
Altensteig 1994

1	e4	c5
2	♘f3	d6
3	d4	cxd4
4	♘xd4	♘f6
5	♘c3	♘c6
6	♗g5	e6
7	♕d2	a6
8	0-0-0	♗d7

8...h6 is examined in Game 12. Other ideas are dubious, e.g.:

1) **8...♕b6** 9 ♘b3 ♗d7 10 ♗e2 ♕c7 11 f4 h6 12 ♗xf6 gxf6 13 ♗h5 is good for White, Panchenko-Csom, Las Palmas 1978.

2) **8...♗e7 9 f4 ♕c7** (9...♘xd4 10 ♕xd4 ♕a5 11 e5 dxe5 12 fxe5 ♘d5 13 ♗xe7 ♘xe7 14 ♗d3 ♘c6 15 ♕h4 ♘xe5 16 ♘e4 f6 17 ♖hf1 with a very dangerous attack for White, Adler-Bannik, USSR 1978) and now:

2a) **10 ♔b1 ♗d7** (10...0-0 11 ♗e2 ♖d8 12 ♗f3 h6 13 h4 ♘xd4 14 ♕xd4 b5 15 ♕f2 ♗b7 16 g4 was good for White in Kavalek-Larsen, Montreal 1979) 11 ♘f3 ♖d8 12 ♗d3 b5 13 ♖he1 b4 14 ♘e2 a5 15 ♘g3 0-0 16 e5 ♘d5 17 ♕e2 was unclear in Przewoznik-Bielczyk, Katowice 1986.

2b) **10 ♗e2 ♘xd4** 11 ♕xd4 b5 12 e5 dxe5 13 fxe5 ♘d5 14 ♗xe7 ♘xc3 15 ♗f3! ♘xd1 16 ♗d6! and White went on to win quickly in Tal-Larsen, Montreal 1979 after 16...♕c4 17 ♕b6! ♘f2 18 ♗c6+ ♗d7 19 ♗xd7+ ♔xd7 20 ♕b7+ ♔d8 21 ♕xa8+ ♕c8 22 ♕a7 1-0.

2c) **10 ♗xf6 gxf6 11 g3 ♗d7 12 f5 ♘xd4 13 ♕xd4 ♖c8?!** (13...0-0 and 13...b5 are possible improvements) 14 ♔b1 b5 15 ♕d2 ♕c5 16 ♗d3 h5? 17 fxe6 fxe6 18 ♘e2 intending ♘f4, Short-Larsen, London 1986, and White has the advantage.

9 f4 *(D)*

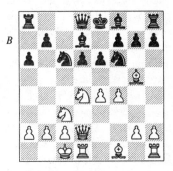

9 ... h6

Black has two major alternatives, 9...b5 and 9...♗e7:

1) **9...b5 10 ♗xf6 gxf6 11 ♔b1**. In *BTS2* 11 ♘xc6 ♗xc6 12 ♕e1 was recommended, but this move order has been abandoned due to 12...b4 13 ♘d5 a5 14 ♖d4 f5! when Black very quickly creates counterplay on the long diagonal. For example, 15 ♖c4 (15 exf5 ♗g7 16 ♖d1 ♗xd5 17 ♖xd5 ♕f6) 15...♗xd5 16 exd5 ♕f6 17 dxe6 fxe6 18 ♖c7 ♔d8! 19 ♖b7 (19 ♖c6 ♗g7 20 ♖xd6+ ♔e7 21 ♕e5 ♕xe5 22 fxe5 ♗xe5 is a little better for Black) 19...♔c8 20 ♖b5 ♗g7 21 c3 bxc3 22 ♗c4 ♖e8 23 ♕e3, which is given as unclear by Poluliakhov, but after 23...♕d4 24 ♗xe6+ ♔c7 White is forced to exchange queens, thereby losing any chance of gaining

the advantage. With 11 ♔b1 White steers clear of this mess and at the same time can aim for similar positions to those analysed in *BTS2*. Black now has:

1a) **11...b4** (rarely played) 12 ♘ce2 ♕b6 13 ♘xc6 ♗xc6 14 f5 e5 (14...♗xe4 15 fxe6 fxe6 16 ♘f4 and now both 16...d5 17 ♗d3 and 16...b3 17 axb3 ♕xb3 18 ♗d3 are good for White) 15 ♘g3 ♕c5 (15...h5 16 h4 gives White a nice target) 16 ♘h5!? ♔e7 (Damljanović didn't like the position after 16...♗e7 17 ♗d3 h6 18 ♖c1) 17 ♗d3 ♖g8 18 ♖hg1! (18 ♕e2 ♗h6) 18...♖g5 19 g4 ♗h6 20 ♕e2 (20 ♘xf6 ♖xg4) 20...♖ag8? (better is 20...♖gg8 when 21 h4 ♗e3 22 ♖g3 ♗d4 23 g5 is unclear according to Damljanović {I prefer White} but also possible is 21 ♖g3, not allowing the bishop to get to d4) and now instead of playing **21 ♖g3?** (Vujaković-Damljanović, Yugoslavia 1991), White could have won the exchange with **21 h4!** ♖xh5 22 ♖h1!. Black has insufficient compensation, e.g. 22...a5 23 gxh5 a4 24 ♗c4 ♖c8 25 b3 a3 26 ♖d3 followed by c3 is winning for White.

1b) **11...♕b6** *(D)* and now:

1b1) For those of you not content with a positional advantage then Wolff's suggestion, **12 ♘f5!?**, might be of interest. His analysis runs 12...exf5 13 ♘d5 ♕d8 (13...♕b7 14 ♘xf6+ ♔d8 15 e5!? or 15 g3) 14 exf5 and now **14...♗xf5** loses to 15 ♕c3 whilst both **14...♗e7** 15 g4! and **14...♗g7** 15 ♖e1+ give White good play for the piece.

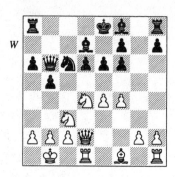

1b2) **12 ♘xc6 ♗xc6 13 ♕e1!** and now Black would like to play ...b4 but for the moment this is met by ♘d5. 13...♗e7 is normal, but as the bishop is often better off on f8 than e7 Black has tried a couple of other moves recently:

1b21) I.Gurevich-Kožul, Biel IZ 1993 continued **13...♖a7** 14 f5 b4 15 ♘e2 e5 16 ♘g3 h5 17 ♗e2! ♖h6 18 ♗c4 a5 19 ♘f1 ♕c5 (19...♗xe4 20 ♗d5 gives excellent positional compensation for a pawn) 20 ♘e3 with advantage.

1b22) Lau-Grosar, Graz 1993 continued **13...0-0-0** 14 ♗d3 h5 15 ♕h4 ♗e7 16 ♖he1 ♖de8 17 ♕h3 ♔b8 18 f5 b4 19 ♘e2 e5 20 ♘c1 a5 21 ♗c4 with a clear advantage for White.

1b23) **13...♗e7** 14 f5 b4 (White has an edge after 14...♕c5 15 fxe6 fxe6 16 ♗d3) 15 ♘e2 e5 (and not 15...♗xe4? 16 fxe6 fxe6 17 ♘g3 ♗d5 18 ♖xd5! exd5 19 ♘f5, which is great for White) 16 ♘g3 ♕c5 17 ♗d3 (17 b3!?) 17...a5 and in an extremely roundabout way we have transposed into the game Ernst-Popović, Subotica IZ 1987, which was featured in *BTS2*. Play continued 18 ♕e2 (now nothing can stop ♗c4-d5) 18...a4 19 ♗c4 0-0 (obviously very risky, but there is no chance of a successful attack against the white king without the other rook) 20 ♘h5 ♔h8 21 ♖hf1 a3? (overlooking that White has an immediate mating threat, but even the best line 21...♖fc8 22 b3 ♖a7 23 ♖f3 axb3 24 ♗xb3 is very unpleasant for Black) 22 ♖f3 (White can afford to abandon the queenside since he has a forced win on the other flank) 22...axb2 23 ♖h3 (intending 24 ♘xf6 ♗xf6 25 ♕h5) 23...♖g8 24 ♘xf6 1-0. After 24...♗xf6 25 ♖xh7+ ♔xh7 26 ♕h5+ ♔g7 27 ♕xf7+ ♔h6 (27...♔h8 28 ♕h5+ ♔g7 29 ♕g6+ and mate next move) 28 ♕xf6+ ♔h7 29 ♕h4+ ♔g7 30 ♕g5+ the rook is the first of many black pieces to disappear.

2) **9...♗e7 10 ♘f3 b5** *(D)* (other moves are inconsistent, for example 10...♕c7 11 e5 dxe5 12 fxe5 ♘d5 13 ♘xd5 exd5 14 ♗xe7 ♘xe7 15 ♗d3 0-0 16 ♕g5 ♘c6 17 ♕h5 or 10...h6 11 ♗xf6 gxf6 12 f5 ♕c7 13 ♔b1 0-0-0 14 ♗c4 with a clear plus for White in both cases) and now:

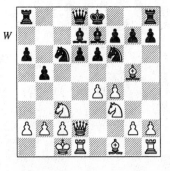

2a) **11 a3!?** (an unusual sideline which gives me the chance to demonstrate one of my better efforts; White allows his queenside to be weakened but he hopes to break through in the centre before Black has time to organise an attack) 11...b4 12 axb4 ♘xb4 13 ♗c4 (not 13 e5?! ♕a5 14 ♔b1 ♘e4) 13...♕c7 (13...♗c6 is given as = by *ECO*, but 14 ♘d4 would be an interesting reply) 14 ♕e2! (White waits for ...♖c8 before playing ♗b3 so that the advance of the a-pawn won't be so dangerous, e.g. 14 ♗b3?! a5 15 e5 a4 16 exd6 axb3 17 dxc7 ♖a1+ 18 ♘b1 ♘a2#) 14...♖c8 15 ♗b3 0-0?! (better is 15...e5) 16 e5 dxe5 17 fxe5 (17 ♘xe5!?) 17...♘fd5 18 ♗xe7 ♘xe7 19 ♘g5 a5 20 ♖hf1 a4 21 ♕e4! ♘g6? *(D)* (Black had to play 21...♘f5, even if White can obtain a strong attack after 22 ♗xa4 ♗xa4 23 ♕xb4 ♗c6 24 ♖xf5! exf5 25 e6)

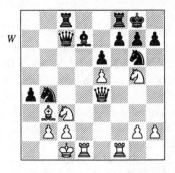

22 ♖xd7! (White is willing to part company with both his rooks if it means landing on e6) 22...♕xd7 23 ♖xf7! axb3? (the best that Black can do is 23...♖xf7 24 ♗xe6 ♕xe6 25

♘xe6 ♘c6 although White should still be winning) 24 ♖xd7 ♖f1+ 25 ♖d1 ♘a2+ 26 ♘xa2 and, in Gallagher-Čabrilo, Royan 1989, Black resigned since he spotted that after 26...bxa2, 27 ♕a4 stops the pawn.

2b) **11 e5 b4** (not 11...dxe5 12 fxe5 b4 13 exf6 bxc3 14 ♕xd7+ and White wins) **12 exf6 bxc3 13 ♕xc3 gxf6 14 ♗h4** *(D)* and now:

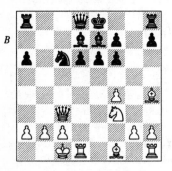

2b1) **14...a5** (14...♕a5 15 ♗xf6 ♘b4 16 ♗c4 ♖c8 17 a3 is good for White) 15 ♔b1 ♘b4 (15...♖b8 16 g4 ♘b4 17 a3 ♖c8 18 ♕b3 ♘d5 19 ♖xd5 with an excellent position for White, Gligorić-Conrady, Dublin 1957) 16 a3 ♖c8 17 ♕b3 ♘d5 18 ♖xd5 exd5 and now either 19 ♘d4 or 19 ♕xd5, with very good compensation for the exchange.

2b2) **14...d5 15 ♔b1** with a further branch:

2b21) **15...a5** 16 ♗b5 ♖c8 17 ♘d4 ♘xd4 18 ♗xd7+ ♕xd7 19 ♕xd4 ♖g8 20 g3 ♕b5 21 ♖he1 is good for White.

2b22) **15...♘b4** 16 ♘d4 ♕a5 (16...♖c8 17 ♕b3 ♕a5 18 ♗e1! ♗a4 19 ♕a3 with a clear plus for White,

Matanović-Jansa, Lugano 1968) 17 a3 ♘c6 18 ♕g3 ♘xd4 19 ♖xd4 ♖b8 20 ♖d3 ♔f8 21 ♗e2 with a small plus for White according to Lukin.

2b23) **15...♕a5** 16 f5 ♖c8 17 ♕d2 ♕c7 18 fxe6 fxe6 19 ♗d3! ♘c4 20 ♗xc4 ♕xc4 21 ♖he1 ♖g8 (after 21...0-0, the simplest reply is 22 g4!) 22 h3 ♖b8 23 ♔a1 h5 24 g3 with a small plus for White, Tseshkovsky-Lukin, USSR 1982.

2b24) **15...♖c8!?** 16 ♘d4 (the a-pawn is not of great interest to either side) 16...♕b6 (16...♘e5?! 17 ♕g3 ♘g6 18 f5 ♘xh4 19 fxe6 fxe6 20 ♕xh4 0-0 21 ♕g4+ ♔f7 22 ♗d3 was very good for White in Rachels-Shirazi, USA Ch 1992) 17 ♘xc6 (17 ♗f2 is certainly worth consideration) 17...♕xc6 18 ♕d2 ♖b8 19 ♔a1 (19 c4!? dxc4 20 ♗xc4 ♕xc4 21 ♕xd7+ ♔f8 22 ♕d4 ♕xd4 23 ♖xd4 f5 24 ♗xe7+ ♔xe7 25 ♖c1 gives White a slightly better rook ending) 19...♕a4 20 b3 ♕a3 21 ♗d3 a5 22 ♕c3 a4 23 ♖b1 is unclear, Adams-Christiansen, Biel 1991.

10 ♗h4 *(D)*

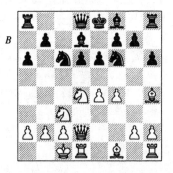

| 10 | ... | g5 |

Or:

1) **10...♗e7** (10...♘xd4 11 ♕xd4 ♗c6 12 ♗c4 is clearly good for White, while 10...♖c8 11 ♘f3 ♕a5 is similar to the note to Black's 9th move) 11 ♘f3! b5 12 e5 (12 ♗xf6 ♗xf6 13 ♕xd6 ♖a7 14 e5 ♗e7 15 ♕d3! ♕a5 16 ♔b1 ♖c7 17 ♕e3! 0-0 18 ♕e4 was also good for White in Georgadze-Makarychev, Nikolaev 1983) 12...b4 13 exf6 bxc3 14 ♕xc3 gxf6 15 f5 and White stands well, Thiemann-Reynolds, Corr. 1966.

2) **10...♘xe4 11 ♕e1** and now:

2a) **11...g5** 12 ♘xe4 ♘xd4 (after 12...gxh4 White can reply 13 ♕c3) 13 fxg5 ♘f5 **14 ♘f6+** ♔e7 15 ♘d5+ ♔e8 16 ♘f6+ ♔e7 17 ♗f2 ♗c6 18 ♗d3 hxg5 19 ♗xf5 ♔xf6 20 ♗d4+ ♔xf5 21 ♗xh8 ♔g6 and by now Black has somehow achieved a quite reasonable position, Jansa-Formanek, Gausdal 1991. I think White would have done better to play **14 ♕c3!**, e.g. 14...♗g7 15 ♘xd6+ ♔f8 16 gxh6! ♗xc3 (16...♗xh6+ 17 ♔b1 +−) 17 ♗xd8 ♖xd8 (17...♘xd6 18 ♗c7!) 18 ♘xb7 and White should be winning.

2b) **11...♘f6 12 ♘f5 ♕a5** (the lines 12...♕b8 13 ♗xf6 gxf6 14 ♘e4, 12...♗e7 13 ♘xd6+ ♔f8 14 ♘xb7 ♕c7 15 ♕d2 and 12...♕c7 13 ♗xf6 gxf6 14 ♘d5 ♕d8 15 ♕e3! are all very pleasant for White) **13 ♘xd6+ ♗xd6 14 ♖xd6** *(D)* with the lines:

2b1) **14...♕c7** 15 ♖d2 is unsatisfactory after **15...0-0-0** 16 ♕f2 ♘e7 17 ♗d3 ♗c6 18 f5 e5 19 ♖hd1 or **15...♕xf4** 16 ♗e2 ♘e4 17 ♘xe4

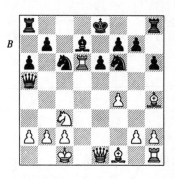

♕xe4 18 ♕f2, Gligorić-Barden, Bognor Regis 1957.

2b2) **14...♘e7** 15 ♖d1 ♘g6 16 ♘e4! ♕xe1 17 ♘d6+ ♔e7 18 ♗xe1 ♘d5 19 ♘xb7 ♘xf4 20 g3 ♘g6 21 ♗g2 ±.

2b3) **14...♘b4** 15 a3 ♘bd5 16 ♕e5 ♗c6 17 ♗c4! is also very good for White.

2b4) **14...0-0-0** 15 ♖d1! ♕c7 (15...♘e7? 16 ♘d5 wins, 15...g5 16 fxg5 hxg5 17 ♗g3 gives White very strong pressure on the dark squares and 15...e5 16 fxe5 ♖he8 17 ♗g3 ♘xe5 18 ♘b5 ♗g4 19 ♖xd8+ ♖xd8 20 ♘a7+ ♔b8 21 ♘c6+ bxc6 22 ♕xe5+ is a very good ending for White) 16 ♕f2 ♘e7 17 ♗d3 ♗c6 18 f5 e5 19 ♖he1 ♘ed5 20 ♘xd5 ♖xd5 (20...♗xd5 21 ♕a7) 21 ♕g3 e4 22 ♕xc7+ ♔xc7 23 ♗xf6 exd3 24 ♗xg7 ♖hd8 25 ♗e5 with good winning chances for White, Spassky-Rabar, Gothenburg 1955.

11   fxg5   ♘g4
12   ♘xc6

In *BTS2* both this and **12 ♘f3** were featured, but this time we have opted for just one variation, but covered it in greater depth. The move order **12 ♗e2 ♘ge5 13 ♘xc6 ♗xc6** is also possible.

12	...	♗xc6
13	♗e2	♘e5
14	g3	♘g6 *(D)*

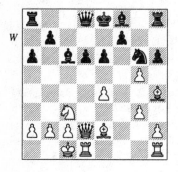

An unusual position with the white bishop incarcerated on h4.

15   ♖hf1

More common is **15 ♔b1**, with the following possibilities:

1) **15...♗e7 16 gxh6** and now:

1a) **16...♗xh4 17 gxh4 ♕xh4 18 ♕xd6 ♖xh6?** (18...♕e7 is better although White stands well) 19 ♗xa6! ♖d8 (19...♖xa6 20 ♕b8+ and mate on d8) 20 ♕c5 ♖xd1+ 21 ♖xd1 ♕e7 22 ♕e3 ♖h4 (22...♖xh2 23 ♕g3!) 23 ♗b5 with a winning advantage for White, Brodsky-Nevednichy, Bucharest 1995.

1b) **16...♘xh4 17 gxh4 ♗f6!?** (Black clearly has some positional compensation for the sacrificed pawns) 18 ♖hf1 ♕e7 19 ♗g4 (with the idea 19...0-0-0 20 ♘d5) 19...♗e5 20 ♕g5 (20 ♗h5 ♕xh4 21 ♗xf7+ ♔e7 is fine for Black, as 22 ♗g6 is met by 22...♖ag8) 20...♕xg5 21 hxg5 (White has straightened out

his pawns but it still doesn't seem to be enough for a significant plus) 21...♔e7 22 h4 f6 23 ♖g1 ♖ag8 24 ♗f3 ♗f4 25 ♖g4 fxg5 26 hxg5 ♗e3 27 ♖e1 (perhaps 27 ♘d5+, but Black could have avoided this with 26...♗xg5) 27...♗xg5 28 ♖eg1 ♖f8! 29 ♖xg5 ♖xf3 30 ♖h5 ♖f6 31 ♖gh1 ♖f4 32 b3 ♖h7 33 ♖e1 ♖f6 34 ♖eh1 ♖f4 35 ♖5h4 ♖xh4 36 ♖xh4 ♔f6 37 ♖h1 ♔e5 with equality, Akopian-Kožul, Moscow OL 1994.

2) **15...h5** *(D)* and now:

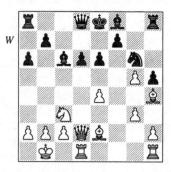

2a) **16 ♕e3 ♗e7** (this is superior to 16...♗g7 17 ♘d5! exd5 18 exd5+ ♕e7 19 ♕xe7+ ♔xe7 20 dxc6 bxc6 21 c3 with an edge for White, as in Chandler-Bellin, Commonwealth Ch 1985, or 16...♕e7 17 ♖hf1 ♗g7 18 ♖f2 ♔f8 19 ♖df1, Mainka-Popović, Dortmund 1988 and White is better) 17 ♖hf1 ♕c7 18 ♕f2 ♘e5 19 h3 0-0-0 20 g4 hxg4 21 ♗xg4 ♘xg4 22 hxg4 ♖h7 with an unclear position, Jansa-Banas, Czechoslovak Ch 1986.

2b) **16 ♖hf1 ♕c7** (16...♗g7!? is better) 17 e5! 0-0-0 18 ♗d3 ♘xh4 19 gxh4 ♗g7 20 ♕f2! and White

stands well, Tseshkovsky-Fahnen-
schmidt, Baden-Baden 1988.

2c) **16 罝df1!?** intending 17 豐d1
attacking h5 is an interesting idea.

15 ... 桌e7

The alternative is **15...h5**, when
16 含b1 transposes into variation
'2b' above. An important question is
whether White can progress without
playing 含b1. One try is **16 e5!?**, for
example 16...公xe5 (16...dxe5 17
豐xd8+ 罝xd8 18 罝xd8+ 含xd8 19
罝xf7 is good for White) 17 g6 (17
含b1 豐c7 18 g6 公xg6 19 桌f6 罝h7
20 豐g5 is good for White, but better is 17...公g6 18 桌d3 公xh4 19
gxh4 桌g7 with an unclear game)
17...桌h6 18 gxf7+ 公xf7 19 桌xd8
桌xd2+ 20 罝xd2 罝xd8 21 罝d4 (the
threat is 罝h4) 21...h4! 22 罝xh4
罝xh4 23 gxh4 含e7 with an unclear
ending. Another try is **16 豐e3**, intending 16...豐c7 17 公d5!. However, Black should play 16...桌e7 so
that his knight is ready to return to e5
if need be.

16 gxh6 公xh4

16...桌xh4 17 gxh4 豐xh4 18
豐xd6 is good for White.

17 gxh4 *(D)*

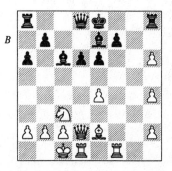

17 ... 桌f8

17...桌xh4 18 罝g1! is given as ±
by Bönsch but matters are not so
clear after **18...桌f6** (the immediate
17...桌f6 would lose to 18 豐f4), with
similar ideas to the Akopian-Kožul
game given above. I have examined
this position in some detail and my
analysis runs: **19 h7 豐e7** *(D)* (forced
as 19...含e7 20 罝df1 桌xc3 21 豐g5+
is crushing)

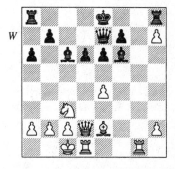

20 公d5!? (20 罝df1 0-0-0 21 豐h6
is also possible, but the text is full of
dangerous pitfalls for Black; another way to introduce the sacrifice
is 20 罝g8+ 含d7 21 公d5, but after
21...exd5 22 exd5 罝axg8! 23 hxg8豐
罝xg8 24 dxc6+ bxc6 25 豐d3 the
situation is far from clear) **20...exd5
21 exd5** and now we have:

1) **21...桌b5** (21...桌xd5 22 罝g8+
含d7 23 豐xd5) **22 罝g8+ 含d7 23
桌g4+ 含c7 24 罝e1** and now:

1a) **24...桌e5?** (this allows White
to play a stunning combination) 25
豐a5+! b6 26 豐c3+!! 含b7 27 罝xe5!
(eliminating the defender of h8)
27...dxe5 (27...豐xe5 28 桌c8+ 含b8
29 豐xe5 dxe5 30 罝xh8) 28 桌c8+

♔a7 (28...♔b8 29 d6! also wins) 29 d6! (clearer than 29 ♖xh8 ♕g5+ 30 ♕d2 ♕g1+ 31 ♕d1 ♕g7) 29...♕xd6 (forced) 30 ♖xh8 and the h-pawn will decide the issue.

1b) 24...♗xb2+! 25 ♔xb2 ♕f6+ 26 ♕c3+! ♕xc3+ 27 ♔xc3 ♖axg8 28 hxg8♕ ♖xg8 29 h3 and White's centralised king and outside passed pawn will make life very unpleasant for Black. An important point is that 29...♔d8, intending ...♗d7, is met by 30 ♖b1 ♔c7 31 ♖f1.

2) 21...♕e5! 22 c3 ♗d7! (after 22...♗xd5 23 ♕xd5 ♕xd5 24 ♖xd5 Black can't take on h7, so he will suffer in this ending; 22...♕xd5 and White has at least the same as above; 22...♗a4 23 ♖de1 ♔d8 24 ♖g8+! ♔c7 25 ♗g4 ♖xh7 26 ♖xa8! {White must be careful, e.g. 26 ♖xe5 ♖xg8 27 ♖f5 ♖xg4 28 b3 ♗g7! 29 bxa4 ♗h6 30 ♖xf7+ ♖xf7 31 ♕xh6 ♖g2 and Black wins} 26...♗g5 27 ♖c8+! ♔b6 28 ♖xe5 ♗xd2+ 29 ♔xd2 dxe5 30 h3 +− with a winning endgame) **23 ♖de1 ♔d8!** *(D)* and now:

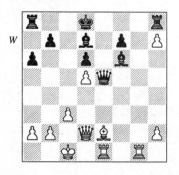

2a) 24 ♖g8+ (24 ♗xa6 ♕h5 25 ♗xb7 ♖xa2 is not recommended)

24...♔c7 25 ♗g4 ♖xh7! 26 ♖xa8 (forced, as 26 ♖xe5 ♖xg8 is winning for Black) 26...♗g5 27 ♖xe5 ♗xd2+ 28 ♔xd2 dxe5 29 d6+ ♔c6 30 ♗f3+ ♔xd6 31 ♗xb7 ♖xh2+ with an unclear endgame.

2b) 24 ♗d1!? ♕f5 25 ♗c2 (if he so wishes, White can take a draw by means of 25 ♖ef1 ♕e5 26 ♖e1) **25...♕h5 26 ♖ef1** *(D)* and I believe White has good compensation for the piece. Here are a few sample variations:

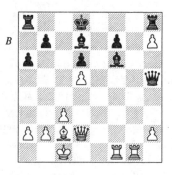

2b1) 26...♕h4 27 ♖g8+ ♔e7 (27...♔c7 28 ♖f4 ♖axg8 29 hxg8♕ ♖xg8 30 ♖xh4 ♖g1+ 31 ♗d1 ♗xh4 32 ♔c2 should be good for White) 28 ♖f4 ♕h5 29 ♖xf6! ♖hxg8 30 hxg8♘+ ♖xg8 31 ♖f1 with advantage to White.

2b2) 26...♗e7 27 ♖g7 ♗e8 28 ♕e3! ♗f8 29 ♕b6+ ♔c8 30 ♗f5+ ♔b8 31 ♖g8 +−.

2b3) 26...♕e5 27 ♕h6 (27 ♖e1 ♕h5 is a draw) 27...♗e7 28 ♖xf7 ♔c7 (28...♗e8 29 ♖fg7) 29 ♖gg7 ♖ae8 (29...♕e1+ 30 ♗d1 ♖ae8 31 ♕f4 is even better for White) 30 b3!?. White attempts to get his king to safety whilst Black is tied down as after 30...♕xc3 31 ♖xe7 ♕a1+ 32 ♔d2 ♕d4+ 33 ♗d3 ♕b2+ 34 ♔d1 the next check is blocked with ♕c1+.

2b4) **26...♗e5** 27 ♖g5 (another idea is 27 ♕e3!?) 27...♕xh2 28 ♕xh2 ♗xh2 29 ♖xf7 ♗e5 30 ♖g8+ (30 ♗f5 ♗f4+) 30...♔c7 31 ♗f5 ♖axg8 (31...♖d8 will only delay the inevitable since Black is in zugzwang) 32 hxg8♕ ♖xg8 33 ♖xd7+ with White having slightly the better of a drawn ending.

Black certainly has to go through a minefield to reach this drawn ending, but objectively speaking White might be better off with the simple **20 ♕h6** 0-0-0 21 ♗d3, followed by ♖df1, maintaining the h7-pawn for the moment. If Black exchanges on c3 White's king becomes slightly exposed, but a more relevant feature is that White's h-pawn becomes far more dangerous once the dark-squared bishop disappears.

18 ♕d4!   **♖xh6**
19 h5

19 ♘d5 deserves investigation.

19 ...   **♕g5+**
20 ♔b1   **♕e5?!**

Better is **20...♕c5**, although after 21 ♕d2 ♖h7 22 ♗g4! White still has good chances of obtaining the advantage. **22...♗g7** can be met by 23 ♖f3 and **22...0-0-0** 23 ♘d5 f5?! 24 b4! ♕a7 25 ♘f6 ♖f7 26 exf5 ♖xf6 27 fxe6 is winning for White.

21 ♕b6!

Not **21 ♕xe5?** dxe5, which gives Black excellent compensation. The

text ensures that the black king will not be able to escape to the queenside.

21 ...   **♖c8**

Bönsch gives **21...♕xh2** 22 ♕c7 and then **22...♖h7** 23 e5! ♕xe5 24 ♗d3, but points out that **22...♗e7** would be a tougher nut to crack.

22 ♕f2   **♖h7**
23 ♗g4   **♕c5**

23...♗xe4? loses after 24 ♘xe4 ♕xe4 25 ♗xe6!.

24 ♕g2   **♗d7**

Defending against ♗xe6 and ♘d5.

25 ♕f3   **♖c7** *(D)*

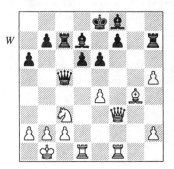

26 e5!

This thematic pawn sacrifice places Black in serious trouble.

26 ...   **d5**

26...♕xe5 27 ♘d5 and **26...dxe5** 27 ♖xd7! ♖xd7 (or 27...♔xd7 28 ♕d3+) 28 ♘e4 are out of the question, but the blocked centre also favours White, not least because Black no longer has control over e5.

27 ♕d3   **♖h6**
28 ♕d2   **♖h8**
29 ♕f4   **♖h7**

30 &e2!

Another point behind 26 e5 was the opening of the b1-h7 diagonal.

30	...	&h6
31	豐h4	豐e7
32	罩f6!	&g7
33	豐g3	豐f8

33...&xf6 34 exf6 罩xc3 35 bxc3 豐f8 36 豐b8+.

34 &d3 罩h6

34...罩h8 also loses: 35 罩xf7! &xf7 36 罩f1+ &g8 37 罩xf8+ &xf8 38 ②xd5 exd5 39 e6 +–.

| 35 | 罩xh6 | &xh6 |
| 36 | ②xd5! | 1-0 |

36...exd5 37 e6 罩c5 38 exd7+ &xd7 39 b4 罩c7 40 &f5+ &c6 41 豐c3+ &b6 42 豐d4+ wins for White.

Game 12
Short – Ljubojević
Amsterdam Euwe mem 1988

1	e4	c5
2	②f3	d6
3	d4	cxd4
4	②xd4	②f6
5	②c3	②c6
6	&g5	e6
7	豐d2	a6
8	0-0-0	h6

Black once again aims to further his queenside ambitions by ...&d7 and ...b5 before committing his king, but in this line he first of all forces White to decide where to put his bishop.

9 &e3 *(D)*

This move is currently thought best. White intends to play f4 and develop his king's bishop to e2 or d3. If

Black castles kingside then White can launch a direct attack by h3 and g4-g5.

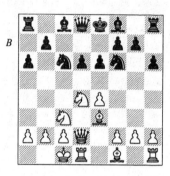

9 ... &d7

Black has a number of possible moves, and although plans with f3 have become quite common for White, we are sticking to the recipe recommended in *BTS2*, which is 'f4 against anything'. The alternatives are:

1) **9...②g4?** is a mistake since 10 ②xc6 bxc6 11 &c5 gives White an advantage.

2) **9...豐c7** is quite often played, but usually transposes to lines considered later. An independent example is 10 f4 &e7 (10...&d7 11 &d3 b5 transposes to the note to Black's 11th move) 11 &e2!? (11 &d3 &d7 12 &b1 b5 transposes to line 3 in the note to Black's 12th move) 11...&d7 (or 11...②a5 12 e5! dxe5 13 fxe5 豐xe5 14 &f4 豐c5 15 ②a4 豐d5 16 &b1! with a very strong attack for the sacrificed pawn) 12 ②b3 ②a5 13 ②xa5 豐xa5 14 &b1 &c6 15 &f3 豐c7 16 罩he1 (the immediate 16 g4 may be even better) 16...罩c8 17 g4

with advantage to White, Chiburdanidze-Lanka, USSR 1980.

3) **9...♗e7 10 f4 ♘xd4 11 ♗xd4 b5** *(D)* and now we have:

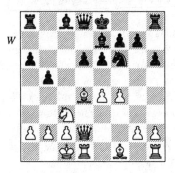

3a) **12 ♗e2!? b4** (12...♗b7 13 ♗f3 b4 14 ♗xf6 ♗xf6 15 ♘e2 ♕a5 16 a3 is good for White) **13 ♘a4 ♘xe4 14 ♕e3 ♘f6 15 ♗f3** and now:

3a1) **15...d5 16 ♔b1** (this move has been played in practice, but in fact 16 g4 0-0 17 ♘b6 ♖b8 18 ♔b1 may be more accurate, transposing into Short-A.Rodriguez below but without allowing Black so much choice) 16...0-0 (16...♗d7 17 ♘b6 ♖b8 18 g4 ♗b5 19 h4 ♔f8 20 g5 ♘e8 21 f5 was also dangerous for Black in Chandler-Kosten, Hastings 1988/9) 17 ♘b6 ♖b8 18 g4 ♗d6?! (18...♘d7 19 ♘xd7 ♗xd7 20 h4 ♗f6 21 g5 ♗xd4 22 ♖xd4 was better, even though White still has a dangerous attack) 19 g5 hxg5 20 fxg5 ♘d7 21 ♘xc8 ♖xc8 22 g6 with a clear advantage for White, Short-A.Rodriguez, Subotica 1987.

3a2) **15...♖b8 16 ♗a7 ♗d7!** (not 16...♖b5 17 ♗b6 ♕d7 18 ♘c5 and White wins, Balashov-Tukmakov,

Sverdlovsk 1987) **17 ♘b6 ♗b5 18 ♔b1!?** (after 18 g4 0-0 19 ♗xb8 ♕xb8 20 g5 hxg5 21 fxg5 ♗d8! 22 gxf6 ♕b6 23 ♕xb6 ♗xb6 Black had sufficient compensation in Khalifman-Ionov, USSR 1988) **18...0-0 19 f5 ♕c7** (the only move) **20 ♗xb8 ♖xb8 21 ♘a8! ♕d8** (not 21...♕c8? 22 ♕a7 ♗f8 23 fxe6 fxe6 24 ♘c7 and the knight escapes, nor 21...♕d7 22 fxe6 fxe6 23 ♖he1 d5 24 ♘b6, followed by taking on e6) **22 ♕a7!** (after 22 fxe6 ♖xa8 23 exf7+ ♔xf7 24 ♗xe4 fxe4 25 ♖xe4 ♗f6 26 ♘c7 Black's active minor pieces are at least as valuable as White's rooks) **22...d5!** (22...exf5 23 ♖he1 ♘e4 24 ♗xe4 fxe4 25 ♖xe4 ♗f6 26 ♘c7 and 22...e5 23 ♖he1! ♗d7 24 ♘c7 ♗xf5 25 ♘xa6 are good for White) **23 ♘c7 ♗c6** (threatening 24...♖b7 and if 24 ♘xa6 then 24...♖a8 wins) **24 fxe6 ♖b7 25 ♘xd5! ♖xa7** (not 25...♘xd5 26 exf7+ ♔f8 27 ♕xa6 ♖c7 28 ♕d3 ♖d7 29 ♕h7 ♘f6 30 ♕h8+ ♔xf7 31 ♕xd8 and wins) **26 ♘xf6+ ♗xf6 27 ♖xd8+ ♗xd8 28 exf7+ ♔xf7 29 ♗xc6** and now:

3a21) In the original game with 18 ♔b1!?, Nunn-Van der Wiel, Lucerne 1989, Black now played the somewhat inaccurate **29...♗f6** and after 30 ♖d1 ♖c7 31 ♗f3 ♗e7 White could have obtained reasonable chances with 32 ♖d5! ♖c5 33 ♖d3.

3a22) After **29...♖f2!**, however, it is very difficult for the white rook to activate itself. 30 ♖e1 ♗f6 31 a3 (obviously White would prefer not to split his queenside but there's no other way to try to make progress)

31...bxa3 32 bxa3 and even though White has an extra pawn his winning chances are minimal. One example is Adams-Serper, Manila OL 1992 which concluded 32...a5 33 h3 ♖f5 34 ♔a2 ♖c5 35 ♗a4 ♔f8 36 ♗b3 h5 37 ♖e4 ♖e5 38 ♖a4 ♖b5 39 ♖c4 ♔e7 40 ♖e4+ ♖e5 41 ♖xe5+ ♗xe5 42 ♗c4 ♔d6 43 ♔b3 ♔c5 44 ♗e2 ½-½. Even so, this is a dangerous line for Black to negotiate and there are few players willing to include such an ending in their repertoire.

3b) **12 ♕e3** *(D)* and now:

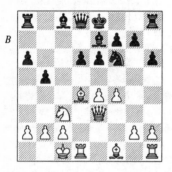

3b1) **12...♕c7** 13 e5 dxe5 14 fxe5 ♘d7 15 ♘e4 0-0 16 ♘f6+! ♘xf6 17 exf6 ♗xf6 18 ♗xf6 gxf6 19 ♕xh6 (19 ♖d4!? is interesting) 19...♕e5 20 h4 ♗b7 21 ♗d3 f5 **22 ♖h3** ♖fd8 23 g4 ♕g7 24 ♕e3 fxg4 25 ♖g3 (Klovans-Makarychev, USSR 1983) and now 25...♖ac8 26 ♖dg1 ♖xd3! 27 ♕xd3 f5 would have been good value for an exchange. However, I think White could have obtained the advantage with **22 ♖he1** ♕g7 23 ♕f4, intending ♖e3-g3. 23...♖fd8, with the idea of ...♖d4, is well met by 24 ♕c7.

3b2) **12...♗b7** 13 ♗xf6 ♗xf6 (13...gxf6 14 f5!? ♕a5 15 a3 ♖c8 16 ♖d3 ♖c5 17 ♗e2 ♖e5 18 ♖f1 ♕c7 19 ♕g3 ♗xe4 20 ♘xe4 ♖xe4 21 ♖c3 gave White good play in Tal-Tukmakov, USSR Ch 1983) 14 e5 ♗e7 15 exd6 ♗xd6 16 ♘e4 ♗xe4 17 ♕xe4 0-0 18 ♗d3 g6 19 h4 and White has good attacking chances, Kovalev-Sjöberg, Ostende 1991.

4) **9...♘xd4 10 ♗xd4 b5 11 f4 ♗b7** (11...b4 12 ♗xf6 ♕xf6 13 ♘e2 ♖b8 14 ♘d4 ♖b6 15 ♗c4 was better for White in Tal-Radulov, Malta OL 1980) **12 ♕e3** *(D)* and now:

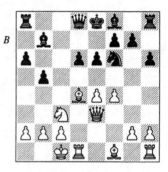

4a) **12...♗e7** transposes to '3b2'.
4b) **12...b4** 13 ♗xf6 gxf6 (the alternative 13...♕xf6 14 ♘b5! ♕d8 15 ♘xd6+ ♗xd6 16 e5 ♗d5 17 ♖xd5 exd5 18 exd6+ ♔f8 19 ♕c5 is very good for White) 14 ♘a4 ♕a5 15 ♘b6 ♖b8 16 ♗c4 is promising for White as **16...♖xe4** 17 ♕xe4 ♕xb6 18 ♖he1 and **16...d5** 17 exd5! ♗c5 18 ♕g3! are both very dangerous for Black.
4c) **12...♕c7** 13 ♗b6 ♕c8? (better is 13...♕c6, although after 14 ♘d5 ♖c8 15 ♘xf6+ gxf6 16 ♗d3

♖g8 17 g3 White still has an edge, Nunn-Lobron, Munich 1991) 14 e5 ♘d5 15 ♘xd5 ♗xd5 16 exd6 ♕c6 17 ♖xd5! (this gives White a murderous attack) 17...♕xd5 18 ♗e2 ♕xa2 (18...♕xd6 also loses after 19 ♖d1, for example 19...♕e7 20 ♕c3 ♕b7 21 ♗f3 ♕xb6 22 ♗c6+! or 19...♕b8 20 ♗f3 ♗e7 21 ♗c6+ ♔f8 22 ♖d7 with an overwhelming position) 19 ♕f3! ♗xd6 (19...♕d5 20 d7+! ♔e7 21 ♖d1 ♕xf3 22 d8♕+ and 19...♖c8 20 d7+ ♔xd7 21 ♕b7+ are both the end) 20 ♕xa8+ ♔e7 21 ♕b7+ ♔f8 22 ♗c5! ♕a1+ 23 ♔d2 ♕xh1 24 ♕b8+ 1-0 Nunn-Fedorowicz, Wijk aan Zee 1991.

10   f4   b5

Against other moves White can adopt the same general plan of ♗d3, ♔b1, followed by a kingside pawn advance, but he has to be careful against 10...♗e7, because 11 ♗d3 allows the awkward 11...♘g4! and 11 h3 b5 12 ♗d3 transposes into the note to White's 12th move. Therefore the best answer to 10...♗e7 is 11 ♔b1 b5 12 ♗d3 and we are back in the main game.

11   ♗d3   ♗e7 (D)

Or:

1) **11...♖c8** 12 ♔b1 ♘a5?! 13 e5! b4! 14 ♘ce2 dxe5 15 fxe5 ♘d5 16 ♖hf1 ♘c4 17 ♗xc4 ♖xc4 18 ♘f4 ♘xe3 19 ♕xe3 ♗c5 20 ♘g6! with a clear advantage for White, Hazai-Szabo, Hungary 1983.

2) **11...♘xd4** 12 ♗xd4 b4 13 ♘e2 ♕a5 14 ♗xf6 gxf6 15 ♔b1, with advantage to White, Psakhis-Ivanović, Sochi 1979.

3) **11...♕c7 12 ♔b1** (the piece sacrifice 12 ♗xb5 also deserves consideration; Yudasin-Greenfeld, Haifa 1993 continued 12...axb5 13 ♘dxb5 ♕b8 14 ♘xd6+ ♗xd6 15 ♕xd6 ♕xd6 16 ♖xd6 ♘a5 17 b3 and such positions often favour White in practice) **12...♘a5 13 ♕e1** (White plans to keep his bishops) and now:

3a) **13...b4** 14 ♘ce2 ♘c4 15 ♗c1 ♗e7 (15...a5 can also be met by 16 ♘g3) 16 ♘g3 (White plans to drive the knight back with ♕e2) 16...♖b8 17 ♕e2 ♘a3+ 18 bxa3 bxa3+ 19 ♘b3 a5 20 ♗xa3 a4 21 ♗c4 axb3 22 cxb3 and Black had no compensation for his pawn, Gallagher-Andreescu, Neuchâtel 1993.

3b) **13...♘c4** 14 ♗c1 ♗e7 15 ♗xc4 bxc4 16 e5 dxe5 17 fxe5 ♘h7 18 ♕g3 ♘f8 19 ♕xg7 ♖h7 20 ♕g3 ♘g6 21 ♘f5! ♕xe5 (21...exf5 22 e6) 22 ♕f3 ♖c8 23 ♘xe7 ♘xe7 24 ♘e4 ♘f5 25 g4 ♗c6 26 ♖he1 ♗xe4 27 ♖xe4 1-0 Smirin-Greenfeld, Elenite 1994.

4) **11...♕a5** can be met by 12 ♔b1 followed by the usual plan.

12   ♔b1

In *BTS2* a strong case was made for starting the kingside offensive at once with **12 h3** but Black may be able to exploit the omission of ♔b1 by playing **12...♘xd4 13 ♗xd4 b4 14 ♘e2 e5!**, the point being that 15 fxe5 dxe5 16 ♗xe5? ♕a5 17 ♗xf6 is met by 17...♕xa2. After 14...e5, several games have continued **15 ♗e3 ♕a5 16 ♔b1 0-0 17 g4** (*D*) and now:

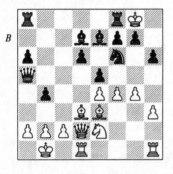

1) **17...♖fd8** 18 fxe5 (18 g5!?, intending to meet 18...exf4 by 19 ♘xf4! hxg5 20 ♘d5, also deserves attention) 18...dxe5 19 ♘g3 ♗e6 20 b3 ♘e8 and now Adams-Shirov, Groningen 1990, continued **21 a4** with unclear consequences. In his notes to the game, Shirov awarded 21 a4 an exclamation mark, claiming that the alternative, **21 ♕f2** is well met by '21...♘d6! 22 ♗b6 ♕a3 23 ♗xd8 ♗xd8, with ...♘b5 to follow.' However, in Dvoirys-Lanka, Gausdal 1991 White played 24 ♕c5! and obtained a winning position after **24...♘b5** 25 ♗xb5 axb5 26 ♖xd8+! ♖xd8 27 ♕xe5 ♖a8 (27...♖d2 28 ♘h5!) 28 ♕b2. If instead Black had played **24...♗e7** then at the very

least White has 25 ♕c6 ♖a7 (or else ♕xa6) 26 ♕a4 ♕xa4 27 bxa4 and with ♘f5 to follow it is unlikely that Black has enough compensation for the exchange.

2) **17...exf4** and White has two recaptures:

2a) **18 ♗xf4 ♗e6** and now:

2a1) **19 b3** d5 20 e5 ♘e4 21 ♗xe4 dxe4 22 ♘d4 ♕c5 23 ♕e2 a5 24 ♖hg1 a4 25 g5 axb3 26 cxb3 hxg5 27 ♗xg5 ♖fd8 28 ♗xe7 ♕xe7 29 ♕xe4 and White won quickly in Wahls-Lutz, Bundesliga 1995.

2a2) **19 ♘c1** d5! (less good is 19...♘d7 20 ♘b3 ♕a4?! {20...♕b6 21 g5 ±} 21 g5 h5 22 ♗e2 with advantage to White, Gallagher-Sher, Antwerp 1992) 20 e5 ♘e4 21 ♕e2 ♕b6! 22 ♗xe4 dxe4 23 ♕xe4 a5 with good play for the pawn, Chandler-Lutz, Bundesliga 1994.

2b) **18 ♘xf4 ♗c6** 19 ♗d4 ♘xe4 20 ♕e3 (20 ♗xe4 ♗xe4 21 ♖he1 d5 22 ♗xg7 ♖fc8! 23 ♖xe4 dxe4 24 ♗xh6 ♗g5! with advantage to Black, Nunn-Greenfeld, Pardubice 1993) 20...d5 21 ♗xe4 dxe4 22 h4 and White has some attacking chances but he is a pawn down, Shabalov-Sher, Biel 1993.

12   ...   b4

This move has been criticised but it isn't clear that the alternatives are better. They are:

1) **12...0-0 13 g4!?** (so far this has only been played by members of the Polgar family but it is an attractive idea in serious danger of spreading; the alternative, 13 h3, is likely to transpose to other lines, for example

13...♘xd4 14 ♗xd4 ♗c6 15 ♕e3
♕c7 is line '2') **13...♘xg4 14 ♖hg1
♘xe3 15 ♕xe3 ♔h8** (D) (this seems
to be forced as 15...♘xd4 16 ♕xd4
♗f6 loses after 17 e5 dxe5 18 ♕e4
g6 19 ♖xg6+ ♗g7 20 ♖xg7+ ♔xg7
21 ♖g1+ ♔f6 22 ♘d5+! exd5 23
♕xe5#) and now:

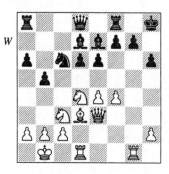

1a) **16 e5** ♘xd4 17 ♕xd4 ♗c6 18
f5 (18 ♕e3 ♖g8 19 ♘e4 ♗xe4 20
♕xe4 g6 21 ♕e3 gave White some
pressure for the pawn in Zso.Polgar-
Groszpeter, Hungarian Ch 1995)
18...dxe5 19 ♕g4 ♗f6 20 fxe6 ♕e7
21 exf7 ♕xf7, J.Polgar-Salov, Madrid 1994, and now 22 ♗g6 ♕e7 23
♘d5 would give White good compensation for the pawn.

1b) **16 ♘f3!?** is Salov's suggestion, which does look quite dangerous for Black. For example, 16...b4
17 ♖xg7 ♔xg7 (17...bxc3 18 ♖dg1!
and the threats of e5 and f5 are hard
to meet, e.g. 18...♗f6 loses to 19 e5!
♗xg7 20 ♕e4) 18 ♖g1+ ♔h8 19 f5
♗g5 20 ♘xg5 hxg5 (20...♕f6 21
e5!) 21 ♖xg5 and the attack crashes
through.

2) **12...♕c7 13 h3** (D) and now:

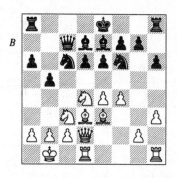

2a) **13...♘a5** 14 g4 and now both
14...b4 15 ♘ce2 ♘c4 16 ♗xc4 ♕xc4
17 ♘g3 a5 18 ♖hf1 ♕a6 19 g5,
Hodgson-Csom, Tel Aviv 1988 and
14...♘c4 15 ♗xc4 ♕xc4 16 ♕g2 b4
17 e5 ♖b8! 18 ♘e4 ♘d5 19 ♗c1
dxe5 20 fxe5, Gallagher-Wells, Neuchâtel 1995, hold promise for White.

2b) **13...♘xd4** 14 ♗xd4 ♗c6 15
♕e3 0-0 16 ♖hf1 (16 e5 is also playable) 16...b4 17 ♘e2 e5 18 fxe5 dxe5
19 ♕g3 ♘xe4 20 ♕xe5 ♕xe5 21
♗xe5 and White has a significant
advantage, Aseev-Shirov, Daugav-
pils 1989.

3) **12...♘xd4** 13 ♗xd4 ♗c6 (or
13...b4 14 ♘e2 ♕b8, Hazai-Lobron,
Rotterdam 1988, 15 h3 and on with
the game) 14 ♕e3 ♕c7 15 e5!? (15
h3 is line '2b') 15...dxe5 16 fxe5
♘d5 17 ♕g3 0-0-0 18 ♘xd5 ♗xd5
19 ♕f2 with an edge for White,
Adams-D.Garcia, Terrassa 1991.

13 ♘ce2   0-0
14 h3

Black's problem is that whilst
White has an automatic attack by h3,
g4, ♘g3 and g5, he will be struggling to create any counterchances at
all. It is curious that Black's troubles

stem from the apparently innocuous
8...h6, which in this type of position
can easily turn into a deadly kingside
weakness.

14 ...	♕c7
15 g4	♕b7
16 ♘g3	♘xd4
17 ♗xd4	♗c6

All Black has achieved is to create
a threat to e4, which delays White's
attack by precisely one move.

18 ♖he1   ♖fe8?

This doesn't help the beleaguered
kingside. The last chance was to play
18...♘d7 intending ...e5 to block the
deadly long diagonal, but in this case
Short gives the line 19 g5 hxg5 20
♖g1 (threatening ♘h5) 20...e5 21
♘f5 ♖fe8 22 fxe5 ♘xe5 23 ♗xe5
dxe5 24 ♖xg5! ♗xg5 25 ♕xg5 f6
26 ♗c4+ ♔f8 27 ♕h5 followed by
mate at h8.

19 g5	hxg5
20 fxg5	♘d7 *(D)*

After this we are treated to a king-
hunt in the style of the 19th century.
20...♘h7 is objectively better (anything is better than being mated), but
21 h4 locking the knight out of play
is very good for White.

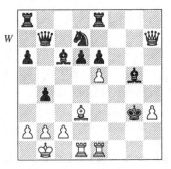

21 ♗xg7!	♔xg7
22 ♘h5+	♔g6

There is no choice as **22...♔g8** 23
g6 fxg6 24 ♕h6, **22...♔f8** 23 g6 ♗f6
24 ♘xf6 ♘xf6 25 ♖f1 ♔e7 26 ♕g5
and **22...♔h8** 23 g6 ♗f8 24 ♖g1
fxg6 25 ♖xg6 ♘e5 26 ♖h6+! all lead
to a disaster.

23 e5+	♔xh5
24 ♕f4	♗xg5
25 ♕xf7+	♔h4
26 ♕h7+	♔g3 *(D)*

The main problem when playing
such positions with White is trying
to keep a broad grin off your face.
The main problem when playing
such positions with Black is to avoid
looking at the broad grin on your opponent's face.

27 ♕h5   ♔h2

Or **27...♖g8** 28 ♕g4+ ♔h2 29
♕g1+ ♔xh3 30 ♗f1+ ♔h4 (30...♗g2
31 ♖d3+ and 32 ♗xg2) 31 ♕h2+
♔g4 32 ♖d4+ ♔f5 33 ♕h7+ ♖g6 34
♗h3# is a nice line given by Short.

28 ♕xg5

In fact White could have forced
mate by **28 ♕e2+ ♔xh3** (28...♗g2
29 ♖h1+ ♔g3 30 ♕g4+ ♔f2 31

Rhf1+ 奧xf1 32 Rxf1+ 含e3 33 Re1+
含f2 34 豐g1+ 含f3 35 Rf1#) 29
豐h5+ 奧h4 30 Re3+ Rf3 (30...含g2
31 豐xh4 or 30...奧f3 31 Rh1+ 含g2
32 豐xh4) 31 Rh1+ 含g2 32 豐xh4
Rxe3 33 奧f1+ 含f3 34 Rh3#, but
there is nothing wrong with winning
Black's queen (and having his king
on h2).

28	...	Rg8
29	Rd2+	奧g2
30	豐f4+	Rg3
31	奧e4	豐xe4
32	豐xe4	1-0

Game 13
Kupreichik – Kuzmin
Minsk 1982

1	e4	c5
2	♘f3	♘c6
3	d4	cxd4
4	♘xd4	♘f6
5	♘c3	d6
6	奧g5 (D)	

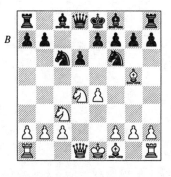

| 6 | ... | 奧d7 |

This is the most popular alternative to 6...e6, but there are other
moves:

1) **6...g6** 7 奧xf6 exf6 8 奧c4 (8
奧b5 奧d7 9 0-0 奧g7 10 ♘de2 is a
more solid alternative) 8...奧g7 (after
this a pawn must be sacrificed, but
the alternative, 8...奧e7 9 豐d2 followed by 0-0-0, is depressing for
Black) 9 ♘db5 0-0 10 豐xd6 f5 11
0-0-0 豐a5 (11...豐g5+ 12 f4 豐xg2
13 e5 is good for White as Stoica's
suggestion, 13...豐g4, can simply be
met by 14 Rhf1! when 14...♘xe5
loses to 15 奧e2! and 14...奧xe5 15
奧xf7+! is no fun either) 12 豐c7 a6
(the lines 12...奧xc3 13 bxc3 豐a4 14
♘d6, 12...豐b4 13 ♘d6 奧xc3 14
bxc3 豐xc3 15 奧xf7+ 含h8 16 含b1
and 12...fxe4 13 豐xa5 ♘xa5 14
奧d5 奧h6+ 15 含b1 are all good for
White) 13 豐xa5 ♘xa5 14 ♘c7 Ra7
15 奧b3 奧xc3 16 bxc3 fxe4 (Khol-
mov-Chernikov, USSR 1982) and
now 17 ♘d5! is good for White according to Kholmov.

2) **6...豐a5** 7 奧xf6 gxf6 8 奧b5
奧d7 9 ♘b3 豐c7 10 ♘d5 豐d8 11
豐h5 e6 12 ♘e3 a6 13 奧e2 豐c7 14
0-0-0 奧e7 15 含b1 0-0-0 16 f4 was
good for White in S.Nikolić-Gufeld,
Kislovodsk 1968.

3) **6...a6** 7 豐d2 ♘xd4 (alternatives transpose into the main variations) 8 豐xd4 e5 9 豐a4+ (White
has no trouble keeping a slight advantage by 9 豐d3 奧e6 10 0-0-0 Rc8
11 ♘d5 奧xd5 12 奧xf6, but with 9
豐a4+ he is playing for more)
9...奧d7 10 奧xf6 豐xf6?! (10...gxf6
11 豐b3 b5 12 奧e2 奧e6 13 ♘d5
奧h6 14 a4, Marjanović-Stoica, Istanbul 1988, is good for White, but
Black has more hope than after

10...♕xf6) 11 ♗b5! ♕d8 12 ♗xd7 ♕xd7 13 ♕b3 0-0 14 ♘d5 with a dream position for White, Kotronias-Kovalev, Debrecen 1992.

4) **6...♕b6 7 ♘b3** (7 ♗e3!? is interesting, e.g. 7...♕xb2 8 ♘db5 ♕b4 9 ♗d2 ♕c5! 10 ♗e2!? ♕b6 11 ♖b1 ♘e5? 12 ♗e3 ♕a5 13 ♖b3 g6 14 ♖a3 ♕d8 15 ♗xa7 ♘ed7 16 f4! and White stands well, Balashov-Petrienko, Voronezh 1987, but 11...♕d8 was the critical test) **7...e6 8 ♗f4!?** ♘e5 (after 8...e5 the bishop returns to g5) **9 ♗e3 ♕c7 10 f4 ♘c6** (10...♘g6 11 ♕f3 ♗d7 12 ♗d3 ♗e7 13 0-0-0 ♗c6 14 ♘d4 was good for White in Greenfeld-Schrenzel, Israel 1983) **11 g4!?** *(D)* (there are a number of reasonable alternatives, such as 11 ♗e2 or 11 ♗d3, but the direct approach often pays off for White in the Sicilian and also avoids drifting into a bad position) and Black has tried several moves:

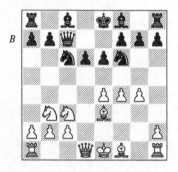

4a) **11...d5** 12 e5 ♘d7 13 ♘b5 ♕d8 (13...♕b8 14 g5 a6 15 ♘5d4 ♕c7 16 ♕f3 ♘xd4 17 ♘xd4 ♗b4 18 ♔f2! ♗e7 19 h4 was better for White in Topalov-Smirin, Burgas 1994)

14 h4 f6, Speelman-Gulko, Hastings 1989-90, and now 15 exf6 ♘xf6 16 g5 ♘e4 17 ♗g2 would have been very good for White.

4b) **11...h6** 12 ♕f3 ♗e7 13 h4 h5 14 gxh5 (14 g5!? is another idea) 14...♘xh5 15 0-0-0 with a pleasant position for White, Gallagher-Gross, Eupen 1991.

4c) **11...a6** 12 g5 ♘d7 13 h4 b5 14 ♕d2 ♘b6 15 ♕f2 ♖b8 16 ♗d3 ♘c4 17 0-0-0 ♘xe3 18 ♕xe3 (perhaps this is a positional gain for Black but he is lagging in development and has a long-term king safety problem) 18...♗e7 19 h5 b4 20 ♘e2 a5 21 ♘bd4 ♘xd4 22 ♘xd4 ♕c5 23 e5! dxe5 (23...d5 24 ♔b1+) 24 fxe5 h6 25 gxh6 gxh6 26 ♔b1 ♗g5 27 ♕e2 ♗d7 28 ♖hf1 ♖f8 29 ♗c4! (a good move, vacating d3 for the queen and lining up the bishop against e6, where something is liable to explode in the not too distant future) 29...a4 30 ♕d3 ♖d8 (30...♕xe5 31 ♘xe6! is one example) 31 ♘b5! ♗xb5 32 ♗xb5+ ♔e7 33 ♕d7+ (strong, even very strong, but not as strong as 33 ♖xf7+! and mate next move) 33...♖xd7 34 ♖xd7+ ♔e8 35 ♖d5+ 1-0 Kovalev-Giffard, Clichy 1991.

7 ♗e2 *(D)*

The main line is 7 ♕d2 when Black continues 7...♘xd4 8 ♕xd4 ♕a5.

The move ♗e2 is well motivated since if Black exchanges on d4 he has lost a tempo over the usual line, so he has to change his plan.

7 ...   a6

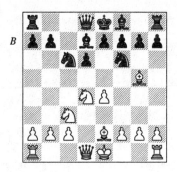

Flexible, but 7...♕a5 may be more critical. This and other options:

1) **7...♕b6 8 ♘db5** (threatening 9 ♗xf6 and 10 ♘d5, while at the same time preventing...e6) **8...♖c8 9 0-0 a6 10 ♗xf6 gxf6 11 ♘d5 ♕d8 12 ♘bc3 e6 13 ♘e3** and White's knights proved well-placed in Vogt-Mascariñas, Polanica Zdroj 1977.

2) **7...e6 8 ♗xf6** (also possible is 8 ♘db5 ♕b8 9 a4 ♗e7 10 ♕d2 a6 11 ♘a3 ♕c7 12 ♖d1 ♖d8 13 ♘c4 ♗c8 14 ♗e3 ♕b8 15 ♘b6 with a slight advantage for White, Spassky-Hort, Moscow 1971) **8...gxf6** (8...♕xf6? 9 ♘db5) **9 0-0** *(D)* and now:

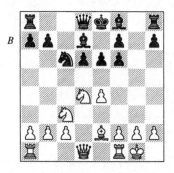

2a) **9...h5 10 ♘db5 ♕b8 11 a4 a6 12 ♘a3 ♕c7 13 ♕d2 f5?** (Black

didn't like the look of 13...0-0-0 14 ♘c4 when White has dangerous attacking chances, but the move chosen seems rather suicidal) **14 ♘c4 ♘a5** (14...0-0-0 15 ♘b5! axb5 16 axb5 ♘b8 17 ♕c3! is decisive and 14...fxe4 15 ♘xe4 d5 16 ♘f6+ ♔d8 17 ♕g5! ♗h6 18 ♕h4 ♔c8 19 ♖ad1 is very good for White) **15 ♕d4!** ♖h6 (Black would prefer to play 15...♖g8 but this is refuted by 16 ♘b6 ♖b8 17 ♘bd5! exd5 18 ♘xd5 with ♘f6+ to follow) **16 ♘b6 ♖b8 17 exf5 e5 18 ♕e3 ♗xf5 19 ♘cd5 ♕d8 20 ♕c3! ♘c6 21 ♗xa6** and White had an overwhelming position, Gallagher-Dubeck, San Bernardino 1994.

2b) **9...a6 10 ♔h1** (following the above game with Dubeck I amused myself with 10 ♗h5 ♕b6 11 ♘f5!?, but I wouldn't dare to suggest such reckless behaviour to readers of *BTS3*) **10...♕c7** (10...♗e7 11 f4 ♘xd4 12 ♕xd4 ♕a5 13 ♖ad1 was better for White in Hort-Geller, Palma de Mallorca 1970) **11 ♗h5!? ♗g7 12 f4 f5** (now or never) **13 ♘xc6 bxc6 14 exf5 exf5 15 ♖e1+ ♔f8 16 ♕d3 ♗e6** (Black does have a couple of nice bishops but the more salient factors in assessing this position are his misplaced king and weak pawn structure) **17 ♖ad1 d5 18 ♘e2 c5 19 ♘g3 ♗xb2 20 ♘xf5 ♖b8 21 ♘g3** (getting out of the f-pawn's way) **21...c4 22 ♕f3 d4 23 f5 ♗c8 24 f6 ♗e6 25 ♘e2 d3 26 cxd3 c3 27 ♘d4! ♗xa2** (de la Villa-Ubilava, Palma 1992) and now White missed the brilliant **28 ♘b5!!** after which Black could have resigned; **28...♖xb5** loses after 29 ♕g4! as now 29...♖g8 is hit by 30 ♕xg8+ and 31 ♖e8#, and 29...♖e5 30 ♖xe5 ♖xe5 31 ♕c8+! leads to mate in a few moves. The main point behind 28 ♘b5!! is revealed after **28...axb5** 29 ♕g4!, when not only is White threatening ♕g7+, but also the devastating ♕b4+. Nor is salvation to be found in refusing the offer as after **28...♕b6**, 29 ♕f4! is decisive.

3) **7...♕a5 8 ♗xf6 gxf6 9 0-0!?** *(D)* and now:

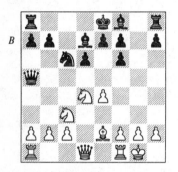

3a) **9...♕g5** 10 ♘f5! ♖g8 (White has the advantage after 10...♗xf5 11 f4 ♕g6 12 ♗h5) 11 ♘g3 with an edge for White.

3b) **9...♕e5** (too ambitious) 10 ♘f3 ♕c5 (10...♕a5 is better even though this is an admission that Black's last move was a mistake) 11 ♘d5 ♖c8 12 c3 a6 13 ♘d4 ♗g7 14 b4 ♕a7 15 ♗h5 with advantage to White, Stoica-Kotronias, Istanbul 1988.

3c) **9...♘xd4 10 ♕xd4 ♕c5?!** (10...♖c8 11 ♘d5! ♕c5 12 ♕d2 ♕xc2 13 ♕e3 ♕c5 14 ♕f4 gives White a

strong initiative in return for the pawn; this was recommended in *BTS2*, but has yet to be tested at the highest level) **11 ♕xc5 dxc5 12 ♘b5!** (even more promising than the 12 ♘d5 of *BTS2*) **12...0-0-0** (12...♔d8 13 ♖fd1 is very unpleasant for Black as White is threatening to double on the d-file, and even 13...a6 can be met by 14 ♖d3!) **13 ♘xa7+ ♔b8 14 ♘b5 ♗g7** and now:

3c1) **15 f4?!** f5 16 e5 f6 17 exf6 ♗xf6 18 c3 ♗c6 19 ♖ad1 ♖hg8 and Black's active bishops gave him reasonable compensation for the pawn, Short-Anand, Amsterdam 1992.

3c2) Anand proposes **15 ♗d3!** because now 15...f5 16 exf5 ♗xb2 17 ♖ab1 is clearly good for White and 15...♗xb5 16 ♗xb5 ♖d4 17 c3 ♖d2 (17...♖xe4 18 ♖fd1 with the idea of a4-a5-a6 is terminal according to Anand) 18 ♖ab1 simply leaves Black a pawn down.

8 ♗xf6   gxf6
9 0-0

There is a second possibility which, like the main line, is based on the move ♘f5, namely **9 ♘f5 ♕a5** 10 0-0 ♖c8 11 ♘d5 ♕d8 12 ♘de3! ♘e5 13 f4 ♘g6 14 ♕d3! h5 15 ♖ad1 b5 16 a4 and White is better, Sznapik-Hawelko, Poland 1984.

9 ...   ♕b6

9...e6 transposes to '2b' in the note to Black's 7th move.

10 ♘f5! *(D)*

Many players would have automatically retreated the knight to b3 but Kupreichik realises that in this situation he can afford to give up his b-pawn. Although Black can organise ...e6 to expel the knight we have already seen in Vogt-Mascariñas above that knights on c3 and e3 can be well placed.

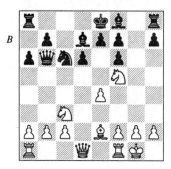

10 ...   0-0-0?!

Black prepares ...e6 but it turns out that this is too slow. He should have tried **10...e6** (10...♕xb2? at once fails to 11 ♘d5 and 12 ♖b1) **11 ♘xd6+ ♗xd6 12 ♕xd6 ♕xb2 13 ♖fd1** and now:

1) **13...♘e5** 14 ♘d5! exd5 15 ♕xf6 ♘c4 (15...♖g8 16 ♖ab1 ♕c3 17 ♖xd5 loses at once) 16 c3 ♖f8 (16...♖g8 17 ♗h5) 17 ♖ab1 ♕xe2 18 ♖e1 followed by exd5+ forcing Black to play ...♗e6, when White continues dxe6 with a winning attack.

2) **13...0-0-0** 14 ♘d5! exd5 15 exd5 ♕c3 (15...♕e5 16 dxc6 ♕xd6 17 ♖xd6 ♗xc6 18 ♖xf6 wins a pawn) 16 dxc6 ♕xc6 17 ♕f4 followed by ♗f3 when Black has problems with his exposed king and his weak f-pawns.

3) **13...♖d8!** 14 ♕g3 (the sacrifice 14 ♖ab1 ♕xc3 15 ♖xb7 flops

after the response 15...♗c8 16 ♖e7+ ♔f8) 14...♕a3 15 ♗h5 and White still has some pressure, although far less than in the game.

11 a4

11 ♘d5 ♕a7 only leaves White with the problem of meeting ...e6.

11 ...   ♘b4

In the Sicilian, Black can normally only contemplate castling queenside when White has also played 0-0-0, since in a race between attacks on opposite wings the missing black c-pawn gives White a large head start.

12 a5   ♕c7
13 ♘a4

Black's ...♘b4 has stopped ♘d5 by White but there are other ways to reach b6.

13 ...   e6 (D)

13...♕xa5 14 c3 ♘c6 15 b4 ♕c7 16 ♕b3 gives White two free tempi and an open a-file for his attack.

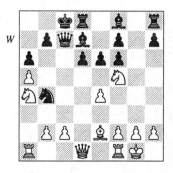

14 ♘d4   ♗xa4

White could not prevent this exchange by playing 14 ♘b6+ ♔b8 15 ♘d4 as then 15...e5 followed by ...♕xc2 would confuse the issue.

15 ♖xa4   d5

Black's only chance is to find some counterplay quickly, or else he will be crushed by c3 followed by b4-b5.

16 c3   ♘c6

Not **16...dxe4** 17 cxb4 e5 when 18 ♕b1 threatening ♖c1 wins.

17 exd5   ♖xd5

18 ♗f3   ♖d6

18...♖xa5 19 ♘xc6 ♖xa4 20 ♕xa4 bxc6 21 ♗xc6 is one of those positions in which the opposite-coloured bishops increase the strength of an attack to alarming proportions.

19 ♖c4   ♖g8?

Black overlooks the threat. **19...e5** was necessary but even then White has the choice of two lines: **20 ♘xc6** ♖xd1 21 ♖xd1 bxc6 22 ♖xc6 gives White an ending with an extra pawn and the better position, while some players might prefer **20 ♗xc6** bxc6 21 ♕g4+ and 22 ♘f5.

20 ♕a4

So simple; c6 collapses and with it Black's position.

20 ...   ♖g5

21 ♗xc6   bxc6

22 ♘xc6   1-0

4 Pelikan Variation

This line arises after 1 e4 c5 2 ♘f3 ♘c6 3 d4 cxd4 4 ♘xd4 ♘f6 5 ♘c3 e5. Black is willing to accept a backward d-pawn in return for active piece play and, in some variations, the two bishops. The historical background to this line is rather obscure since many players have adopted it over the years with different ideas in mind. The names of Lasker and Pelikan are associated with it, but the modern handling probably owes most to the Russian grandmaster Sveshnikov. We have given Pelikan's name to the whole system with 5...e5, reserving that of Sveshnikov for the 8...b5 variation, today considered the main line. It has gained many other adherents in recent years and is regarded as an excellent way to play for a win with Black, since unbalanced positions arise in almost every line.

There is a second move order by which the Pelikan can arise, namely 1 e4 c5 2 ♘f3 ♘c6 3 d4 cxd4 4 ♘xd4 ♘f6 5 ♘c3 e6 (or 2...e6 and 5...♘c6) 6 ♘db5 d6 7 ♗f4 e5 8 ♗g5, reaching the same position as after 1 e4 c5 2 ♘f3 ♘c6 3 d4 cxd4 4 ♘xd4 ♘f6 5 ♘c3 e5 6 ♘db5 d6 7 ♗g5, but in one extra move. To avoid the confusion of having two different move numbers in each position we will take the 5...e5 order as standard,

even though in practice the two move orders are equally common.

Since Black is incurring strategic weaknesses White's most logical (and best) lines are those in which he limits his immediate ambitions to nullifying Black's piece play and only later turns his mind to the exploitation of his long-term advantage. Our recommendation for White runs 6 ♘db5 d6 7 ♗g5 a6 8 ♘a3 b5 (the less common line 8...♗e6 is considered in Game 14) 9 ♗xf6 gxf6 10 ♘d5 when Black chooses between 10...f5 and 10...♗g7. Both lines lead to unbalanced position where Black pits his two bishops and central pawn majority against White's control of d5 and superior pawn structure. The offside knight on a3 can be an important factor, and White usually aims to bring knight back into the game by playing c3 or c4. All the lines of the Sveshnikov (8...b5) are covered in Game 15.

Game 14
Karpov – Nunn
London 1982

1	e4	c5
2	♘f3	♘c6
3	d4	cxd4
4	♘xd4	♘f6
5	♘c3	e5

6 ♘db5 *(D)*

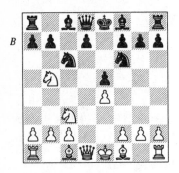

6 ... d6

All Black's 6th move alternatives give White a clear plus:

1) **6...a6** 7 ♘d6+ ♗xd6 8 ♕xd6 ♕e7 9 ♕xe7+ ♘xe7 (9...♔xe7 10 ♗g5 ♘b4 11 0-0-0 is similar) 10 ♗g5 and White has undisputed control of d5.

2) **6...♗c5** 7 ♗e3!? (7 ♘d6+ is also good) 7...♗xe3 8 ♘d6+ ♔f8 9 fxe3 ♕b6 10 ♘c4 ♕c5 11 ♕d6+ ♕xd6 12 ♘xd6 and f7 is about to come under heavy attack by ♗c4.

3) **6...♗b4** 7 a3 ♗xc3+ 8 ♘xc3 d6 9 ♗g5 h6 (9...a6 10 ♘d5 is also very pleasant for White) 10 ♗xf6 ♕xf6 11 ♘b5 and Black will lose his d-pawn for insufficient compensation.

4) **6...h6** (by preventing ♗g5 Black avoids the loss of control of d5 as in line 1, but the move is really just too slow) 7 ♘d6+ ♗xd6 8 ♕xd6 ♕e7 9 ♘b5 (Spassky introduced this pawn sacrifice – the older lines 9 ♕xe7+ ♔xe7 10 b3 and 10 ♗e3 also give White a favourable ending) 9...♕xd6 (9...0-0 10 ♕xe7 ♘xe7 11

♘d6 or 10 b3 ♘xe4 11 ♕xe7 ♘xe7 12 ♗a3) 10 ♘xd6+ ♔e7 11 ♘f5+ ♔f8 12 b3 d5 (12...♘xe4 13 ♗a3+ ♔g8 and now 14 f3 or 14 ♘d6) 13 ♗a3+ ♔g8 14 exd5 ♘xd5 15 ♘d6 ♖b8 16 ♗c4 ♗e6 17 0-0-0 and White has a very pleasant position, Spassky-Gheorghiu, Bath 1973.

7 ♗g5 a6

Black must meet the threat of ♘d5 so the only other move is **7...♗e6**, but then White does not have to retreat his b5-knight to the bad square a3 and can gain the advantage by 8 ♘d5 ♖c8 (8...♗xd5 9 exd5 ♘e7 is good for White after 10 ♕f3 or 10 c3 a6 11 ♕a4) 9 c3 a6 10 ♘a3 ♗xd5 11 ♗xf6 gxf6 12 ♕xd5 ♕a5 13 ♗c4, Jansa-Danek, Czechoslovak Ch 1982, with a grip on d5.

8 ♘a3 ♗e6

8...b5 is the line popularised by Sveshnikov and is examined in Game 15. Other moves are definitely inferior:

1) **8...♗e7** (Black commits the bishop too soon) 9 ♘c4 ♗e6 (after 9...♘d4 10 ♗xf6 ♗xf6 11 ♘d5 b5 12 ♘cb6 ♖b8 13 ♘xc8 ♖xc8 14 c3 ♘e6 15 a4! White has a clear advantage, Averbakh-Korchnoi, semi-final USSR Ch 1950, 9...0-0 10 ♗xf6 ♗xf6 11 ♕xd6 doesn't give Black enough for the pawn and 9...b5 10 ♗xf6 gxf6 11 ♘e3 gives White a crushing bind) 10 ♗xf6 gxf6 11 ♘e3 (thanks to Black's ...♗e7 he cannot now dislodge the knight by ...♗h6) 11...♕d7 12 ♘cd5 followed by ♗d3 and ♕h5, once again with a total light-squared bind.

2) **8...d5** (not correct) 9 ♘xd5 ♗xa3 10 bxa3 ♕a5+ 11 ♕d2 ♕xd2+ 12 ♗xd2 ♘xd5 13 exd5 ♘d4 14 ♗d3 followed by 0-0 and f4, when White has two bishops in an open position and a moderately relevant extra pawn.

9 ♘c4   ♖c8 *(D)*

9...♗e7 transposes to line '1' of the last note, while the alternative **9...♘d4** (9...b5 10 ♗xf6 ♕xf6 11 ♘e3 and 12 ♘cd5 is very good for White) often leads to the knight being driven back with loss of time, e.g. 10 ♗xf6 gxf6 (10...♕xf6 11 ♘b6 ♖b8 12 ♘cd5 ♕d8 13 c3 leaves Black a tempo down on Karpov-Nunn) 11 ♘e3 ♖c8 12 ♗d3 ♗h6 (12...h5 13 0-0 h4 14 ♘cd5 ♗g7 15 c3 ♘c6 16 ♕f3 is excellent for White, Bronstein-Pilnik, Moscow 1956) 13 0-0 0-0 14 ♘cd5 and again Black's knight is expelled by c3, Dely-Flesch, Hungarian Ch 1965.

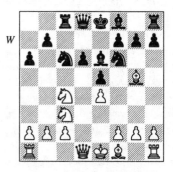

10 ♗xf6   ♕xf6

With this move Black accepts a loss of time to avoid damage to his pawn structure but as a result he is driven into a passive position. The important alternative **10...gxf6** is met by **11 ♗d3 ♘e7** (11...♘d4 12 ♘e3 transposes to the last note while 11...♖g8?! 12 0-0 ♗h6 13 ♘d5 f5 14 ♕h5! ♗f8 15 ♘cb6 f4 16 ♘xc8 ♗g4 17 ♕xh7 ♖g7 18 ♕xg7! ♗xg7 19 ♘cb6 gave White too much for the queen in Matulović-Arnason, Zeman 1983) **12 ♘e3 ♗h6** (12...♕b6 13 0-0! ♕xb2 14 ♘cd5 ♗xd5 15 ♘xd5 ♘xd5 16 exd5 ♕d4 17 ♕f3 ♔e7 18 a4! ♖c7 19 ♖fd1 ♕c3 20 ♖ab1 ♕a5 21 ♕e4 gave White more than enough for the pawn in Mednis-Lombardy, USA Ch 1978 – this type of pawn sacrifice in return for light-squared pressure and attacking chances occurs frequently in the 10...gxf6 line) **13 0-0 ♗xe3 14 fxe3 ♕b6** and now:

1) **15 ♕f3 h5** (15...♕xb2? 16 ♘d5 ♗xd5 17 exd5 is bad for Black) 16 ♘d5 ♗xd5 17 exd5 ♖h6 18 ♖ab1 ♕a5!? (18...♖c7 19 c4 was good for White in Tseshkovsky-Chandler, Minsk 1982) 19 e4 f5 (19...♕xa2? 20 ♕e3 ♖h8 21 ♕b6 wins) 20 exf5 (20 a3 f4 is not as clear) 20...♘xd5 21 ♔h1 ♕c5 22 ♖be1 ± Am.Rodriguez-Espinoza, Cali 1990. White has the more effective minor piece and Black's rook is misplaced on h6.

2) **15 ♕c1!?** was preferred in Anand-Morović, Las Palmas 1993, not with the idea of defending the b-pawn but to force Black to defend his f-pawn; after 15...♘g8 16 ♔h1 ♕c5 17 ♕d2 h5 18 ♖ad1 h4 19 h3 ♔f8 20 ♕e2 ♖h6 21 ♘d5 White had the better game.

11 ♘b6

It is very dangerous for White to take the pawn by **11 ♘xd6+ ♗xd6 12 ♕xd6** when 12...♖d8! 13 ♕c5 ♘d4 14 ♗d3 ♕g5 15 ♔f1 ♖c8 16 ♕b4 b5 gives Black adequate compensation.

| 11 | ... | ♖b8 |
| 12 | ♘cd5 | ♕d8 |

12...♕g6 13 ♕d3 ♗e7 14 ♘c7+ ♔d8 15 ♘cd5 followed by 0-0-0 gives White a dangerous attack.

| 13 | c3 | ♗e7 |

Attempting to develop the bishop more actively runs into trouble after **13...g6** 14 ♕a4! ♗xd5 15 ♘xd5 ♗g7 16 ♗xa6 ♖a8 17 ♕b5! (even more effective than 17 ♗xb7, as given in *BTS2*) 17...♖xa6 18 ♕xb7 with a winning position for White.

| 14 | ♗c4 |

Karpov correctly steers clear of the complications resulting from the win of a pawn by **14 ♘c4** 0-0 15 ♘xe7+ ♕xe7 16 ♕xd6 ♕h4, and quietly consolidates his grip on d5. White's knights are rather clumsily placed but Black's possibilities for active play are very limited and aiming for ...f5 is his only constructive plan.

14	...	0-0
15	0-0	♗g5
16	a4	♔h8

Chekhov suggests the imaginative **16...♕e8** intending 17...♗d8, but after 17 a5 (with the queen on e8 Black can no longer meet this move by ...♘xa5) 17...♗d8 18 b4 ♔h8 19 ♖a2 f5 20 exf5 ♗xf5 21 ♘e3 White has the better chances.

| 17 | ♕e2 | *(D)* |

This move and the next are evidence of Karpov's understanding of the position. White would like to play **17 a5** defending the b6-knight and thereby freeing the tangle of minor pieces, but at the moment it just allows 17...♘xa5! 18 ♖xa5 ♗xd5. It seems natural, therefore, to prepare a5 with **17 b4** but in Sznapik-Simić, Smederevo 1981 Black obtained active play by 17...f5 18 b5 ♘a5 19 ♗d3 g6 and equalised comfortably.

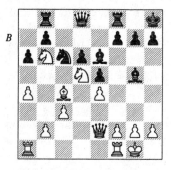

Karpov's first concern is to take the sting out of ...f5 by preparing to answer it with exf5 and f4. For this purpose ♕e2, which pins the e-pawn against the loose bishop on e6, and his next move ♔h1, removing the king from the vulnerable diagonal, are excellent preparation. Only when Black's counterplay is completely neutralised does White return to the exploitation of his queenside space advantage and d5 control.

| 17 | ... | g6 |

I made use of Karpov's chess lesson five years later in the game Nunn-Manor, London Lloyds Bank 1987, which continued **17...a5!?** 18

🏜ad1 🏜h6 (after 18...g6 19 🏜a2! Black should avoid 19...♘e7 20 ♕b5 and 19...🏜h6 20 ♘c4 f5 21 exf5 gxf5 22 ♘db6 with a clear plus for White, but even his best line 19...f5 20 exf5 gxf5 21 ♘c4 f4 22 f3 is slightly better for White) 19 ♔h1 ♘e7?! (19...g6 is more solid, as in Karpov-Nunn) 20 ♘xe7 ♕xb6 (the alternative 20...♕xe7 21 🏜xe6 fxe6 22 ♕b5 is very bad for Black) 21 ♘f5 and Black had no compensation for his serious weaknesses. White went on to win.

18	♔h1	🏜h6
19	b4?!	

Afterwards Karpov thought that this was still too soon and that **19 🏜ad1** or **19 🏜ae1** would have been better.

19	...	f5
20	exf5	gxf5
21	f4	🏜xd5

Black hopes for salvation in the drawing tendencies of opposite-coloured bishops, but White's bishop has a fine outpost at d5 whereas Black's is rather useless.

22	♘xd5	e4?!

22...♘e7 at once is more logical, based on the fact that White cannot win a pawn by 23 fxe5 ♘xd5 24 🏜xd5 dxe5 25 ♕xe5+ because of 25...🏜g7 26 ♕e6 🏜f6.

23	a5	🏜g7
24	🏜ac1	♘e7
25	🏜fd1	♘xd5
26	🏜xd5	♕c7
27	🏜c2	♕e7
28	♕e3	🏜bc8
29	c4	🏜c7

White has two ways of making further progress. He can either play b5 to leave Black with an isolated pawn on the queenside, which will be hard to defend when his bishop is operating only on the kingside, or he can prepare g4 to attack Black's king. For the moment White is not sure which plan offers the best chances.

30	g3	🏜e8
31	🏜g2	♕f6 *(D)*

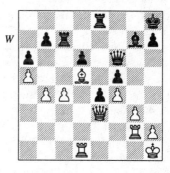

32 g4

This doesn't have the desired effect and it would probably have been better to try the other plan. If Black moved his forces to the queenside White could then have contemplated g4 later.

32	...	fxg4
33	🏜xg4	♕c3
34	🏜g3	♕xb4

If Black swaps queens Karpov gives the line 34...♕xe3 35 🏜xe3 🏜ce7 36 b5! 🏜h6 37 🏜f1 🏜f8 38 🏜xe4 🏜xe4 39 🏜xe4 🏜xf4 40 🏜xf4 🏜xf4 41 🏜xb7 and wins.

35	🏜dg1	♕b2

Stopping White's threat of ♕d4.

36	♖g5	♛f6
37	♖1g4	♛a1+
38	♔g2	♛b2+
39	♔h3	♖ce7
40	f5	♛f6?

This was the sealed move (move 41 in the game, which started with the 2...e6 move order) and, as so often happens, after a long period of difficult defence a player's relief at reaching the time control results in a casual sealed move. White obviously has considerable pressure for the pawn but after 40...♖f8 (Karpov suggests 40...♛a1 threatening ...♛f1+) it is likely that Black can draw. Black's passive queen move gives White the freedom of action he needs to mount the decisive assault.

41	♖h5	♖f8
42	♖gh4	h6

White cannot now play 43 ♖xh6+ ♗xh6 44 ♖xh6+ due to 44...♛xh6+ 45 ♛xh6 ♖h7.

43	♖g4	♖e5
44	♖gg5	♖c8 *(D)*

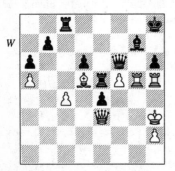

There isn't much Black can do to meet the threat of ♔g4 followed by ♖g6.

45	♔g4!	♔h7?

Going under without a fight. I should have tried 45...♖xd5 46 cxd5 ♖c2 although White is winning even after this.

46	♖g6	♛f8
47	♛g5	♛xf5+

Otherwise 48 ♖gxh6+ ♗xh6 49 ♛g6+ is the end.

48	♛xf5	♖xf5
49	♖xg7+	♔xg7
50	♖xf5	1-0

Game 15
Short – Sax
Saint John Ct (1) 1988

1	e4	c5
2	♘f3	♘c6
3	d4	cxd4
4	♘xd4	♘f6
5	♘c3	e5
6	♘db5	d6
7	♗g5	a6
8	♘a3	b5
9	♗xf6	gxf6

9...♛xf6 10 ♘d5 ♛d8 11 c4 ♘e7 (after 11...b4 12 ♛a4 ♗d7 13 ♘b5! axb5 14 ♛xa8 ♛xa8 15 ♘c7+ White wins material) 12 cxb5 ♘xd5 13 ♛xd5 (13 exd5 is also an effective move) 13...♗e6 14 ♛d2 d5 15 bxa6 ♗xa3 16 ♗b5+! gives White a clear advantage.

10	♘d5 *(D)*	
10	...	f5

This is a already an important moment for Black. At one time 10...f5 was the only move played in this position, but recently the alternative 10...♗g7 has become popular. The

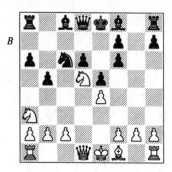

idea behind this move is to delay Black's thematic break ...f5, giving first priority to removing the powerful knight from d5 by ...♘e7. At the time of *BTS2* the theory of this line was still very much in its infancy, which made it difficult to recommend one line ahead of another. This time we have taken the plunge and are suggesting the solid continuation 11 ♗d3 followed by c3.

Before investigating this line in detail, it is worth mentioning the possibility **10...♗e6** 11 c3 ♗g7 12 ♘c2 and now **12...f5** 13 exf5 ♗xf5 14 ♘e3 leaves Black a tempo down over a normal line, while **12...♗xd5** 13 exd5!? (13 ♕xd5 ♘e7 14 ♕d2 f5 15 exf5 d5 16 ♕g5 0-0 17 f6 ♘g6) 13...♘e7 14 a4! 0-0 15 axb5 axb5 16 ♖xa8 ♕xa8 17 ♘b4 ♕b7 18 g3! was good for White in Gallagher-Korpics, Oberwart 1993.

After **10...♗g7 11 ♗d3 ♘e7 12 ♘xe7 ♕xe7 13 c3 f5 14 0-0!?** (14 ♘c2 is more common, but the move order we are proposing rules out a number of extra options for Black and reduces considerably the quantity of theory one has to know)

14...0-0 15 ♘c2 *(D)* we arrive at the basic position of this line:

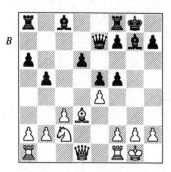

1) **15...fxe4?!** 16 ♗xe4 ♖b8 17 ♘b4! with a clear plus for White.

2) **15...♖b8** 16 exf5 e4 17 ♖e1 ♗xf5 18 ♘d4 ♗xd4 (better than 18...♗g6, which turned out very badly for Black in Kramnik-Nunn, Monaco 1994 after 19 ♗xe4! ♗xe4 20 f3 d5 21 fxe4 dxe4 22 ♕g4! ♕c5 23 ♔h1 when 23...f5 is impossible because of 24 ♕xg7+!) 19 cxd4 d5 20 ♕d2 ♖b6, Magem-San Segundo, Madrid 1994, and now Magem gives 21 ♗f1 ♕h4 22 ♖e3 ♖h6 23 ♖g3+ ♔h8 25 h3 as slightly better for White.

3) **15...d5** 16 exf5 e4 17 ♗e2 ♖d8 18 ♘d4 ♗xd4 and now in Psakhis-Dolmatov, Klaipeda 1988 White, for some reason, recaptured with the pawn and agreed a draw a couple of moves later. 19 ♕xd4 looks more natural, and after 19...♗xf5 20 a4 White has a distinct positional advantage.

4) **15...♗b7 16 exf5** *(D)* and now:

4a) **16...e4** 17 ♖e1 d5 18 ♗f1 ♕g5 19 ♘d4 ♗xd4 20 ♕xd4 ♕xf5

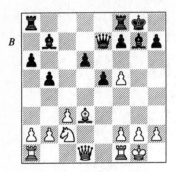

21 a4 is even better for White than the similar position in line 3 just above as Black's bishop is more passively placed. The game de la Villa-Anglada, Ibercaja 1993 finished rather abruptly: 21...♗c6 22 axb5 ♗xb5 23 c4! (opening the third rank) 23...♗c6? 24 ♖a3! f6 25 cxd5 and Black resigned as 25...♕xd5 loses to 26 ♗c4 and 25...♗xd5 to 26 ♖a5 followed by ♗c4.

4b) 16...♕g5 17 ♘e3 (17 f3 deserves consideration) with a further branch:

4b1) 17...d5 18 f4! (destroying the black centre) 18...♕h6 (18...exf4 19 ♕g4! ♕xg4 20 ♘xg4 f6 {20...h5 21 f6} 21 ♖xf4 with a winning ending for White, Topalov-Spasov, Budapest 1993) 19 f6 ♕xf6 20 fxe5 ♕b6 21 ♖e1 ♖fe8 22 ♔h1 ♖xe5 23 ♘f5 with advantage to White, Mithrakanth-Prasad, Indian Ch 1992.

4b2) 17...h5!? (Black invests a tempo to secure control over g4) 18 ♗e2 d5 19 ♗f3 ♖ad8 20 ♕b3 (obviously not 20 ♗xd5 ♖xd5! 21 ♘xd5 ♖d8) 20...e4 21 ♗e2 d4 22 cxd4 ♖xd4 23 ♖ad1 ♖fd8 24 ♖xd4 ♖xd4 25 ♕c2! and Black has insufficient

compensation for the pawn, Topalov-Vaiser, Mesa 1992.

11 ♗d3   ♗e6

11...♕g5 (11...f4 12 g3! is also good for White) 12 g4! ♔d8 13 gxf5 ♗xf5 14 ♘e3 ♗e6 15 ♕d2 gives White a positional advantage.

12 0-0   ♗g7

Or:

1) **12...f4?!** 13 c4! ♖g8 (13...bxc4 14 ♗c2! ♗g7 15 ♗a4 ♖c8 16 ♘xc4 and 13...b4 14 ♕a4! ♗d7 15 ♘b5 are very good for White) 14 f3 b4 and now Timman-I.Sokolov, Amsterdam 1994 was agreed drawn after **15 ♘c2?!** a5 16 b3 ♗e7 17 ♖f2, but White should have played **15 ♕a4 ♖c8!** 16 ♘c2 (thanks to the inclusion of f3 and ...♖g8, 16 ♘xb4? loses a piece) 16...a5 17 a3 with some advantage. He will always be able to defend his kingside with ♖f2 and ♗f1.

2) **12...♗xd5 13 exd5 ♘e7 14 c3**. *BTS2* concentrated on 14 ♘xb5, which wins a pawn but allows Black some positional compensation. This time we are opting for the quieter continuation. White plans to concentrate his forces against Black's weakest point, f5, by playing ♕h5 followed by ♘c2-e3 and if Black plays ...e4 White will be looking to break up Black's centre with f3. **14...♗g7 15 ♕h5** *(D)* and now:

2a) **15...♕d7** 16 ♖ad1 ♖c8 (hoping to generate some counterplay against d5 by playing ...♖c5) 17 ♘c2 ♖c5 (17...e4 18 ♗e2 followed by f3 is favourable to White; 17...0-0 18 g3! e4 19 ♗e2 ♖c5 20 ♘e3 f4!?

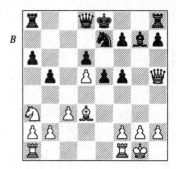

21 gxf4 f5 22 f3 ♕a7! was unclear in Renet-T.Horvath, European Club Ch 1993, as 23 fxe4 is met by 23...♖c4! but perhaps White should have played 22 ♔h1 as 22...♘g6 23 ♕g5 looks in his favour) 18 ♘e3 e4 19 ♗b1 0-0 (19...f4 20 ♘g4 ♕f5 21 ♕xf5 ♘xf5 22 f3! is good for White) 20 g3! (not 20 f3 f4 21 ♗xe4 f5) 20...b4?! (Black should have prepared this with 20...♖b8) 21 cxb4 ♖b5 22 a3 ♗xb2 23 ♔h1! (23 f3 is still too early because of 23...♕a7) 23...♖c8 24 f3 ♖c3 25 fxe4 ♖xa3 (not 25...♖xe3? 26 ♕g5+) 26 ♘xf5 ♘xf5 27 e5!! ♘xg3+ 28 hxg3 ♗xe5 29 ♕xh7+ ♔f8 30 ♖c1! ♖b7 31 ♗f5 ♕b5 32 ♗e6 1-0 Dolmatov-Chekhov, Germany 1992.

2b) **15...e4 16 ♗c2** and now:

2b1) **16...♕a5?!** 17 ♖ae1 ♖a7 (or 17...♗xc3 18 bxc3 ♕xa3 19 ♗xe4! fxe4 20 ♖xe4 ♖a7 21 ♖ae1 ♕xc3 22 ♕g5 ♕c7 23 h4!, followed by h5-h6, with a strong attack according to Kramnik) 18 ♔h1 (18 ♗b3 is also good) 18...♗xc3 19 bxc3 ♕xa3 20 ♗b3 ♕b2 21 f3 with excellent prospects for White, Zso.Polgar-Kramnik, Guarapuava 1991.

2b2) **16...0-0** 17 ♖ae1 ♖c8 18 ♗b3! (a strong move, neutralising ...b4, clearing c2 for the knight and protecting the d-pawn) 18...♖c5 19 ♘c2 ♕d7 20 f3! with advantage to White, Kovalev-Palac, Neu Isenburg 1992.

2b3) **16...♕c8!?** 17 ♖ae1 0-0 18 ♔h1 ♘g6! (in a previous outing Krasenkov had got into trouble after 18...b4?! 19 cxb4 ♗xb2 20 ♖e3 f6 21 g4! ♗xa3 22 gxf5 ♖f7 23 ♖g1+ ♖g7 24 ♖xg7+ ♔xg7, Tseshkovsky-Krasenkov, Voskresensk 1992, and now 25 ♖g3+ ♔h8 26 ♕f7 ♕f8 27 ♕xf8+ ♖xf8 28 ♖xa3 ♘xd5 29 ♗xe4 ♘xb4 30 ♖a4 would have given White a very good ending) 19 ♗b1 (19 f3 is met by 19...b4 but ♗b3 deserves attention, either here or on the previous move) 19...♖e8 20 f4 exf3 21 ♕xf3 ♖xe1 22 ♖xe1 f4, Almasi-Krasenkov, Malmö 1994, and now 23 ♗xg6 hxg6 24 ♕xf4 looks a little better for White, as long as he spends the next few moves bringing his knight back into the game.

13 ♕h5   f4

Not **13...0-0?** 14 exf5 ♗xd5 15 f6 e4 16 fxg7 ♖e8 17 ♕xd5, nor **13...h6?!** 14 f4! opening the position while Black's king is still in the centre.

14 c4   bxc4

After **14...b4** (14...♗xd5 15 exd5 ♘e7 16 ♖ad1 b4 17 ♘b1 ♘g6 18 g3 with advantage to White, Vogt-Georgadze, Halle 1978) 15 ♘c2 ♖b8 White has a variety of promising ideas, since with d5 secured he can play on the queenside with b3 and a3, or on the kingside with g3. Finally ♘e1-f3-h4-f5 can be awkward.

The speculative **14...0-0** 15 cxb5 ♘d4 16 ♘c2 ♘xb5 (16...♘xc2 17 ♗xc2 axb5 18 ♗b3 is a safe positional plus for White) is dubious after 17 a4 (17 ♘cb4 ♘d4 18 ♖c1 is also promising) 17...♖a7 18 a5 ♘c6 19 b4 f5 20 ♘b6 ♖a7 21 exf5 ♗f7 22 ♕h3 ♕f6 23 ♗e4 ♘e7 24 ♖ad1 and White keeps control of d5.

15 ♗xc4   0-0
16 ♖ac1 *(D)*

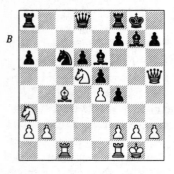

16 ...   ♘e7

The position after 16 ♖ac1 is the key to the whole line and one of the most important in the Sveshnikov Variation. Black has a wide range of options:

1) **16...♘d4?!** 17 ♘c2! ♘xc2 (the line 17...f3 18 ♘xd4 fxg2 19 ♘f5! gxf1♕+ 20 ♔xf1 ♗xf5 21 exf5 h6 22 ♖c3! ♕g5 23 ♕xg5 hxg5 24 ♘e7+ ♔h7 25 ♖h3+ ♗h6 26 f6 e4 27 ♗d5 wins for White) 18 ♖xc2 ♔h8 19 ♖fc1 ♖a7 20 b4 ♖g8 21 a4 with an excellent position for White, Mokry-Vodichka, Dečin 1979.

2) **16...♖a7!?** with the alternatives:

2a) **17 ♘xf4!?** exf4 (17...♗xc4? 18 ♖xc4 ♘a5 19 ♖a4 exf4 20 ♖xa5 ♗xb2 21 ♘c4 is good for White) 18 ♗xe6 ♘e7! (not 18...fxe6 19 ♖xc6) 19 ♗c4! (after 19 ♗d5 or 19 ♗f5 Black can take the bishop and then play 20...♗xb2, when the sacrifice 21 ♖b1 ♖xa3 22 ♖b3 ♗c5 23 ♖h3 doesn't work because Black can advance his f-pawn and defend the second rank) 19...♘g6 (not now 19...♗xb2? 20 ♖b1 ♗g7 21 ♖b3 intending ♖h3) 20 ♖c2 ♖e7 21 ♗d5 ♖e5 22 ♕d1 ♕h4 23 ♘c4 ♖h5 24 h3 ♖g5 25 ♔h1 ♗e5 and Black has enough for the pawn, Dvoirys-Bašagić, Šibenik 1988.

2b) **17 ♖fd1 ♕b8!?** (17...♔h8? 18 ♘xf4 exf4 19 ♗xe6 really does work because f7 hangs after ...♘e7) 18 b3 (18 ♘xf4 exf4 19 ♗xe6 ♘e7 is still unclear) 18...♘d4 19 ♘c2 ♘b5 and now 20 ♘cb4! is good for White.

3) **16...♔h8** 17 ♖fd1 ♘d4 18 ♘c2 is slightly better for White.

4) **16...♖b8** (the main line) **17 b3** *(D)* and now:

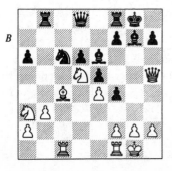

4a) **17...♔h8** 18 ♘xf4!? exf4 19 ♗xe6 ♘d4 20 ♗f5! ♘xf5 21 ♕xf5 ♗b2 22 ♘c4 ♗xc1 23 ♖xc1 is a very promising exchange sacrifice.

4b) **17...♗xd5** 18 ♗xd5 ♘b4 19 ♖fd1 ♘xa2 20 ♖c6, followed by ♘c4, and Black is very badly placed.

4c) **17...♕a5 18 ♘b1!?** (18 ♘c2 ♕xa2 should lead to a draw after 19 ♕h4 h6! 20 ♘f6+ ♗xf6 21 ♕xf6 ♗xc4 22 ♕xh6 ♗xf1 23 ♕g5+) **18...♔h8** (not 18...♕xa2? 19 ♘bc3 ♕a5 20 ♖a1 ♕c5 21 ♖xa6) **19 ♘bc3** *(D)* and now:

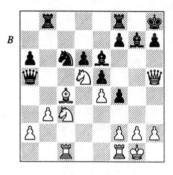

4c1) **19...f5** 20 ♘e7 ♘xe7 21 ♗xe6 ♖f6! (not 21...fxe4? 22 ♘xe4 d5 23 ♖c5 ♕b4 24 ♘g5 h6 25 ♖c7 breaking through) 22 exf5 e4! 23 ♕e2! (23 ♘xe4? ♖xe6 24 ♘g5 ♕xf5 and Black wins) 23...d5, Estevez-Timoshchenko, Managua 1988, and now 24 ♕d2! f3 (24...♘xf5 25 ♕xd5 ♕xd5 26 ♗xd5 e3 27 ♘e4 is very good for White) reaches the critical position. Black has some compensation for the pawn after **25 ♘xe4** ♕xd2 26 ♘xd2 fxg2 27 ♔xg2 ♘xf5, but **25 g4!** appears quite unpleasant for Black (25...♗h6 26 ♕d4).

4c2) **19...♘d4** 20 ♖fd1 (20 ♘xf4 ♗xc4 21 bxc4 ♕c5 is much less clear) 20...f5?! (20...f3!?) 21 ♘e7! ♗xc4 22 bxc4 ♖f6 23 ♘xf5 ♘xf5 24 exf5 ♖g8 (24...♖bf8 25 ♘e4 ♖xf5 26 ♘g5! h6 27 ♖xd6! is also winning for White) 25 ♘e4 ♖h6 26 ♘xd6! 1-0 Varavin-Cherniaev, Moscow 1992.

4d) **17...♕d7 18 ♖fd1 ♔h8** (not 18...♗g4? 19 ♕g5, while 18...♘d4 19 ♘c2 ♘xc2 20 ♖xc2 ♔h8 21 ♖d3 ♗g4 22 ♕h4 f5 23 f3 fxe4 24 fxe4 is a little better for White) **19 ♕h4** *(D)* and now:

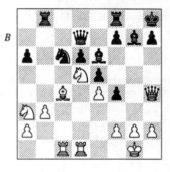

4d1) **19...f5!?** 20 ♘xf4 exf4 21 ♗xe6 ♕xe6 22 ♖xc6 fxe4 (not 22...♖bc8? 23 exf5 ♕e2 24 ♖cxd6 ♖ce8 25 h3 ♕xa2 27 f6 1-0 Dolmatov-Figuero, Seville 1993) 23 ♖cxd6 ♕e8 and now both **24 ♘c4** e3 25 fxe3 (not 25 ♖e1 ♗c3) 25...fxe3 26 ♖e1 ♕f7! 27 ♘xe3 ♖be8 28 h3!, Turzo-Shaked, World U-16 1994 and *BTS2*'s suggestion **24 ♕g4**, with the idea 24...e3 25 ♕f3 (25 ♕e2!?) followed by ♘c4, leave Black having to prove that he has sufficient compensation.

4d2) **19...♗xd5 20 ♗xd5!** (better than the old continuation 20 ♖xd5) **20...♘b4** (after 20...♘d4 21 ♖c4! both 21...f3 22 ♘c2 ♘e2+ 23 ♔f1 ♘f4 24 gxf3 and 21...f5 22 ♘c2 fxe4 23 ♘xd4 exd4 24 ♗xe4, Sveshnikov-Vyzhmanavin, Protvino 1987, are good for White) and now:

4d21) **21 ♖d2** f5 22 ♘c4 (22 ♕h3 should be met by 22...♘xd5 23 ♖xd5 ♕b7 24 ♕d3 fxe4 25 ♕xe4 f3 rather than 22...♕e7 23 exf5 e4 24 ♘c4 ♖f6 25 ♖e1 e3 26 fxe3 ♖h6 27 ♕g4 ♗c3 28 ♕xf4 ♖f6 29 ♖ed1 ♗xd2 30 ♖xd2 with an advantage for White, Klovans-Vyzhmanavin, USSR 1987) 22...♘xd5 (22...♖b5 23 ♖cd1 ♘xd5 may be better) 23 ♖xd5 fxe4 24 ♖xd6 ♕f5 25 h3! h5 26 ♕e7 e3 27 fxe3 fxe3 28 ♖d7!, Renet-Korchnoi, Lugano 1988, and several sources, including *BTS2*, consider White to be better here. However, I (JG) am not so sure; for example Renet gives 28...♕f2+ 29 ♔h1 ♕g3 30 ♘xe3 ♖f2 31 ♖f1 as a clear advantage to White, but Black should continue **30...♖be8** 31 ♕c5 ♖f2 32 ♖f1 ♖xg2! 33 ♖xg2 ♕xh3+ with fair drawing chances.

4d22) **21 ♖c3!** (Renet's suggestion in his notes to the above game with Korchnoi) 21...♘xa2 (after 21...f5 22 ♖h3 ♗f6 23 ♗e6! both 23...♕e7 24 ♕h5 fxe4 25 ♘c4 d5 26 ♘d6 and 23...♗xh4 24 ♗xd7 are good for White) 22 ♖h3 h6 23 ♘c4 ♖bd8 24 g4! and White has dangerous attacking chances since if Black exchanges on g3 the route is open for White's knight to move to f5.

17 ♖fd1

There is an interesting alternative in **17 ♘c7!?** ♗xc4 (17...♕xc7 18 ♗xe6 ♕b7 19 ♗b3! is good for White since 19...♕xe4 loses to 20 ♗c2) 18 ♖xc4 ♖c8 19 ♖fc1; perhaps 19...♕d7 is the best reply.

17 ...   ♖c8
18 ♘xe7+   ♕xe7 (D)

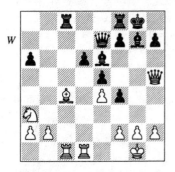

Up to this point the game has followed Matanović-Sax, Buenos Aires OL 1978, which continued 19 ♕e2 ♔h8 20 ♗xa6 f5! with dangerous counterplay. Black went on to win and later it was suggested that 20 ♖c2 followed by doubling rooks on the c-file would have been good for White. Short prefers to double rooks on the d-file with his queen still actively posted on h5.

19 ♖c3!

Black has no immediate threats, so White can afford to take time out to prepare b3 followed by ♖cd3. Black must aim for ...f5, since this provides the only possible counterplay to offset the backward d-pawn. The immediate 19...f5 fails to 20 exf5.

19 ...   &h8

Short's innovation caused Sax to use a lot of time over this and his next few moves, so that before long White was an hour ahead on the clock. **19...Ʀc6?** 20 &xe6 Ʀxc3 21 &f5 wins.

20 b3   f5

20...d5 21 exd5 &xd5 22 Ʀxd5 ♕xa3 fails after 23 &d3 e4 (23...h6 24 ♕f5 and 23...f5 24 &xf5 are even worse) 24 &xe4 h6 25 Ʀxc8 Ʀxc8 26 h3.

Black could have tried **20...&d7**, but then White can keep the advantage by 21 ♘b1! (intending Ʀcd3 and ♘c3) 21...f5 22 Ʀcd3 fxe4 23 Ʀxd6 followed by ♘c3.

21 Ʀh3   h6
22 &xe6   ♕xe6
23 Ʀhd3   Ʀcd8

Although this looks passive it is the best way to defend the d-pawn, for example **23...Ʀc6** 24 ♕f3 or **23...fxe4** 24 Ʀxd6 ♕e7 25 ♘c4 with a clear plus for White in both cases. There is little point leaving a rook on the c-file when it will soon be blocked by ♘c4.

24 ♕e2!

It is easy to win a pawn but if this involves allowing Black to advance his central pawns Black's powerful bishop may well provide enough compensation. One such line is 24 ♘c4 (24 ♕f3? ♕g6! 25 exf5 ♕xf5 followed by ...e4 is also dubious) 24...fxe4 25 Ʀxd6 Ʀxd6 26 Ʀxd6 ♕e7 27 Ʀxa6 e3 28 fxe3 fxe3 and the threats to White's king practically force him to play 29 Ʀxh6+ (29

♘xe3 ♕c5 30 ♕e2 e4 threatening ...&d4 is awkward) 29...&xh6 30 ♕xh6+ &g8 31 ♕xe3 but 31...♕f6 32 h3 ♕f1+ 33 &h2 ♕f4+ is a likely draw because the knight and queenside pawns cannot assume a stable defensive configuration. White correctly prefers to keep the bind, and cash in later.

24 ...   fxe4

24...♕g6 25 f3 d5 (25...fxe4 26 ♕xe4 is good for White) 26 Ʀxd5 Ʀxd5 27 exd5 e4 28 ♘c4 e3 may seem unclear, but White's passed pawn is just as far advanced as Black's and he has an extra pawn in hand.

25 ♕xe4   f3
26 ♘c4! *(D)*

Much better than **26 Ʀxf3** d5 27 ♕h4 (27 Ʀxf8+ &xf8 attacks a3) 27...Ʀfe8 followed by the advance of the central pawns, with good compensation for the pawn.

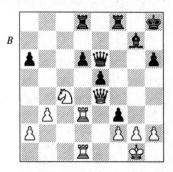

26 ...   Ʀf4

26...fxg2 27 Ʀxd6 Ʀxd6 28 Ʀxd6 ♕f7 29 Ʀd2 and 30 ♘e3 is also very good for White.

27 ♕d5   ♕g4

Black cannot avoid a miserable ending. Although he now succeeds in playing ...d5 his bishop remains blocked by the e5-pawn.

28	♖xf3	♖xf3
29	♕xf3	♕xf3
30	gxf3	d5
31	♔f1	♗f6

Despite White's doubled pawn the position should be a win since Black's d-pawn is easily blockaded by White's king and the bishop will be impeded by the central pawns. Moreover, White possesses a powerful queenside pawn majority.

32	♘b6	d4
33	♔e2	

33 ♖c1! was more accurate, activating the rook before Black can play ...♗g5. Then 34 ♖c8 is a threat, and after 33...♔g7 34 ♖c7+ ♔g6 35 ♖d7 White plays his rook behind Black's passed pawn and follows up with ♔e2-d3. However the move played should also be sufficient to win.

33	...	♗g5
34	♘c4	♗f4
35	h3	♖g8

Black will have to play this sooner or later, for otherwise White plays ♔d3 and ♖g1, seizing the open file for his own use.

36	b4	♖g2

The rook must move up the g-file to allow the black king to cross, and at g2 it delays White's ♔d3.

37	a4	♔g7
38	b5	axb5
39	axb5	♔f6
40	b6	♔e6

41	b7	♖g8
42	♖b1	♖b8 (D)

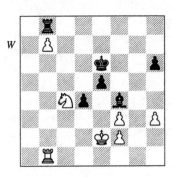

The win still requires some work. White first secures the advanced pawn and moves his king up. Black is paralysed and can only adopt a waiting strategy.

43	♖b5	♔d7
44	♘a5	♔c7

White's only worry is that Black might try to liquidate to a rook and pawn ending by ...♗g5-d8xa5. This might prove awkward to win as White would be left with only f- and h-pawns. The immediate **44...♗g5 45 ♖xe5 ♗d8** fails to 46 ♖d5+ ♔e6 47 ♖xd8.

45	♔d3	♔d6
46	h4	

Definitely ruling out ...♗g5.

46	...	♔c7
47	♖b2	♗h2
48	♔e4	

White's plan is to play ♖c2+ at a moment when Black must reply ...♔d7 to prevent ♖c8. Then White will seize the g-file by ♖c1-g1. Finally the penetration of the rook combined with the advance of the white king to c4 and b5 will decide the game. The immediate **48 ♖c2+** fails to 48...♔b6! 49 ♖c8 ♔xa5, so White must blockade the e-pawn before starting his plan.

    48   ...   **♗f4** *(D)*

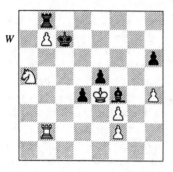

Black can only delay the end. This move covers c1 in order to prevent ♖c1-g1.

    49 ♖c2+   **♔d7**

Or **49...♔b6** 50 ♖c8 ♖xb7 51 ♘xb7 ♔xb7 52 ♖f8 (threatening ♖xf4) 52...♗h2 53 ♖f6 and wins.

    50 ♔d3!

Black is in zugzwang. The rook cannot move because of ♘c6, the king cannot move because of ♖c8 and ...h5 doesn't help.

    50   ...   **♗h2**
    51 ♖c1   **♗f4**

The same again! Black has to free g1.

    52 ♖g1   **♔d6**
    53 ♔c4   **1-0**

The finish might be **53...♖f8** 54 ♘b3 (if White gets the chance to play ♘b3-c5 the winning process is simplified) 54...♖b8 55 ♘c5 ♖h8 56 ♖g6+ ♔c7 57 ♔b5 d3 58 ♖c6+ ♔b8 59 ♔b6 mating, or **53...♔c7** 54 ♖g6 ♖h8 55 ♔c5 d3 56 ♖g7+ ♔b8 57 ♔b6 with a similar conclusion.

5 The Dragon

The Dragon is characterised by the initial moves 1 e4 c5 2 ♘f3 d6 3 d4 cxd4 4 ♘xd4 ♘f6 5 ♘c3 g6, intending to develop Black's bishop actively at g7. If White plays quietly and castles kingside the bishop will still be useful in supporting Black's minority attack on the queenside, while if White aims to attack the enemy king and plays 0-0-0 the Dragon bishop comes into its own. Hosts of players have seen their queensides disintegrate under the laser-like power of the g7 bishop, often supported by ...♕a5 and ...♖c8 to step up the pressure on c3. The true Dragon player will analyse six exchange sacrifices on c3 before breakfast, and White needs to be constantly on the alert for combinations based on blowing open the long diagonal.

The Dragon is one of the most controversial lines in the Sicilian. At various times over the years it has appeared to be in its death throes, only to be suddenly revived by the discovery of new ideas for Black. Practitioners regard the variation as their private property, and defend it with an almost religious fervour against the many players who wish to commit the heresy of mating Black down the h-file. BTS2 proposed the main line of the Yugoslav Attack, 9 ♗c4 followed by attempting to mate Black down the h-file, but this time we are opting for 9 0-0-0 followed by attempting to mate Black down the h-file. The advantage of this approach is clearest if Black insists on getting involved in a mutual king-hunt, when the tempi White has saved on ♗c4-b3 are very valuable. The slight catch is that Black can reply 9...d5, somewhat changing the character of the game. This pawn sacrifice has a very respectable reputation but thanks to the injection of several interesting new ideas White has been coping quite well with it recently. This is examined in Game 17, whilst Game 16 deals with 9...♘xd4 and all the other alternatives for Black.

General principles aren't much help in the Dragon, since success or failure is determined mainly by tactical considerations.

Game 16
I. Gurevich – Ward
London Lloyds Bank 1994

1	e4	c5
2	♘f3	d6
3	d4	cxd4
4	♘xd4	♘f6
5	♘c3	g6
6	♗e3	

If White intends castling queen-side this move is the most usual. **6 ⍾e2** only fits in with 0-0, since the bishop is usually better placed at f1 or c4 in the more aggressive lines resulting from castling on opposite wings.

6 ... ⍾g7

The Dragon differs from many other Sicilian systems in that Black often omits the typical move ...a6. Time is of particular importance in the Dragon and Black simply cannot afford the tempo spent on preparing ...b5, which can often be played without ...a6 in case White castles queenside. The idea of playing ...a6 and ...b5 before castling has been tried, but after **6...a6** (not 6...⍾g4?? losing material after 7 ⍾b5+) 7 f3 ⍾bd7 8 ⍟d2 b5 9 a4! bxa4 (9...b4 10 ⍾d5 is also very good for White) 10 ⍖xa4 ⍾g7 11 ⍾e2 0-0 12 0-0 ⍾c5 13 ⍖a3 ⍾b7 14 ⍖fa1 ⍟c8 15 ⍾b3 White had strong queenside pressure in Kavalek-Bilek, Sousse IZ 1967.

7 f3 (D)

This is more or less forced as 7 ⍾c4 and 7 ⍟d2 can both be met by 7...⍾g4.

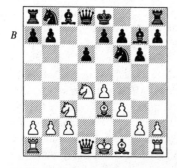

7 ... 0-0

Or:

1) **7...a6** (7...⍾bd7 puts no pressure on d4 so simply 8 ⍟d2 followed by 0-0-0, ⍾c4 and ⍾h6 gives White a strong attack) **8 ⍟d2 ⍾bd7** (8...b5 9 a4! is similar to Kavalek-Bilek above) and now:

1a) **9 ⍾h6** (9 0-0-0 is also good) 9...⍾xh6 (9...0-0 is suicidal since White's intended h4-h5 attack is much stronger than usual) 10 ⍟xh6 b5 11 0-0-0 ⍾b7 12 ⌖b1, Bastrikov-Khasin, USSR 1961, and Black's king is stuck in the centre.

1b) **9 g4 ⍾b6 10 0-0-0 ⍾fd7 11 ⍾h6 ⍾xh6 12 ⍟xh6 e5 13 ⍾b3 ⍾f6 14 ⍟d2 ⌖e7 15 ⍾e2 ⍟c7 16 f4!** exf4?! 17 g5 ⍾e8? 18 ⍟d4! 1-0 was the game Arakhamia-Chiburdanidze, Belgrade 1992. White has the double threat of 19 ⍟xh8 and 19 ⍟xb6.

2) **7...⍾c6** (this can transpose into the main line if Black castles quickly, so we only explore lines in which Black plays ...⍾d7 and ...⌖c8 before ...0-0) 8 ⍟d2 ⍾d7 9 0-0-0 ⌖c8 10 g4 ⍾e5 (10...0-0 transposes to line '2' in the note to Black's 9th move) 11 h4 h5 (11...0-0 is variation '2a4' in the note to Black's 9th move) 12 g5 ⍾h7 13 f4 ⍾g4 and now P.Littlewood-Mestel, London 1978, continued **14 ⍾g1 0-0 15 ⌖b1** e5 16 ⍾f3 ⍾e6 17 fxe5 ⍾xe5 18 ⍾xe5 ⍾xe5 19 ⍾b5 ⌖e8 and Black had no problems. However, White can improve by playing f5 at some point, for example **15 f5** or, more provocatively, **14 f5!?** since even

though 14...♘xe3 15 ♕xe3 0-0 exchanges off White's dark-squared bishop, it isn't easy to see a constructive plan for Black after 16 ♗h3.

8   ♕d2   ♘c6

Or **8...d5** (other moves meet with common-sense replies, e.g. 8...♗e6 9 ♘xe6 fxe6 10 e5 or 8...a6 9 0-0-0 b5 10 h4) **9 e5** *(D)* and now:

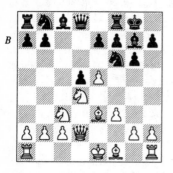

1) **9...♘e8** 10 f4 f6 11 0-0-0 fxe5 (11...♘c6 12 ♘f3) 12 fxe5 ♘c6 (after 12...♗xe5 13 ♘f3 White either regains the pawn with advantage or, after 13...♗xc3 14 ♕xc3 e6 15 h4, gets an enormous attack) 13 ♘f3 ♗g4 (13...e6 14 ♗h6 leaves Black with a very bad bishop) 14 ♘xd5 ♖xf3 15 gxf3 ♗xf3 16 ♗g2 ♗xd1 17 ♖xd1 ♗xe5 18 ♗c5 e6 19 ♘e7+ ♔g7 20 ♘xc6 ♕xd2+ 21 ♖xd2 bxc6 22 ♖d7+ with advantage to White.

2) **9...♘fd7** 10 f4 ♘c6 11 0-0-0 (11 ♘b3 e6 12 0-0-0 f6 13 ♘xd5! fxe5 14 ♘c3 ♕e7 15 ♔b1 exf4 16 ♗xf4 gave White a clear positional plus in L.Milov-Afek, Konsumex 1992) 11...♘b6 12 ♘f3 (this suggestion of Afek's is perhaps even stronger than the usual 12 ♘b3 or

12 ♗e2) 12...e6 (12...♘c4 13 ♗xc4 dxc4 14 ♕e2+) 13 h4 h5 14 ♗c5 ♘e7 15 ♘b5 a6 16 ♘bd4 and now White's position is preferable.

9   0-0-0 *(D)*

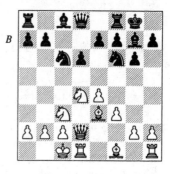

9   ...   ♘xd4

9...d5 is the subject of the next game whilst the other alternatives are examined below:

1) **9...♗e6** and now:

1a) **10 ♔b1** leaves Black with no better continuation than **10...♘xd4** 11 ♗xd4 ♕c7 transposing to the main line. If instead **10...♖c8**, then 11 ♘xe6 fxe6 12 ♗c4 ♕d7 13 ♗b3 ♘e5 14 ♕e2 a6 15 ♘a4!, threatening ♘b6, ♘c5 and f4-f5, is excellent for White.

1b) White can also try **10 ♘xe6** fxe6 11 g3! (11 ♗c4 ♕c8! is not so clear) when Romero-Martin, Spanish Ch 1990 continued 11...♕d7 12 ♗h3 ♘e5 13 ♕e2 b5 14 f4 ♘c4 15 e5 ♘e8 16 ♗d4 ♘c7 17 ♘e4 d5 18 ♘c5 ♕c6 19 ♗g4 b4 20 h4 a5 21 h5 a4 22 hxg6 h6! 23 ♖h2 ♖a5 24 ♖dh1 b3 25 a3 ♖xc5 26 c3! and with the queenside blocked, Black can only await his fate on the other wing.

2) **9...♗d7** *(D)* is thought to be a little slow when White hasn't wasted time on ♗c4. White now has:

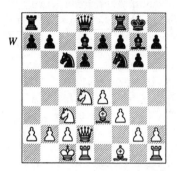

2a) **10 g4 ♖c8 11 h4** (11 ♔b1 is interesting as after 11...♘e5 12 h4 we have transposed to line '2a4' cutting out lines '2a', '2a2' and '2a3', while 12 ♗h6 is recommended by Miles and Moskow who give 12 ♗h6 ♘c4 13 ♗xc4 ♖xc4 14 ♘de2 followed by h4 and h5 as good for White) and now Black has:

2a1) **11...b5** 12 ♘cxb5 ♘e5 13 h5 ♘xf3 (once Black has started sacrificing he must continue) 14 ♘xf3 ♗xg4 15 ♕g2 (15 ♗e2 ♘xe4 16 ♕e1! would be a safe answer to Black's aggression) 15...♕a5 16 a3 ♖xc2+! 17 ♔xc2 ♕a4+ 18 ♔d2 ♕b3 19 ♘c3 ♕xb2+ 20 ♔d3 ♕xa3 with horrendous complications in the game Mestel-Christiansen, Hastings 1978/9. This remarkable game concluded 21 ♗c1 (21 ♖c1 was probably better) 21...♕b4 22 ♗d2 ♖c8 23 hxg6 hxg6 (23...h5!? reserving h6 for the bishop was possible) 24 ♖h4 ♖xc3+ 25 ♗xc3 ♕xe4+ 26 ♔d2 ♘d5? (the line 26...♗xf3 27

♖xe4 ♘xe4+ 28 ♔e3 ♗xg2 29 ♗xg7 ♔xg7 30 ♗xg2 ♘c5 was best for Black; the weird ending resulting appears to be better for White) 27 ♗xg7 ♕e3+ 28 ♔c2 ♗xf3 29 ♗b2! e5 30 ♕d2 ♘c5+ 31 ♔b1 ♘e3 32 ♖c1 ♕b6 33 ♕h2 ♘f5 34 ♖c8+ ♔g7 35 ♖b4 1-0.

2a2) **11...♕a5** 12 ♔b1 (12 h5 allows 12...♘b4, with ...♖xc3 to follow, but 12 ♘b3 ♕c7 13 h5 is an interesting alternative) 12...♖fd8? (12...♘e5 transposes to line '2a4' and 12...♘xd4 13 ♗xd4 ♖fd8 is assessed as slightly better for White by Hübner) 13 ♘b3 ♕c7 14 h5 ♗e6 15 hxg6 fxg6, Hübner-Hort, match 1979 and now 16 ♘d5! would have given White a clear plus according to Hübner.

2a3) **11...h5** 12 ♗e2 (it is by no means certain that this is White's best; Ligterink-Sosonko, Dutch Ch 1978 went 12 gxh5 ♘xh5 13 ♖g1 ♔h7 14 ♗e2 ♘xd4 15 ♗xd4 ♗h6 16 ♗e3 ♗g7 17 ♗d4 ♗h6 ½-½ but 14 ♔b1 avoiding the draw may be good for White) 12...♘e5 13 gxh5 ♘xh5 14 ♖dg1 (14 ♖hg1 is an alternative, but whether better or worse is not easy to decide) 14...♘c4 15 ♗xc4 (a defect of 12 ♗e2 is that this capture will involve a loss of a tempo) 15...♖xc4 16 ♖g5 (threatening 17 ♖xh5 gxh5 18 ♖g1) 16...♖c5 17 ♘d5 e6 18 ♖xh5 exd5 19 ♖xd5 ♖xd5 20 exd5 and White was just a little better in Speelman-Liu Wenzhe, China 1981.

2a4) **11...♘e5 12 ♔b1** (after 12 h5 ♕a5 13 ♔b1, Seirawan and Jim

Gallagher {probably a long-lost cousin to judge from his chess style} give 13...♖xc3! 14 ♕xc3 ♕xc3 15 bxc3 ♘xf3! 16 ♘xf3 ♗xg4 17 ♗g2 ♘xe4 with a lot of play for the rook) **12...♕a5** (12...b5 13 ♘cxb5 ♘xf3 is not so effective with the king on b1) **13 ♘d5 ♕xd2 14 ♘xe7+ ♔h8 15 ♗xd2! ♖ce8** (D)

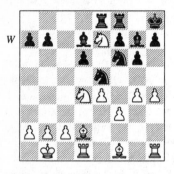

2a41) The game Timoshenko-Jim Gallagher, Jacksonville 1990 continued **16 ♗b4?!** (16 ♘d5 ♘xd5 17 exd5 ♘xg4) 16...♘xf3! 17 ♘xf3 ♘xe4 18 ♘d5 ♗xg4 19 ♗g2 ♘f2 20 ♗xd6 ♖g8 21 ♘g5 h6 22 ♘xf7+ ♔h7 23 ♖df1 ♘xh1 24 ♖xh1 ♖e2 25 ♘f4 ♖xg2! 26 ♘xg2 ♗f3 27 ♖h2 (27 ♖g1 ♗d4 28 ♘e1 ♗xg1 29 ♘xf3 ♗f2 is OK for Black) 27...♖e8 28 ♗g3 ♖f8! 29 ♘g5+ hxg5 30 hxg5+ ♔g8 and the bishop pair compensated for the missing pawn.

2a42) However, I believe that **16 h5!** would refute Black's interesting concept. If now **16...♖xe7**, then 17 h6! traps the bishop and after **16...gxh5** White can simply recapture or play 17 ♘ef5! as 17...hxg4 18 ♘xg7 costs Black the exchange. Nor

can Black save himself by means of **16...♘xe4** 17 fxe4 ♖xe7 (17...♗g4 18 h6) as 18 h6 ♗f6 19 g5 still traps the bishop. There remains the attempt to block the h-pawn's further advance with **16...h6**, but then 17 g5! looks crushing, e.g. 17...♘xh5 18 gxh6 ♖xe7 (18...♗f6 19 ♘d5) 19 hxg7+ ♔xg7 20 ♗b4!.

2b) **10 h4 ♖c8 11 h5 ♘xh5 12 ♕f2!?** (12 ♘xc6 ♖xc6 13 ♗h6 ♗xc3 14 bxc3 ♕a5 looks good for Black) 12...♘e5 13 g4 ♘f6 14 ♘d5 with a strong attack for White. In Shaked-Leonard, Philadelphia 1993 Black sacrificed unsoundly by 14...♘fxg4 and lost quickly after 15 fxg4 ♘xg4 16 ♕h4 h5 17 ♘xe7+ ♔h8 18 ♗g5 ♗h6 19 ♗xh6 ♘xh6 20 ♕f6+ ♔h7 21 ♘f3 ♘g4 22 ♘g5+ ♔h6 23 ♘xf7+ 1-0.

3) **9...♘e5** and now:

3a) **10 g4** e6 11 ♗e2 d5 12 g5 ♘h5 13 f4 ♘c4 14 ♗xc4 dxc4 15 e5 ± Z.Almasi-Szalanczy, Kecskemet 1993.

3b) **10 ♗h6 ♗xh6 11 ♕xh6 ♔h8 12 ♕d2 ♗d7 13 f4 ♘c6 14 ♗e2 ±** Luther-Szalanczy, Kecskemet 1993.

10 ♗xd4   ♗e6
11 ♔b1!

This prevents 11...♕a5, which would now be met by the standard trick 12 ♘d5 ♕xd2 13 ♘xe7+, and White wins a pawn. However, Black doesn't really have an alternative plan so he is forced first to play ...♕c7 and ...♖fc8 and only then ...♕a5 (with f8 available for the king the trick doesn't work).

11 ...   ♕c7 (D)

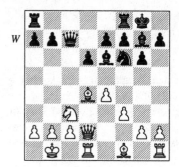

12   g4

Or **12 h4 ♖fc8 13 h5 ♕a5** (after 13...♘xh5 14 ♗xg7 ♔xg7 15 g4 ♘f6 16 e5 dxe5 17 ♕h6+ ♔g8 18 g5 ♘h5 19 ♗d3! White had a decisive attack in Evans-Zuckerman, New York 1987, which concluded 19...e4 20 ♘xe4 ♕f4 21 ♖xh5! gxh5 22 ♘f6+ exf6 23 ♗xh7+ ♔h8 24 ♗f5+ ♔g8 25 ♕h7+ ♔f8 26 ♕h8+ 1-0) **14 hxg6 hxg6 15 a3 ♖ab8 16 ♗d3** and now:

1) **16...b5?!** 17 ♕g5! (a strong move which both slows down the opposing attack and brings the queen into the vicinity of the black king) 17...♗c4 (17...♕c7 18 e5 dxe5 19 ♗xe5 ♕c5 20 f4 ♖b7?! 21 ♗xg6 fxg6 22 ♕xg6! ♗f7 23 ♖h8+! 1-0 Van der Wiel-Sax, Plovdiv 1983) 18 f4 e5 19 fxe5 b4 20 exf6! ♕xg5 21 fxg7 f6 22 ♗xc4+ ♔xg7 (22...♖xc4 23 ♖h8+ ♔xg7 24 ♖xb8 bxc3 25 ♖b7+ ♔f8 26 ♗xc3 is good for White as the black king is simply too exposed) 23 ♘d5! ± Cuipers-Berendse, Holland 1984.

2) **16...♗c4!** 17 ♗xc4 ♖xc4 18 ♗xf6 ♗xf6 19 ♘d5 ♕xd2 20 ♘xf6+ ♔g7 led to equality in the game

Marjanović-Mesing, Bela Crkva 1984. 17 ♗xc4 and 18 ♗xf6 was not a very critical test, but for the moment sharper continuations such as **17 f4** or **17 g4** remain unexplored. Against either Black will start his counterattack with 17...b5.

12   ...   ♖fc8
13   h4   ♕a5
14   ♕g5!

First played in a quickplay game by Ivanchuk, this move virtually forces an exchange of queens on g5, which is very favourable for White. Previously **14 a3** had been played and after 14...♖ab8 15 h4 b5 a sharp struggle arose with chances for both sides.

14   ...   ♕xg5

If Black plays **14...♕c7**, then the simplest would be to play 15 ♗d3 quickly and await with curiosity Black's next move.

15   hxg5   ♘d7
16   ♗xg7   ♔xg7 *(D)*

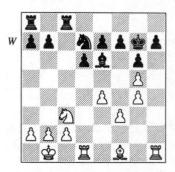

17   ♖h4!

In the original game with 14 ♕g5!, Ivanchuk-Kir.Georgiev, Tilburg 1993, White played the less accurate **17 ♗e2**. Gurevich's move, which protects g4 so that the f-pawn can advance and gives White the option of doubling on the h-file, is more powerful.

17 ...   f6

Black must grab some space before it's too late.

18 gxf6+   ♘xf6
19 g5   ♘d7

Or **19...♘h5 20 f4 ♖f8 21 f5 ♘g3 22 fxe6 ♘xf1 23 b3! ♖f2 24 e5!** with a clear advantage for White according to Gurevich.

20 f4   ♖c5
21 ♘b5!

The knight heads for its ideal square, d4.

21 ...   ♘f8
22 ♘d4   ♗d7
23 ♗d3 *(D)*

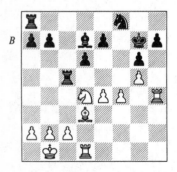

White has an extremely pleasant position. All his pieces are more active than their counterparts and he also has a superior pawn structure. Black now takes some drastic action, reasoning that if White is going to get f5 in then he might as well have a big centre in return. Objectively

speaking though, Black's next move probably changes the assessment of his position from bad to lost.

23 ...   e5

I can sympathise with someone who's not willing to defend the position after **23...♘e6 24 ♖dh1 ♖h8 25 ♘xe6+ ♗xe6 26 b3**, when White can slowly build up his position until he feels like striking, safe in the knowledge that Black has nothing to do but wait.

24 ♘b3   ♖c7
25 f5   gxf5
26 exf5   d5
27 c3   a5

Of course **27...e4**, which is met by 28 f6+, concedes control of the central dark squares and facilitates the knight's entry into the game.

28 ♗c2   a4
29 ♘c1   ♖a5
30 ♘e2!

Once the knight reaches the kingside Black will be in serious danger of getting mated, notwithstanding the reduced material.

30 ...   ♗e8
31 a3   ♔g8
32 ♖g1   ♖a6
33 ♘g3   ♖g7
34 ♘f1!

Black has done the best he can over the last few moves but a knight on g4 will be too much to cope with. Note how White is in no hurry to push his kingside pawns. On f5 and g5 they severely restrict the black minor pieces.

34 ...   b5
35 ♘e3   ♖d6

| 36 | ♘g4 | e4 |

36...♖xg5 loses to 37 ♘h6+.

37 ♖h2?!

The immediate **37 ♖h6!** would have been more to the point.

| 37 | ... | ♘d7 |
| 38 | ♖h6! | ♖b6 |

38...♖xh6 39 gxh6 ♖e7 40 ♘f6+ ♔f8 41 ♘xd5 ♖e5 42 ♘e3 is also hopeless.

| 39 | ♖xb6 | ♘xb6 |
| 40 | ♘f6+ | ♔f7 |

40...♔f8 41 ♖h1 and Black can't take on g5.

41	♘xh7	♘d7
42	♗d1	♔g8
43	g6	♖xh7
44	gxh7+	♔xh7
45	♔c1	♘f6
46	♔d2	1-0

Game 17
Luther – M. Hoffmann
Lippstadt 1994

1	e4	c5
2	♘f3	d6
3	d4	cxd4
4	♘xd4	♘f6
5	♘c3	g6
6	♗e3	♗g7
7	f3	0-0
8	♕d2	♘c6
9	0-0-0	d5 *(D)*
10	♕e1	

A logical move hoping to take advantage of the fact that the black queen is on the same line as the white rook. Although Black's last move is theoretically a pawn sacrifice, White should not even consider taking it.

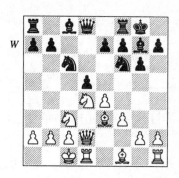

After **10 exd5 ♘xd5 11 ♘xc6 bxc6 12 ♘xd5** (12 ♗d4!) **12...cxd5 13 ♕xd5 ♕c7!** Black has too much for a pawn.

White does have one interesting alternative though, **10 ♔b1!?**, which has recently been introduced into practice by L.Milov.

1) The far from obvious idea is to meet **10...♘xd4** with **11 e5!** *(D)*.

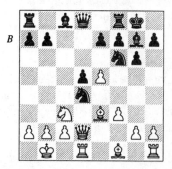

Experience is still very limited, but what we've seen so far suggests that White is doing well here.

1a) For example, L.Milov-Golubev, Biel 1994 continued **11...♘d7 12 ♗xd4 ♘xe5** (12...e6 13 f4 f6 14 exf6 ♗xf6 15 ♕e3 ♘b6 16 h4 was distinctly better for White in the game Milov-Cirkvenčić, Nagykanizsa Open 1993) 13 ♕e3! ♘c6 14 ♗xg7 ♔xg7 15 ♘xd5 ♕a5 (15...♗e6 16 ♕c3+ f6 17 ♗c4 is good for White) 16 b4! ♕a4 17 b5 ♖b8! 18 ♕b3 (18 ♔c1!?) 18...♕xb3 19 axb3 e6 20 bxc6 exd5 and now instead of the inaccurate **21 c7?**, which allowed Black to equalise after 21...♖a8 22 ♖xd5 ♗e6 23 ♖c5 ♖fe8! 24 ♗d3 ♖ac8 25 ♖a5 a6, the straightforward **21 ♖xd5 bxc6 22 ♖a5** would have left Black with a difficult defensive task.

Alternatives to 11...♘d7 also look good for White, e.g.:

1b) **11...♘xc2?** 12 exf6 +−.

1c) **11...♘f5** 12 exf6 exf6 13 ♗c5 ±.

1d) Perhaps **11...♘xf3** is most critical. After 12 gxf3 ♘d7 White can play either 13 f4 followed by the advance of the h-pawn, or 13 ♘xd5 as 13...♘xe5 allows 14 ♘f6+ and after 13...♗xe5 14 ♗h6 White has a dangerous initiative.

2) Golubev assesses **10...e6** as ±.

It is too soon for any definitive judgement of 10 ♔b1, especially without any examples of 10...e6.

10   ...   e6

Or:

1) **10...♖e8?!** 11 ♗b5 ♗d7 12 ♗xc6! bxc6 (12...♗xc6 13 e5 ♘d7 14 e6 ±) 13 e5 c5 14 ♘b3! c4!? (14...d4 15 ♘xc5 dxc3 16 exf6 ♕b6 17 ♕xc3 ♕xf6 18 ♘d7 +−) 15 ♘c5 (15 ♘d4) 15...♗c6 16 exf6 ♗xf6 17 ♕f2 and Black didn't have enough for the piece, Jansa-W.Watson, Prague 1992.

2) **10...e5** (this has been out of favour recently but it seems to cause White at least as many problems as the main line) **11 ♘xc6 bxc6 12 exd5 ♘xd5** (12...cxd5 looks more natural, but after 13 ♗g5 ♗e6 14 ♗c4! White has the advantage; the best that Black can do is 14...♕c7 15 ♗xf6 dxc4 16 ♗xg7 ♔xg7 17 ♕e3 ♖ab8 18 ♖he1 f6 19 ♘e4 with an edge for White, Kuporosov-A.Kovačević, Vrnjačka Banja 1992) **13 ♗c4 ♗e6 14 ♘e4 ♕c7** (Black can also try 14...h6 with the idea of meeting 15 ♗c5 by 15...f5; Dragon players normally don't even hesitate for a moment before playing such exchange sacrifices, but in this case White seems to be able to gain the advantage after 16 ♗xf8 ♕xf8 17 ♘f2 ♕e7 18 ♘d3! when 18...♘b6 19 ♕b4! is good for White, as are 18...♕f6 19 ♖d2 ♖e8 20 ♖e2 ♗f7 21 ♕f2! and 18...♗f7 19 ♕a5 e4 20 ♖he1 e3 21 ♕c5 ♕xc5 22 ♘xc5 f4 23 g3 g5 24 h4 ♗f6 25 hxg5 hxg5 26 gxf4 gxf4 27 ♖h1 ±; analysis by Perez Cruz) **15 ♗c5 ♖fd8** (D) and in this position White has at least three reasonable tries:

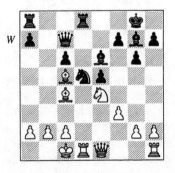

2a) **16 ♕h4** h6 17 g4 ♘f4! (better than 17...♖ab8 18 g5 h5 19 ♕f2 ♕b7 20 b3 with an edge for White, Kramnik-Rosselli, Maringa 1991; or 17...♖d7 18 g5 h5 19 ♘f6+!? ♘xf6 20 ♗xe6 ♖xd1+ 21 ♖xd1 ♘d5 22 ♗xd5 cxd5 23 ♖xd5 ♕a5 24 a3 ♕b5 25 ♕e4! and Black had no compensation for the pawn in Mainka-Lindemann, Oberwart 1991) 18 ♗d6? (18 ♖xd8+ ♖xd8 19 ♗xe6 ♘xe6 20 ♗e7 might be better for White as 20...♖d4 is met by 21 ♘f6+ ♔h8 22 ♘e8, but Black should prefer 18...♕xd8 with a roughly balanced position) 18...♖xd6! 19 ♘xd6 ♗d5! 20 ♗xd5 cxd5 21 ♘b5 ♕c5 22 ♘c3 ♖c8 with an excellent game for Black, Baron-Komljenović, Ibercaja 1993.

2b) **16 g4** ♘f4 17 ♕c3 ♖d5! 18 ♔b1 ♖ad8 19 ♗xd5 cxd5 20 ♗e3 (20 ♘g5 d4! 21 ♗xd4 ♕d6! is good for Black) 20...♕e7 21 ♕c5 ♕b7 22 ♕a3 ♕c6 23 ♕c3 ♕a8! 24 ♗xf4 ♖c8! 25 ♕a5 exf4 and Black's strong bishops give him ample compensation for the exchange, Xie Jun-Gufeld, Kuala Lumpur 1994.

2c) **16 ♘g5 ♗c8 17 g4** *(D)* (a suggestion of Dvoirys) with the possibilities:

2c1) After **17...h6**, the sensible continuation is **18 ♘e4 ♗e6 19 ♕f2**, and the pressure against a7 makes it hard for Black to allow an exchange on d8. The crazy continuation is **18 h4** hxg5 (18...♖b8 19 ♘e4 f5 20 ♘c3!? ♗e6 21 gxf5 gxf5 22 ♖g1 looks dangerous for Black) 19 hxg5, but after 19...♗b7 (19...♘e7 20

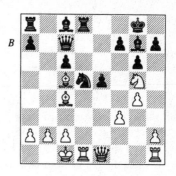

♖xd8 ♕xd8 21 ♕h4 ♕c7 22 ♕h7+ ♔f8 23 ♖h6!, with the threat of 24 ♖xg6, is much more dangerous) 20 ♕h4 ♘e7 21 ♕h7+ ♔f8 White may not have enough compenastion for the piece since Black is already preparing to liquidate rooks.

2c2) **17...♖b8 18 ♗a3 ♗h6!?** (or 18...h6 19 ♘e4 ♗e6 20 ♘c5 ±; Greenfeld suggests 18...♕b6) **19 ♕h4** (19 h4? f6) **19...♔g7 20 f4!** and now:

2c21) **20...f6** (20...♘xf4 21 ♖xd8 ♕xd8 22 ♕xh6+! wins) 21 ♖d3! exf4 (21...♘xf4 22 ♖xd8 ♕xd8 23 ♕xh6+ and wins) 22 ♖h3! fxg5 23 ♕xh6+ ♔f6 24 b3! with dangerous threats.

2c22) **20...♖e8 21 fxe5!? ♖xe5 22 ♗f8+!** is very good for White.

2c23) **20...♗xg5 21 fxg5 ♗e6 22 ♖de1! ♘f4 23 ♗xe6 ♘xe6 24 ♖e3! ♕a5!?** (24...♕d7 25 ♖d3! ♘d4 26 ♖e1±) 25 ♕f2! ♖d4 (25...♕d5! ±) 26 ♖he1! ♖b5 27 ♕f6+ ♔g8 28 c3 ± Svidler-Alterman, Haifa 1995.

11 h4!

Until recently **11 g4** was the normal move here, but then it was discovered that ...e5 is much stronger once White has weakened his king-side. For example, the game Mor-ozevich-Savchenko, Moscow 1991 continued 11...e5! 12 ♘xc6 bxc6 13 exd5 cxd5 14 ♗g5 ♗b7 (with the pawn on g2, 15 ♗c4! would give White the advantage, and it would still have been better than the course Morozevich took) 15 ♕xe5? h6 16 ♗h4 (16 ♗xf6 ♗xf6 is tremendous for Black) 16...g5 17 ♗e1 ♘xg4 18 ♕g3 ♘e3 19 ♖d2 ♕a5 20 ♕f2 ♗xc3 21 ♔b1 ♕b4 0-1.

After 11 h4, which has the merit of not weakening the kingside so much, White plans to start an attack on the h-file which his queen on e1 is particularly well placed to join in. In many lines ♕h4 will prove difficult for Black to meet.

11 ...   ♕c7 (D)

Alternatives are:

1) **11...♕e7** 12 ♘b3 ♖d8 (on 12...b6, the reply 13 h5 looks strong) 13 exd5 ♘xd5 14 ♗g5! ♘f6 15 ♖xd8+ ♕xd8 16 ♘e4 a5 17 a3 a4 18 ♘bc5 h6 19 ♘xf6+ ♗xf6 20 ♗xf6 ♕xf6 21 ♘e4 ♕d4 22 ♗b5 ♔g7 23 ♕c3! and the weakness of the a-pawn proved decisive in Sax-Piket, Tilburg 1989.

2) **11...♖e8** 12 ♘b3 ♘a5 13 h5 ♘xb3+ 14 axb3 ♕a5 (14...♘xh5 15 g4 ♘f6 16 ♕h4 is extremely dangerous for Black) 15 hxg6 fxg6 16 ♔b1 dxe4 17 fxe4 ♘g4 18 ♗d4 e5 19 ♗g1 ♕c7?! 20 ♘b5 ♕e7 21 ♗c4+ ♔h8 22 ♘d6 (Smagin-Raj-ković, Bundesliga 1991) with a win-ning advantage for White as 22...♖f8 fails to stop 23 ♘f7+! on account of

23...♖xf7 24 ♗xf7 ♕xf7 25 ♖d8+ ♗f8 26 ♗c5.

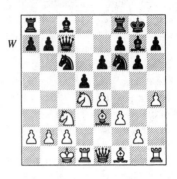

12 h5

A case can also be made out for continuing in positional vein. For ex-ample, **12 exd5 exd5** 13 ♕d2 ♖e8 14 ♗f4 ♕a5 15 ♘b3 ♕b4 16 a3 ♕e7 17 ♗g5 ♗e6 18 ♘b5 was quite good for White in Dvoirys-Los, Gronin-gen 1993.

12 ...   ♘xh5

12...♘xd4 13 ♗xd4 e5 14 ♘b5 ♕e7 15 ♗c3 ♘xh5 16 exd5 was bet-ter for White in Sirigos-Alterman, Komotini 1992.

13 exd5

Knaak's proposal, **13 g4**, is very interesting. He gives **13...♘xd4** 14 ♗xd4 ♗xd4 15 ♖xd4 ♕g3 (after 15...♕e5 16 ♕d2 ♘g3 17 ♖g1 dxe4 18 f4 ♘xf1 19 ♖xf1 ♕g7 20 g5 e5 21 ♖d6 e3 22 ♕xe3 exf4 23 ♕xf4 ♗h3 24 ♖f2 ♖ae8 25 ♘d5 ♖e1+ 26 ♔d2 ♕e5 27 ♖h2! White gained material in the game R.Mainka-Al-terman, London Lloyds Bank 1994) 16 ♕d2 ♘f4 17 exd5 e5 18 ♖e4 ♕xf3 19 ♕h2 h5 20 gxh5 as being clearly better for White, but perhaps

13...♘g3 would be a more critical test of Knaak's idea.

13 ... **♘xd4?!**

13...exd5! is better, as **14 ♘xd5 ♛e5** is unclear and Luther's suggestion **14 g4** fails to **14...♘xd4!** 15 ♗xd4 ♛f4+ 16 ♗e3 ♛xf3. Therefore in Almasi-Kir.Georgiev, Groningen 1994 White tried **14 ♘db5** and instead of **14...♛e7?** 15 ♘xd5 ♛e5 16 ♘bc3 with advantage to White, Black should have played **14...♛g3!**, which Almasi assesses as equal. So unless an improvement is found for White here, the alternatives to the 12th and 13th moves given above look more promising.

14 ♗xd4 **♗xd4**

14...♛g3 15 ♛d2 ♗xd4 16 ♛xd4 e5 (16...♛f4+ 17 ♛xf4 ♘xf4 18 d6 is good for White) 17 ♛g1! ♗f5 18 ♔b1 ♖fc8 19 d6 is clearly better for White according to Luther.

15 ♖xd4 **♛g3** *(D)*

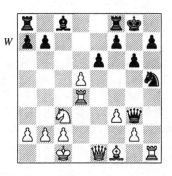

16 ♛e3 **exd5**

After **16...e5** 17 ♖dh4 the black queen is in trouble. Luther points out 17...♗f5 18 ♘e4 ♗xe4 19 ♖g4! ♗xd5 20 ♖xh5.

17 ♘xd5

17 ♖xh5 was tempting, but White correctly figures that he can gain a strong attack without parting with any material.

17 ... **♔h8**

Black can't have enjoyed playing this ugly move, but the problem is that the natural **17...♗e6** would present White with the brilliancy prize after 18 ♖xh5! gxh5 19 ♖g4+!! hxg4 20 ♛g5+ ♔h8 21 ♛f6+ ♔g8 22 ♘e7#.

18 ♖e4!

By opening the long diagonal for the queen White prevents **18...♗e6** which would now lose to 19 ♛c3+.

18 ... **♗f5**
19 ♖e5

Threatening ♖xf5 or ♖xh5.

19 ... **f6!** *(D)*

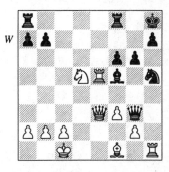

The only chance.

20 ♖e7?

White is bluffed out. **20 ♖xf5!** was still very strong because after **20...gxf5** 21 ♖xh5 ♖ae8, 22 ♘xf6! is immediately decisive. **20...♖ae8** at once is a better try although after 21 ♖fxh5! gxh5 (after 21...♖xe3 22

Rxh7+ Kg8 23 Ne7+! Rxe7 24 Bc4+ White forces mate) 22 Qd4 Re1+ 23 Kd2 Ra1 24 Nc3 Qe1+ 25 Kd3 the black attack has run out of momentum and White remains with his material plus.

| 20 | ... | Rad8 |
| 21 | f4 | |

White sensibly opts for an exchange of queens, avoiding 21 c4 b5! and 21 Qh6 Rf7!.

| 21 | ... | Qxe3+ |

Not 21...Rxd5?? 22 Qxg3 Nxg3 23 Rhxh7+ Kg8 24 Reg7#. The alternative 21...Qg4 loses, but in a less obvious fashion: 22 g3! and now 22...Rxd5 23 Be2 wins as 23...Qxg3 24 Qxg3 leads to the same mate as above, and 22...Bxc2 23 Nc3! defends against Black's threats and prepares Be2.

22	Nxe3	Bc8
23	g4	Ng7
24	Bd3?!	

Luther prefers 24 Bb5, retreating the bishop to d3 only after Black has weakened his queenside with ...a6.

24	...	f5
25	gxf5	gxf5
26	Nc4	Rfe8
27	Ne5	

I believe this is where White let his remaining advantage slip. He should have played 27 Rxe8+ as Black cannot recapture with the rook: 27...Rxe8 28 Nd6 Rf8 29 Rh6 and Black is in virtual zugzwang, not to mention the concrete threat of 28 Bc4. Therefore Black has to play

27...Nxe8 and after 28 Ne5 White retains a nagging edge. His pawn structure is superior and his king is ready for a quick march to the centre.

27	...	Rxe7
28	Ng6+	Kg8
29	Nxe7+	Kh8
30	Rh6	Be6
31	Rf6	Re8
32	Nxf5	Nh5
33	Rh6	Nxf4
34	Be4	Bxf5
35	Bxf5	Re7
36	Kd2	

The game is now level. The simplest would have been 36...Kg7 37 Rxh7+ Kf6 38 Rxe7 Kxe7 with a dead drawn position.

The remainder of the game is given in brief with Black making error after error and somehow contriving to lose an ending that was almost impossible to lose: 36...Kg8 37 c4 Rf7 38 Be4 Re7 39 Bc2 Kf8? 40 Rxh7? (40 Bxh7 would give some chances) 40...Rxh7 41 Bxh7 Ke7 42 Ke3 Nh5 43 Kd4 Nf6 (43...b6!) 44 Bf5 Kd6 45 c5+ Kc6 46 b4 b6 47 Ke5 Ne8 48 Be4+ Kd7 49 b5 Nc7?! (49...bxc5 50 Bc6+ Kd8 51 Bxe8 Kxe8 52 Kd5 Kd7 53 Kxc5 Kc7 54 a4 Kb7 55 a5 a6 =) 50 cxb6 axb6 51 a4 Ke7?? (Black could still have saved himself with a stalemate trick: 51...Kc8 52 Kd6 Kb8 53 Kd7 Ka7! and 54 Ba8 is met by 54...Kb8) 52 Bf5 1-0. Nothing can be done to stop the white king penetrating.

6 Kan Variation

This line, which starts 1 e4 c5 2 ♘f3 e6 3 d4 cxd4 4 ♘xd4 a6, is notable for the flexibility afforded to Black, since by delaying his piece development he keeps the maximum possible range of options open. Because there are many reasonable choices at each move it is pointless to give precise lines against all possible move-orders, so in this chapter there will be a greater emphasis on general principles. The continuation recommended in this chapter, 5 ♗d3, is the most common line in practice. At the moment Black's most popular reply is to set up a 'hedgehog' position by 5...♘f6 6 0-0 d6 (or 6...♕c7 7 ♕e2 d6). After 7 c4 Black may choose to develop his bishop on e7 immediately, but he sometimes brings the queenside out first in order to retain the possibility of ...g6 and ...♗g7. The 'hedgehog' name is derived from the way Black curls up on the first two ranks, moves like ...♘bd7, ...b6, ...♗b7, ...♖e8, ...♕c7, ...♗f8, ...♖ac8 and ...♕b8 being typical. Black's slow development invites White to attack, but experience has shown that the unwary attacker can easily impale himself on Black's spines, and such attacks have to be well-organised if they are to stand much chance of success. Moreover White has to watch out for

Black's ...b5 and ...d5 breaks. Game 19 deals with the lines arising after 5...♘f6, including the 'hedgehog'. All Black's other 5th moves, such as 5...♗c5, 5...♘c6, 5...♘e7 and 5...g6, are in Game 18.

Game 18
Yakovich – Emms
Cappelle la Grande 1993

1	e4	c5
2	♘f3	e6
3	d4	cxd4
4	♘xd4	a6
5	♗d3 *(D)*	

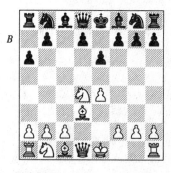

5	...	♗c5

Black's alternatives are arranged in descending order of importance:

1) **5...♘c6** (it is surprising that this solid line is not played more frequently; although the symmetrical position gives Black few winning

chances, it is quite hard for White to prove any advantage) **6 ♘xc6** and now:

1a) **6...dxc6** 7 ♘d2 e5 8 ♕h5 ♗d6 9 ♘c4 ♗c7 (9...♘f6 10 ♘xd6+ ♕xd6 11 ♕e2 ♗e6 12 0-0 gives White the opportunity to make his dark-squared bishop a potent force, as in Jansa-Cebalo, Smederevska Palanka 1978 after 12...♘d7 13 ♖d1 ♕e7 14 b3 0-0 15 a4 a5 16 ♗a3 ♘c5 17 ♗c4!) 10 ♗g5 ♘f6 11 ♕e2 h6 12 ♗h4 ♕e7 13 0-0-0 (13 0-0?! allowed Black to stir up trouble by 13...g5 14 ♗g3 h5 15 f3 h4 in Ligterink-Miles, Lone Pine 1979) 13...♗e6 14 f4 ♗xc4 (14...♗g4 15 ♗xf6 ♗xe2 16 ♗xe7 ♖xd1 17 ♗d6 ♗xd6 18 ♘xd6+ ♔d7 19 ♘xf7 wins material for White) 15 ♗xc4 b5 16 ♗b3 0-0 17 ♗xf6 ♕xf6 18 ♖d7 and White's pressure against f7 gives him an advantage, Tseshkovsky-Miles, Bled-Portorož 1979.

1b) **6...bxc6** (out of favour ever since the famous Fischer-Petrosian game mentioned below) **7 0-0 d5** (7...e5 8 f4 ♗c5+ {8...d6 is more solid} 9 ♔h1 ♘e7 10 ♕h5 ♘g6 11 f5 ♘f4 12 ♗xf4 exf4 13 f6 ♗d4 14 fxg7 ♗xg7 15 ♖xf4 ♕e7 16 ♘c3 is very good for White, Ravinsky-Vorotnikov, USSR 1963, while 7...g6?! 8 e5 ♗g7 9 f4 d6, Van der Wiel-Anand, Thessaloniki OL 1984, should have been met by 10 exd6 ♕xd6 11 ♘d2 ♕d4+ 12 ♔h1 ♘f6 13 ♘c4 ♘d5 14 ♘d6+ ♔e7 15 c3 with a fine position for White) **8 c4 ♘f6 9 cxd5 cxd5 10 exd5 ♘xd5** (10...exd5 11 ♘c3 ♗e7 12 ♕a4+ ♕d7 13 ♖e1!

♕xa4 14 ♘xa4 ♗e6 15 ♗e3 0-0 16 ♗c5 is Fischer-Petrosian, Buenos Aires Ct (7) 1971, which was won by Fischer, while 10...♕xd5 11 ♘c3 ♕d7 12 ♗g5 ♗e7 13 ♕e2 ♗b7 14 ♖ac1 0-0 15 ♖fd1, although keeping Black's pawns intact, gave White a dangerous initiative in Mikhalchishin-Gorchakov, USSR 1972) **11 ♗e4** *(D)* and now:

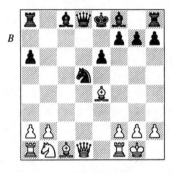

1b1) **11...♖b8** 12 ♕f3 f5 13 ♗xd5 ♕xd5 14 ♕xd5 exd5 15 ♖d1 ♗e6 16 ♘c3 ♖d8 17 ♗g5 ♖d7 18 ♘e2 gives White the better ending.

1b2) **11...♗e7** 12 ♘c3 ♗b7 13 ♕a4+ ♕d7 14 ♕xd7+ ♔xd7 15 ♖d1 is also promising after **15...♖ad8** 16 ♘xd5 ♗xd5 17 ♗xd5 exd5 18 ♖xd5+ ♔e6 19 ♖xd8 ♖xd8 20 ♗e3, Matanović-Roos, Le Havre 1966, or alternatively **15...♗f6** 16 ♘xd5 ♗xd5 17 ♗xd5 exd5 18 ♖xd5+ ♔e6 19 ♖d2 ♖hd8 20 ♖e2+, Averbakh-Taimanov, USSR Ch 1960.

1b3) **11...♖a7** 12 ♕d4 ♖d7 13 ♘c3 ♘xc3 (13...♗b7 14 ♘xd5 ♗xd5 15 ♗xd5 ♖xd5 16 ♕a4+ wins the a-pawn) 14 ♕xc3 and Black's uncastled king gives him plenty of problems, Beliavsky-Kurajica, Sarajevo 1982.

2) **5...g6 6 c4 ♗g7** (this is an attempt to reach a kind of hedgehog position, but with the bishop more actively deployed at g7) **7 ♘b3** *(D)* and now:

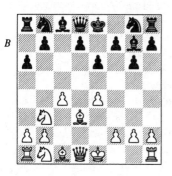

2a) **7...♘e7 8 ♘c3 0-0** (8...d5 9 cxd5 exd5 10 ♗g5 h6 11 ♗xe7 ♗xc3+ 12 bxc3 ♕xe7 13 0-0 dxe4 14 ♗xe4 0-0 15 ♖e1 and White has a big lead in development, Donchev-Prié, Toulon 1988) 9 0-0 ♘bc6 10 ♗e2 b6 (10...f5 11 c5 b6 12 cxb6 ♕xb6 13 ♗e3 ♕d8 was unclear in Psakhis-Oratovsky, Tel Aviv 1993 but perhaps 11 exf5 is better) 11 ♗g5 h6 12 ♗e3 f5 13 ♕d2 ♔h7 14 f3 with an edge for White, Anand-Bologan, Calcutta 1992.

2b) **7...d6 8 ♘c3 ♘f6 9 ♗f4** (9 0-0 followed by ♗f4 transposes to lines given in Game 19, but White can do better here because Black has no time for ...♘c6 and ...♘e8) 9...0-0 10 ♗e2 e5 (10...♘e8 11 c5 is particularly unpleasant when Black's queen is undefended) 11 ♗e3 ♗e6 12 0-0 ♘c6 13 f3 ♖c8 14 ♖c1, with a

favourable position for White in the game Ljubojević-Rajković, Yugoslavia 1980. The plan of directly attacking the d-pawn by ♗f4 and ♗e2 is a logical way to exploit Black's ...♗g7, and in this case it gives White the advantage.

3) **5...♘e7** (Black aims to play ...♘c6, but only when he can recapture with a piece) and now:

3a) **6 0-0 ♘ec6** (or 6...g6 7 c4 ♗g7 8 ♗e3 ♘bc6 9 ♘xc6 bxc6 {9...♘xc6 ± is better} 10 c5! ♗xb2 11 ♘d2 0-0, Topalov-J.Polgar, Las Palmas 1994, and now 12 ♗h6 ♗g7 13 ♗xg7 ♔xg7 14 ♘c4 would have given White a permanent positional bind) 7 c3 ♗e7 8 ♗e3 0-0 9 f4 d6 10 ♘f3 ♘d7 11 ♘bd2 gave White a small but enduring plus in Georgiev-Peev, Bulgarian Ch 1980/1.

3b) **6 ♘c3 ♘ec6 7 ♘b3 ♗e7 8 ♕h5!** d6 9 ♗e3 ♘d7 10 f4 b5 11 0-0-0 b4?! 12 ♘a4! e5 13 f5 0-0 14 g4! gave White an automatic attack, Mikhalchishin-Dorfman, Lvov 1983.

4) **5...♕c7 6 0-0** and now Black can transpose into Game 19 by **6...♘f6**, or try:

4a) **6...♘c6?!** 7 ♘xc6 ♕xc6 (or else Black has an inferior version of variation 1 above) 8 c4 (8 ♘d2 is probably also good) 8...g6 9 ♘c3 ♗g7 10 ♖e1 ♘e7 11 ♗g5 d6 12 ♕d2 with a very good position for White.

4b) **6...♗c5 7 ♘b3 ♗e7 8 ♕g4** (White could also develop normally) **8...♘f6** and now:

4b1) Nunn-I.Gurevich, Hastings 1992/3 continued 9 ♘c3 h5 10 ♕e2

♘c6 11 f4 d6 12 ♗e3 (12 ♗d2 may be better) 12...♗xc3 13 bxc3 ♘f6 with an unclear game.

4b2) In his notes to the game Gurevich gives **9 ♗f4!?** h5 (forced) 10 ♕g3 h4 11 ♕g4 ♗e5 12 ♗xe5 ♕xe5 13 ♘c3 ♘f6 **14 ♕xg7 ♖g8** 15 ♕h6 ♕xh2+ 16 ♔xh2 ♘g4+ 17 ♔h1 ♘xh6 as equal, but I (JG) don't see what's wrong with **14 ♕e2** when White has a healthy lead in development and will be able to gain further time with f4.

5) **5...b6 6 0-0 ♗b7 7 ♘c3** (7 c4 also led to a good game for White in Benjamin-Dizdarević, Manila OL 1992 after 7...d6 8 f4 ♘d7 9 ♘c3 g6 10 f5 ♗g7 11 ♗c2 ♕e7 12 fxe6 fxe6 13 ♘f3! ♘gf6 14 ♗f4 e5 15 ♗g5) **7...d6 8 f4** *(D)* and now:

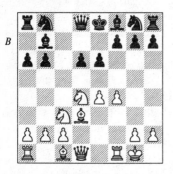

5a) **8...♘d7?** 9 f5 e5 10 ♘e6! (the main drawback of the early queenside fianchetto is that it weakens e6) 10...fxe6 (10...♕c8 11 ♘d5! is very strong as 11...fxe6 loses to 12 ♕h5+ ♔d8 13 fxe6 ♘df6 14 ♕f7 and 11...♗xd5 12 exd5 fxe6 13 ♕h5+ ♔d8 14 fxe6 ♘df6 15 ♕f7 ♘e7 16 ♗g5 is also winning for

White) 11 ♕h5+ g6 (11...♔e7 12 fxe6 g6 13 ♗g5+ ♘df6 14 ♕f3 ♗g7 15 ♘d5+ ♗xd5 16 exd5 leaves Black in a terrible tangle) 12 fxg6 ♘gf6 13 g7+ ♘xh5 14 gxh8♕ ♕e7 15 ♕g8 and Black had no real compensation for the exchange in Fogarasi-Portisch, Hungary 1994.

5b) On **8...♘f6**, Fogarasi recommends 9 g4! and after 9...d5 10 e5 ♘e4 11 ♕f3 ♗xc3 12 bxc3 ♘d7 13 ♗d2 ♗e7 14 ♖ae1 White has a clear advantage.

6) **5...b5** 6 0-0 ♗b7 7 a4 b4 8 ♘d2 ♘e7 9 f4 ♘ec6 10 ♘4f3 d6 11 ♕e1 with advantage to White, Wedberg-Dzindzihashvili, New York 1991. One of the main advantages of 5 ♗d3 as opposed to 5 ♘c3 is that an early ...b5 by Black is hardly ever a worry, since White may undermine Black's queenside pawns by a4 without fearing a loss of time after ...b4.

7) **5...♕b6** 6 c3! d6 (6...♘c6 7 0-0 ♘xd4 8 cxd4 ♕xd4 9 ♘c3 is dangerous for Black) 7 0-0 ♘f6 8 a4 ♗e7 9 ♘d2 ♕c7 10 a5 0-0 11 ♘c4 ♘bd7 12 ♕e2 ♖e8 13 ♗g5! ♗f8?! (13...h6 14 ♗h4 b5 is just slightly better for White) 14 ♗h4 with a good game for White, Lazić-Martinović, Yugoslavia 1987.

6 ♘b3   ♗a7

6...♗b6 is also possible but then Black will have little choice but to exchange on e3.

6...♗e7 appears from time to time, the idea being akin to that of the ...♕b6, ...♕c7 ploy seen in many lines of the Sicilian, namely to force the knight to retreat from its active central post. White can try **7 ♕g4** but the simplest seems to develop normally. For example **7 0-0 d6 8 c4** followed by ♘c3, f4, ♔h1, etc.

7 ♕e2

7 0-0 ♘c6 8 ♕g4 *(D)*, hoping to take advantage of the fact that the dark-squared bishop has deserted the kingside, is worthy of attention.

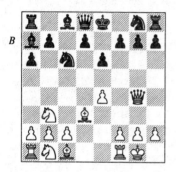

Black has:

1) **8...♕f6 9 ♘c3 ♘ge7 10 ♗g5 ♕g6 11 ♕h4** (*ECO* assesses this position as ±) and now in Popović-Schlosser, Brno 1992 Black produced a real howler, 11...♘e5??, with the obvious idea of 12 ♗xe7?? ♘f3+ but after 12 ♗e2! he felt obliged to resign as he couldn't deal with the double threat of 13 ♗xe7 and 13 ♗h5.

2) **8...♘f6! 9 ♕xg7** (9 ♕g3 or 9 ♕h4 are reasonable alternatives) **9...♖g8 10 ♕h6** and now:

2a) **10...♘e5 11 ♗e2! b5** (11...d5 12 ♘c3 dxe4 13 ♗g5 ♖g6 14 ♕h4 ♗d7 15 ♘xe4 ♗c6 16 ♗xf6! and White was already winning in Hellers-Sjöberg, Malmö 1994) **12 ♗g5** (Ljubojević gives 12 ♗e3 ♖g6 13

♕h3 as a clear advantage for White, but perhaps Black can try 13...♘xe4 since 14 ♗xa7 ♖xa7 15 ♕e3 is met by ♕g5! when 16 ♕xe4 loses after 16...♗b7! and 16 ♕xg5 ♘xg5 17 f4? ♘h3+ 18 ♔h1 ♗b7! is also immediately decisive) 12...♖g6 13 ♕h4 ♗b7 14 ♘1d2 h6 (or 14...♖c8 15 c3 ± Oll-Stangl, Tilburg 1994) 15 ♗xf6 ♖xf6, Ljubojević-Lobron, Plovdiv 1983, when Ljubojević gives **16 c3** as ±, but I like **16 a4** as 16...b4 can be met by 17 ♘a5!.

2b) **10...♖g6 11 ♕h3 e5!** led to a draw by repetition in J.Horvath-Farago, Budapest 1987 after 12 ♕h4 ♖g4 13 ♕h6 ♖g6 **14 ♕h4**, etc. and it has to be said that it would be extremely risky for White to try to continue the game. For example, if he continues **14 ♕d2**, then 14...d6 (threatening ...♗h3) 15 ♔h1 ♘g4 looks very strong as 16 g3 is met by 16...♘xh2! 17 ♔xh2 ♕d7! and 16 h3 ♕h4! looks crushing. To sum up, this could be an interesting line to have in your repertoire if you are willing to take the risk of a quick draw.

7 ...   ♘c6

8 ♗e3 *(D)*

8 ...   ♘f6

Up until about four years ago Black regularly exchanged bishops on e3, but since then he has almost invariably invited White to exchange bishops on a7, in the belief that his rook will be more active on the second rank. Perhaps this is just a quirk of fashion so we still have to examine the older lines in some detail:

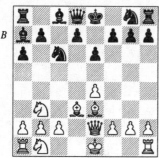

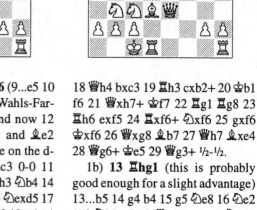

1) **8...⌴xe3 9 ⌴xe3 d6** (9...e5 10 ⌺c3 ⌺ge7 11 0-0-0 d6, Wahls-Far-ago, Altensteig 1987, and now 12 ⌳d2 followed by ⌳hd1 and ⌴e2 creates awkward pressure on the d-file and 9...⌺ge7 10 ⌺c3 0-0 11 0-0-0 ⌴c7 12 f4 d6 13 ⌴h3 ⌺b4 14 ⌳hf1! e5 15 f5 d5 16 exd5 ⌺exd5 17 ⌺xd5 ⌺xd5 18 ⌴h4 ⌺f6 19 g4 e4 20 g5 exd3 21 ⌳xd3 ⌴e5 22 gxf6 ⌴xf6 23 ⌴xf6 gxf6 24 ⌳d6 gave White a very good ending in Korlov-Batakov, Corr 1984) **10 ⌺c3 ⌺f6 11 0-0-0 0-0** (moves such as 11...b5 and 11...⌴c7 are well met by 12 g4 and 11...e5 led to a promising position for White in Lekander-Schoneberg, Corr 1980 after 12 ⌳d2 ⌴e6 13 ⌳hd1 ⌴c7 14 ⌴e2 ⌳d8 15 g4! 0-0 16 ⌴g3 ⌴xb3 17 cxb3! ⌺d4 18 ⌺b1 b5 19 ⌴d3 ⌴c6 20 f3 ⌳fe8 21 ⌴g2 b4 22 g5!) **12 f4 ⌴c7** *(D)* and White has a number of attacking ideas:

1a) **13 ⌴h3 ⌺b4 14 g4 b5 15 g5 ⌺xd3+** (15...⌺e8 16 ⌴h4 f6 17 a3 fxg5 18 fxg5 ⌺xd3+ 19 ⌳xd3 ⌳b8 was unclear in Vogt-Velikov, E.Ger-many-Bulgaria 1987) 16 ⌳xd3 ⌺e8 17 f5 b4 led to a sharp finish in Bron-stein-Suetin, Moscow Ch 1982 after

18 ⌴h4 bxc3 19 ⌳h3 cxb2+ 20 ⌺b1 f6 21 ⌴xh7+ ⌺f7 22 ⌳g1 ⌳g8 23 ⌳h6 exf5 24 ⌳xf6+ ⌺xf6 25 gxf6 ⌺xf6 26 ⌴xg8 ⌴b7 27 ⌴h7 ⌴xe4 28 ⌴g6+ ⌺e5 29 ⌴g3+ ½-½.

1b) **13 ⌳hg1** (this is probably good enough for a slight advantage) 13...b5 14 g4 b4 15 g5 ⌺e8 16 ⌺e2 (16 ⌺b1 a5 17 ⌳g4!? a4 18 ⌺3d2 ⌴a6 19 ⌴xa6 ⌳xa6 20 ⌳h4 g6 21 ⌴h3 f5 22 gxf6 ⌳xf6 23 ⌺c4 may be slightly better for White, Wed-berg-Spraggett, New York Open 1987) 16...⌴a7 (16...a5 17 ⌺bd4 ⌺xd4 18 ⌴xd4 ⌴a6 19 ⌺b1 was a little better for White in Arnason-Suetin, Sochi 1980) 17 ⌴h3! g6 18 f5 exf5 19 exf5 ⌺e7 20 ⌺g3! ⌴e3+?! (20...a5 is better, but still favours White) 21 ⌺b1 ⌴xf5 22 ⌴xf5 ⌺xf5 23 ⌳de1 ⌴f4 24 ⌳gf1 ⌴h4 25 ⌴xh4 ⌺xh4 26 ⌳e4 with an excellent ending for White, Arnason-Kirov, Plovdiv 1986.

1c) **13 g4** with a further branch:

1c1) Accepting the offer must be a critical test of White's willingness to play g4 without the preparatory ⌳hg1. In Short-Velikov, European Club Ch 1987 the continuation was

13...♘xg4 14 ♕g3 ♘f6 15 ♖hg1 ♘e8 **16 ♔b1** (16 f5!? is natural) 16...♘e7?! (16...b5 and 16...f6 have been suggested as possible improvements) 17 ♘d4 ♕c5 18 ♘f3 f6 19 e5! with a very strong attack for White. Velikov must have found an improvement because he repeated this line in a later game Ivanović-Velikov, Saint John Open 1988. Unfortunately Ivanović varied by **16 ♕h4**, so we don't know what Velikov's intention was. Despite this hint, I (JN) believe White has good compensation for the pawn and it would require a brave player to take this line on as Black.

1c2) **13...b5 14 g5 ♘d7 15 f5!? b4 16 ♘e2 a5** (positions in which the players are attacking on opposite wings are extremely difficult to assess; unless one of the players is well in front it is likely that a single tempo will decide the race and obscure tactical points will often have a crucial influence on the play) **17 ♕h3** (attacking e6 directly, and generating a concealed threat to h7) **17...exf5 18 exf5 ♘de5 19 ♘f4** (the pin along the c8-h3 diagonal is awkward for White and bringing the knight to d5 is the only way to make progress) **19...a4 20 ♘d5 ♕d8** (now that b3 and g5 are under attack, White is committed to the sacrificial path) **21 ♖hg1!** *(D)* and now:

1c21) In the game Kengis-Nevednichy, USSR 1979 Black continued **21...♘xd3+?** (eliminating one of the attacking pieces, but in doing so activating the d1-rook) 22 ♖xd3

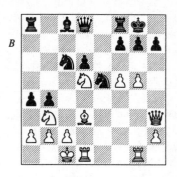

♘e5 (now White wins by force) 23 ♘f6+ gxf6 24 ♕h6! (24 gxf6+ ♘g6 repulses the attack) 24...♘xd3+ (now 24...♘g6 loses to 25 ♖h3 ♖e8 26 fxg6 fxg6 27 ♕xh7+ ♔f8 28 ♕h8+ whilst 24...♔h8 25 ♖h3 ♗xf5 26 g6! ♗xg6 27 ♖xg6 is also mate) 25 ♔b1! (Black was hoping for 25 cxd3 ♔h8 when 26 gxf6 ♖g8 27 ♖g7 ♗xf5 defends, as does 26 g6 fxg6 27 fxg6 ♕c7+ and 28...♕g7) 25...fxg5 (25...♔h8 26 g6 fxg6 27 fxg6 threatens both 28 ♕xh7# and 28 g7+, while 25...♕b6 26 ♖g3 only makes matters worse) 26 f6 ♕xf6 27 ♕xf6 g4 (although rook, bishop and two pawns amount to enough material to balance a queen, Black still suffers from his bad king position) 28 ♕g5+ ♔h8 29 ♕f6+ ♔g8 30 ♘d4 ♘e5 31 h3 (intending 32 hxg4 followed by ♘f5) 31...h5 32 ♕g5+ ♘g6 33 ♕xh5 gxh3 34 ♕d5 (attacking a8 and g8) 34...♗e6 35 ♘xe6 h2 36 ♖xg6+ 1-0 (36...fxg6 37 ♘xf8+ and ♕xa8 wins all the black pieces). An extremely energetic performance from White.

1c22) Black's best defence is **21...axb3! 22 ♘f6+ gxf6 23 ♕h6!**

(23 gxf6+ ♘g6 leads nowhere as the f5-pawn is pinned while 24 ♕h6 ♕xf6 25 fxg6 fxg6 26 ♗xg6 ♕f4+ 27 ♕xf4 ♖xf4 28 ♗e8+ ♔f8 29 ♗xc6 bxa2 30 ♔d2 ♖d4+ wins for Black) **23...♘g6!** (23...♔h8 24 gxf6 ♖g8 25 ♖g7 ♘xd3+ 26 ♖xd3 ♗xf5 27 ♖h3! results in mate at h7) **24 fxg6 fxg6 25 ♗xg6 ♖a7! 26 gxf6 hxg6** (26...♕xf6 27 ♗xh7+ ♔h8 28 ♖g8+! ♖xg8 29 ♗g6+ mates, or 27...♔f7 28 ♖df1) **27 ♖xg6+** (27 ♕xg6+ ♔h8 leads to nothing as the d1 rook cannot reach the h-file, ♖d5 being met by ...♘e5) **27...♔f7** *(D)* reaching a remarkable position in which it appears that White must mate, but it isn't certain that he can do so.

1c221) In the second edition I (JN) commented that I couldn't see a mate after **28 ♖g7+ ♔e6** (28...♔e8 29 ♕e3+ ♘e5 30 ♕xa7 ♕xf6 31 axb3 is very good for White, with material equality but weak black pawns and an exposed black king) 29 ♕h3+ ♔xf6 30 ♕h6+ ♔e5 (after 30...♔f5 31 ♖g2! White does mate), for example 31 ♖g3 ♗f5 32 c4

♗e4!. I still don't see a mate, (nor can Fritz – JG) and nobody wrote to me suggesting one.

1c222) If we return to the position after 27...♔f7 White can gain a massive advantage by **28 ♖e1 ♘e5 29 ♖g7+ ♔e6** (29...♔e8 30 ♖xa7 ♕xf6 31 ♕h5+ ♔d8 32 axb3 is similar) 30 ♖xa7 bxa2 (30...♕xf6 31 ♕h3+ and ♕xb3+) 31 ♕h3+ ♔d5 32 ♕b3+ ♔c6 33 ♕xa2, with a slight material plus for White together with a raging attack.

2) Black can also develop his knight to e7 rather than f6. Against this plan we are recommending that White castles short, not getting involved in the habitual pawn storming competition as his attack won't have as much momentum without a knight on f6 for the g-pawn to sink its teeth into. Moreover with the knight on e7 Black won't have as much control over squares like h5 and g4, both in the vicinity of his castled king, so White may be able to develop an attack merely by piece play; and if he's not going to pawn-storm, his own king will be much safer on the kingside, well out of the way of Black's queenside counter-play. A good example of this strategy is the game Kindermann-Zso.Polgar, Münster 1994: **8...♘ge7** (if Black refuses to commit this knight then White can also wait, playing moves like 9 ♘c3 and 10 f4 before deciding on which side to castle) 9 ♘c3 ♕c7 (9...d6 10 f4 0-0 11 ♗xa7 ♖xa7 12 0-0 b5 13 ♖ae1 leads to very similar play) 10 f4 d6 11 ♗xa7 (perhaps this

exchange could have been made earlier) 11...♖xa7 12 0-0 b5 13 ♖ae1 b4 14 ♘d1 0-0 15 ♘e3 d5 16 e5 f5 17 exf6 ♖xf6 18 ♕h5 g6 19 ♕g5 ♖f7 20 ♘g4 and White had a clear positional advantage as well as good attacking chances against the black king.

9 ♘c3   d6 (D)

10 0-0-0   b5

10...0-0 11 f4 e5 12 ♗xa7 ♖xa7 13 f5 b5 transposes back into the main game, but in Spraggett-Illescas, Spain 1994 White tried **13 ♕f2!?** and achieved some advantage after **13...♘g4?!** 14 ♕g3 exf4 15 ♕xf4 ♘ge5 16 ♗e2! b5 17 ♘d4 ♘xd4 18 ♖xd4 ♗e6 19 ♖hd1, but Black would have done better to play **13...exf4**.

11 ♗xa7

White should make this exchange sooner rather then later, for example **11 f4 b4 12 ♘a4 ♗d7 13 ♗xa7?** loses a piece after **13...♘xa7!**. This is precisely what happened to Michael Adams in his game against Hjartarson from the Paris leg of the 1994 Intel Rapid Grand Prix, with

the slight difference that the black knight was on e7 instead of f6.

11 ...   ♖xa7
12 f4   b4

When Black has exchanged on e3 he usually meets the threat of e5 by playing ...♕c7, but with the rook on a7 this would seriously hamper the co-ordination of his forces; therefore he has to play ...e5 himself, but first he should drive the white knight away from its control of d5. Neglecting to do so leads to a good game for White, for example: **12...e5** 13 f5 b4 (or 13...0-0 14 g4 ♘d4?, Yudasin-Nikolaev, Podolsk 1991 and now White should have played 15 ♘xd4 exd4 16 ♕f2! when 16...♕b6 17 ♖hg1! followed by ♘e2 and 16...♘xg4 17 ♕xd4 are both very good for him) 14 ♘d5 ♘xd5 15 exd5 and now Yudasin considers **15...♕g5+** 16 ♔b1 ♘e7 17 h4!, **15...♘a5** 16 ♘xa5 ♕xa5 17 ♔b1 ♕xd5 18 ♗e4 ♕c5 19 ♖d5 ♕b6 20 ♖hd1 ♖d7 21 f6! and **15...♘e7** 16 f6! gxf6 17 ♕f2 all to be in White's favour.

13 ♘a4

This is of course a very double-edged square for the knight, but the alternative, **15 ♘b1**, allows Black an automatic attack by ...a5-a4 etc.

13 ...   e5
14 f5   0-0

The immediate **14...♗d7** would be met by 15 ♕e3.

15 g4

This doesn't require any explanation.

15 ...   ♗d7

16	g5	♘e8
17	♕e3!	

White is now threatening to solve all his problems by playing 18 ♘b6, so Black has no choice but to give up his a-pawn. 17 ♖hg1, ignoring the plight of the knight on a4 in favour of an immediate kingside attack has also been tried. Icelandic Grandmaster Stefansson analysed the position to a draw: 17...♘b8! 18 ♕h5 ♗xa4 19 ♖g3 ♗b5 (19...♘d7 20 ♗c4) 20 ♖h3 h6 21 ♖g1! (in Prié-Stefansson, Reykjavik 1993 White played the awful 21 f6?? and was lost after 21...♘xf6 22 gxf6 ♕xf6) 21...♕b6 22 ♖g2 f6 23 gxh6 ♗xd3 24 cxd3 ♖c7+ 25 ♔b1 ♘c6 26 hxg7 ♖xg7 27 ♕h7+ ♔f7 28 ♖xg7+ ♘xg7 29 ♕g6+ ♔g8 30 ♕h7+ with perpetual check.

17	...	♖b7
18	♗xa6 *(D)*	

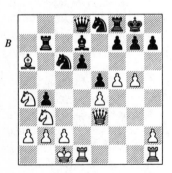

18	...	♖b8

Although this position has been reached on several occasions nobody has played (or considered in their notes) 18...♖a7, which appears to me at least as critical as the text.

After **19 ♗b5** (not 19 ♕b6? ♕a8) **19...♘d4 20 ♗xd7 ♕xd7 21 ♘b6 ♕c6!**, White is forced to play **22 ♖xd4!**, although this does seem to be good enough for some advantage, e.g.:

1) **22...♕xb6 23 ♖d3 ♕a6** (the line 23...♕xe3+ 24 ♖xe3 ♖xa2 25 ♖d1 is excellent for White) 24 ♕e1! so that moves such as ...♕c4 or ...♖c7 can be met by ♔b1 followed by ♘c1 if Black attacks a2 again.

2) **22...exd4 23 ♕xd4 ♖c7** (after 23...♖xa2 24 ♔b1 followed by ♘d5 White has tremendous play for the exchange) and now **24 c3 bxc3 25 bxc3 ♕xc3+ 26 ♕xc3 ♖xc3+ 27 ♔d2** is unclear, so White should probably swallow his pride and play **24 ♘a1**. Of course this is not an ideal square for the knight but Black's kingside pieces are also in a bit of a huddle and White is hoping to relieve the pressure on the c-file by ♘d5, thereby enabling him to return the knight on a1 to a more desirable square. There is also no need to fear 24...b3 as after 25 axb3 ♖a7 White can block the a-file with 26 ♘a4.

19	♗c4! *(D)*	

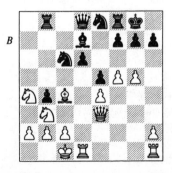

Much stronger than the previously played 19 ♕d2 or 19 ♔b1. White wastes no time placing his bishop on its most effective diagonal, thereby creating dangerous kingside threats based on g5-g6.

19 ... ♔h8

Black removes his king from the sensitive diagonal as after **19...♘d4** 20 g6! ♘f6 (20...♗xa4 21 gxf7+ is good for White) 21 gxf7+ ♔h8 22 ♘xd4 exd4 23 ♖xd4 ♗xa4 24 e5 White's attack crashes through the middle. Nor can he block the g-pawn's advance with **19...g6** as the opening of the h-file by 20 fxg6 hxg6 21 h4! and h5 will prove far more important than any piece that may be lost on the queenside.

20 ♕d2!

A very good move, introducing ideas of ♘ac5 and defusing the threat of ...♘d4, which can now be met by 21 ♘xd4 exd4 22 b3 as the queen will not be *en prise* as it would have been on e3.

20 ... ♘a5

The alternative is **20...♖a8** when 21 ♘ac5! ♖xa2 22 ♔b1 ♖a7 23 ♘xd7 ♕xd7 24 ♕f2! followed by ♖d3-h3 should be very good for White.

21 ♘xa5 ♕xa5

22 b3 ♖c8 *(D)*

After **22...♗xa4** 23 bxa4 ♕xa4 24 ♖hg1! White's attack will triumph as he is able to combine attack and defence. A possible continuation: 24...♘c7 25 ♖g3 ♘b5 26 ♗xb5 ♖xb5 27 ♕xd6 ♖g8 28 ♖h3 ♕xa2 29 g6! and White wins because **29...fxg6** loses to 30 ♖xh7+!, **29...h6**

to 30 ♖xh6+! and **29...♖e8** to 30 ♕d7.

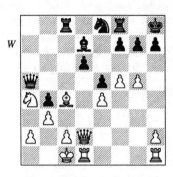

23 ♕d5!

Now Black will even be denied the pleasure of dreaming about an attack on the white king. As the ending is completely hopeless he is forced to retreat leaving White with an extra pawn and a positional bind. The game is essentially decided.

23 ... ♕a7

24 ♔b1 ♕e3

25 ♖he1!

White temporarily returns the pawn in order to simplify into a technically won position.

25 ... ♕xg5

26 ♘b6 ♗c6

27 ♕a5 ♕d8

28 ♗d5! ♗xd5

On **28...♘f6**, White wins by 29 ♕xb4 ♖b8 30 ♗xc6 ♖xb6 31 ♗b5! followed by a4.

29 ♖xd5 ♖c6

30 ♘c4 ♕h4

The queen returns to the kingside in search of counterplay as the ending after **30...♘f6** 31 ♕xd8 ♖xd8 32 ♘xe5! is lost.

31	♕xb4	♕xh2
32	♖c1!	♔g8

Leaving aside the fact that **32...h5** allows 33 ♘xe5, it would be dangerous for Black to push his h-pawn with all four rooks on the board as White may be able to start an attack with ♖dd1 and ♖h1.

33	♘xd6	♖xd6
34	♖xd6	♘xd6
35	♕xd6	h5
36	a4 (D)	

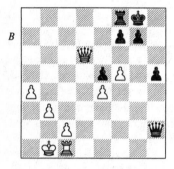

This sort of pawn race is not uncommon in the Sicilian, usually resulting in both players having to give up their rook for the opposing passed pawn. Here, this will mean that White's b-pawn will be left to carry the day.

36	...	h4
37	a5	h3
38	a6	♕f4
39	♕d5	h2
40	a7!	♕xc1+
41	♔xc1	h1♕+
42	♔b2	

Black won the race but loses the game. His next move slightly accelerates his resignation.

42	...	g5
43	fxg6	♔g7
44	a8♕	♖xa8
45	♕xf7+!	1-0

Game 19
Nunn – Gheorghiu
Hamburg 1984

1	e4	c5
2	♘f3	e6
3	d4	cxd4
4	♘xd4	a6
5	♗d3	♘f6
6	0-0 (D)	

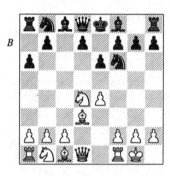

| 6 | ... | d6 |

6...d5 7 e5 is very bad for Black since the natural 7...♘fd7 loses to 8 ♘xe6!.

The surprising move **6...e5** was unveiled in Fedorowicz-Dorfman, New York 1989, and now 7 ♗g5! exd4 (7...h6 8 ♗xf6 ♕xf6 9 ♘e2 d6 10 ♘bc3 ♗e6 11 f4 is good for White) 8 e5 ♗e7 (8...♕a5 9 ♗d2! and 8...h6 9 exf6 hxg5 10 ♖e1+ are very bad for Black) 9 exf6 ♗xf6 10 ♗xf6 ♕xf6 11 ♖e1+ ♔f8 12 ♗e4 is a little better for White since Black will still have an isolated pawn after White regains the front d-pawn.

Black has a major alternative in **6...♕c7 7 ♕e2** *(D)* (7 c4 ♘c6 8 ♘xc6 dxc6 is now considered satisfactory for Black because White has spent a move on c4, which in this position only serves to weaken d4) and now we examine several possibilities which are distinct to an early ...♕c7:

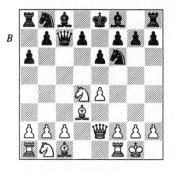

1) **7...♘c6** is bad because of 8 ♘xc6 and 9 e5.

2) **7...♗c5** is (or was) a speciality of Eingorn and I.Gurevich but it has now been discovered that the simple 8 ♘b3 ♗a7 (8...♗e7 is also met by 9 e5; for example, 9...♘d5 10 c4 ♘b4 11 ♗f4 ♘xd3 12 ♕xd3 with a clear advantage for White) 9 e5! gives White an edge. Ulybin-I.Gurevich, Santiago jr Wch 1990 continued 9...♘d5 10 c4 ♘b4 11 ♗f4 ♘xd3 (11...♘8c6 12 ♘1d2 ♘xd3 13 ♕xd3 f5 14 ♕g3 0-0 15 c5! was very good for White in Kudrin-I.Gurevich, Philadelphia 1990) 12 ♕xd3 f6 (otherwise Black will suffocate) 13 ♕f3! (better than 13 ♕g3 g5!) 13...fxe5 14 ♕h5+ g6 15 ♕xe5 ♕xe5

16 ♗xe5 0-0, and now White should have played 17 ♘c3 as **17...b5** 18 cxb5 axb5 19 ♘xb5 ♗a6 20 a4 doesn't give Black enough for the pawn and **17...♘c6** 18 ♗d6 ♖f5 19 ♘e4 leaves him struggling to complete his development.

3) **7...♗d6** 8 ♔h1 ♘c6 9 c3 (9 ♘xc6 dxc6 10 f4 e5 11 f5 also gives White an edge according to Anand) 9...♘e5 10 f4 ♘xd3 11 ♕xd3 ♗e7 12 c4! d6 13 ♘c3 0-0 14 b3 and White's extra space gave him some advantage in Anand-Ljubojević, Linares 1993.

4) **7...d6 8 c4 g6** (8...♗e7 will be similar to the main line) has become quite a popular way for Black to play. The kingside fianchetto reduces White's prospects of a direct kingside attack but on the other hand d6 is weakened. **9 ♘c3** (it is also worth considering b3 and ♗b2) **9...♗g7 10 ♖d1** (White's idea is to attack d6 by ♘f3, ♗f4, ♖ac1 and ♗b1) **10...0-0 11 ♘f3** *(D)* (11 ♗c2 is less accurate; the bishop is better placed on b1 so White should not retreat it until he has played ♖ac1) and now:

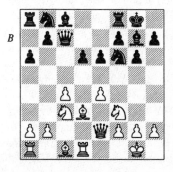

4a) **11...♘c6** and now there is a further branch:

4a1) **12 ♗f4 e5!?** (12...♘g4 13 ♖ac1 ♘ge5 14 ♕e3!? ♕e7 15 ♗e2 ♗d7 16 ♘e1! ♖ad8 17 ♗h6 was already very pleasant for White in Milos-Motwani, Manila OL 1992; Black should probably have played 14...♘xd3 with just an edge for White) 13 ♗e3 ♗g4 is a new idea from Black who hopes to equalise the game by gaining control of d4. After 14 h3 ♘d4 (14...♗xf3 15 ♕xf3 ♘d7 16 ♘d5 ♕d8 17 b4! {preventing the d7-knight reaching e6 and d4 via c5} 17...♘d4 18 ♕g3 gave White an edge in Kotronias-Stefansson, Komotini 1993) 15 ♗xd4 exd4 16 ♘d5 ♗xf3 17 ♕xf3 a draw was agreed in Almasi-Farago, Hungary 1992, although White still has at least a small edge.

4a2) **12 h3!?** avoids the above simplifications and is in fact quite a useful waiting move. For example, 12...♘d7 13 ♗e3 (now that Black has committed himself to the ...♘d7-e5 manoeuvre there is no need for White to play ♗f4) 13...b6 14 ♖ac1 ♗b7 15 ♗b1 ♘ce5 16 ♘xe5 ♘xe5 17 b3 ♖fe8 18 ♕d2 ♗f8 19 ♘a4 ♘d7 20 ♘xb6! (an important tactical point which is also relevant to the very similar lines considered in '4b') 20...♘xb6 21 ♕a5 ♘d5 22 ♖xd5! gave White a clear advantage in Luther-Von Gleich, Bonn 1993.

4b) **11...♘bd7 12 ♗f4 ♘g4** (another way to relieve the pressure on d6 is 12...♘h5, one example being Gallagher-Goldstern, Bad Zurzach

1995 which continued 13 ♗e3 b6 14 ♕d2 ♖e8 15 ♗e2 ♗f8 16 ♗h6 ♗e7 17 ♗g5 ♘hf6 18 ♖ac1 ♗b7 19 ♕f4 ♔g7 20 ♕h4 with an edge for White) **13 ♖ac1 ♘ge5 14 b3** (14 ♘xe5!? ♘xe5 15 ♗e3 ♗d7 16 f4 ♘xd3 17 ♕xd3 ♖fd8 18 ♕xd6 ♕xc4 19 ♗b6 ♗f8 20 ♕d4! ♕c8 21 ♔h1 won for White in Moutousis-Van Wely, Dortmund 1992 but Black's play was poor; 14...dxe5 seems the most obvious alternative) **14...b6 15 ♗b1** *(D)* and now:

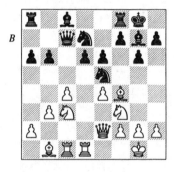

4b1) **15...♗b7?** (if Black wishes to avoid the exchange on f3 he should play 15...♖e8) 16 ♕d2! (this move unexpectedly wins a pawn) 16...♖fc8 (after 16...♘xf3+ 17 gxf3 ♘e5 18 ♕xd6 ♘xf3+ 19 ♔g2 ♘h4+ 20 ♔g3!, 20...♕xd6 loses the exchange and on 20...♕c8 White can play 21 ♔xh4 with impunity) 17 ♕xd6 ♕xd6 18 ♖xd6 ♘xf3+ 19 gxf3 ♗c6 20 ♘e2 left Black with no compensation for the pawn in Armas-Bosboom, Groningen 1991.

4b2) **15...♘xf3+ 16 ♕xf3 ♘e5 17 ♕e2 ♗b7** (17...♖b8 is similar) **18 ♕d2 ♖fd8** and now:

4b21) **19 ♗g5** f6 (better than 19...♖d7 20 h3, intending f4, with advantage to White in the game Armas-Ionescu, Romanian Ch 1988) 20 ♗e3 ♖b8 (not 20...g5, 21 ♘a4!) 21 h3 g5 22 ♘e2 was unclear in Wolff-Sadler, London 1991.

4b22) **19 ♗e3** was answered by **19...♖ab8** 20 h3 ♗a8 21 f4 ♘c6 22 ♕f2, which gave White an edge in Armas-Gheorghiu, Romanian Ch 1987. Perhaps Black could have tried **19...♘g4**. He did well, however, to avoid **19...♗f8**, which runs into 20 ♘a4 ♘d7 21 ♘xb6! ♘xb6 22 ♕a5 ♘d5 23 ♖xd5!.

4b23) **19 h3 ♗f8** 20 ♗e3 ♖ac8 21 ♗g5!? ♗e7 22 ♗xe7 ♕xe7 23 f4 ♘c6 24 ♕f2 with some advantage for White, Velička-Bosboom, Groningen 1991.

7   c4 *(D)*

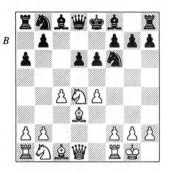

7   ...   ♗e7

Other moves:

1) **7...g6** 8 ♘c3 ♗g7 9 ♘b3! 0-0 10 ♗e2 ♘c6 11 ♗f4 ♘e8 (Black has little choice as 11...♘e5 12 c5 is very awkward) and after **12 ♕d2** b6 13 ♖fd1 ♘e5 14 ♖ac1 ♕c7 Black

equalised in Nunn-Gheorghiu, Vienna 1986. However **12 c5!** is unpleasant for Black, for example 12...dxc5 13 ♕xd8 ♘xd8 14 ♘a4! or 12...e5 13 ♗e3 ♗e6 14 ♘d5.

2) **7...♗d7** 8 ♘c3 ♘c6 9 ♘xc6 ♗xc6 10 ♕e2 ♗e7 11 b3 0-0 12 ♗b2 and now:

2a) **12...♖c8** 13 ♔h1 ♘d7 14 f4 ♗f6 15 ♖ad1 ♕c7 16 ♗b1 b5 17 cxb5 axb5 18 e5 dxe5 19 ♘xb5 ♗xb5 20 ♕xb5 ♖fd8 21 f5! was very good for White in Howell-Aldama, Capablanca mem 1993.

2b) After **12...♕b8** 13 a4 ♖e8 14 ♖ae1 ♘d7 15 f4 ♗h4! 16 ♖d1 ♗f6 17 b4!? the position was unclear in Nunn-Bischoff, Dortmund 1987; **14 f4!** was more accurate, not committing the a1-rook for the moment.

2c) **12...♖e8** 13 f4 d5!? 14 cxd5 exd5 15 e5 ♘e4 16 ♘xe4! dxe4 17 ♗xe4 ♗b5 and now **18 ♕g4?!** ♕d2! 19 ♗xh7+!? was unclear in Arnason-Toshkov, Jurmala 1987. White can draw by **18 ♕c2** ♗xf1 19 ♗xh7+ ♔h8 20 ♔xf1 ♖c8 21 ♕d3! g6 22 ♗xg6 hxg6 23 ♕xg6 ♕d2, but **18 ♕f3!?** is the most promising, not only playing for a possible attack by ♕h3, but also lining up against the b7-pawn.

3) **7...b6** normally transposes to lines considered below.

8   ♘c3

White has two main attacking plans, which are distinguished by the development of his queen's bishop. Firstly he may build up a slow kingside attack by b3, ♗b2, ♘c3, ♕e2, f4, ♖ae1 and so on, with the ultimate aim of a breakthrough by f5. The other plan is to prepare for e5 by ♘c3, ♕e2, f4, ♗d2 and ♖ae1. The important point is that with the bishop on b2 the e5 plan is much less effective, because White ends up with a pawn on e5 and this would block the bishop on b2.

8 ...   0-0
9 ♕e2

Moves such as ♕e2, ♔h1 and f4 are logical because they do not commit White to one plan or the other. My (JN) view is that the e5 plan is most effective against ...♘bd7 by Black, because then the queen's knight blocks the retreat of the one on f6. Therefore it is often useful to delay committing the c1-bishop until Black has moved his b8-knight. Against ...♘c6 White will take on c6, then play b3 and ♗b2, and against ...♘bd7 White will continue with ♗d2 and ♖ae1.

9 ...   b6

Black also delays for as long as possible. An example where he didn't is Vehi-Robović, Biel 1993, which continued **9...♘bd7** 10 f4 ♕c7 11 ♔h1 ♖e8 12 ♗d2 (12 ♘f3!?) 12...♗f8 13 ♖ae1 e5 14 fxe5 dxe5 15 ♘f5 ♔h8 16 ♗g5 with a strong initiative for White.

10 f4

Despite the above (rather subjective) comments it is quite reasonable to play b3 straight away, the advantage being that White can sometimes manage without ♔h1. After **10 b3 ♗b7 11 ♗b2** *(D)* there are two variations:

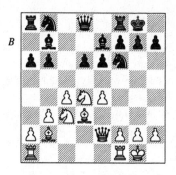

1) **11...♘c6** (as the earlier explanation makes clear, this move plays into White's hands since we reach positions similar to the main line below, but with White having saved about half a tempo by missing out ♔h1) **12 ♘xc6 ♗xc6** and Black has been highly unsuccessful from this position:

1a) **13 ♖ad1 ♕b8?!** 14 a3 (what on earth is this for?) 14...♖d8? (it doesn't matter about the tempo spent on a3 in view of the way Black plays) 15 f4 ♘d7 16 ♘d5! ♗f8 17 ♖f3! ♖e8 18 ♖h3! g6 19 ♕g4 ♕d8 20 ♖f1 ♗g7 21 ♗xg7 ♔xg7 22 f5! with a massive attack, Ivanović-Ermenkov, Plovdiv Echt 1983.

1b) **13 f4 ♘d7** 14 ♖ad1 b5? 15 cxb5! axb5 16 ♗xb5 ♕b6+ 17 ♖f2! ♗xb5 18 ♕xb5 ♕xb5 19 ♘xb5 ♖xa2 20 ♗xg7 ♖fa8 21 ♖xa2 ♖xa2 22 ♗d4 e5, Hellers-Adamski, Eeklo 1985, and now 23 ♗c3 gives White a won ending.

1c) **13 ♖ae1 ♖e8** 14 f4 g6 15 e5! dxe5 16 fxe5 ♗c5+ 17 ♔h1 ♘g4 18 ♗e4! ♘xe5 19 ♗xc6 ♘xc6 20 ♕f3 with a tremendous attack for White, Ermenkov-Gheorghiu, Prague 1985.

2) **11...♘bd7** 12 ♖ad1 (12 f4 is also playable) 12...♖e8 (12...♕c7 13 ♗b1 ♖fe8 14 f4 ♖ac8 15 ♘f3 ♗f8 16 ♔h1 ♗c6 is less accurate, and 17 e5! ♗xf3 18 ♖xf3 dxe5 19 fxe5 ♘g4 20 ♖xf7! gave White a very dangerous attack in Plachetka-Ravikumar, Copenhagen 1980) 13 ♗b1 ♕b8 14 f4 ♗f8 15 ♔h1 ♖a7 16 ♘f3 ♗a8 with a double-edged position, Åkesson-Mestel, Copenhagen 1980, although I (JN) still favour White.

10	...	♗b7
11	♔h1 (D)	

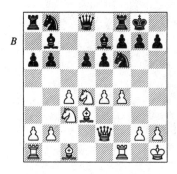

11	...	♘c6

Or:

1) **11...♘bd7** 12 ♗d2 ♕c7 13 ♖ac1 (13 ♖ae1 ♖fe8 14 ♖f3 g6 15 ♖g3! ♔h8 16 ♖h3 e5 17 ♘f3 exf4 18 ♗xf4 ♗f8 19 ♕f2 ♘c5 20 ♗c2 was also good for White in Ivanović-Peev, Balasiha 1977) 13...g6 14 b4 ♖ac8 15 a3 ♕b8 (the advantage of playing f4 is that the weakening of c4 created by White playing b4 cannot be exploited by ...♘e5) 16 ♘f3 ♖fe8 17 ♖ce1 ♗f8 18 ♘g5 h6 (18...e5 19 f5 gave White a dangerous attack at no material cost in the game Commons-Najdorf, Lone Pine 1976) 19 ♘xf7! ♔xf7 20 e5 ♘g8 21 ♕g4 ♘e7 22 ♗xg6+! ♘xg6 23 f5 ♘dxe5 24 fxe6+! (24 fxg6+ ♔g8 is unclear) 24...♔e7 (24...♔g7 25 ♖xe5 dxe5 26 ♖f7+ mates) 25 ♕xg6! (the climax of a magnificent combination) 25...♔d8 26 ♖xe5 dxe5 27 ♗xh6 ♖xc4 (27...♗xh6 28 ♖d1+ mates) 28 ♕xe8+ (White gives up his queen after all!) 28...♔xe8 29 ♖xf8+ ♔e7 30 ♖xb8 ♗c6 31 ♘d1 b5 32 ♔g1 ♔xe6 33 ♖b6 1-0 Commons-Peev, Plovdiv 1976.

2) **11...♖e8** (dubious as it allows White to play for e5 without delay) 12 ♘f3 g6 (12...♘bd7 13 e5 dxe5 14 fxe5 ♘g4 15 ♗f4 ♗xf3 16 ♖xf3 and 12...♘c6 13 e5 dxe5 14 fxe5 ♘g4 15 ♗f4 are good for White) 13 e5! ♘h5, Sax-Bellon, Dubai OL 1986, and now Sax recommends 14 ♗e4 ♘c6 15 g4 ♘g7 16 f5!, when **16...exf5** 17 gxf5 dxe5 18 fxg6 hxg6 19 ♘xe5, **16...gxf5** 17 gxf5 ♘xf5 (or 17...exf5 18 ♗d5) 18 ♗xf5 exf5 19 ♘d5 and **16...dxe5** 17 fxg6 f5 (or 17...hxg6 18 ♘xe5) 18 gxf5 exf5 19 ♗d5+ ♔h8 20 ♘xe5 are all good for White.

12	♘xc6	♗xc6
13	b3	♘d7

Or 13...♕c7 14 ♗b2 ♖ad8 and now:

1) **15 ♖ad1** g6 16 ♗b1 ♘h5 17 ♖d3 (17 g4 ♘g7 18 f5! exf5 19 gxf5 was probably better) 17...e5! 18 fxe5 dxe5 19 ♖xd8 ♖xd8 20 ♘d5 with just an edge for White, Matulović-Tringov, Vrnjačka Banja 1986.

2) **15 ♖ae1** (threatening ♘d5) 15...♗b7 16 ♗b1 ♘d7? (16...g6 is

probably better, when 17 ♕d3 is only a slight plus for White) and now **17 ♕h5 ♖fe8 18 ♗e3 ♘f6 19 ♕h3 g6 20 f5!** gave White a decisive attack in Nunn-Gheorghiu, Biel 1983, which is annotated in detail in *Secrets of Grandmaster Play* by John Nunn and Peter Griffiths. For some reason Gheorghiu repeated the entire line in the game Mokry-Gheorghiu, Prague 1985. That game continued **17 ♕g4 ♗f6 18 ♖e3 g6 19 ♖h3** and then **19...♔h8??** 20 ♘d5! winning, as 20...exd5 is met by 21 ♕h4. Of course **19...♖fe8** is better, but 20 ♕g3 intending f5 gives White a dangerous attack in any case.

14 ♗b2 *(D)*

14 ... g6

14...♗f6 leaves d6 weak and after 15 ♖ad1 ♕c7 (15...♕b8 16 ♗b1 b5 17 cxb5 axb5 was Mainka-Espig, Bundesliga 1991, and now it seems to me (JG) that the sacrificial line 18 e5! dxe5 19 ♖xd7 ♗xd7 20 ♕d3 ♖d8 {20...e4 21 ♘xe4!} 21 ♕xh7+ ♔f8 22 ♘e4 would have left White with a very powerful attack) 16 ♗b1 ♖fd8?! (16...♖ad8 offered better

chances) 17 ♖d3 g6 18 ♖fd1 ♘c5 19 ♘d5! exd5 20 ♗xf6 ♘xd3 21 exd5! ♘xf4 22 ♕f3 ♘h5 23 ♗xd8 ♖xd8 24 dxc6 White had a clear advantage in the game Marjanović-Rajković, Yugoslav Ch 1983.

15 ♖ad1

The purpose of this (rather than ♖ae1) is to prevent the development of Black's e7-bishop to the long diagonal. After 15...♗f6, for example, 16 ♗b1 ♕c7 17 ♕d2 attacks d6.

15 ... ♖e8

16 ♗b1 *(D)*

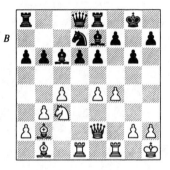

16 ... ♕c7

The alternatives are:

1) **16...♖a7** 17 a4 (the direct 17 ♖d3 was also tempting) 17...♗f8 18 ♗c2 ♕a8 19 ♕f2 ♘c5? (19...♖c7 was better) 20 ♘d5! exd5 21 cxd5 ♗xa4 22 bxa4 ♗g7 23 ♗xg7 ♔xg7 24 e5! and White stands well, Popović-Kotronias, Pucarevo 1987.

2) **16...♕b8** 17 f5 (17 a4!? is possible, but I (JN) like 17 ♕d3 b5 18 cxb5 axb5 19 ♘e2! b4 20 ♘d4 ♗b7 21 ♕h3 with dangerous threats on the kingside) 17...b5 18 fxe6 fxe6 19 cxb5 axb5 20 ♘d5!? ♗xd5 (and

not 20...exd5 21 exd5 ♗f6 22 ♕d2 ♗xb2 23 dxc6 with advantage to White) 21 exd5 e5 22 ♕g4 ♘f6 23 ♕e6+ ♔g7 was unclear in Prasad-Gheorghiu, Biel 1985.

3) **16...♗f8** 17 e5! dxe5 18 ♗e4! gives White a dangerous attack. The game Vogt-Gheorghiu, E.Germany-Romania 1984 continued 18...♕c7 (18...♗xe4 19 ♘xe4 ♗g7 20 ♗xe5 ♗xe5 21 fxe5 ♔g7 22 ♕f2 wins after 22...♕e7 23 ♕f6+! ♔g8 24 ♕xe7 ♖xe7 25 ♖xd7 or 22...♖e7 23 ♘g5 ♕g8 24 ♘xf7 ♖f8 25 ♖xd7!) 19 ♕f3 ♗xe4 20 ♘xe4 f5 (20...♗g7 21 fxe5 ♘xe5 22 ♘f6+ ♔h8 23 ♗xe5 wins material) 21 ♖xd7 fxe4 22 ♕d1 ♕c6 23 ♗xe5 ♖ac8 24 ♕d4 ♗e7 (24...♖e7 25 ♖d6 drops the b-pawn, while 24...b5 25 ♕a7! and 24...♗c5 25 ♖g7+ ♔f8 26 ♗d6+ lead to mate) 25 f5! (the immediate 25 ♗h8 ♗f8 26 ♖g7+ ♔xh8 27 ♖xg6+ is met by ...e5, but if Black now plays 25...exf5 this line wins) 25...♖cd8 (25...gxf5 26 ♗h8 ♗f8 27 ♖xf5! exf5 28 ♖g7+ mates) 26 ♖xe7! (26 fxg6! ♖xd7 27 gxh7+ ♔xh7 28 ♖f7+ ♔h6 29 ♕e3+ ♗g5 30 ♕h3+ also wins) 26...exf5 (26...♖xd4 27 ♖g7+ is mate next move) 27 ♖xe8+ ♕xe8 28 ♕xb6 1-0.

17 ♕d3

A flexible move attacking d6 and preparing ♕d4 or ♕h3 according to circumstance.

17 ... ♗f8 *(D)*

This move cost Black forty minutes, presumably checking that the line 18 ♕d4 e5 (18...♗g7 19 ♕xg7+ wins) 19 ♘d5 ♗xd5 20 ♕xd5 exf4

21 ♖xf4 ♘e5 22 ♖df1 ♖a7 presented no dangers.

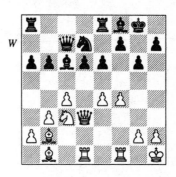

18 ♘b5!?

A shock for Black. The point is that after 18...axb5 19 ♕c3 e5 20 cxb5 ♖ac8 21 bxc6 ♕xc6 22 ♕f3 Black cannot exchange at f4 since he has no satisfactory way to cover f7, so White gets to play 23 f5, when Black's light squares look very sickly.

18 ... ♗xb5
19 cxb5 axb5

19...a5 20 ♖c1 ♘c5 21 ♕c3 is much worse as Black has to play the weakening ...e5.

20 ♕xb5 ♕b7

The upshot of White's mini-combination is that he has the two bishops and a queenside pawn majority. Now **21 a4!** would have been logical, relieving the b1-bishop of its defensive duty and pinning down the b6-pawn. If Black remains passive the b1-bishop can eventually move to b5. During the game I was concerned about the reply 21...♘c5 22 ♕c4 ♖ac8, but 23 f5 e5 24 ♖f3 gives Black no way to exploit the position of White's queen (24...♘e6 25 fxe6!), and consolidation by 25 ♕e2 will be good for White.

21 ♕e2?!   b5!

Black takes the chance to prevent a4. Now ...b4 would permanently cripple White's queenside pawns, so...

22 b4

Black cannot transfer his knight to c4 because b5 is weak, for example 22...♕a6 (threatening ...♘b6) 23 ♗d3 ♕xa2 24 ♗xb5 ♕a7 (24...♖ed8 25 ♗xd7 and ♖a1) 25 ♗c6 followed by ♗d4 and b5, with an excellent position for White.

22 ...   ♖a6 (D)

Another useful defensive move, covering d6 in preparation for ...♗g7. Here I thought for a long time trying to find a way to keep the advantage.

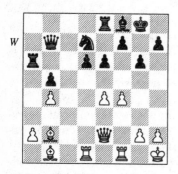

23 ♖f3!	**♗g7**
24 ♗xg7	**♔xg7**
25 ♖fd3	**♕c7**
26 ♖h3	

The point of White's manoeuvre is that he gains a tempo by attacking b5 to transfer his rook to the h-file,

thereby reviving his threats against Black's king.

26 ...   ♖b6

Not 26...♕c4? 27 ♕b2+ followed by 28 ♖c3, when Black's queen is suddenly trapped.

27 ♕d2

The threat is 28 e5 d5 29 f5 and the queen gets to h6.

27 ...   ♘f6

Once again Black finds a good defence, relieving the pin down the d-file.

28 f5   exf5

28...e5 29 ♕h6+ ♔g8 30 g4! is very unpleasant.

29 exf5   d5!

All these difficult moves were very time-consuming, so that Black had only a couple of minutes left to reach move 40. At first sight White can win by 30 fxg6 fxg6 **31 ♕h6+** ♔g8 32 ♗xg6 hxg6 33 ♕h8+ (33 ♕xg6+ ♕g7 34 ♕f5 ♖ce6 defends) 33...♔f7 34 ♖h7+ ♔e6 35 ♖e1+ (35 ♕xf6+ ♔xf6 36 ♖xc7 ♖be6 gives Black enough for the pawn in view of his active rooks and king), but then comes 35...♔f5! 36 ♖f1+ ♔g5! 37 h4+ ♔g4 and White's queen is trapped.

30 fxg6?!

The immediate **30 ♖f1!** was much better, when the defence Black plays in the game would have been prevented.

30 ...   fxg6

31 ♖f1

Now truly threatening 32 ♕h6+ ♔g8 33 ♗xg6.

31 ...   ♘g4!

Suddenly Black exploits White's vulnerable back rank. If **32 ♕xd5?** then 32...♘f2+ wins.

32 ♕d4+ ♖f6 *(D)*

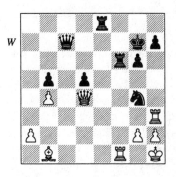

White cannot take the rook or the knight, nor can he play ♖hf3. The move played supports the weak back rank and simultaneously attacks the knight.

33 ♗d3 h5

Forced, but effective. The draw would now be in sight if it were not for Black's time-trouble.

34 ♖xf6 ♘xf6
35 ♖f3 ♖e1+
36 ♗f1 ♕e7?!

36...♕e5 37 ♕xe5 ♖xe5 38 ♗xb5 gives White good winning chances as the d-pawn cannot pass over the d3-square. However, **36...♕d6!** was more accurate, for example 37 ♔g1 (37 h3 ♖e4 38 ♕c3 ♖xb4 39 ♖xf6 ♕xf6) 37...♖e4 38 ♕c5 (38 ♕c3 d4 39 ♕d3 ♘g4! 40 g3 ♖e1 threatening ...♘e5 is unpleasant) 38...♕xc5 39

bxc5 ♖e1 and the draw is inevitable (40 ♖c3 d4).

37 ♔g1 ♖e4

Black can also choose to wait, since progress isn't easy for White, but in time-trouble it is very natural to break the pin.

38 ♕c3 d4

Not **38...♖xb4** 39 ♖xf6 d4 because of 40 ♖e6!.

39 ♕d3

With two moves still to make Black suddenly finds himself in trouble over the b5-pawn. **39...♕xb4** loses to 40 ♖xf6, so the best chance is **39...♘d5** 40 ♕xb5 ♘xb4. Then 41 ♗c4 ♖e1+ 42 ♔f2 ♔h6 isn't dangerous, so White's winning prospects are very slight.

39 ... ♘g4?
40 h3

and Black's flag dropped before he could make his 40th move. After 40...♘e3 41 ♕xb5 ♘xf1 42 ♖xf1 ♖e2 43 ♕d3 ♕e3+ 44 ♕xe3 dxe3, suggested by Black after the game, White can win by 45 a4! (but not 45 b5 ♖xa2 46 ♖b1 ♖d2! 47 ♔f1 ♖f2+ 48 ♔e1 ♖xg2 49 ♖b4 ♖d2 50 b6 ♖d8 51 b7 ♖b8 when Black has drawing chances) 45...♖b2 46 b5 ♖a2 47 b6 ♖xa4 48 ♖b1 ♖d4 49 ♔f1! (49 b7 e2) 49...♖d8 50 b7 ♖b8 51 ♔e2, etc. Obviously Black has other ways to play, but the two connected passed pawns give White good winning chances in any case.

7 Maroczy Bind

This most commonly arises if Black plays an early ...g6, for example 1 e4 c5 2 ♘f3 ♘c6 3 d4 cxd4 4 ♘xd4 g6, aiming to reach a Dragon position without having played ...d6. This restricts White's options quite severely, since he has to be careful not to allow Black to play ...d5 in one go, saving a crucial tempo. An effective way out of this dilemma is to continue 5 c4, setting up the formation of pawns on c4 and e4 known as the Maroczy Bind. The asset of this formation is the automatic restraint of ...b5 and ...d5, Black's basic freeing thrusts. Black does sometimes succeed in organising ...b5, but this is normally only good when White has made a mistake. White's main asset is his space advantage, leading to the corollary that he should avoid exchanges which would relieve the cramp in Black's position. If Black does succeed in liquidating to an ending, White's c4-pawn and dark-squared weaknesses can become a liability. Play often becomes a matter of slow manoeuvring as White tries to increase his space advantage and force weaknesses in the black position while his opponent remains crouched on the first couple of ranks waiting for the first sign of over-extension to launch a counterattack. The Maroczy Bind can also occur if Black adopts an unusual move order, for example 1 e4 c5 2 ♘f3 ♘c6 3 d4 cxd4 4 ♘xd4 d6 and now 5 c4 will probably transpose to this chapter after 5...♘f6 6 ♘c3 g6. Although the Maroczy Bind is slightly passive for Black, players such as Larsen, Petursson and Velimirović have shown that by patiently waiting for a lapse of concentration from White this line can offer winning chances for Black. The theoretical opinion is that White should maintain a slight advantage, but no one should believe that this is a line in White cannot lose.

Game 20
Karpov – Kavalek
Nice OL 1974

1	e4	c5
2	♘f3	♘c6
3	d4	cxd4
4	♘xd4	g6
5	c4	

Here Black has two possibilities. He may play 5...♗g7 in order to force White's ♗e3, but in doing this he forfeits the chance to take on d4 at a moment when White must recapture with the queen. The alternative is 5...♘f6, which will often transpose to 5...♗g7 if Black does not take up the chance to play ...♘xd4.

The 5...♗g7 systems are examined in Game 21, while in this game we look at 5...♘f6.

5 ... ♘f6
6 ♘c3 *(D)*

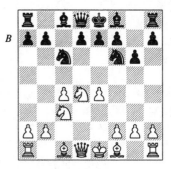

6 ... d6

If Black adopts the move order 6...♘xd4 7 ♕xd4 d6 (possibly to rule out ♘c2) then White has an interesting alternative based on playing ♗d3 rather than ♗e2, providing the e4-pawn with useful extra protection, for example **6...♘xd4 7 ♕xd4 d6 8 ♗g5 ♗g7 9 ♕d2 0-0** (9...♗e6 10 ♖c1 ♖c8 11 b3 ♕a5 12 f3 h6 13 ♗e3 0-0 14 ♗d3 ♔h7 15 0-0 a6 16 h3 ♘d7 17 f4 f5 18 exf5 ♗xf5 19 ♗e2! was good for White in Polugaevsky-Beliavsky, USSR Ch 1975) and now:

1) **10 f3** is interesting, for example after 10...♗e6 11 ♖c1 ♕a5 12 b3 and now rather than **12...a6?** 13 ♘d5! ♕xd2+ 14 ♔xd2 ♗xd5 15 cxd5 ♖fc8 16 ♖xc8! ♖xc8 17 g3 ♔f8 18 ♗h3 ♖c7 19 ♖c1 ♖xc1 20 ♔xc1 which left White winning in Byrne-Garcia Padron, Torremolinos 1977, **12...♖fc8** was better, when 13

♗e2 a6 14 ♘a4 transposes to Karpov-Kavalek.

2) **10 ♗d3 ♗e6** (10...a5 11 0-0 a4 12 ♖ac1 ♗e6 13 ♕c2 gave White his usual comfortable space advantage in Portisch-Reshevsky, Petropolis IZ 1973) 11 0-0 (more accurate than 11 ♖c1 as ...♕a5 would now allow ♘d5) 11...♖c8 12 b3 a6 13 ♖ac1 ♘d7 (perhaps 13...♖e8 is better, with the idea of meeting 14 f4 with 14...b5, although even here it's unclear whether Black has sufficient compensation for the pawn after 15 cxb5 axb5 16 ♗xf6 ♗xf6 17 ♘xb5; if this position is not to White's liking then he can try 14 ♔h1 or 14 ♖fe1) 14 f4 f6 15 ♗h4 ♗h6 16 ♘d5 ♘c5 17 ♗b1 b5 18 cxb5 axb5 19 b4 ♘a4 20 ♖xc8 ♗xc8 21 ♕e2 e6? (21...♗d7 is preferable, when White should not play 22 e5 dxe5 23 fxe5 on account of 23...♗c6!, but 22 f5 with advantage) 22 ♕xb5 ♗d7 23 ♘xf6+! ♕xf6 24 ♕xd7 ♕xh4 25 g3 ♕g4 26 ♕xa4 ♗xf4 27 ♕b3 with a clear advantage for White, Psakhis-Kagan, Tel Aviv 1992.

7 ♗e2 ♘xd4

This is Black's last chance to force White to recapture on d4 with his queen. If he plays 7...♗g7 White should transpose to Game 24 by 8 ♗e3. At one time 8 ♘c2 was thought the best reply to 7...♗g7, but after 8...♘d7 9 ♗d2 a5! (not 9...♘c5?! 10 b4 ♘e6 11 ♖c1 0-0 12 0-0 f5 13 exf5 gxf5 14 f4 ♘ed4 15 ♘xd4 ♘xd4 16 ♗e3 with a positional advantage for White, Nunn-Rind, Manchester 1980) 10 0-0 0-0 11 ♖c1 ♘c5 Black has a much better version of the Maroczy Bind than in other lines. In Nunn-Petursson, Wijk aan Zee 1990 I made matters worse by playing 12 b3? ♘b4!, when Black had a clear advantage.

    8 ♕xd4   ♗g7

    9 ♗g5 *(D)*

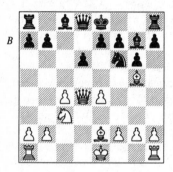

    9 ...   0-0

There is little to be gained by delaying castling:

1) **9...♗d7** 10 ♕d2 h6 (10...♗c6 should be met by 11 f3) 11 ♗f4 a6 12 0-0 ♗c6 13 f3 0-0 14 a4 ♘d7 15 a5! ♘c5 16 ♖a3 with a slight advantage for White, Pomar-Cordovil, Malaga 1972.

2) **9...h6** 10 ♗e3 0-0 11 ♕d2 ♔h7 (11...♕a5 12 0-0 forces ...♔h7 in any case) **12 0-0 ♗e6 13 f4** (13 ♗d4 ♖c8 14 b3 a6 15 ♕e3 ♘d7 16 ♗xg7 ♔xg7 17 f4 ♕b6 18 ♕xb6 ♘xb6 19 f5 ♗d7 20 ♖ad1 only gave White a slight edge in Timman-Ribli, Amsterdam 1973) **13...♖c8** (after 13...♕a5 14 f5 forces 14...♗d7 since 14...gxf5 15 exf5 ♗xf5 allows 16 ♖xf5, so White avoids wasting a tempo on b3) **14 b3** *(D)* and now:

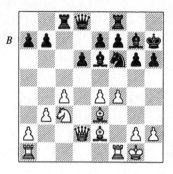

2a) **14...a6** 15 ♖ad1 ♕a5 16 ♗d4 is good for White after both **16...b5** 17 f5 ♗d7 18 ♗xf6! exf6 19 ♘d5 ♕xd2 20 ♖xd2, Nunn-van der Sterren, Groningen 1974/5 and **16...♗d7** 17 ♗xf6 exf6 18 ♘d5 ♕c5+ 19 ♔h1 a5 20 f5, Nunn-I.Ivanov, London 1987, so it makes sense for Black to try to force White's rook to the less active square c1.

2b) **14...♕a5** 15 a3 (15 ♖ac1 is also possible, although 15...a6 16 f5 ♗d7 17 h3 ♗c6 18 ♗d3 ♘d7 was unclear in Gulko-Petrosian, Biel IZ 1976) 15...a6 16 f5 ♗d7 17 b4 ♕e5 (Larsen-Fischer, Denver Ct (2) 1971) and now, according to various analyses of this famous match, 18 ♖ad1 would have been good for White.

3) **9...♗e6** 10 ♖c1 ♕a5 11 ♕d2 ♖c8?! (11...0-0 is more accurate) **12 f3!** leaves Black in a rather awkward situation since he has committed the wrong rook to c8. The point is that after ...0-0 and ...♖fc8 White is never threatening to play ♘d5, because the sequence ...♕xd2, ♘xe7+ ♔f8 costs White his errant knight. With the a8-rook on c8, however,

Black will sooner or later have to waste time meeting this threat.

3a) So, **12...0-0** 13 b3 a6 14 0-0 is good for White.

3b) It is also too dangerous to snatch the c-pawn, e.g. **12...♗xc4** 13 ♘d5! ♕xa2 **14 0-0** ♘xd5 15 ♖xc4! ♖xc4 16 ♕xd5 ♖a4 17 ♗b5+ ♔f8 18 ♖c1! and in Geller-Stean, Teesside 1975 Black resigned because of 18...♗d4+ 19 ♕xd4! ♖xd4 20 ♗h6+ mating. In fact White had an even more convincing win by **14 ♘b4**, since 14...♕b3 15 ♗d1 traps the queen.

3c) If Black doesn't castle he will soon run out of things to do, e.g. **12...a6** 13 b3 b5 14 ♘d5! ♕xd2+ 15 ♔xd2 ♗xd5 16 cxd5 ♔d7 17 a4 h6 18 ♗e3 ♖xc1 19 ♖xc1 ♖b8 20 ♖c6 with a very good ending for White, Nunn-Reuben, London 1978.

10 ♕d2

10 ♕e3 is an important alternative which has the advantage of firmly defending the e-pawn; this makes the lines with a quick ...a6 and ...b5, which can easily cause problems after 10 ♕d2, much less effective. After **10...♗e6 11 ♖c1!?** *(D)* Black has:

1) **11...a6** 12 0-0 b5 13 cxb5 axb5 14 a3! ♕b8?! (14...♖a5 is suggested by Petursson, but he hasn't repeated this line) 15 ♗xb5 and Black didn't have enough for the pawn in Arnason-Petursson, Reykjavik 1990.

2) **11...♕b6 12 ♕d2 ♕b4 13 f3** and now:

2a) **13...♗xc4** 14 a3 ♕b3 15 ♗xc4 ♕xc4 16 ♘d5 ♕b3 17 ♘xe7+

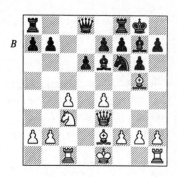

♔h8 is given as unclear by Petursson, but I (JG) prefer White. A sample variation: 18 0-0 ♕b6+ 19 ♖f2 ♖fe8 20 ♗xf6 ♗xf6 21 ♘d5 ♕d4 22 ♖c7 ±.

2b) **13...♖fc8** 14 b3 a6 15 ♘a4 ♕xd2+ 16 ♔xd2 and we are back in Karpov-Kavalek, although judging from the notes in various sources nobody else seems to have noticed. Donaldson and Silman, for example, in *Accelerated Dragons* (Cadogan 1993) give 11...♕b6 and 12...♕b4 exclamation marks and consider the position after 16 ♔xd2 to be equal, whilst two pages earlier in their book they give the same position as better for White (albeit after 15 ♔xd2).

3) **11...♕a5 12 0-0** and now:

3a) **12...♖fc8** 13 b3 a6 14 f4 ♕c5 15 ♕xc5 ♖xc5 16 ♗f3 ♖b8 17 e5 (17 ♘a4 followed by c5 is also interesting) 17...dxe5 18 fxe5 ♘e8 19 ♗xe7 ♖xe5 20 ♗h4 with a clear advantage for White, Ciocaltea-Spiridonov, Timisoara 1982.

3b) **12...♖fe8** 13 b3 ♘d7 14 ♗h6 (White's problem is that 14 f4 ♕c5 15 ♕xc5 ♘xc5 is very awkward for him and after 14 ♖fd1 he has to

take into account 14...♗xc3 and
15...♛xa2) **14...♛c5** (14...♗h8 15
♖fd1) **15 ♛d2 ♛d4** and now:

3b1) **16 ♛xd4 ♗xd4 17 ♖fd1
♗c5 18 ♘d5 ♗xd5 19 exd5 a5 20
♗d2 ♗b4!** with an equal game,
Stangl-Espig, Dortmund 1991.

3b2) I (JG) prefer **16 ♘b5!** as
after 16...♛xd2 17 ♗xd2 ♖ec8 18
♗e3 White retains an edge.

10   ...   ♗e6

Black cannot do without this
move so 10...a6, for example, is of
no independent significance and will
transpose to lines considered below.

11   ♖c1

Perhaps this move is not the most
accurate as in several variations
when Black plays ...a6 and ...b5 he is
able to follow up with ...♗xa2. The
main alternative is **11 0-0** *(D)*, with
the following possibilities:

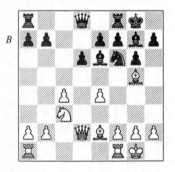

1) **11...♖c8 12 ♖ad1!? ♛a5** (not
12...♗xc4 13 e5 ♘e8 14 ♗xc4 ♖xc4
15 ♛e2! ♖c7 16 exd6 ♘xd6 17 ♘d5
+−) **13 b3 a6 14 ♘d5 ♛xd2 15
♘xe7+ ♔h8 16 ♗xd2 ♖ce8 17 ♗b4
♖xe7 18 ♗xd6 ♖ee8 19 e5 ♘g4 20
♗xf8 ♖xf8 21 ♗f3 ♖b8 22 h3 ♘xe5**

23 ♗xb7 a5 24 ♗d5 with a clear
advantage for White, J.Polgar-Dzin-
dzihashvili, New York 1992.

2) **11...a6 12 ♖ad1!?** (12 ♖c1
transposes into the note to Black's
11th move) 12...♛a5 (12...b5 13 e5!?
dxe5 14 ♛xd8 ♖fxd8 15 ♖xd8 ♖xd8
16 cxb5 axb5 17 ♗xb5 should be
better for White) **13 ♗xf6!? ♗xf6**
(perhaps Black can try 13...exf6 14
♛xd6 f5) **14 ♘d5 ♛xa2 15 ♘xf6+
exf6 16 ♛c3! ♛a4 17 ♖xd6 ♖ac8
18 b3 ♛a3 19 ♖fd1** with advantage
to White, Tiviakov-Polak, Oakham
1992. In fact, the game only lasted
another three moves: 19...♖c7 20 h4
♔g7 21 h5 gxh5? 22 ♖xe6 1-0.

3) **11...♛a5 12 f3** (12 ♖ad1 a6
transposes to '2') 12...a6 13 ♖fd1
(13 ♘d5?! ♛xd2 14 ♘xe7+ ♔h8 15
♗xd2 ♖fe8 16 ♘d5 ♘xd5 17 cxd5
♗xd5 18 ♗c3 ½-½ Short-Anders-
son, Novi Sad OL 1990) 13...♖fc8
14 ♘d5 ♛xd2 15 ♖xd2 ♗xd5 (after
15...♘xd5? 16 exd5 ♗d7 17 ♗xe7!
♗h6 White should play not 18 ♖c2
♗f5 and 19...♖e8, but 18 ♖ad1!
♗xd2 19 ♖xd2 ♖e8 20 ♗xd6 with a
clear plus for White, Britton-Don-
aldson, Rhodes 1980) 16 cxd5 ♔f8
and White can only claim a very
slight plus. In general these end-
ings with an open c-file are very
drawish unless Black has weakened
his queenside by playing ...b5, which
both allows a4 and gives White an
entry point at c6 (see Nunn-Reuben,
line '3' in the note to Black's 9th
move for a demonstration). Another
way for White to obtain some pressure is to seize the c-file by playing

his bishop to the h3-c8 diagonal. As neither situation exists here, White's advantage is insignificant and in practice Black would have few problems reaching the draw.

Now we return to the main line after 11 ♖c1 *(D)*:

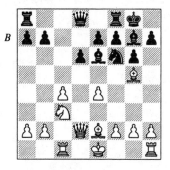

11 ... ♕a5

11...a6 is more critical; White has several sensible looking replies, but against each one of them Black seems to be able to gain reasonable play with 12...b5, e.g.

1) **12 0-0** b5 13 cxb5 axb5 14 ♗xb5 (against 14 a3, Andres proposes 14...♕a5 15 ♗xb5 ♘xe4 16 ♘xe4 ♕xb5 17 ♗xe7 ♖fb8 with enough compensation for the pawn) 14...♗xa2 15 ♗c6 ♖a6 16 ♘xa2 ♖xa2 17 ♖c2 ♕b8 with an equal game, Ortega-Andres, Cuba 1984.

2) **12 f3** b5 13 cxb5 axb5 14 a3 ♘d7! 15 b4?! (15 ♘b5 and ♗xb5 are met by the awkward 15...♘c5, but are still probably better than this odd move) 15...♖xa3 16 ♘xb5 ♖a2 with a very active game for Black, Topalov-Antunes, Candas 1992.

3) **12 b3** and now:

3a) **12...♖c8** with two possibilities for White:

3a1) **13 0-0** b5 14 cxb5 axb5 15 ♗xf6 (*BTS2* recommended 15 ♗xb5 ♕a5 16 ♗d3 ♖xc3 17 ♕xc3 {17 ♖xc3 ♘xe4! is good for Black}, unfortunately overlooking 17...♕xg5) 15...♗xf6 16 ♘xb5 ♕b6. This position has been reached on several occasions and it is unclear whether Black's bishop pair provides sufficient compensation for the pawn. The latest example, Gufeld-Konguvel, Calcutta 1994 suggests not: **17 b4!?** ♕b7 (perhaps Black should be looking to improve upon this) 18 a4! ♕xe4 19 ♘c7 ♖b8 20 ♘xe6 fxe6 21 ♖c4 ♕d5 22 ♕c2 and White's passed pawns give him the advantage.

3a2) **13 f3** b5 14 cxb5 axb5 15 ♘xb5 (15 ♗xb5 ♕a5) 15...♖xc1+ 16 ♕xc1 ♕a5+ 17 ♕d2 ♖a8 18 ♘c3! *(D)* (this is an improvement over 18 ♕xa5 ♖xa5 19 a3 ♗xb3 =) and now:

3a21) Frolov-Tangborn, Kobanya 1992 continued **18...h6** 19 ♗e3 ♘g4 20 ♗d4 ♗xd4 21 ♕xd4 ♖c8

22 ♔d2 ♖xc3 (22...♘e5 23 ♖c1 is very good for White) 23 ♕xc3 ♕xa2+ 24 ♔e1 ♘e5 25 ♔f2 ♕a7+ 26 ♕e3 when Black's compensation was obviously insufficient.

3a22) **18...♖c8** is a more natural try, but this also seems good for White after 19 ♘a4 ♖c1+ 20 ♗d1 ♕xd2+ 21 ♔xd2 ♖a1 22 ♘c3 h6 (22...♔f8!?) 23 ♗e3 ♘d7 24 ♖g1!.

3b) **12...b5!** 13 cxb5 axb5 14 ♗xb5 (14 ♗xf6 ♗xf6 15 ♘xb5 ♕a5 looks fine for Black) 14...♕a5 15 0-0 ♖ac8 16 ♗d3 ♖xc3 17 ♖xc3 ♘xe4 18 ♗xe4 ♗xc3 19 ♕e3 d5 with an excellent game for Black, Lukov-Brendel, Krumbach 1991.

If the above variations are really true then White should try either 10 ♕e3 or 11 0-0.

12 f3 ♖fc8
13 b3

By securely defending c4 and e4 White has prevented any tricks based on an immediate ...b5 so Black has nothing better than to prepare this thrust with ...a6.

13 ... a6
14 ♘a4

White chooses a favourable moment to exchange queens. Black's last move weakened b6 and he must waste a tempo preventing White's knight fork.

14 ... ♕xd2+

After **14...♕d8** White may play:

1) **15 c5!?** (as suggested by Karpov) 15...♖c6 (the main idea is that after 15...dxc5 16 ♕xd8+ ♖xd8 17 ♘b6 ♖ab8, 18 ♗f4 wins material) 16 ♔f2! ♕f8 17 ♕b4 ♘d7 18 cxd6 ♖xd6 19 ♕xb7 ♗d4+ 20 ♗e3 ♖b8 21 ♕c7 with advantage to White, Krasenkov-Hernandez, Palma 1989 as after 21...♗xe3+ 22 ♔xe3 Black has no way to exploit the advanced position of the white king.

2) **15 ♗e3** is a quieter continuation which promises White an edge, e.g. 15...♖ab8?! (15...♘d7) 16 ♗a7 ♖a8 17 ♗b6 ♕f8 18 ♗e3 ♖ab8 19 ♘b6 ♖c7 20 0-0 ♘d7 21 ♘d5 with an excellent position, Nunn-Blum, London 1979.

15 ♔xd2 (D)

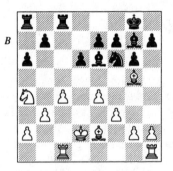

15 ... ♖c6

After Black lost with this move in Karpov-Kavalek attention turned to **15...♘d7**, but this doesn't seem to be much better, for example **16 g4!** (16 h4 f6 17 ♗e3 f5 allows Black more freedom) and now:

1) **16...f6** 17 ♗e3 f5 18 exf5 gxf5 19 h3! ♖f8 20 f4 d5 21 cxd5 ♗xd5 22 ♖hd1 ♖ac8 23 gxf5 b5 24 ♖xc8 ♖xc8 25 ♔e1! with advantage to White, Beliavsky-Tiviakov, Groningen 1993.

2) **16...♔f8** 17 h4 ♖c6 18 ♖c2 ♘c5 19 ♘c3 a5 20 ♘d5 ♖e8 21 ♗e3

♗c8 22 h5 e6 23 ♘c3 f5 24 hxg6 hxg6 25 exf5 exf5 26 gxf5 ♗xf5 27 ♖cc1 with a favourable ending for White, Averbakh-Popov, Polanica Zdroj 1976. It is curious that the exchange of queens is just what White needs to start a kingside attack. The explanation is that Black's counterplay by ...b5 would be very dangerous with queens on the board, since it would lead to an attack against the centralised white king. With queens off this counterplay is relatively harmless.

16 ♘c3 ♖ac8

Karpov suggested **16...♖e8** as a possible improvement, so as to trap White's bishop in case of 17 ♘d5 ♘d7 18 ♘xe7+?! ♖xe7 19 ♗xe7 f6 20 ♗d8 b6. **16...♖cc8** was played in Sakharov-Pereira, Corr. 1976, which finished in a draw after 17 ♘a4 ♖c6!. I don't suppose Karpov would have agreed a draw if Kavalek had 'found' 16...♖cc8!.

17 ♘d5 ♔f8
18 ♗e3 ♘d7

Defending such an ending is an unpleasant task at the best of times, doubly so against Karpov. White has the choice of expanding on the queenside by a timely b4, or of gaining space on the other flank by g4 and h4, as in the note to Black's 15th move. Until White shows his hand Black can only wait.

19 h4 ♗xd5

Black resolves to do away with the dangerous knight. **19...h5** would be well met by 20 ♘f4 and Karpov's suggestion of **19...f5** would require

strong nerves in view of Black's king position.

20 exd5 ♖6c7
21 h5 ♔g8?! *(D)*

This move is probably a mistake. **21...♖e8** followed by ...e6 would have opened the position up for White's two bishops, but by activating his rooks on the central files Black would have developed counterplay against White's king.

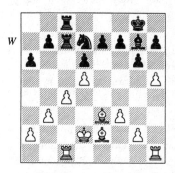

22 f4!

Most players would have rejected this as it allows Black's knight to settle at e4 (supported by ...f5). Karpov, however, is actually aiming to provoke ...f5, which gives him the lever g4 by which he can prise open Black's kingside.

22 ... ♘c5
23 ♗g4 ♘e4+
24 ♔d3 f5
25 ♗f3 b5

It looks as though Black's counterplay has got off the ground at last but White defuses it adroitly.

26 g4 bxc4+
27 ♖xc4 ♖xc4
28 bxc4 ♘c5+

Black had little choice as he could not allow the white rook to occupy the b-file, nor could he play ...♖b8 without losing a pawn at e4.

29 ♗xc5!

If there are rooks on the board opposite-coloured bishops tend to lose their drawish influence. Here Black runs into trouble because his king is badly placed and he will have two or even three pawns stuck on light squares, where they cannot be defended by his bishop.

29 ... ♖xc5

Black plays for a counterattack by ...♖a5. **29...dxc5** 30 h6 ♗d4 31 ♖b1 is also unpleasant, the a6-pawn being particularly weak.

30 h6 ♗f8

It looks awful to bury the bishop but Black lacked a reasonable alternative, for example **30...♗f6** 31 ♖b1 threatens 32 gxf5 gxf5 33 ♖b8+ ♔f7 34 ♗h5#, or **30...fxg4** 31 ♗xg4 ♗f8 (31...♗f6 32 ♗e6+ ♔f8 33 ♖b1) 32 ♗e6+ ♔h8 33 f5 ♖a5 34 ♖b1 ♖a3+ 35 ♔e2 ♖xa2+ 36 ♔f1 ♗xh6 37 f6 and the pawn slips through (37...exf6 38 ♖b8+ wins a piece).

31 ♔c3

Karpov also analyses **31 g5 ♖a5 32 ♖b1** as good for White, but the variations are by no means simple and in practice it is not surprising that he chose to prevent 31...♖a5 by simple means (32 ♔b3, and the rook has to go back).

31 ... fxg4
32 ♗xg4 ♔f7?! *(D)*

Black resolves to extract his king, even at the cost of the h7-pawn. In spite of its dangerous appearance, he would probably have done better to try **32...♖c7** 33 ♗e6+ ♔h8 34 f5 ♖b7! (preventing 35 ♖b1 ♗xh6 36 f6 exf6 37 ♖b8+), when White finds it hard to make progress because of Black's attack on the h6-pawn.

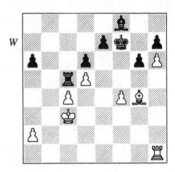

33 ♗e6+ ♔f6
34 ♗g8 ♖c7

34...♗xh6 35 ♖xh6 ♔g7 leads to a lost rook and pawn ending after 36 ♖xh7+ and 37 ♖xe7.

35 ♗xh7 e6

35...♔f7 is refuted by 36 f5 g5 37 f6! exf6 38 ♗f5 ♔g8 39 h7+ ♔h8 40 ♖b1 and 41 ♖b8.

36 ♗g8 exd5
37 h7

Not 37 ♗xd5? ♖h7.

37 ... ♗g7?

Loses by force. After **37...♖xc4+** 38 ♔d3 ♗g7 39 ♗xd5 (39 h8♕ ♗xh8 40 ♖xh8 ♖c8 and 41...♔g7) 39...♖c8 we reach the same position as in the game but with White having a pawn less. Black would still be worse, but he would have chances of a draw.

38 ♗xd5 ♗h8

39	ⵁd3	ⵁf5
40	ⵁe3	⧠e7+
41	ⵁf3	a5
42	a4	⧠c7
43	⵻e4+	ⵁf6
44	⧠h6	ⵁg7

44...ⵁg7 45 ⧠xg6+ ⵁxh7 46 ⧠g1+ ⵁh6 47 ⧠h1+ and 48 ⧠h7+ wins the rook.

| 45 | ⵁg4 | 1-0 |

Black is totally paralysed.

Game 21
Vaganian – Ivkov
Moscow 1985

1	e4	c5
2	⵻f3	⵻c6
3	d4	cxd4
4	⵻xd4	g6
5	c4	⵻g7
6	⵻e3 *(D)*	

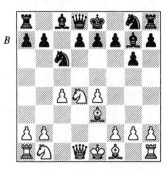

| **6** | **...** | **⵻f6** |

Black can also play ...⵻h6 followed by ...f5, either with or without ...d6, but this idea does not equalise:

1) **6...d6** 7 ⵻c3 ⵻h6 8 ⵻e2 0-0 9 0-0 f5 10 exf5 gxf5 (10...⵻xd4 11 ⵻xd4 ⵻xd4 12 ⵼xd4 ⵻xf5 13 ⵼d2

⵻d7 was good for White after both 14 ⵻f3, Tal-Kupreichik, Sochi 1970 and 14 ⵻g4, Vilela-Estevez, Cien-fuegos 1980 and 10...⵻xd4 11 ⵻xh6 ⧠xf5 transposes to '2') 11 f4 ⵼b6 (11...⵻d7 12 ⵼d2 ⵻g4 13 ⵻xg4 fxg4 14 ⵻d5 gave White an edge in the game Szabo-Larsen, Vinkovci 1970) 12 ⵻xf5 ⵼xb2 13 ⵻xh6+ ⵻xh6 14 ⧠c1 (or 14 ⵻d5 ⵻f5 15 ⵻d3 ⵼g7 16 ⵁh1 with advantage for White, Yermolinsky-Chepukai-tis, USSR 1980) 14...⵻g7 15 ⧠c2 (15 ⵻d5 sacrificing the a-pawn was possible) 15...⵼a3 16 ⵼d2 with an edge for White, Spassov-Ničevski, Sofia 1976.

2) **6...⵻h6 7 ⵻c3 0-0 8 ⵻e2 f5 9 exf5 ⵻xd4 10 ⵻xh6 ⧠xf5 11 0-0 d6** *(D)* (11...⵼b6 is answered by 12 ⵻d5!). This position was reached no less than four times by Afifi in the 1990 Manila Interzonal.

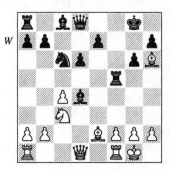

2a) Two games continued **12 ⵻f3**:

2a1) The first of the two games, against Hübner, was a bit of a dis-aster. There followed **12...⵻g7** 13 ⵻xg7 (13 ⵻e3 is also quite good)

13...♔xg7 14 ♗e4 ♖f7 15 ♕d2 ♕b6 16 ♗d5 e6 17 ♗xc6! ♕xc6 18 ♖ad1 ♕xc4 19 ♕xd6 White had a positionally won game.

2a2) Later in the tournament Afifi preferred **12...♗xc3** and after 13 bxc3 ♘e5 14 ♗e4 ♖h5 15 ♗e3 (Rachels-Afifi, Manila IZ 1990) 15...♕c7 would have left the situation unclear.

2b) White can avoid the doubling of his pawns with **12 ♕d2** and this should be good enough to give him an edge. For example, **12...♕a5** 13 ♔h1 ♖f7 14 f4 was promising in Shamkovich-Vasiukov, USSR 1965 and **12...♗g7** 13 ♗xg7 ♔xg7 (Hakki-Afifi, Bahrain 1990) 14 ♗d3!? ♖f7 15 ♗e4 would transpose to Hübner-Afifi given above.

7 ♘c3   0-0

Black has a major alternative in 7...♘g4, which has recently become more popular. This new respectability has been based partly on a new idea for Black involving kingside pawn expansion, and partly on a realisation that the older lines are not so bad for Black as had been thought. White has his typical space advantage, but Black's position is solid and Larsen in particular has achieved quite good results for Black.

After **7...♘g4 8 ♕xg4 ♘xd4** (or 8...♗xd4 9 ♗xd4 ♘xd4 10 0-0-0 e5 11 ♕g3 d6 12 f4 f6 13 f5! ♔f7 14 ♘b5 ♘xb5 15 cxb5 with an excellent position for White, Mestel-Karlsson, Las Palmas 1982) **9 ♕d1** *(D)* Black has three possibilities:

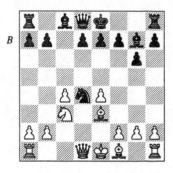

1) **9...e5** and now White has the choice between a complicated and a safe line, both of which promise him some advantage:

1a) **10 ♘b5** (the sharp continuation) 10...0-0 11 ♕d2! (11 ♘xd4? exd4 12 ♗xd4 ♕a5+ is what Black is hoping for; a recent example of this old trap being Brunner-Ekström, Suhr 1990 which continued 13 ♔e2 ♖e8 14 f3 d5! 15 ♗xg7 ♖xe4+! 16 ♔d3 ♖xc4 17 ♔e3 ♕c5+ 18 ♔d2 ♔xg7 19 ♗xc4 dxc4 with a winning attack for Black) 11...♕h4 (11...♕e7 12 f3 f5 13 ♗d3 d6 14 ♗g5 ♗f6 15 ♗xf6 ♕xf6 16 ♘xd4 exd4 17 0-0 left Black's d-pawn fatally weak in Yebelin-Silman, Budapest 1994) 12 ♗d3 d5 13 cxd5 ♘xb5 14 ♗xb5 ♕xe4 15 0-0 ♖d8 16 ♖fd1 and White is clearly better. Note that 16...♗e6 fails to 17 f3 ♕xd5 18 ♕e2 trapping Black's queen.

1b) **10 ♗d3** (the solid continuation) 10...0-0 11 0-0 d6 12 ♕d2 (12 a4!? deserves attention; Spraggett-Garcia Ilundain, Candas 1992 continued 12...♗e6 13 ♘b5 a6 14 ♘xd4 exd4 15 ♗d2 ♖c8 16 b3 f5 17 exf5 ♗xf5 18 ♕f3 with advantage to

White) 12...♗e6 (or 12...f5 13 exf5 gxf5 14 f4 ♘c6 15 ♖ad1 ♕e7 16 ♗e2 ♘d4 17 ♗xd4 exd4 18 ♘d5 with a clear plus for White, Andersson-Rogers, Malta 1980) 13 ♖ac1 a6 14 b3 ♖c8 15 f3 and now both **15...f5** 16 exf5 gxf5 17 f4 ♕f6 18 ♘e2 ♖cd8 19 ♘xd4 exd4 20 ♗f2, Ghitescu-Radovici, Romania Ch 1977, and **15...♕a5** 16 ♖fd1 f5 17 exf5 ♘xf5 18 ♗e4, Tal-Partos, Nice 1974, were very good for White.

2) **9...♘c6** 10 ♕d2 ♕a5 11 ♖c1 0-0 12 ♗e2 d6 13 0-0 ♗e6 14 b3 ♖ac8 15 f4 with a good position for White, Polugaevsky-Suetin, Kislovodsk 1972.

3) **9...♘e6** (the main line) **10 ♖c1** *(D)* and now:

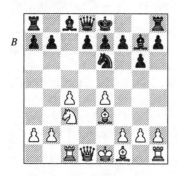

3a) **10...♕a5** and it is unclear whether White should develop his bishop at d3 or e2:

3a1) **11 ♗d3** leads to a further branch:

3a11) **11...♗xc3+** 12 ♖xc3 ♕xa2 13 ♕c1 ♕a5 14 c5 is extremely dangerous for Black.

3a12) **11...d6** 12 0-0 (better than 12 ♕d2 ♗d7 13 0-0 ♗c6 14 ♖fe1

0-0 15 ♗h6 ♕e5! 16 ♗xg7 ♕xg7 17 ♖cd1 ♘c5 18 ♗f1 a5 with equality, Nogueiras-Korchnoi, Montpellier Ct 1985) 12...0-0 13 ♗b1 ♗d7 14 f4 ♗c6?! (14...♘c5 15 ♘d5 is better for White, but not as bad as the game) 15 f5 ♘c5 16 f6! (the start of an extremely surprising combination) 16...♗xf6 17 ♖xf6! exf6 18 b4! ♕xb4 19 ♕xd6 ♘a6 20 ♕xf6 (this is the point; now Black is getting mated on the dark squares) 20...♖fe8 (20...♖fd8 21 ♗h6 ♕c5+ 22 ♔h1 ♕d4 23 e5 wins) 21 ♗d4! (not 21 ♗h6?? ♕c5+ 22 ♔h1 ♕e5) 21...♔f8 22 a3! ♕a5 23 ♖f1 ♕c7 24 ♕g7+ 1-0 Filipenko-Kliukin, Biel 1993.

3a13) **11...b6** 12 0-0 ♗b7 (if Black plays 12...g5, then White can continue as in '3a2' with f3, ♖f2 and ♗f1) 13 f4!? (probably better than 13 ♕d2 g5 14 ♖fd1 d6 when 15 f3 ♗e5 16 ♔h1 ♗f4 17 ♗xf4 ♘xf4 18 ♗f1 ♘e6 19 a3 ♕e5 20 ♘d5 h5 21 b4 ♔f8 22 ♖e1 ♖c8 was equal in Popović-Cebalo, Yugoslavia 1988, and 15 a3 h5 16 ♖c2 ♗d4 17 b4 ♕e5 18 ♘d5 ♗xe3 19 fxe3 ♖c8 20 ♖f1 ♘g7 21 ♕f2 f6 was unclear in Ljubojević-Korchnoi, Tilburg 1987) 13...0-0 14 ♗b1 d6 15 ♖f2 ♖ac8 16 ♘d5 ♗xd5 17 exd5 ♘c5 18 a3 and White is better, A.Rodriguez-Hernandez, Cuban Ch 1988.

3a2) **11 ♗e2 b6 12 0-0 ♗b7 13 f3 g5** (Larsen's plan increases the dark-squared pressure and reserves e5 for the queen, but the obvious danger is that Black's king has to stay in the centre) **14 ♖f2!** (a number of other games had continued with

♕d2, but the rook transfer to d2 appears to be the best way of meeting Black's double-edged plan) **14...h5 15 ♗f1** *(D)* and now:

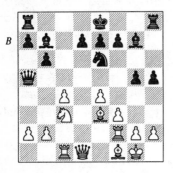

3a21) 15...♗xc3?! 16 ♖xc3 g4 backfired horribly in Chandler-Larsen, Hastings 1990 after 17 f4! ♗xe4 18 f5! g3 (18...♗xf5 19 ♗d4! ♘xd4 20 ♕xd4 e5 21 ♖e3! wins material) 19 hxg3 ♘c5 (perhaps Larsen had intended 19...♗g4, overlooking 20 ♕f3) 20 ♖a3 ♕b4 21 ♕d4 ♖g8 22 ♗d2 and Black's queen is trapped.

3a22) 15...♕e5 16 ♖d2 with a couple of examples:

3a221) 16...d6 17 ♘d5 ♔f8 18 b4 ♗h6 19 ♕b3 g4 20 ♗xh6+ ♖xh6 21 ♕e3 ♕g7 22 f4 with a distinct advantage for White, Short-Larsen, Hastings 1987/8.

3a222) 16...♗c6 (Black refrains from ...d6 as he hopes to build up pressure on the b8-h2 diagonal by playing ...♕b8 and ...♗e5; an interesting, if somewhat optimistic idea) 17 b4 ♖d8 18 ♘d5 ♕b8 19 c5 bxc5 20 bxc5 ♗e5 21 h3 ♖g8 22 ♕b3 g4 23 ♕xb8 ♗xb8 24 hxg4 hxg4 25 f4! ♗xd5 26 exd5 ♗xf4 27 ♗xf4 ♘xf4

28 ♖d4 ♘h5 29 ♖a4 and notwithstanding his pawn minus White has much the better of this ending, Stangl-Becker, Bundesliga 1991/2.

3b) 10...b6 11 ♗d3 (11 b4 is also good, for example 11...♗b7 12 ♗d3 0-0 13 0-0 ♘d4 14 ♗b1 ♘c6 15 a3 d6 16 ♕d3 ♖c8 17 f4 and White has consolidated his space advantage, Suba-Taimanov, Bucharest 1979, or 13...♖c8 14 f4 with attacking chances for White) 11...♗b7 12 0-0 ♕b8 (Black intends a variant of Larsen's plan to dominate the dark squares on the kingside; normal development would lead to positions similar to Suba-Taimanov above) 13 ♕d2 ♕d6 14 ♘d5 g5 15 b4 h5 16 ♖fd1 ♗e5 17 h3 ♗f4 18 ♗f1! and Black's attack has become bogged down while White has all sorts of threats against Black's king and queen, Mochalov-Kapengut, USSR First League 1976.

3c) 10...d6 11 b4! (when Black's knight is on e6 White should in general aim to play b4 as quickly as possible, preventing Black cementing his knight on c5 by ...a5) **11...0-0 12 ♗e2** *(D)* and now:

3c1) **12...b6** 13 0-0 ♗b7 14 ♘d5 ♘c7 (14...♕d7 15 ♗g4! f5 16 ♗h3 ♘c7 17 ♘xc7 ♕xc7 18 exf5 gxf5 19 c5! with advantage to White, Adorjan-Larsen, Hastings 1986/7) 15 ♗g5 f6 16 ♗e3 ♔h8 17 ♕b3 ♕d7 18 ♖fd1 and White enjoyed a large space advantage, C.Hansen-Larsen, Esbjerg 1988.

3c2) **12...a5** 13 a3 axb4 14 axb4 ♗d7 (14...♖a3 15 ♘d5) 15 0-0 ♗c6 16 ♕d2 ♖a3 (16...♗xc3 17 ♕xc3 ♗xe4 fails to 18 ♗h6 ♖e8 19 ♖ce1 followed by ♗g4 with a catastrophe at g7) 17 ♘d5 ♔h8 18 ♗b6 ♕d7 19 f4 with a fine position for White, Portisch-Pfleger, Manila 1974.

3d) **10...0-0** 11 b4 will quickly transpose into '3b' or '3c'.

8 ♗e2 *(D)*

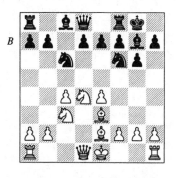

8 ... d6

Black may try to do without this move:

1) **8...a5** 9 0-0 a4 10 c5!? (an attempt at outright refutation; 10 ♘db5 would be similar to 9...a5 below) 10...d5 11 cxd6 ♕xd6 12 ♘db5 ♕b4 (12...♕xd1 13 ♖axd1 gives White some endgame advantage) 13 a3

♕a5 14 f4 e5 15 fxe5 ♘xe5 16 ♖xf6! ♗xf6 17 ♘d5 ♗d8? (Black should have tried 17...♗a6! 18 ♖c1! ♗d7 19 ♖c5 ♕d8, although White has an ominous initiative) 18 ♗d4! f6 19 ♗c3 ♕a6 20 ♘bc7 ♕a7+ 21 ♗d4 ♕b8 22 ♘xa8 with a clear plus for White, Nunn-Haik, Paris 1983.

2) **8...b6** (an important alternative) **9 0-0 ♗b7 10 f3** *(D)* (when Black develops his bishop at b7 the extra protection of the e-pawn afforded by f3 is usually a good idea) and now Black has an extensive range of possibilities:

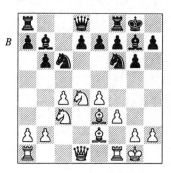

2a) **10...♘h5 11 ♘xc6!?** with a choice of recaptures:

2a1) **11...♗xc6** 12 ♖c1 f5 13 exf5 gxf5 14 f4 ♘f6 15 ♗f3 ♖c8 16 b3 ♕e8 17 ♘d5 ♕f7 18 ♘xf6+ ♕xf6 19 ♖c2 ♗xf3?! 20 ♖xf3 d6 21 ♖d2 ♔h8 22 ♗d4 gave White his standard favourable position in Nunn-Ristoja, Malta OL 1980.

2a2) **11...dxc6** 12 c5 b5 13 g4!? (13 f4 b4 14 ♘a4 ♘f6 is considered as harmless for Black by Donaldson and Silman, but they only take 15 ♗f3 and 15 ♗d3 into account when the natural 15 ♕c2 should give White an edge) 13...♘f6 14 ♕c2 (14 e5!?) 14...e5 with only a small plus for White, Khuzman-Hergott, Biel 1993.

2b) 10...d6 (this is inconsistent with the choice of ...b6) 11 ♕d2 ♕d7 12 a4!? e6 13 ♖fd1 ♖fd8 14 ♘xc6 ♕xc6 15 a5 bxa5 16 ♘b5 with threats to d6, a7 and a5, Gheorghiu-Bellon, Las Palmas 1976.

2c) 10...♖c8 11 ♕d2 ♘h5 (the alternative 11...♖e8 12 ♖ac1 ♕c7 13 b4! ♘h5 14 ♘xc6 ♗xc6 15 ♘d5 ♕b8 16 f4 ♘f6 17 ♗f3 d6 18 ♗d4 was very good for White in Nunn-Karlsson, Helsinki 1981) **12 ♖fd1 ♘e5 13 b3 f5 14 exf5 gxf5 15 ♘d5!** *(D)* and now:

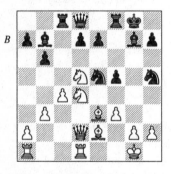

2c1) 15...♕e8?! (Kir.Georgiev-Kristensen, Saint John 1988) 16 f4! ♗xd5 (16...♘g4 17 ♘xf5 ♘xe3 18 ♘xg7 ♘xg7 19 ♕xe3 wins) 17 cxd5 ♘g4 18 ♘xf5! ♗xa1 19 ♗xg4 ♘f6 (19...♗f6 20 d6! e6 21 ♘e7+ ♗xe7 22 dxe7 ♖f6 23 ♕xd7 wins and 19...♗c3 20 ♕d3 ♘g7 21 d6 are no better) 20 ♘h6+ ♔g7 21 ♖xa1 ♔xh6 22 f5+ ♔g7 23 ♗h6+ ♔h8 24 ♗xf8

♘xg4 25 ♕d4+ ♘f6 26 ♗h6 wins for White.

2c2) 15...♗xd5 16 cxd5 f4 17 ♗f2 ♕e8 and now **18 ♗d3?!** ♘xd3 19 ♕xd3 ♕g6 20 ♕xg6 hxg6 21 ♖ac1 ♖xc1 22 ♖xc1 ♗xd4! 23 ♗xd4 ♖f5 left White fighting for a draw in Sherzer-Edelman, New York 1993. However, White's 18th move was a bit panicky. Much better would have been **18 d6** when both **18...exd6** 19 ♘b5 ♕g6 20 ♖ac1 and **18...e6** 19 ♘b5 ♕g6 20 ♖ac1 are good for White.

2d) 10...♘xd4 11 ♗xd4 d6 12 ♕d2 ♘d7 13 ♗xg7 (13 ♗e3 is a promising alternative) 13...♔xg7 14 f4 ♖c8 15 ♖ad1 ♘f6 16 e5 dxe5 17 fxe5 ♘g8 18 ♕e3! with some advantage for White, Cvetković-Cebalo, Yugoslavia 1985.

2e) 10...♘e8 11 ♕d2 ♘c7 12 ♖ad1 ♘e6 13 ♘db5 d6 14 ♘d5 ♖b8 15 f4 ♘c5 16 ♗f3 a6 17 ♘d4 ♘xd4 18 ♗xd4 ♗xd4+ 19 ♕xd4 b5, Agapov-Kimelfeld, USSR 1985, and now 20 e5 would have kept some advantage for White.

2f) 10...e6 11 ♕d2 (11 ♘db5 is probably also good, e.g. 11...d5 12 cxd5 exd5 13 exd5 ♘e7 14 d6 ♘f5 15 ♗f2 ♘e8 16 d7 ♘f6 17 g4 ♘e7 18 ♗h4 with advantage, A.Rodriguez-Pinal, Sagua la Grande 1984) 11...d5 (11...♕e7 is more solid, as in Panno-Bellon, Buenos Aires 1994, which continued 12 ♖fe1 ♖fd8 13 ♗f1 ♘xd4 14 ♗xd4 ♘e8 15 ♗f2 ♘c7 16 ♖ad1 d6 17 a4 with an edge for White) 12 ♘xc6 ♗xc6 13 cxd5 exd5 14 e5 ♘d7 15 f4 ♘c5 16 ♖ad1!

f6 (16...♘e4 17 ♘xe4 fxe4 18 ♕d6! ♗b7 19 ♗c4 is also unpleasant) 17 ♘xd5 fxe5 18 ♗c4 ♔h8 19 fxe5 ♖xf1+ (19...♗xe5 20 ♗d4 ♕d6 21 ♗xe5+ ♕xe5 22 ♖fe1 ♘e4 23 ♖xe4! 1-0 Kuporosov-Yakovich, USSR 1984) 20 ♖xf1 ♕h4 21 ♖f4! ♕h5 22 ♘e7 ♗b7 23 b4 ♘e4 24 ♕d7 ♖b8 25 ♘c8! ♖xc8 26 ♕xb7 ♖d8 27 ♕xe4 ♗xe5 28 ♗e2 1-0 Kuporosov-Malishauskas, USSR 1985.

2g) **10...♕b8** 11 ♕d2 ♖d8 12 ♖fd1 d6 13 ♘b3!? (13 ♕e1 ♖d7 14 ♕h4 is another possibility) 13...♖d7 14 a4 ♕d8 15 a5 bxa5 16 ♘b5 ♗a6 17 ♘xa5 ♗xb5 18 cxb5 ♘xa5 19 ♕xa5 ♕xa5 20 ♖xa5 with a winning endgame for White, Arakhamia-Canela, Novi Sad OL 1990.

9   0-0 *(D)*

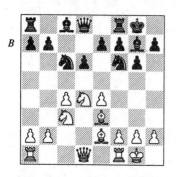

9   ...   ♗d7

Or:

1) **9...♘xd4** (and not 9...♘g4? losing a piece after 10 ♗xg4 ♗xg4 11 ♘xc6) 10 ♗xd4 ♗e6 11 f4 ♖c8 (11...♕c8 12 b3 ♖d8 {12...♗g4 13 e5!} and now 13 h3, keeping Black's pieces out of g4 gives White a good game) 12 b3 ♗d7 13 e5 dxe5 14 fxe5 ♘e8 15 ♕d2 ♗c6 16 ♕e3 with advantage to White, A.Sokolov-Nemet, Bern 1992.

2) **9...♘d7** 10 ♖b1 ♘c5 11 ♕d2 ♘xd4 12 ♗xd4 a5 13 b3 ♗xd4 14 ♕xd4 b6 15 ♖fe1 ♗b7 16 ♖bd1 f6 17 ♗g4 ♗c6 18 h4! with a slight advantage for White, Anand-Morović, Novi Sad OL 1990.

3) **9...a5** 10 f3 ♘d7 11 ♘db5 ♘c5 12 ♕d2 a4 13 ♖fd1 ♕a5 14 ♖ac1 ♗e6 15 ♘d5 ♕xd2 16 ♖xd2 ♗xd5? (16...♖fd8 is only slightly better for White) 17 cxd5 ♘b4 18 ♖xc5! dxc5 19 ♗xc5 ♘xa2 20 ♗xe7 and Black is in trouble, Andersson-Larsen, Linares 1983.

4) **9...♖e8**, another Larsen idea, is the most important alternative to 9...♗d7. White has several tries:

4a) **10 ♖c1** ♘xd4 11 ♗xd4 ♗h6! 12 ♖c2 b6 (12...e5 13 ♗e3 ♗xe3 14 fxe3 is unclear) 13 f3 ♗b7 14 ♕e1 ♘h5 was fine for Black in Pyhälä-Rantanen, Pori 1986.

4b) **10 ♖b1** a6 11 f3 ♗d7 12 ♘c2 ♘e5 13 a4 ♕c7 14 ♘a3 e6 15 f4 with some advantage for White, Wolff-Larsen, New York 1990.

4c) **10 ♘b3** ♗e6 11 f3 ♘e5 12 ♘d5 ♗d7 13 ♕d2 ♘xd5 14 cxd5 b5 15 ♖ac1 a5 16 ♘d4 and White stood very well in Wahls-Vanscura, Budapest 1988, but Black played the opening horribly.

4d) **10 ♘c2**, also avoiding the knight exchange and preparing solid development by ♖c1 was recommended in *BTS2* but has still not been tested.

10   ♕d2

It is also possible to move the knight on d4, thereby frustrating Black's plan of ...♘xd4 and ...♗c6. In the game Korchnoi-Soos, Rome 1982, White continued 10 ♘b3 ♘a5 (10...a5 11 a4 ♘b4 12 f3 ♗c6 13 ♕d2 ♖c8 14 ♔h1 ♘d7 15 ♘d5 was also better for White, Tarjan-Strauss, USA 1982) 11 f3 ♘xb3 12 axb3 a6 13 b4 ♗e6 14 ♕d2 ♖c8 15 b3 ♘d7 16 ♖a2, while Schmidt-Kagan, Lucerne 1982, went 10 ♘c2 ♗e6 11 ♕d2 a5 12 f4 a4 13 ♖ab1 ♗g4 14 ♗d3 ♗c8 15 h3 ♘d7 16 ♗e2 and in both cases White had a good position. It could well be that these lines are as strong as the traditional continuations 10 ♖c1 and 10 ♕d2, but they do not seem to have been tested in recent years.

A separate question is whether White should play 10 ♖c1 or 10 ♕d2. We are concentrating on the latter move for two reasons. Firstly, the rook on c1 is sometimes vulnerable to unwelcome attacks by ...♘xd4 and ...♗h6, and secondly White often starts a queenside advance by a3 and b4 later on. If Black plays ...a5 White needs a rook on b1 to force through b4, but playing the rook to c1 and then to b1 loses a tempo.

10   ...   ♘xd4

10...♖c8 11 f3 a6 12 ♖ac1 ♘xd4 13 ♗xd4 ♗e6 14 b3 is too passive and White has a very comfortable position, Smejkal-Diez del Corral, Skopje OL 1972.

11   ♗xd4   ♗c6
12   f3   a5

The move-order is flexible, but White always answers ...♘d7 by ♗e3 (to avoid freeing exchanges) and ...a5 by b3 (or else Black plays ...a4 followed by ...♕a5, with an active position).

13   b3   ♘d7 (D)

Or 13...♖e8 (13...♘h5?! 14 ♗e3! f5 15 exf5 gxf5 16 f4 was promising for White in Kavalek-Larsen, USA-Nordic match 1986) 14 ♖fd1 ♘d7 15 ♗e3 ♘c5 16 ♖ac1 (16 ♖ab1 appears more consistent) 16...♕b6 17 ♘b5 ♖ec8 18 ♕e1 (18 ♘d4 is better) 18...♗xb5! 19 cxb5 ♗h6 with an equal position, Arnason-Karlsson, Helsinki 1986.

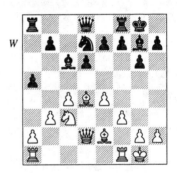

14   ♗e3

14 ♗f2!? is an interesting alternative. After 14...♘c5 15 ♖ab1 Black has:

1) 15...♕b6 16 a3! ♕d8 (as 16...♘xb3, which would win with the white bishop on e3, now fails to 17 ♕d1! Black has no choice but to retreat his queen without having accomplished the main point behind ...♕b6, namely to play ...♖fc8) and now:

1a) **17 ⟐fc1 a4!**.

1b) **17 b4** (premature) 17...axb4 18 axb4 ⟐a4 19 ⟐xa4 ⟐xa4 20 ⟐fc1 ⟐a8 with a very comfortable game for Black, Arnason-Larsen, Östersund Z 1992.

1c) **17 ⟐d1** (often a useful move in this variation as it allows White to play b4 under more favourable circumstances) 17...b6 18 b4 ⟐d7 19 ⟐b3 ± Wells-McElligott, Dublin 1993.

2) **15...⟐c7** 16 ⟐fc1 ⟐fc8 17 ⟐d1 ⟐d8 18 a3 b6 19 b4 axb4 20 axb4 ⟐d7 21 ⟐b3 ⟐f8 22 ⟐e3 is similar to '1c' and gave White an edge in Renet-Spangenberg, Buenos Aires 1994.

3) **15...e6** 16 ⟐b5!? ⟐e5 17 ⟐d4 ⟐f6 was played in Hellers-Cebalo, Debrecen Echt 1992, and now 18 g3! would threaten to push back the black pieces. Note that 18...⟐xe4 19 fxe4 ⟐xe4 20 ⟐e3 ⟐xf2 fails to 21 ⟐c2!.

4) **15...f5** 16 exf5 gxf5 17 a3 ⟐h8 18 b4 axb4 19 axb4 ⟐a4 20 ⟐xa4 ½-½ Bagirov-Yudasin, USSR 1991. Perhaps 18 b4 was a little hasty, but even so I would have thought that the final position was in White's favour, e.g. 20...⟐xa4 21 b5!? ⟐d7 22 c5 dxc5 23 ⟐xc5 leaves him with the better pawn structure.

14 ...   ⟐c5

15 ⟐ab1 *(D)*

In order to make progress White must expel the knight from c5, and so he needs to play a3 and b4. 15 ⟐ab1 appears the most logical, and this intuitive assessment is supported

by the fact that with the alternative **15 ⟐ac1** (this position can also arise via 10 ⟐c1), White is struggling to gain any advantage. After **15...⟐b6** (15...f5 16 exf5 gxf5 17 ⟐d5 ⟐f7 18 ⟐fd1 b6! 19 ⟐g5 ⟐a7 was unclear in Vaganian-Yudasin, USSR Ch 1988) **16 ⟐b5 ⟐fc8 17 ⟐fd1 ⟐d8** there is:

1) **18 ⟐f1 ⟐f8** 19 ⟐c3 b6 20 ⟐d5 ⟐ab8 21 ⟐b1 ⟐e5 22 ⟐h6 ⟐g7 23 ⟐g5 ⟐b7 24 ⟐e1 ⟐e6 25 ⟐e3 ⟐c5! with a level game, Sax-Petursson, Reykjavik 1988.

2) **18 ⟐d4** was answered by **18...⟐f8?!** 19 ⟐b1 ⟐f6 20 a3 ⟐g7 21 b4 axb4 22 axb4 ⟐e6 23 ⟐xe6 fxe6 24 b5 ⟐e8 25 f4 with a clear plus for White in Nunn-Velimirović, Dubai OL 1986. However, Black should have played **18...⟐d7** 19 ⟐b1 ⟐e6 20 ⟐xe6 ⟐xe6 with equality.

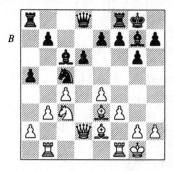

15 ...   ⟐b6

After **15...e6** 16 ⟐d1! intending ⟐e2-d4, a3 and b4 Black's panic reaction 16...f5 17 exf5 ⟐xf5 18 ⟐e2 was good for White in Tringov-Haik, Vrnjačka Banja 1986.

15...b6 16 ⟐d1 (White's problem is that the immediate a3 may be met by ...a4; the idea of ♗d1 is to be able to take the black knight when it arrives at b3, but White has other ways to nullify ...a4, for example with the slow preparatory plan of ♖fc1-c2, ♗f1 and ♕f2 to line up against Black's weak pawn on b6) 16...♕b8 17 a3 ♖c8 18 ♘d5 ♗xd5?! (probably bad, but White is slightly better in any case) 19 exd5 a4 20 b4 ♘b3 21 ♕e2 gave White an excellent position in Anand-Larsen, Cannes 1989.

16 ♖fc1

Or 16 ♘b5 (not 16 a3? ♘xb3! 17 ♕d3 ♗d4) 16...♖fc8 17 ♖fd1 ♕d8 18 ♘d4 (18 ♔h1 ♕f8 19 ♘c3 b6 20 a3 ♖ab8 21 ♗f1 h5 22 ♘d5 ♖b7 23 b4 axb4 24 axb4 ♘d7 25 c5! gave White a good game in Greenfeld-Bruk, Israel 1992, but it's hard to believe that ♘c3-b5, followed shortly by ♘b5-c3 is White's best course of action) 18...♕f8 19 a3 (19 ♗f1 may be better, but I doubt that White has more than a tiny edge) 19...♗d7! (not 19...♗f6? 20 b4 axb4 21 axb4 ♘e6 22 ♘xe6 fxe6 23 f4 with the same White advantage as in Nunn-Velimirović above) 20 b4 axb4 21 axb4 ♘e6 22 ♖a1 ♖xa1 23 ♖xa1 ♖a8 24 ♖xa8 ♕xa8 25 ♘xe6 ♗xe6 with complete equality, Jansa-Petursson, Næstved 1988.

16 ...   ♖fc8

17 ♖c2

Again this is useful preparation for a3 and b4. Now Black cannot meet 18 a3 by 18...♘xb3 because 19 ♘d1! wins material.

17 ...   ♕d8

There is no point to **17...♕b4** because after 18 ♕c1 Black will be driven back by a3 with great loss of time.

18 ♗f1   ♗e5

White intends ♕f2, followed by a3 and b4, so Black has to organise some counterplay. With ...♗e5 he hopes to become active with ...e6 and ...♕h4, but the exposed bishop on e5 is a target which causes White to switch plans away from his queenside pawn advance to a more aggressive idea.

19 ♘d1!?

The knight transfer to h6, which gains time along the way when ♘g4 hits the bishop, is not a very thematic approach, but chess cannot always be played according to the recipe book.

19 ...   ♕e8 *(D)*

Preparing ...b5 is the most natural way to counter White's slow build-up towards a kingside attack. Moreover the queen defends the f7-pawn which might come under fire after ♘f2-g4-h6+.

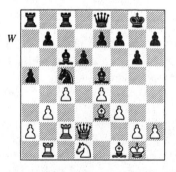

20 ♘f2   b5?!

It would have been better to play **20...♗g7**, so as to meet 21 ♘g4 by 21...h5. Then White could hardly venture into the lion's den by 22 ♘h6+ ♚h7, so the knight would have to return to f2. After 20...♗g7 White should switch plans again by 21 ♘d3 b6 22 ♕f2, followed by a3 and b4.

21	♘g4	♗g7
22	cxb5	♗xb5
23	♘h6+	♚f8 *(D)*

Unfortunately Black has to go to f8 because **23...♚h8** loses a pawn after 24 ♘xf7+, while **23...♗xh6** 24 ♗xh6 gives White a permanent advantage.

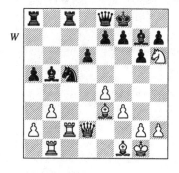

24	♗xb5	♕xb5
25	♕d5	♕e8
26	e5!	♖d8?!

In a difficult position Black fails to offer the most resistance. He should try to give up a pawn to reach an ending in which the offside knight on h6 gives White problems. Therefore **26...♘e6** was best (26...♖a6 27 exd6 is bad since 27...♖xd6 28 ♕xf7+! wins a clear pawn), with the idea 27 ♖xc8 ♖xc8 28 exd6 exd6 **29 ♕xd6+ ♕e7 30 ♕xe7+ ♚xe7** with excellent counterplay. White should prefer **29 ♘g4!**, whereupon the weak pawns on d6 and a5 make Black's position unattractive, but his chances would certainly be much better than in the game.

27	exd6	exd6
28	♖e1	♖ac8?

The final collapse. **28...♘e6** was necessary to meet the threat of 29 ♖xc5, when 29 ♘g4 gives White a positional advantage but nothing decisive.

29	♖xc5!	♖xc5
30	♕xc5	1-0

8 Taimanov Variation

The first moves of this system run 1 e4 c5 2 ♘f3 e6 3 d4 cxd4 4 ♘xd4 ♘c6 (or 2...♘c6 and 4...e6). In a way this resembles the Kan Variation, since Black keeps the f8-b4 diagonal open for his bishop, but here White cannot play ♗d3 so there are fewer options for the first player.

BTS2 recommended the Maroczy set-up starting with 5 ♘b5, but this time we are opting for 5 ♘c3. There are several reasons for this change but I'll just give one example from my own practice. After 5 ♘b5 d6 6 c4 ♘f6 7 ♘1c3 a6 8 ♘a3 ♗e7 9 ♗e2 0-0 10 0-0 b6 11 ♗e3 ♘e5 12 f4 ♘ed7 13 ♗f3 ♗b7 14 ♕e2 White's main idea, perhaps after some further preparatory moves such as ♖ac1 and ♖fd1, is to play g4-g5 gaining space on the kingside and relieving some of the pressure against e4. However, in Gallagher-Cramling, Bern 1991, this idea was nipped in the bud by 14...h6!. Now any subsequent g4 can be met by ...♘h7 and ...g5 causing White some positional difficulties as Black will gain control of e5. Deprived of my only active plan I floundered around for a few moves before settling on a draw.

The new system, 5 ♘c3, is also not without its drawbacks mainly because the Classical Scheveningen is not part of the repertoire we are proposing in this book. Therefore we have to rely on some slightly less common systems, but as you will see they are also quite dangerous for Black. Game 22 deals with 5...a6, against which we are recommending 6 ♘xc6, and 5...d6, against which we suggest 6 g4 inviting transposition to the Keres Attack of Chapter 2. Game 23 deals with 5...♕c7; to avoid transposition to the Scheveningen we are suggesting 6 f4.

Game 22
Gallagher – Rufener
Bern 1994

1	e4	c5
2	♘f3	e6
3	d4	cxd4
4	♘xd4	♘c6
5	♘c3 (D)	

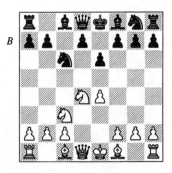

5	...	a6

After **5...d6** we suggest **6 g4!?**. Of course there are many other good moves such as 6 ♗e3 or 6 ♗e2 but these involve being ready to play lines in the Scheveningen that do not form part of our repertoire. 6 g4 caused astonishment when it was first adopted by no less than Anatoly Karpov during the 1985 World Championship match. Black has:

1) **6...♘f6** transposing to Chapter 2.

2) **6...h6** 7 h4 (consistent) 7....a6 8 ♗g2 (8 ♗e3 is quite playable but after 8...♘f6 we have transposed to a line in the Keres Attack that is not discussed in Chapter 2) 8...♗e7 9 ♗e3 ♘xd4 (9...♗xh4 10 ♘xc6 bxc6 11 ♖xh4! ♕xh4 12 ♕xd6 ♗d7 13 g5! is much too risky for Black) 10 ♕xd4 e5 11 ♕d1 ♗e6 (11...♗xh4? 12 ♘d5!, threatening ♗b6 is very strong and 11...♘f6 12 ♗f3! is also good for White) 12 ♘d5 ♖c8 13 c3 ♘f6 14 ♘xe7 ♕xe7 15 g5 (15 ♗f3, maintaining the tension, deserves consideration) 15...hxg5 16 hxg5 ♖xh1+ 17 ♗xh1 ♘g4 18 ♗d2 ♕f8! 19 ♕f3 (19 ♗f3 would have been met by 19...♕h8!) 19...♕h8 20 ♗g2 ♕h4 21 b3! (threatening ♔e2 and then ♖h1) 21...d5! 22 ♕g3 ♕xg3 23 fxg3, Karpov-Kasparov, Moscow Wch (14) 1985, with a rather strange ending in which Black was able to maintain the balance despite having an awkwardly placed knight on g4.

3) **6...♘xd4** 7 ♕xd4 ♘e7 8 ♗e3 ♘c6 9 ♕d2 ♗e7 10 0-0-0 a6 11 ♔b1 0-0 12 g5 b5 13 f4 leads to a fairly normal Sicilian position with White

attacking on the kingside and Black advancing on the queenside. In the game Lobron-Schulze, Bundesliga 1993 White gained the upper hand after 13...b4 14 ♘a4 ♖b8 15 h4 ♕a5 16 b3 d5 17 exd5 exd5 18 ♗d3 ♗g4 19 ♖dg1 ♗f3 20 ♖h3 ♗e4 21 f5 ♖fe8 22 f6 ♗xd3 23 ♕xd3 ♗d6 24 h5.

4) **6...a6** 7 ♗e3 ♘ge7 (this is the most popular way for Black to play; alternatively 7...♗d7 8 g5 ♘ge7 9 ♘de2!? is slightly better for White according to Ehlvest) **8 ♘b3** (8 g5!? is also possible, with a probable transposition to line '3') **8...b5** *(D)* (or 8...♘g6 9 ♕e2 ♗e7 10 0-0-0 b5 11 f4 h6 12 ♕f2 ♗d7 13 ♔b1 ♖b8 14 ♗e2 ♘a5 15 ♘xa5 ♕xa5 16 ♗d3 with an edge for White, Bologan-Frolov, USSR Ch 1991) and now:

4a) **9 f4 ♗b7 10 ♕f3?!** (10 ♗g2 ♘a5 11 ♘xa5 ♕xa5 12 ♕e2 transposes to line '4b', but if White employs this move order Black may try 10...♘g6) **10...g5!** (Black gives up a pawn to gain control of e5, not an uncommon idea in the Sicilian) 11 fxg5 ♘e5 12 ♕g2 b4 13 ♘e2 h5! (to give you an idea of modern preparation,

Judit Polgar says that she had this position on the board in her room on the morning of the game) 14 gxh5? (Shirov heads straight into the trap; 14 gxh6 ♗xh6 15 ♗xh6 ♖xh6 gives Black good play, but 14 0-0-0 would have been unclear) 14...♘f5! 15 ♗f2?! (a better chance was to sacrifice the queen by 15 exf5 ♗xg2 16 ♗xg2 although Black must be doing well after 16...♖xh5) 15...♕xg5! 16 ♘a5 (Shirov had been relying on this counterstroke) 16...♘e3! (played instantly) 17 ♕g3 (17 ♕xg5 ♘f3# and 17 ♗xe3 ♕xe3 18 ♘xb7 ♘f3+ 19 ♔d1 ♕d2# are the attractive points to Black's combination) 17...♕xg3 18 ♘xg3 ♘xc2+ 19 ♔d1 ♘xa1 20 ♘xb7 b3! and the knight escaped, leaving Black a clear exchange up, Shirov-J.Polgar, Buenos Aires 1994.

4b) 9 ♕e2 ♘a5 10 ♘xa5 (this looks better than 10 0-0-0 ♘c4, as played in Shirov-Salov, Linares 1993) 10...♕xa5 11 ♗g2 ♗b7 12 f4 ♘c6 13 0-0 ♗e7 14 g5 ♕c7 15 ♕f2 ♗d8 16 ♘e2! 0-0 17 h4 ♘e7, Lanka-Yermolinsky, Lucerne Wcht 1993, and now 18 ♘d4! d5 (18...e5 19 fxe5 dxe5 20 ♘e6!) 19 e5 would have been very promising for White according to Lanka.

6   ♘xc6   bxc6

6...dxc6 is just bad for Black and is never seen in practice.

7   ♗d3 *(D)*

7   ...   d5

Black has a couple of important alternatives; he can set up a small centre with 7...d6 or he can delay any central action until he sees what

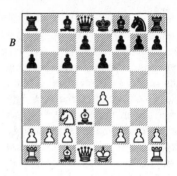

set-up White has adopted, by playing 7...♕c7.

1) **7...d6 8 0-0 ♘f6 9 f4** with the branch:

1a) **9...♗e7** (9...e5 10 ♔h1 ♗e7 11 fxe5 dxe5 12 ♗e3 0-0 13 ♘a4 gave White an edge in Van der Wiel Zapata, Palma 1989) **10 ♕e2** (10 ♕f3 should be considered) **10...♘d7 11 ♔h1 ♕c7** and now:

1a1) The game Reeh-J.Horvath, Mitropa Cup 1990 continued **12 ♗d2** 0-0 13 ♖ae1 ♘c5 14 e5 d5 15 ♗xh7+!? (good enough for a draw) 15...♔xh7 16 ♕h5+ ♔g8 17 ♖e3 f5 18 ♖h3 ♗d7 19 ♖ff3 ♗e8 20 ♕h7+ ♔f7 21 ♕h5+ ♔g8 22 ♕h7+ ♔f7 23 ♕h5+ ♔g8 ½-½.

1a2) **12 ♘a4!?** (often a good idea when Black has played an early ...♘d7 as it prevents ...♘c5) 12...0-0 13 c4 and after a continuation such as 13...c5 14 b3 ♗b7 15 ♗b2 White has an edge.

1b) **9...♕c7 10 ♕e2** (10 ♕e1 is also quite a promising move and in Gallagher-Landenbergue, Martigny 1993 I tried 10 ♕f3, achieving a clear advantage after 10...♗b7 11 b3 c5 12 ♗b2 ♗e7 13 ♖ae1 ♘d7 14

♘d1! ♗f6 15 ♗xf6, when 15...♘xf6 16 ♕g3 0-0 17 e5 gives White a formidable attack, and my opponent's choice, 15...gxf6 left him with a miserable position after 16 ♕h5) 10...d5 (it may seem strange to play ...d5 so soon after having played ...d6 but Black is arguing that f2-f4 doesn't help White's position as it limits the scope of his queen's bishop; 10...e5 can be met in similar fashion to the Van der Wiel-Zapata game in '1a' above) 11 ♗d2 ♗e7 (it would require a brave man to take the b-pawn with ...♕b6+, but if White doesn't feel like risking this he could first play ♔h1) 12 ♖ae1 0-0 13 ♔h1 ♖e8 14 e5 ♘d7 15 ♘a4 (this, followed by c4, is very common in these lines and ensures that White can at least hold his own on the queenside) 15...♘c5 16 ♘xc5 ♗xc5 17 c4 a5 18 ♖c1 ♕b6 19 b3 (the last solid move) 19...♗d7 20 ♖f3 g6 21 ♗e1 (heading for h4 and f6) 21...♗e7 22 ♖h3 f5 (this fatally weakens g6, but it's unlikely that Black could have held the kingside in the long run; he really needs a knight on f8) 23 exf6 ♗xf6 24 ♗f2! c5 (24...♕c7 loses after 25 ♖xh7! ♔xh7 26 ♕h5+ ♔g8 27 ♕xg6+ ♗g7 28 ♕h7+ ♔f7 29 ♗g6+ ♔e7 30 ♗c5+ ♔f6 31 ♗h5! and mate in a few moves) 24...c5 25 ♕g4! ♖e7 (White was threatening ♖xh7!) 26 ♗xg6! hxg6 (of course 26...♖g7 allows 27 ♗xh7+) 27 ♕xg6+ ♗g7 28 cxd5! ♖c8 29 f5! and White soon won, Kosten-Collinson, British Ch (Plymouth) 1989.

2) **7...♕c7 8 0-0 ♘f6** (8...c5 9 ♕e2 ♗b7 10 0-0 ♘e7 11 b3 ♘g6 12 ♗d2 ♗e7 13 ♕h5 0-0-0 14 ♘a4 d5 15 exd5 ♖xd5 16 ♕e2 ♕c6 17 ♗c3 ♖h5?! 18 ♖ae1 ♗f6 19 ♗xf6 gxf6 20 ♗e4 ♕xe4 21 ♕xe4 ♗xe4 22 ♖xe4 ♖d8 23 ♖c4 gave White a very good ending in Gallagher-Zviagintsev, Loosdorf 1993, but I have to admit that ♗xa6!, either on move 18 or on move 20, simply never occurred to me) **9 f4** (9 ♕e2!?) **9...d5** (9...d6 is '1b') **10 ♕f3 ♗e7** *(D)* with a couple of examples:

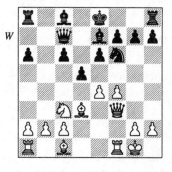

2a) **11 b3** 0-0 12 ♗b2 ♖d8 13 e5 ♘d7 14 ♕h3 g6 15 ♘d1! (having forced a weakening on the dark squares around the black king, White sends his knight off on a long journey to try to exploit them) 15...c5 16 c4 ♘b6 17 ♘f2 dxc4 18 bxc4 ♗b7 19 ♘g4 h5 20 ♘h6+ ♔g7 21 f5! ♕c6 (or 21...♔xh6 22 fxg6 fxg6 23 ♖f7 with a crushing attack) 22 fxg6 ♔xh6 23 ♖xf7 ♖xd3 24 ♖h7+ 1-0 Rohde-Spraggett, San Francisco 1987. A model attack from White.

2b) **11 ♔h1 ♗b7** (11...0-0 could be met by 12 e5 ♘d7 13 ♕h3) 12 f5!?

e5 13 ♕g3 d4 14 ♘b1 c5 15 ♘d2 0-0 16 ♘c4! ♚h8 (16...♗xe4 is met by 17 ♗h6 and 16...♘xe4 by 17 ♗xe4 ♗xe4 18 f6! ♗xf6 19 ♖xf6) 17 ♖e1 (now White has a big positional plus) 17...♘d7 18 ♗d2 a5 (Black is worried about White playing ♗a5 at some point) 19 a4! (fixing the weakness on a5 and preparing to swing the queen's rook to the kingside) 19...♗f6 20 ♖a3! ♘b8 21 ♕g4 ♘c6 22 ♗e2 (White's last two moves have cleared the third rank for the rook) 22...♖fd8 23 ♖h3! ♚g8 24 ♖h6! g6 25 ♕h3 ♘e7 26 ♗d3 ♖a6 (now it's Black's turn to try to swing his rook into the defence – but to no avail) 27 ♖xh7 ♗g7 28 ♖xg7+! ♚xg7 29 ♕h6+ ♚g8 30 ♗xa5! (a nice point) 30...♕c6 (30...♖xa5 31 f6 mates) 31 ♗xd8 ♘xf5 32 ♕g5 1-0.

Undoubtedly Black's play in these two games can be improved upon but they illustrate well White's ideas in this system. The lines where Black plays ...♕c7 are of particular importance as they can equally be reached via Game 23.

8 0-0   ♘f6 *(D)*

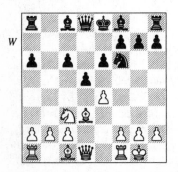

9 ♖e1

9 ♕e2 is much less explored than the text but it has made a few successful appearances recently. For example, Smyslov-C.Hansen, Biel IZ 1993 continued 9...♗e7 10 b3 0-0 11 ♗b2 a5 (11...♘d7 12 ♘a4 ♗f6 was an incredibly bad idea from the system's originator, and after 13 e5 ♗e7 14 c4 a5 15 cxd5 cxd5 16 ♖ac1 White had a clear plus in the game David-Taimanov, Prague 1993; perhaps Black can try 11...c5) 12 ♖ad1 ♕c7 13 ♘a4!? (White wishes to play c4 even if it costs him the bishop pair) 13...♗b7 14 c4 ♖fd8 (14...dxe4 15 ♗xe4 ♘xe4 16 ♕xe4 c5 17 ♕e3 ♖fd8 18 ♗e5 ♕c6 19 f3 is what Black should have played according to Smyslov, even if White is still slightly better) 15 e5 ♘d7 16 cxd5 cxd5 17 ♖c1 ♕b8 18 ♗d4 with a very promising position for White. It's worth seeing a bit more of this game as the veteran Smyslov soon transformed his positional advantage into a devastating kingside attack: 18...♗a3 19 ♖c3! (threatening ♗xh7+) 19...h6 20 ♗b5 ♘f8 21 ♖g3 ♘g6 22 ♘b6 ♖a7 23 ♘d7 ♕a8 24 ♖xg6! fxg6 25 ♕g4 ♗a6 26 ♕xe6+ ♚h7 27 ♗xa6 ♖xa6 28 ♕f7 ♖xd7 29 ♕xd7 ♕c6 30 ♕f7 ♕e6 31 ♕xe6 ♖xe6 32 f4 and White won.

9 ...   ♗e7

9...♗b7 (a major alternative) 10 e5 ♘d7 11 ♘a4 *(D)* and now Black has a choice:

1) 11...♕h4 (11...♕a5 12 b3 ♗b4 13 ♖e2 is slightly better for White according to Sax, who also believes

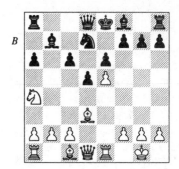

that 12 c3 is worthy of attention) 12 b3 ♞c5 13 ♖b1! ♞xd3 (Black is in no position to open the b-file by ♞xa4) 14 cxd3 (if Black now continues passively White can aim for a good knight v bad bishop position by ♗e3-c5) 14...♗b4? (a strange decision forcing White to activate his rook; better is 14...c5, upon which Sax recommends 15 ♖e3) 15 ♖e3 g6 (15...0-0 loses to 16 ♖g3) 16 ♖g3 ♗e7 17 ♗e3 f5 (17...d4 18 ♖h3) 18 exf6 ♛xf6 19 ♖f3 ♛h4 20 ♛e2 ♗c8 (20...e5 21 ♗c5) 21 ♛b2, Sax-Zapata, Subotica IZ 1987, and not only has White a strategically won game but he also collected some material after 21...♖f8 22 ♖xf8+ ♗xf8 23 ♞b6 ♖b8 24 ♛e5.

2) **11...♗e7** 12 ♛g4 g5 13 b3 h5 14 ♛e2 c5 15 c4 d4 16 ♗e4 ♛c7 17 ♗xb7 ♛xb7 18 ♞b2 gave White an edge in Sierro Gonzalez-Nogueiras, St Clara 1987. White has a safer king and should eventually aim to open the position by playing b4.

3) **11...♛c7!** 12 ♗f4 c5 13 c4 **dxc4** and now:

3a) Adams-Andersson, Cannes 1989 continued **14 ♗e4 ♗e7 15 ♖c1**

0-0 16 ♖xc4 ♗xe4 17 ♖cxe4 ♖fd8 18 ♛c2 ♞b6 19 ♞xb6 ♛xb6 20 ♗e3 ♛a5 21 ♖a1 ♖d5 22 h3 ♖ad8 23 ♖c1 h6 24 b3 ♛b5 with an equal game.

3b) Perhaps White should simply have played **14 ♗xc4,** which gives him some chances of an edge. For example 14...♛c6 (14...♗e7 should not be met by 15 ♛g4 on account of 15...g5!, but by 15 ♞c3 when 15...♞b6 16 ♗b3 looks a little better for White) 15 ♗f1 (better than 15 f3 which would make it virtually impossible for White to develop any sort of kingside attack) 15...♗e7 16 ♞c3 0-0 17 ♛g4 ♖fd8 18 ♗h6 and now **18...♗f8** can be met by 19 ♖e3, threatening 20 ♗xg7 and **18...g6** by 19 ♗g5! when White can hope to exploit the weakened dark squares around the black king.

10 e5   ♞d7
11 ♛g4 *(D)*

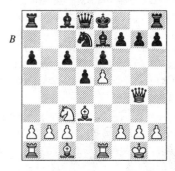

11 ...   g6
Black can also play **11...♔f8**. After 12 ♗d2 f5?! (12...♞c5 13 ♞a4 h5 14 ♛d4 ♞xa4 15 ♛xa4 c5 16 c4 was slightly better for White in Rogers-Razuvaev, Tilburg 1993 and

12...h5 13 ♕f3 ♔g8 14 ♘a4 ♗g5 15 ♕e2 ♗xd2 16 ♕xd2 g6 17 ♖ac1 also gave White an edge in J.Horvath-Van Mil, Budapest 1989 but both these continuations are more solid than 12...f5) 13 exf6 ♘xf6 14 ♕g3. Black has an impressive centre but it's not going anywhere and his king is not ideally placed. In Mestel-Daly, British Ch 1992 White eventually triumphed in a cascade of sacrifices: 14...♔f7 15 ♘a4 ♗d6 16 f4 c5 17 c4 ♗d7 18 ♘c3 ♖e8 19 ♖e2 ♗c6 20 ♖ae1 ♕d7 21 ♕h3 g6 22 f5! exf5 23 cxd5 ♗b5 24 ♘xb5 axb5 25 ♖e6! c4 26 ♗c3! ♗c5+ 27 ♔h1 ♘h5 28 ♗xf5 ♕xd5 29 ♗xg6+! hxg6 30 ♖f1+ ♔g8 31 ♖xg6+ ♔h7 32 ♖g7+ ♔h6 33 ♖f6+! ♔xg7 34 ♕g4+ 1-0.

12 ♗h6 *(D)*

If White wishes to avoid the complications of the following note then he should play **12 b3**. One example is the game Spraggett-A.Sokolov, Saint John Ct (10) 1988, which continued 12...a5 13 ♘a4 ♘c5 14 ♗h6 ♘xa4 15 ♕xa4 ♗d7 16 ♕f4 ♗f8 and now 17 h4 would have given White an edge.

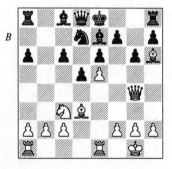

12 ... ♗f8?!

This tamely accepts a worse position. The critical line is **12...♖b8**:

1) White has usually sacrificed his b-pawn with **13 ♕h3!?**, giving rise to the following possibilities:

1a) **13...♖g8** 14 ♗d2!? (14 b3 is also quite good) 14...h5 15 ♘a4 ♘c5 16 ♘xc5 ♗xc5 17 b3 a5 18 ♕f3 ♕b6 19 c4 ♗b4 20 ♗xb4 ♕xb4 21 ♖ec1 and White had his customary edge in Rogers-Small, Wellington 1988.

1b) **13...♖b4** 14 ♗g7 ♖h4 15 ♕g3 ♖g8 16 ♗f6! with a clear plus for White according to Sax. A possible continuation is 16...♗xf6 17 exf6 ♖b4 18 ♕d6 ♖xb2 19 ♖ab1!? with excellent attacking prospects for White.

1c) **13...♖xb2!** 14 ♗g7 ♖g8 15 ♕xh7 ♖xg7 16 ♕xg7 ♗b4! *(D)* is perhaps going to force a reassessment of this line. White has:

1c1) **17 ♘a4 ♗xe1** 18 ♘xb2 ♗c3 (18...♗xf2+!?) 19 ♖b1 (19 ♗xg6 ♕e7!) 19...♕b6 and now Black is going to win the knight on b2, and I can't see how White will be able to exploit the resulting pin along the b-file.

1c2) **17 &xg6** and now:

1c21) **17...fxg6?** 18 ♕xg6+ ♚e7 19 ♕g5+ ♚e8 20 ♕h5+ ♚e7 21 ♖e3 is very good for White as **21...♘f8** 22 ♘a4! ♖xc2 23 ♕h4+ picks up the bishop and **21...&xc3** 22 ♖xc3 ♕b6 23 ♕g5+ ♚e8 24 h4 will leave Black struggling to stop the h-pawn.

1c22) But **17...♕e7!** gives Black a good game after both **18 ♖e3** fxg6 19 ♕xg6+ ♕f7 and **18 ♕g8+** ♘f8 19 ♘a4 &xe1 20 ♘xb2 (20 ♖xe1 ♖b4) 20...&c3.

1c3) Socorro-Lebredo, Cabaigun 1990 continued **17 ♖e3 &xc3** 18 &xg6 ♘xe5 19 ♖xe5 (perhaps 19 &xf7+ ♘xf7 20 ♕xc3 with a mess is the best that White can do) 19...fxg6 20 ♕xg6+ ♚e7 with a not too dissimilar position to certain lines of the famous Poisoned Pawn Variation where the black king also gets booted around, only for White to see it find sanctuary amongst a central pawn mass (21 ♖h5 ♕f8 22 ♖h7+ ♚d6 23 ♕g3+ &e5 24 ♕a3 c5, for example). I have examined this position in some detail and can't see any way for White to get at the black king but the passed h-pawn did enable him to maintain the balance on a number of occasions. I think it's best if I leave you to form your own conclusions.

2) In view of the above lines it is worthwhile re-examining the solid **13 b3**. *ECO* dismisses this as equal after 13...♖b4 14 ♕e2 &g5 (this is not forced) **15 a3 ♖b8 16 &xg6**

♕xg5, but does Black really have enough for the pawn after **15 &xg5** ♕xg5 16 &xa6 &xa6 17 ♕xa6 in this line? I doubt it.

13	&xf8	♚xf8
14	♘a4	♚g7
15	c4	♖b8
16	b3	♕e7 *(D)*

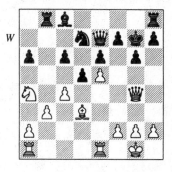

17	♖ac1	♘b6
18	♘xb6	♖xb6
19	h4	

The last few moves are fairly typical for this variation and require little explanation (if you've looked at the variations above). White stands better as Black is restricted by the weak squares on his kingside and must also take care that White can't open the queenside at a moment favourable to him. These factors, combined with White's extra space and more active minor piece, mean that it will take an extremely resolute performance from Black to avoid being overstretched at some point.

| 19 | ... | h5 |

Weakens g6, but Black can't allow White to play h5.

| 20 | ♕f4 | a5 |

21 罝e3   罝b4

Black plans to activate his bishop by ...奧a6, but this couldn't be done at once in view of 22 c5.

22 罝g3   奧a6? *(D)*

Black should have reinforced the g6 square with **22...罝h6**, although this does of course leave him very passively placed. The move chosen meets a tactical refutation.

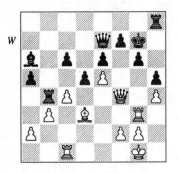

23 罝c3!

The first point behind this move is that it defends b3 so White is now threatening 24 a3 罝bb8 25 cxd5 奧xd3 26 d6!. That is what would happen on **23...罝h6**, for example. So Black played...

23 ...   dxc4

...and discovered the second point behind 罝c3...

24 奧xg6!   cxb3

Taking the bishop leads to mate: **24...fxg6** 25 罝xg6+ 奧xg6 26 罝g3+ 奧h7 27 豐e4+ 奧h6 28 豐g6#.

25 奧e4+   奧f8
26 axb3

Black is quite lucky to be on the board at all but with his king position destroyed and several pawn weaknesses he will still need a miracle to avoid his fate.

26 ...   c5
27 豐e3

Breaking the pin and eyeing up the c5-pawn.

27 ...   罝d4
28 奧f3!

With d1 protected and his bishop on a more secure square White is now ready for positive action. If Black takes on h4, White simply takes on c5 opening up the queenside.

28 ...   奧e8
29 豐c1   c4
30 bxc4   豐xh4

If Black had tried to blockade with **30...豐c5**, White wins with 31 豐e3!; the threat is 罝d3 and since **31...豐a7** loses after 32 罝d3 罝d7 33 奧c6, Black must try **31...奧xc4** when there follows 32 奧e2 豐d5 33 豐c1! 奧a6 (33...罝xe2 34 罝c8+ 奧e7 35 豐c7+ 豐d7 36 豐c5+) 34 罝c8+! 奧xc8 35 豐xc8+ 豐d8 36 奧b5+ 奧f8 37 豐c5+ 豐e7 38 豐xd4 and White wins.

31 豐a3!   罝xc4
32 奧c6+   1-0

Game 23
Gallagher – Cramling
Biel 1990

1	e4	c5
2	奌f3	e6
3	d4	cxd4
4	奌xd4	奌c6
5	奌c3	豐c7
6	f4 *(D)*	

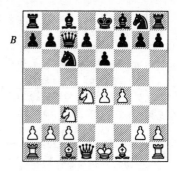

6 ...   ♞xd4

6...d6 is an attempt to reach a Scheveningen, but White has some dangerous plans based on castling queenside. For example 7 ♗e3 (7 ♘xc6 is not so good when Black hasn't wasted a tempo on ...a6) 7...♘f6 8 ♗e2 (perhaps 8 ♕f3 is more natural when White achieved a good game in Lau-Andonov, St John 1988 after 8...♗d7 9 0-0-0 ♘xd4 10 ♗xd4 a6 11 g4 e5 12 ♗e3 exf4 13 ♗xf4 ♗c6 14 g5 ♘d7 15 ♗c4 ♘b6 16 ♗b3, but if I were to recommend only that, then I wouldn't be able to show off the following game) 8...♗e7 9 ♕d2 0-0 10 0-0-0 a6 11 g4 d5 (11...♘xd4 12 ♗xd4 e5 13 ♗e3 ♗xg4 14 ♗xg4 ♘xg4 15 ♘d5 ♕d8 16 ♗b6 ♕d7 17 ♖hg1! is winning for White) 12 e5 ♘d7 (the position now resembles a French Defence) 13 h4 ♘b6 14 h5 ♘a5 15 ♘f5!? ♘bc4 (15...gxf5 16 ♗xb6 ♕xb6 17 ♘xd5 and White will regain his piece with interest) 16 ♘xe7+ ♕xe7 17 ♗xc4 ♘xc4 18 ♕d4 f6 (18...♕b4 19 ♘e2 and everything is under control) 19 h6 fxe5 20 fxe5 g6? 21 ♘e4! b6 (21...♘xe3 22 ♘f6+) 22 ♘f6+ ♔h8

23 b3 ♘xe3 24 ♕xe3 (White has a positionally won game) 24...b5 25 ♖hf1 ♗b7 26 ♕b6 ♖ac8 27 ♕d6! ♕xd6 28 exd6 ♖cd8 29 ♘d7! ♖xf1 30 ♖xf1 ♔g8 31 ♘f6+ ♔h8 32 g5 e5 33 ♘d7! (White returns to d7 for his fourth knight sacrifice of the game) 33...♔g8 34 ♘xe5 ♖xd6 35 ♖f7 ♖e6 36 ♖g7+ 1-0 Gallagher-Jansa, Royan 1989.

6...a6 is the main alternative to the text; **7 ♘xc6! ♕xc6** (7...bxc6 is played with about equal frequency and transposes to lines considered in Game 22) **8 ♗d3** *(D)* (8 ♗e2 b5 9 ♗f3 is another reasonable system which doesn't form part of our repertoire) and now:

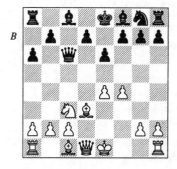

1) **8...♗c5?!** (a dubious move order) 9 ♕e2 ♘e7 10 ♗d2 b5 11 e5!? d5? (better is 11...♗b7, when 12 ♗e4 ♕c7 13 ♗xb7 ♕xb7 14 ♘e4 ♕c6 15 b4 is unclear but 12 ♘e4 should be good enough for an edge) 12 exd6 (perhaps Black expected 12 ♘xb5, which is not so clear after 12...♖b8) 12...♕xd6 13 ♘e4 ♕c6 14 ♘xc5 ♕xc5 15 ♗c3 ♔f8 (15...0-0 16 0-0-0 and Black will be subjected

to a massive attack) 16 ♗e4 ♖a7 17 0-0-0 ♖d7 18 ♖xd7 ♗xd7 19 ♖d1 ♗e8 20 ♕d2 and White had a winning position in Gallagher-Meulders, Eupen 1992. In fact after only seven more moves Black was in total zugzwang: 20...f5 21 ♗f3 ♔f7 22 ♕d6! ♕xd6 23 ♖xd6 h5 24 ♖xa6 ♖h7 25 ♖a7 g6 26 ♗b4 ♔f6 27 h4 and any move Black makes loses at least the exchange, including 27...e5 28 fxe5+ ♔e6 29 ♗xe7 ♔xe7 30 ♗d5+.

2) **8...b5 9 ♕e2 ♗b7** (9...b4 is met by 10 ♘d5 and after 10...♕d6 White can choose between 11 e5 ♕c6 12 ♘e3 with a nice square on c4 awaiting the knight, or 11 ♘e3 ♕xf4 12 ♘c4 ♕c7 13 e5 with a lot of pressure for a pawn) **10 ♗d2** *(D)*. Of course White doesn't play 10 ♗e3, which would deprive him of the answer ♘d5 in reply to ...b4. White is now ready to castle either side depending on developments. There haven't been many practical examples from this position, but what we've seen so far suggests that White is doing quite well. Black's main moves are:

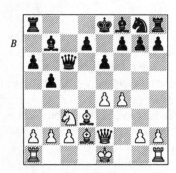

2a) **10...♘e7** (10...♗e7 is very passive and after 11 a4!? b4 12 ♘a2 a5 13 c3 bxc3 14 ♘xc3 ♘f6 15 ♖c1, White was already much better in Hector-Gorrotaxtegi, San Sebastian 1991) 11 a3 (11 a4 and 11 0-0 come into consideration, but now that ...b4 can't be met by ♘d5 it's not a bad idea to secure the knight on c3) 11...♘g6 (11...♘c8 should also be met by 12 0-0) 12 0-0 ♗e7 (after 12...♗c5+ 13 ♔h1 White follows the same plan as in the game) 13 ♖f3! ♕c7 14 ♖af1 h5 (14...0-0 15 ♖h3 gives White a very strong attack as long as he remembers to play ♔h1 before ♕h5 in view of ...♕c5+ exchanging queens) 15 ♔h1 h4 16 ♖h3 e5? (a mistake in a poor position) 17 f5 ♘f4 (17...♘f8 18 ♕g4 ♗f6 19 ♗g5 is also very bad) 18 ♗xf4 exf4 19 e5 f3 20 ♖hxf3! (of course) 20...♗xf3 (flicking in 20...h3 would make no difference after 21 g3) 21 ♕xf3 ♖b8 22 ♖e1 with an overwhelming position for White, Yudasin-Balashov, Minsk 1982.

2b) **10...♗c5** 11 0-0-0 ♘e7 (playing 11...b4 is still risky; after 12 ♘d5 ♕d6 13 ♘e3 ♕xf4 14 ♘c4 ♕c7 15 ♕g4 White has a very strong initiative) 12 ♕h5! b4?! (12...♖c8 13 ♔b1 0-0 14 ♖hf1 ♕b6 15 g4 with an edge for White, Tolnai-C.Horvath, Hungarian Ch 1989) 13 ♘a4! d5 (the only move as both 13...♕xa4 14 ♕xc5 ♕xa2 15 ♗xb4 and 13...♗d6 14 ♕a5! are very bad for Black) 14 ♘xc5 ♕xc5 15 ♖he1 ♖c8 16 ♔b1 a5 (Black is in difficulties as he can't castle) 17 ♗e3 ♕c7 18 exd5 ♘xd5

19 f5! 0-0 (forced) 20 fxe6 g6 21 ♕h6 and White had a clear advantage in Gallagher-Illescas, French League 1990.

7 ♕xd4 a6
8 ♗e2 b5

8...♘e7 is well met by 9 ♕f2. One example is the game Am.Rodriguez-Zapata, Bayamo 1987, which continued 9...b5 (more accurate than 9...♘c6 as in that case White will be able to omit a3, for example 10 ♗e3 b5 11 0-0 ♗e7 12 e5 0-0 13 ♘e4 ♗b7 14 ♗b6 ♕c8 15 ♗c5 with a clear advantage for White according to Boleslavsky) 10 ♗e3 ♗b7 (10...b4 11 ♘a4 ♕xc2 12 ♘b6 ♖b8 13 ♘c4! ♘c6 14 e5 followed by 0-0 gives White tremendous play for the pawn) 11 a3 ♘c6 12 0-0 ♗e7 13 ♗b6 ♕c8 14 ♖ad1 0-0 15 ♗f3 f6 16 ♖fe1 with a pleasant position for White.

9 ♗e3 ♗b7

Black can try 9...♘e7 here as well. After 10 0-0 ♘c6 11 ♕d3 ♗b7 12 e5 ♗e7 13 ♖ad1 ♖c8 14 a3 ♘a5 15 ♔h1 ♘c4 16 ♗c1 ♗c6 17 ♘e4 0-0 18 ♗f3 White had a slight advantage in Chandler-Zapata, Amsterdam 1987.

10 0-0-0

Of course this is quite risky but the results with **10 0-0** have been uninspiring. Black is thought to be able to equalize by 10...♖c8 11 ♖fd1 (11 ♖ad1 ♘f6 12 ♗f3 h5 is also OK for Black) 11...♗c5 12 ♕xc5 ♕xc5 13 ♗xc5 ♖xc5 14 ♖d4 ♘e7! 15 ♖ad1 and now both 15...♗c6 and 15...d5 are roughly level. This ending is not

as promising for White as the one we consider later (note to Black's 12th move). There White castled queenside, which in effect gains a tempo as the rook reaches the d-file in one go and the black knight didn't have the opportunity to develop to the superior e7-square. One may also argue that the white king is better off on c1 than g1.

10 ... ♖c8
11 ♖d2 (D)

This may appear artificial, but White must protect the c2-square.

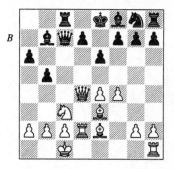

11 ... ♘f6

11...♗c5 12 ♕xc5 ♕xc5 13 ♗xc5 ♖xc5 14 ♖hd1 ♗c6 (14...♖c7 15 ♗xb5! and 14...♘f6 15 e5 ♘d5 16 ♘e4 are very good for White) 15 a3 ♘f6 16 ♗f3 is ± according to Kupreichik.

12 ♗f3 ♕a5

12...♗c5 13 ♕xc5 ♕xc5 14 ♗xc5 ♖xc5 15 ♖e1 is considered to be a little better for White.

12...♕c4 is well met by 13 e5.

12...b4 13 ♘a4 ♕c4 14 b3! ♕xd4 15 ♖xd4 gave White an edge in Kupreichik-Kotronias, Lvov 1988.

That leaves **12...♗e7** *(D)* as the main alternative. White then has:

1) **13 ♖hd1 0-0 14 e5** and now:

1a) **14...♗xf3?** 15 gxf3 b4? 16 exf6 bxc3 17 ♖g2! ♕b7 18 ♖xg7+ ♔h8 19 ♖g8+! and Black resigned in Ehlvest-Andersson, Belfort 1988 in view of 19...♖xg8 20 fxe7+ ♖g7 21 ♖g1 ♕xb2+ 22 ♔d1 ♕b1+ 23 ♗c1 when mate follows shortly.

1b) **14...b4!** 15 exf6? (15 ♘a4 is better, when 15...♗xf3 16 gxf3 ♘d5 17 ♘b6 ♘xb6 18 ♕xb6 ♕c4 19 b3 ♕c3 20 ♕d4 leads to a roughly level endgame) 15...bxc3 16 ♕xc3 (16 fxe7 cxd2+ 17 ♖xd2 ♖fe8 18 ♗xb7 ♕xb7 19 ♕xd7 ♖xe7 is good for Black) 16...♕xc3! 17 fxe7 (17 bxc3 ♗a3+ 18 ♔b1 ♗xf3 followed by ...♖b8+ wins for Black) 17...♕xe3 18 exf8♕+ ♔xf8 19 ♗xb7 ♖b8 and Black soon won, Hector-P.Cramling, Valby 1991. A word of advice: if you find yourself facing a male Swedish grandmaster then you should head for this variation, regardless of colour, as they seem to find a way to lose all their pieces or get mated within 20 moves.

2) **13 g4!?** is thought to allow Black to equalise with **13...♗c5 14 ♕xc5 ♕xc5 15 ♗xc5 ♖xc5**, the idea being that the tempo White has gained, g2-g4, actually harms his position. However, I'm not so sure about this theory; admittedly the pin on the e-pawn can prove annoying but White does have new possibilities based on playing g5. I (JG) have looked at this position in some depth and found some fascinating variations. My analysis runs **16 ♖hd1!** *(D)* (White must be careful not to play g5 too early as Black can sometimes develop counterplay by ...♘g8 and ...h6, while in this particular position the exchange sacrifice on c3 is also interesting) and now:

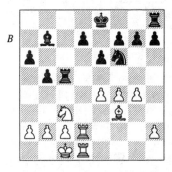

2a) **16...b4** 17 ♘a4 ♖c7 18 ♖d4 looks very good for White, for example 18...a5 19 g5 ♘g8 20 ♘b6 ♗c6 21 ♘c4 with a clear advantage.

2b) **16...♖c7** 17 ♖d4 ♗c6 18 a4! also promises White a slight advantage.

2c) **16...♗c6** looks like the critical line as 17 ♖d4 can now be met by 17...e5 and 17 a3 a5 doesn't solve

White's problems with his vulnerable e-pawn. Therefore **17 g5** and now:

2c1) After **17...b4** 18 ♘d5! both **18...exd5** 19 exd5 ♘xd5 20 ♗xd5 and **18...♘xd5** 19 exd5 ♗b7 20 ♗g2! are better for White, an important point in the latter variation being the tactic 20...0-0 21 dxe6! ♗xg2 22 exd7.

2c2) **17...♘g8 18 ♘e2!** *(D)* (now that the pressure on e4 has been relieved the knight is free to find a square with more potential) with a further branch:

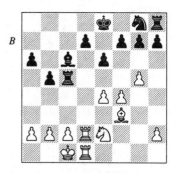

2c21) **18...h6?** (what could be more natural?) **19 ♘d4** when Black has three moves:

2c211) **19...♗b7** 20 ♘xe6!! fxe6 (obviously 20...dxe6 allows mate in two) 21 ♖xd7 and Black is defenceless. **21...♗c6** gets mated in a few moves after 22 ♗h5+ and **21...♗d5** 22 ♖xg7 only delays the inevitable. The best he can do is **21...hxg5** (preventing ♗h5+) 22 ♖xb7 ♖xh2 23 c3 when **23...gxf4** loses a piece after 24 ♖b8+ and **23...♘f6** 24 e5 ♘d5 25 ♗xd5 gives White a won ending.

2c212) **19...♗a8** 20 ♘xe6!! fxe6 21 ♖xd7 (21 ♗h5+ g6! 22 ♗xg6+ ♔f8 23 ♖xd7 ♘e7 is less clear-cut) 21...hxg5 22 ♖d8+ ♔f7 23 ♖xa8 (23 ♖d7+ is also promising) and now **23...♖xh2** 24 c3 is winning for White as Black is liable to lose his knight and **23...gxf4** is well met by 24 h4! with a fatal pin on the eighth rank.

2c213) **19...hxg5** (Black may try this if he spots 20 ♘xe6 in time) 20 ♘xc6 ♖xc6 21 ♖xd7 ♖c8 22 e5! (the most important thing is to activate the bishop; now 22...♖xh2 loses to 23 ♗c6!) 22...♘e7 23 ♗b7 ♖b8 24 fxg5 and now both **24...♘g6** 25 ♗xa6 ♘xe5 26 ♖c7! with the idea of ♖c5 and **24...♖xh2** 25 ♗xa6 ♘d5 26 ♖b7! are good for White.

2c22) **18...f5?!** (another case of Black looking for active play before he's ready for it) **19 ♘d4** and now:

2c221) **19...♗xe4** 20 ♘xe6! dxe6 21 ♖d8+ ♔f7 22 ♗h5+! g6 23 ♖1d7+ ♘e7 24 ♖xh8 ♖xc2+ 25 ♔d1 and White wins.

2c222) **19...fxe4** when White can gain the advantage in prosaic fashion by 20 ♘xc6 exf3 21 ♘e5 d5 22 ♘xf3 followed by ♘d4, or in more spectacular fashion by 20 ♗h5+ g6 21 ♘xc6 ♖xc6 22 ♖xd7 gxh5 23 g6!! ♘f6 (23...hxg6 24 ♖d8+ ♔f7 25 ♖1d7+ ♔f6 {25...♘e7 26 ♖xh8 +-} 26 ♖f8#!) 24 ♖d8+ ♔e7 25 ♖xh8 hxg6 when Black has some compensation for the exchange.

2c23) **18...♘e7!** 19 ♘d4 ♗b7 when after a normal continuation like **20 ♘b3 ♖c7** 21 ♘a5 ♗c8 it's difficult to see how White can step up the pressure. However, he does have an abnormal continuation at his disposal, **20 ♘xe6!?**, which is nowhere near as devastating as in the above lines but still poses Black some problems. After **20...fxe6 21 ♖xd7 ♗d5! 22 ♖a7** (22 ♖d6 loses to 22...♖c6! and 22 ♖xe7+ ♔xe7 23 exd5 ♖c4 looks at least OK for Black) there are two possibilities:

2c231) **22...♗c6?** 23 ♖d6! ♔f7 (Black can't bail out with 23...0-0 on account of 24 ♖xe7 ♖xf4 25 ♖d8+ while 23...h6 24 ♗h5+ g6 25 ♖xe6 ♗d7 26 ♗xg6+ ♔d8 27 ♖d6 is also very good for White) 24 ♗g4! and the black position is caving in; on **24...e5**, 25 b4! is the most efficient while **24...♗xe4** 25 ♗xe6+ ♔e8 26 ♖dd7! is also the end.

2c232) **22...♗xa2! 23 ♖dd7 ♘c6!** (not 23...♘c8 24 ♗h5+! g6 25 ♖xh7 ♖xh7 26 ♗xg6+ ♔f8 27 ♖xh7 when White's passed pawns should prove decisive) and now:

2c2321) **24 ♗h5+!?** (if you are a raving lunatic, then here is your winning attempt) 24...g6 25 ♖xh7 ♖xh7 26 ♗xg6+ ♔d8! 27 ♖xh7 ♘d4 28 ♔d2 ♖xc2+ 29 ♔d3 ♖c4 30 h4 and the race is on between the white pawns and the black mating attack.

2c2322) **24 ♖ac7** (sensible) and now **24...♖f8** loses to 25 ♖xg7 ♖xf4 26 ♖g8+ ♖f8 27 ♖c8+, **24...♗b3** to 25 ♖xg7! while **24...♘b8** 25 ♗h5+! g6 26 ♖xh7 is also good for White. However, Black has just one saving move, **24...♘b4!**, after which White

has nothing better than to take a draw by perpetual check.

So, perhaps theory is right and the position after 13 g4 can be assessed as =, but there is certainly plenty of rope for Black to hang himself by!

Returning to the position after 12...♕a5 *(D)*:

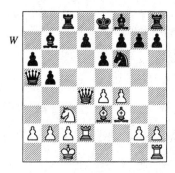

13   ♕a7!

This required careful calculation as Black has a dangerous looking exchange sacrifice. Instead 13 e5 led to great complications in Polihroniade-J.Polgar, Thessaloniki wom OL 1988 after 13...♗c5 14 ♕d3 ♗xe3 15 ♕xe3 b4 16 ♗xb7 (16 exf6? bxc3 17 bxc3 ♕xa2) 16...bxc3 17 ♖d3 (17 ♗xc8? cxd2+ 18 ♕xd2 ♕xa2 is very good for Black) 17...♘g4 and now White should have played 18 ♕g3 when Judit and Zsuzsa Polgar give the variation 18...♕b5 19 ♗xc8 ♕xb2+ 20 ♔d1 ♕b1+ 21 ♔e2 ♕xc2+ 22 ♔e1 ♕b1+ 23 ♔e2+ with a draw by perpetual check.

13   ...   ♕c7

13...♗a3 fails to 14 ♘b1, but **13...♖xc3** is more complicated. My idea was 14 bxc3 ♕xc3 (14...♗a3+ 15 ♔d1) 15 ♖d3! and after 15...♕a1+ 16 ♔d2 ♗b4+ 17 ♔e2 ♕xh1 18 ♖d1 ♕xh2 19 ♕b8+ ♔e7 20 ♕xb7! White has a very strong attack. A sample variation runs: 20...e5 21 c3! ♗d6 (21...♗a3 22 ♕xa6) 22 ♖xd6! ♔xd6 23 ♗c5+! and now the lines **23...♔xc5** 24 ♕c7 and **23...♔e6** 24 f5 are checkmate.

14 e5!?

I was a bit nervous about my queen on a7 so I opted for the ending at once. However **14 ♖e1** deserves serious consideration: **14...b4** can be met by 15 ♘d5! and **14...♗b4** by 15 ♗b6! (15 ♗d4 ♖a8) 15...♕b8 (15...♕c6 16 e5 ♘d5 17 ♖xd5! wins for White) 16 ♕xb8 ♖xb8 17 ♗d4 with an edge for White.

14	...	♗xf3
15	♕xc7	♖xc7
16	gxf3	♘g8

I was quite surprised by this retreat and had been expecting **16...b4**, after which I intended 17 ♘a4 ♘d5 18 ♖xd5! exd5 19 ♖d1 with good long-term compensation for the exchange.

17	♘e4	♘h6
18	♖hd1	

I was not interested in **18 ♘d6+** ♗xd6 19 ♖xd6 ♘f5 20 ♖xa6 0-0 when Black has good play for the pawn.

18	...	♘f5
19	♗b6	♖b7
20	♗c5	♖c7
21	♗b6	♖b7

22	♗c5	♖c7 *(D)*

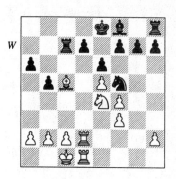

23 ♗xf8

I overestimated my chances in the resulting double rook ending. I should have played **23 b4!** and after 23...♗e7! 24 ♗xe7 ♘xe7 25 ♘c5 ♘d5, 26 ♖xd5 is another promising exchange sacrifice.

23	...	♖xf8
24	♘d6+	♘xd6
25	♖xd6	♖a7
26	♖b6	♔e7
27	♖dd6	f6!

Now Black will get a rook loose amongst my weak kingside pawns. I didn't like the look of **28 ♖xa6** ♖xa6 29 ♖xa6 fxe5 30 fxe5 ♖xf3 31 ♖b6 g5 32 ♖xb5 g4! when anything can happen, so I played the solid...

28 ♖d3

...and offered a **draw**, which was accepted. After 28...fxe5 29 fxe5 ♖f5 30 ♖e3 ♖h5 31 ♖e2 ♖h3 32 ♖f2 g5 33 ♖d6 the game is level. Both players have one active rook and one passive rook tied down to their weak pawns.

9 Sicilian Four Knights

This rather antiquated system has never really caught on as the generally passive nature of Black's position has proved unattractive to most players. Black plays 1 e4 c5 2 ♘f3 e6 3 d4 cxd4 4 ♘xd4 ♘f6 5 ♘c3 ♘c6 (of course this can arise from other move orders, in particular via 2...♘c6). In some ways this is akin to the Kan and Taimanov Systems since Black leaves the f8-b4 diagonal open for his bishop, but instead of playing ...a6 he develops a piece. Naturally this is in Black's favour unless White has some direct method of exploiting the omission of ...a6, so 6 ♘db5 is the only move to cause problems. Black then very often continues 6...d6 and after 7 ♗f4 e5 8 ♗g5 we have transposed to the Pelikan, considered in Chapter 4. The point of this move order is that Black avoids the possibility that after 1 e4 c5 2 ♘f3 ♘c6 3 d4 cxd4 4 ♘xd4 ♘f6 5 ♘c3 e5 6 ♘db5 d6 White might play 7 ♘d5 or 7 a4. Since we are recommending the main line with 7 ♗g5 this transposition is not a worry and therefore 6...d6 just leads to the earlier chapter on the Pelikan. After 6 ♘db5, 6...d5 loses to 7 exd5 exd5 8 ♗f4 and 6...♗c5 7 ♗f4 followed by ♗d6 is unpleasant for Black, so we need only consider 6...♗b4 in the current chapter. The tactical line recommended in the first edition has suffered a serious setback in recent years, so this time (as in *BTS2*) we only analyse the positional continuation 7 a3 ♗xc3+ 8 ♘xc3 d5 9 exd5, which either gives Black an isolated pawn after 9...exd5 or gives White a lead in development after 9...♘xd5 10 ♗d2. This is a safe line for White in which he is likely to secure a small but permanent advantage. In practice it is easy for White to allow the position to slide towards a draw, and in some ways it is an annoying line to meet because instead of the sharp struggle typical of most Sicilian lines, White is trying to exploit a slight positional edge. Nevertheless it is even more unpleasant for Black, who can only win if White takes exceptional risks, and so this line is relatively unpopular.

Game 24
Mokry – B. Stein
Gausdal 1988

1	e4	c5
2	♘f3	e6
3	d4	cxd4
4	♘xd4	♘f6
5	♘c3	♘c6
6	♘db5	♗b4
7	a3	♗xc3+

8 ᐁxc3 d5
9 exd5 *(D)*

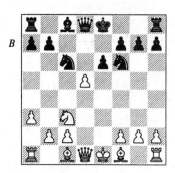

9 ... exd5

The knight capture is quite rare these days, but it's interesting to note that Ulf Andersson seems quite happy to defend the unpleasant ending that arises from line '1' below. After **9...ᐁxd5 10 ♗d2** Black has:

1) **10...ᐁxc3** 11 ♗xc3 ♕xd1+ 12 ♖xd1 f6 (12...e5 13 ♗d3 ♗e6 14 0-0 f6 15 f4 is similar, Ivkov-Gligorić, Amsterdam 1964) 13 f4 (for some reason Ehlvest preferred the passive 13 f3 and after 13...♗d7 14 ♗d3 0-0-0 15 ♖d2 e5 16 ♗e4 ♗e6 17 ♔e2 ♖xd2+ 18 ♔xd2 ᐁe7 19 ♗b4 ᐁd5 20 ♗xd5 ♗xd5 21 ♔e3 the players agreed to a draw in Ehlvest-Andersson, Skellefteå 1989) 13...♗d7 14 ♗c4 0-0-0 15 0-0 ♖he8 (15...♔c7 16 ♖de1 ♖he8 17 ♖f3 ♗c8 with a very unpleasant position for Black, Fischer-Addison, USA Ch 1962/3) and now instead of **16 b4** ᐁe7 17 b5 ᐁd5 18 ♗d2 ᐁb6 19 ♗d3 ᐁa4 20 ♖b1 ᐁc5! (the fifth successive move by this knight) which led to a roughly level game

in Psakhis-Andersson, Manila OL 1992, I would suggest **16 ♖de1**, *à la* Fischer, which prevents ...e5 (unless Black doesn't mind a rook penetrating to f7) without making a mess of the queenside.

2) **10...♕h4** 11 ♕f3 0-0 (playing 11...ᐁe5 12 ♕g3 and 11...ᐁd4 12 ♕d3 just make matters worse) 12 0-0-0 ᐁxc3 13 ♗xc3 e5 14 ♗d3 ♗g4 (14...♕g4 15 ♗e4 ♕xf3 16 ♗xf3 with the typical favourable ending for White, Minić-Gerusel, Halle 1967) 15 ♕e4 ♕h6+ 16 ♗d2 ♕g6 17 f3 ♗e6 18 ♕xg6 hxg6 19 ♗e3 and again White has a promising ending, Tal-Matulović, Kislovodsk 1966.

3) **10...♕b6** 11 ᐁb5 ᐁd4 12 ᐁxd4 ♕xd4 13 ♗b5+ ♗d7 14 ♗xd7+ ♔xd7 15 0-0 left Black's king badly placed in Kaplan-Siaperas, Siegen OL 1970.

4) **10...♕f6** 11 ♕h5 0-0 12 0-0-0 ᐁxc3 (12...♕xf2 13 ᐁxd5 exd5 14 ♗d3 is no better) 13 ♗xc3 ♕f4+ 14 ♖d2 e5 15 ♗b5 with advantage, Matulović-Kokkoris, Athens 1969.

5) **10...0-0** 11 ♕h5 ᐁf6 12 ♕h4 ♕d4 13 ♗g5 ♖d8 14 ♕xd4 ♖xd4 15 ♗d3 b6 16 0-0-0 is the same story as in all the other lines, Gufeld-Khasin, USSR Ch 1966.

10 ♗d3 0-0

Or **10...d4** (after 10...♕e7+ 11 ♕e2 ♕xe2+ 12 ᐁxe2 ᐁe5 13 ♗b5+ ♗d7 14 ♗xd7+ ♔xd7, Liberzon-Bronstein, USSR 1972, White could have played 15 ♗e3 ♖he8 16 ♗d4 with a slight advantage) with the variations:

1) **11 ♕e2+ ♗e6 12 ♘e4 ♘xe4 13 ♕xe4 ♕d5** *(D)* and now:

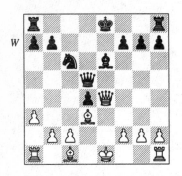

1a) **14 ♕xd5 ♗xd5 15 ♗f4 0-0 16 0-0 ♖fe8 17 ♖fe1** f6, Fernandez-Illescas, Pamplona 1991, and now instead of **18 ♖xe8 ♖xe8 19 ♗g3** g5!, which was followed up with ...♗f7-g6, White should have prevented Black's kingside expansion by **18 h4!**, after which he could have claimed an edge.

1b) **14 ♗f4 0-0-0 15 0-0 g5 16 ♗d2 h6** (16...♘e5 17 ♕xd5 ♗xd5 18 ♗f5+) **17 ♕xd5 ♗xd5 18 f4 g4 19 ♖ae1 h5 20 b4** and White is better, Illescas-Sorokin, Palma 1989.

2) **11 ♘e2 ♗f5** (11...0-0 12 0-0 transposes into the main line) **12 0-0 ♗xd3 13 ♕xd3 0-0** and now:

2a) **14 b4!?** (White plans to help himself to the d-pawn) **14...♕b6** (14...♖c8?! 15 ♗b2 ♖e8 16 ♖ad1 ♘e5 17 ♕xd4 ♕c7 18 ♘c3 was very good for White in Jonsson-Kristjansson, Akureyri 1994) **15 ♗b2** (15 ♗g5!?) **15...♖fd8 16 ♖fd1** (perhaps 16 ♖ad1, but then White won't be able to play the ending given below) **16...♘e5** (16...a5 17 b5 ♘e5 18

♗xd4! is very good for White) and now:

2a1) **17 ♗xd4 ♘xd3 18 ♗xb6 axb6 19 cxd3** with an extra pawn for White but also positional problems which will make this advantage extremely hard to realise.

2a2) **17 ♕g3 ♘c6 18 c4** (18 ♕h4 looks strong, but Black has the unpleasant reply 18...♖e8!) **18...dxc3 19 ♗xc3 ♖xd1+ 20 ♖xd1 ♖d8!** with just a small plus for White.

2b) **14 ♗g5 h6 15 ♗h4 ♖e8 16 ♖ad1 ♖c8 17 c3!** (a more dynamic move than 17 ♖fe1 ♖e6 18 ♔f1 ♕c7 19 ♗g3 ♕b6 20 b4 with just a microscopic advantage for White, Karpov-Kuzmin, Leningrad 1977) **17...dxc3 18 ♕h3 ♕e7 19 ♘xc3 ♕e6** (19...♕e5 20 f4 ♕e3+ 21 ♕xe3 ♖xe3 22 ♗xf6 gxf6 23 ♘d5 is very good for White) **20 ♕xe6 fxe6** (20...♖xe6 21 ♗xf6 ♖xf6 22 ♖d7 b6 23 ♖e1 favours White) **21 ♗xf6 gxf6 22 ♘e4** with an endgame advantage for White, Estevez-Chaviano, Santa Clara 1983.

11 0-0 *(D)*

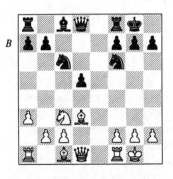

11 ... d4 *(D)*

This is the most logical because it forces White to decide where his knight is going immediately. In order to avoid liquidation it seems that 11...d4 should be met by the relatively passive ♘e2; after other 11th moves White can usually arrange to meet ...d4 by the more active ♘e4, for example:

1) **11...a6** 12 ♗f4 (12 ♗g5 is also promising) 12...d4 13 ♘e4 ♘d5 (the line 13...♗f5 14 ♗c7! illustrates why Black should not have delayed) 14 ♗d6 ♖e8 15 ♗g3 f5? (suicide, but even 15...♗f5 16 ♘d6 ♗xd3 17 ♕xd3 ♖e7 18 ♘f5 is very awkward) 16 ♘d6 ♖f8 17 ♗c4 ♗e6 18 ♖e1 ♕d7 19 ♘xb7 ♕xb7 20 ♖xe6 ♘a5 21 ♗a2 1-0 Vukcević-Ervin, USA 1976.

2) **11...h6** 12 ♗f4 d4 13 ♘b5 (13 ♘e4 as in line '1' is also possible) 13...♘d5 14 ♕f3! ♗e6 15 ♖fe1 (15 ♖ad1 ♕d7 16 h3 ♖ad8 17 ♗h2 ♕e7 18 ♕g3 also gave White some advantage in Cirić-Rossolimo, Vršac 1969) 15...♕d7 16 ♗e5! ♘xe5 17 ♖xe5 ♘e7 (17...♘f6 looks more resilient but Black is still in difficulties after 18 ♕f4 ♖fd8 19 ♖d1) 18 ♕e4 ♖fd8 19 ♕h7+ ♔f8 20 ♕h8+ ♘g8 21 ♖ae1 (threatening ♗h7, as ...f6 is no longer a defence) 21...♗d5 22 ♖xd5! ♕xd5 23 ♘c7 ♕d7 24 ♗h7 1-0 Timoshenko-Chernov, Bucharest 1993.

3) **11...♗g4 12 f3** and now:

3a) **12...♗e6** 13 ♗g5 h6 (both 13...♖e8 14 ♕d2 d4 15 ♘e2 a6 16 ♘g3, Planinc-Andersson, Sombor 1970 and 13...♕b6+ 14 ♔h1 ♘d7

15 f4! f5 16 ♕f3, Matulović-Benko, Vrnjačka Banja 1973 were also bad for Black) 14 ♗h4 g5 15 ♗f2 ♘h5 16 ♘b5 and according to Taimanov White has a clear plus.

3b) **12...♗h5** 13 ♗g5 ♕b6+!? 14 ♔h1 ♘e4 (this is imaginative play by Black but it fails to equalize) 15 ♘xe4 dxe4 16 ♗xe4 ♕xb2 17 ♕b1! ♕xb1 18 ♖fxb1 f5 19 ♗d3 b6 20 ♖b5 ♗g6 21 ♖d1 with a somewhat better ending for White, Ehlvest-Romero, Logroño 1991.

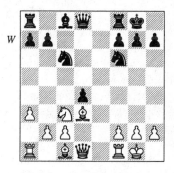

12 ♘e2

The available evidence suggests that this offers the best chances for an advantage. After **12 ♘e4 ♗f5** 13 ♗g5 ♗xe4 14 ♗xe4 ♕d6 (the diehards of this system currently favour this move over 14...h6, which allows White to gain a small advantage after 15 ♗h4 g5 16 ♗xc6 bxc6 17 ♗g3 ♕d5 18 f4!, as in Kir.Georgiev-Chandler, Leningrad 1987) 15 ♗xf6 (nobody has tried to keep the bishop pair) 15...♕xf6 16 ♕d3 (16 ♕h5 g6 17 ♕b5 ♖ae8 followed by 18...♖e7 is also OK for Black, but perhaps 16 ♕f3 is a better try for the advantage)

16...g6 17 ♖ad1 ♖ad8 18 ♕b5 ♖d7 19 ♖fe1 ♔g7 with an equal game, Westerinen-Khenkin, Gausdal 1991.

12 ...　　　♗g4

There are several alternatives, with line '3' recently proving the most popular of Black's 12th move choices.

1) **12...♖e8** is an interesting new idea:

1a) The main point is to meet the standard **13 ♗g5** with 13...♖e5. For example, Kamsky-Lautier, Paris Immopar rapid 1992 continued 14 ♗f4 (14 ♕d2 ♗f5!) 14...♖d5 15 ♘g3 ♘e5 16 ♗xe5 ♖xe5 17 ♕d2 ♕b6 18 ♖ae1 ♖xe1 19 ♖xe1 ♗e6 20 b3 ♖d8 and Black was very close to equality.

1b) **13 b4**, launching an immediate assault on the d-pawn, seems to pose Black the most problems. For example, Yudasin-Sorokin, Moscow 1992 continued 13...♗g4 14 f3 ♗h5 15 ♗b2 a6 16 ♖f2! (threatening ♘xd4) 16...♘e5 (on 16...♔h8, 17 g4 would be a risky way to win a pawn, but I can't see an adequate reply to 17 ♗c4!, as 17...♘e5 18 ♗b3 d3 fails to 19 ♗xe5) 17 ♗xd4 ♘xd3 18 ♕xd3 ♗g6 19 ♕d2 ♖c8 20 c3 and White was a pawn up for nothing.

2) **12...h6** 13 b4! (if this is good against ...♖e8 then it must be at least as strong against the slow ...h6) 13...a6 14 ♗b2 ♔h8 15 ♕d2 (15 ♗c4!?, as above, looks good to me) 15...b5?! (15...♕d6 is only ± according to Bangiev) 16 ♕f4 ♘d5 17 ♕g3 (17 ♕f3!?) 17...♘de7 18 ♖ad1 ♖a7 19 c3 ♖d7 20 cxd4 ♘d5 (Petrushin-Bangiev, Simferopol 1989) and now

21 ♗b1 would have been very good for White.

3) **12...♕d5** *(D)*, and now White has several ways to handle the position:

3a) **13 c4** (aiming for active piece play) 13...dxc3 14 ♘xc3 ♕a5 15 ♗d2!? (15 ♗f4 is more common but has not been extremely successful) 15...♖d8 16 ♘b5 ♕a6 (16...♕b6 17 ♗e3 ♕a5 18 b4) 17 ♕c2 ♘e5 18 ♗e2 ♗g4 19 ♗c3 ♖ac8 20 ♖ad1 ♘d5 21 ♗xg4 ♘xg4 22 ♕d3 ♖d7 23 ♕f5 ♕e6 24 ♕xe6 fxe6 25 h3 (25 ♘xa7 is only equal after 25...♘xc3! 26 bxc3 {26 ♖xd7?? ♘e2+ 27 ♔h1 ♘xf2+! mates} 26...♖xd1 27 ♘xc8 ♖d3 28 ♖c1 ♖d2 29 h3 ♘xf2 30 ♖f1 ♖d8! 31 ♘e7+ ♔f7 and White has no square for his knight) 25...a6 26 ♘a7 ♖cd8 27 ♗a5 ♖a8 28 hxg4 ♖xa7 29 ♗c3 ♖a8 30 ♖fe1 ♖ad8 31 ♗e5 with an edge for White, Dvoirys-Maliutin, USSR 1991.

3b) **13 ♘f4 ♕d6 14 ♘h5 ♘xh5** (14...♘g4 15 ♗f4 ♕d5 16 ♘g3 ♗e6 17 ♖e1 ♖ad8 18 h3 ♘f6 19 ♕d2 was also a little better for White in Schlemermeyer-Stein, Bundesliga 1993)

15 ♕xh5 h6 16 ♖e1 ♗d7 *(D)* and now:

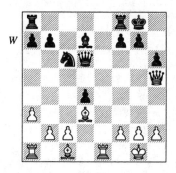

3b1) **17 ♕f3 ♖fe8 18 ♗f4 ♕f6 19 ♕g3 ♔h8 20 h3 ♗f5! 21 ♗xh6!?** gxh6 (21...♖xd3 22 ♗g5) **22 ♕f4 ♘e7 23 g4 ♕g6! 24 ♗xf5 ♘xf5 25 ♕xf5 ♕xf5 26 gxf5 ♔g7 27 ♖ad1** ½-½ Smirin-Khenkin, Elenite 1993. White's extra pawn is meaningless.

3b2) **17 ♕h4** (again White plans ♗f4 and this is probably more accurate than '3b' as the black queen is kept away from her ideal square, f6) 17...♖ae8 18 ♗f4 ♕d5 19 ♕g3 ♖e6 (preferable was 19...♔h8 although White would still have an edge) **20 ♖xe6 ♕xe6 21 ♗d2 ♕e5** (21...♖e8 22 h3 ♕e5 would have been better than the game) **22 ♖e1 ♕xg3 23 hxg3 ♖e8?** (this turns a difficult endgame into a lost one – without rooks on the board White's king will become too active; the last chance for Black to mount a successful defence was 23...♗e6 followed by ...♖d8) **24 ♖xe8+ ♗xe8 25 f4 ♗d7 26 ♔f2 ♔f8 27 ♗e4 ♔e7 28 ♔e2 ♔d6 29 ♔d3 b6 30 ♗b4+ ♔e6 31 ♗f3 f5 32 ♔c4 a5 33 ♗d5+ ♔f6 34** ♗d6 and faced with the destruction of his queenside by ♗c7 Black called it a day, Tiviakov-Sorokin, St. Petersburg 1993.

3c) **13 ♘g3** was recommended in *BTS2* but has still not been tested in a serious game. The only example is Cavello-Mellado, from the Oviedo rapid 1991. Play continued 13...♘e5 **14 ♗f4 ♘xd3 15 ♕xd3 ♗e6 16 ♖ad1 ♖fd8 17 ♖d2 ♖ac8 18 ♖e1 ♕c4 19 ♕xc4 ♖xc4 20 c3?** ♘d5 21 ♗g5 dxc3! with advantage to Black. White should have tried **20 ♗e5** with the threat of 21 b3; **20...♖dc8** can be met by 21 ♖ee2 and I (JG) suspect that after **20...♘g4 21 b3 ♘xe5 22** bxc4 ♘xc4 **23 ♖d3** that Black doesn't have quite enough for the exchange.

Returning to the main line after 12...♗g4 *(D)*:

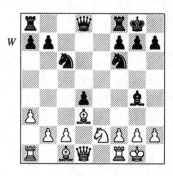

13 f3

This appears best, because the exchange on e2 usually simplifies Black's defensive task:

1) **13 ♗f4 ♖e8 14 ♖e1 ♕b6 15 b4 ♘e5 16 ♗xe5 ♖xe5 17 ♕d2 ♗xe2 18 ♖xe2 ♖xe2 19 ♗xe2 g6 20 ♖d1**

⬜d8 21 ♗f3 gave White a small but lasting advantage in Lobron-Chandler, Biel 1987.

2) After **13 ♗g5 ♕d6 14 ⬜e1** (14 ♕d2 ♗xe2 15 ♕xe2 ⬜fe8 16 ♕d1 ♘e5 offers White nothing, Short-Wiedenkeller, Esbjerg 1984) Black has tried:

2a) **14...a5** 15 ♕d2 ♘d5 16 h3 ♗xe2 17 ♗xe2 h6 18 ♗h4 was the continuation of R.Mainka-B.Stein, Dortmund 1987. Black now tried to imprison White's bishop by 18...f5 19 c4 ♘f4 20 ♗f3 ♘g6 21 ♗g3 f4 but this rebounded badly: 22 ♗d5+ ♔h7 23 ⬜e6 ♕d7 24 ♕d3 ♘ce7 25 ♗h2 ♘f5 26 ⬜ae1 ⬜ab8 27 ♕e4 b6 28 g3 ♕d8 29 h4 h5 30 ♕f3 ♔h6 31 ♕xf4+ ♔h7 32 ♕e4 ⬜c8 33 ♕f3 ♔h6 34 ⬜1e5 1-0.

2b) **14...⬜e8** 15 ♕d2 (15 f3 ♗h5 16 ♘f4 h6 17 ♘xh5 hxg5 18 ♘xf6+ ♕xf6 19 ♕d2 ♘e5 20 ⬜e4 ½-½ Short-Chandler, Hastings 1987/8) 15...♗xe2 (better than 15...⬜ac8 16 ♘g3 with a clear edge for White) 16 ⬜xe2 ⬜xe2 17 ♕xe2 ⬜e8 18 ♕f3 ♘e5 19 ♕f4 ♕b6 20 ♗xf6 ♘xd3 21 ♕g3 ♕xf6 22 ♕xd3 ♕b6 and Black drew easily in Kudrin-Rogers, London 1988.

13 ...   ♗h5
14 ♗g5   ♕d6

The position is the same as in Short-Chandler above, except that the moves ⬜e1 and ...⬜fe8 have been omitted. This difference favours White, as we shall see.

15 ♕e1

This is a good square for the queen. The immediate threat is ♕h4,

but White also intends to step up the pressure on d4 by ♕f2 and ⬜ad1. **15 ♕d2** is an interesting alternative if White plans to meet 15...⬜ad8 by 16 ♕f4!; Fishbein-Langua, Chicago 1991 continued 16...♗g6 17 ♗xf6 gxf6 **18 ♕xd6 ⬜xd6** 19 f4 ♗xd3 20 cxd3 ⬜e6 21 ♘g3 ♘e7! 22 ⬜ac1 ♘d5 23 ⬜c5 ⬜d8 and with his hole on e3 White had no real advantage to speak of. I (JG), personally, would have been loathe to exchange queens off after wrecking my opponent's kingside; **18 ♕h6** and **18 ♕h4** both look much more testing.

15 ...   ♗g6 (D)

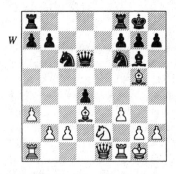

16 ⬜d1   ⬜fe8

Black must not exchange on d3 as this gives White a free tempo to increase the pressure on d4 by ♕f2 and ⬜fd1.

16...♘d5 was tried in Topalov-Sion, Leon 1993 but after 17 ♕f2 ♘b6 18 ♗c1! ⬜ac8 19 b3 ⬜fd8 20 ♗b2 the d-pawn was already ripe for plucking. Perhaps Black's best plan is to put a rook on the c-file to try to exploit the fact that White's queen is no longer defending the c2-pawn.

| 17 | ♕f2 | ♖ad8 |
| 18 | ♖d2 | ♖d7 |

Black decides to meet White's plan passively, even though being forced on the defensive is usually a sign that an isolated pawn position has gone wrong. However Mokry's suggestion of **18...♖e5** appears no better after 19 ♗h4 threatening ♗g3.

| 19 | ♖fd1 | ♖ed8 |

In the line **19...♗xd3** 20 ♖xd3 ♕e5 21 ♗xf6 ♕xe2 22 ♕xe2 ♖xe2 23 ♗xd4 ♖xc2 24 ♗c3 Black succeeds in exchanging his weak isolated pawn, but only at the cost of giving White a dominant bishop and chances of penetrating to the seventh rank.

| 20 | ♗b5! | |

Removing a vital defender increases the pressure on d4 intolerably. Black's reply leads to material loss, but even **20...♕e5** 21 ♗xc6 bxc6 22 ♗xf6 gxf6 23 f4 ♕b5 24 ♘g3, threatening f5, is unpleasant.

| 20 | ... | h6 *(D)* |
| 21 | ♘xd4! | hxg5 |

Black's moves are all forced, since **21...♘xd4** loses to 22 ♗xd7.

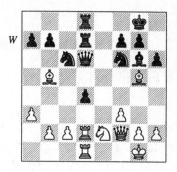

22	♘xc6	♕xd2
23	♖xd2	♖xd2
24	♘xd8	♖xf2
25	♔xf2	♗xc2
26	♘xb7	

White is a pawn up and his active king makes the task of converting his material plus into a point relatively simple.

26	...	♗b3
27	♘a5	♗d5
28	♘c6	♗xc6
29	♗xc6	♔f8
30	♔e3	♔e7
31	♔d4	♔d6
32	♗b5	1-0

Black did not wish to see the technical phase of the game.

10 Löwenthal and Kalashnikov Variations

These lines start 1 e4 c5 2 ♘f3 ♘c6 3 d4 cxd4 4 ♘xd4 e5 and are slightly akin to the Pelikan in its use of an early ...e5. The 'old' Löwenthal runs 5 ♘b5 a6 6 ♘d6+ ♗xd6 7 ♕xd6 ♕f6 and Black hopes that his lead in development will compensate for his dark-square weaknesses and lack of the two bishops. Current theory suggests that this is a vain hope and White should be able to maintain an advantage. This is the subject of Game 25.

Black has an interesting and dynamic alternative, which has been pioneered by Sveshnikov and other Soviet players. This runs 5 ♘b5 d6, and is generally known as the Kalashnikov Variation. Here White has the choice between 6 c4, aiming for a firm grip on d5, or 6 ♘1c3 as in the Pelikan. In BTS2 both lines were examined but with theory developing rapidly it was time to make a choice – and the solid 6 c4 has emerged on top. This is examined in Game 26.

Game 25
Liberzon – Franzoni
Biel 1980

1	e4	c5
2	♘f3	♘c6
3	d4	cxd4
4	♘xd4	e5
5	♘b5	a6
6	♘d6+	♗xd6
7	♕xd6	♕f6 *(D)*

7...♕e7 8 ♕d1 ♘f6 9 ♘c3 threatening ♗g5 is good for White because he will secure control of d5.

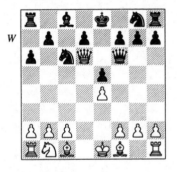

| 8 | ♕d1 |

White has a wide variety of queen moves and most of them are good! There seems little doubt that 8 ♕c7, which has always been highly regarded theoretically, gives White a good game but I have not recommended it here because White must always be careful that his queen is not trapped. The simpler ♕d1 seems preferable. One should note that 8 ♕xf6 is also quite good, for example 8...♘xf6 9 ♘c3 and now:

1) **9...d5** 10 ♗g5 d4 (10...♘b4 11 ♗xf6 gxf6 12 ♘xd5 ♘xc2+ 13 ♔d2 ♘xa1 14 ♘c7+ ♔e7 15 ♘xa8 ♗e6 16 ♘b6 ♗xa2 17 ♔c3 and 10...♘xe4 11 ♘xd5 0-0 12 ♗e3 are also good for White) 11 ♗xf6 dxc3 12 ♗xg7 ♖g8 13 ♗h6 ♘b4 14 0-0-0 ♘xa2+ 15 ♔b1 ♗e6 16 ♖d6 ♖g6 17 ♗e3 ♘b4 18 ♗c5 with advantage for White according to Gligorić.

2) **9...♘b4** *(D)* and now:

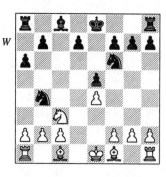

2a) **10 ♗d3** ♘xd3+ (10...h6 11 b3 d6 12 ♗a3 ♘xd3+ 13 cxd3 ♔e7 14 f4 ♔e6 15 f5+ ♔e7 16 ♖d1 ♖e8 17 d4 exd4 18 ♖xd4 ♔f8 19 ♗xd6+ ♔g8 20 0-0 b5 21 e5 1-0 was a drastic finish, Byrne-Evans, USA Ch 1981) 11 cxd3 h6 12 b3 with an edge for White.

2b) **10 ♔d2** d5 11 a3 d4 12 axb4 dxc3+ 13 ♔e3 ♘g4+ 14 ♔e2 f5 15 bxc3 ♘f6 16 ♖a5 ♘xe4 17 f3! ♘d6 18 ♖xe5+ and Black has very little for the lost pawn, Velimirović-Ristić, Yugoslavia 1979.

8 ... ♕g6

8...♘ge7 9 ♘c3 0-0 (9...♕g6 will transpose to the next note) 10 ♗e3 b5 11 ♕d2 ♕g6 12 f3 d6 13 0-0-0

♖d8 14 ♔b1 ♗b7 15 g4 f6 16 ♘d5 ♘xd5 17 ♕xd5+ is also promising for White, Gligorić-Benko, Dublin 1957.

9 ♘c3 *(D)*

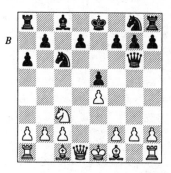

9 ... d5!?

For a time this move caused a revival of the Löwenthal, but now White has found a way to defuse the complications and liquidate to a favourable ending. The older line runs **9...♘ge7 10 h4! h5** (10...d5 11 h5 ♕d6 12 h6! g6 13 exd5 and now both 13...♘d4 and 13...♘b4 allow the reply 14 ♘e4, while 10...h6 11 h5 ♕f6 12 ♗e3 0-0 13 ♕d2 b5 14 0-0-0 b4 15 ♘a4 a5 16 ♘b6 ♖b8 17 ♕d6 gave White an excellent ending in Boleslavsky-Sakharov, USSR 1957) **11 ♗g5 d5** (the only move that makes sense; e.g. 11...b5 12 ♕d3 ♗b7 13 0-0-0 ♖d8 14 ♕d6 ♕xd6 15 ♖xd6 f6 16 ♗e3 ♘c8 17 ♖d2 ♘e7 18 ♗d3 d6 19 ♖hd1 was very good for White in Hazai-Csom, Warsaw 1987) **12 exd5** (the tempting 12 ♗xe7 is met by 12...d4!) and now we have:

1) **12...♘d4** 13 ♗d3 ♗f5 14 ♗xf5 ♘exf5 15 ♕d3 ♖c8!? (this move is

an interesting new try; 15...f6 16 ♗e3 is known to be good for White) 16 0-0-0 0-0 17 ♔b1 b5 18 ♘e2?! and now 18...e4?! 19 ♕xe4 ♖ce8 20 ♕xe8 ♖xe8 21 ♘xd4 f6 22 ♗f4 ♘xd4 23 ♖xd4 ♕xg2 24 ♖hd1, despite his queen minus, gave White the advantage in Gažik-Gross, Stary Smokovec 1991. However, I can't see anything wrong with 18...♘xc2, as 19 ♖c1 runs into 19...♘b4 20 ♕e4 ♘xd5!. I think White should have played the calm 18 ♖c1, e.g. 18...b4 19 ♘e2 ♘xe2 20 ♕xe2 ♘d4 21 ♕d3 ♖xc2 22 ♕xg6 ♖xc1+ 23 ♖xc1 fxg6 24 d6 with an excellent ending; or 18...f6 19 ♗e3 ♕xg2 20 ♘e4, with the idea of c3, should be favourable for White. It would be interesting to see further tests of this line.

2) 12...♘b4 13 ♗xe7 ♔xe7 14 ♗d3! (much better than the often-recommended 14 d6+, since White reaches the same type of ending, but with his d-pawn securely defended) 14...♘xd3+ 15 ♕xd3 ♕xd3 16 cxd3 (D) and now:

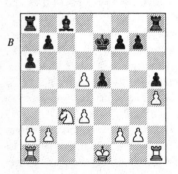

2a) 16...b5 17 a3 and Black cannot recover his pawn, for example

17...♗f5 18 ♔d2! ♖h6 19 ♖he1 ♔d6 20 ♖ac1, Sveshnikov-Panchenko, USSR 1977 or 17...♗b7 18 0-0-0 ♔d6 (suggested by Sveshnikov) 19 d4, or finally 17...♖b8 (suggested by Baumbach) 18 0-0-0 b4 19 axb4 ♖xb4 20 ♖he1 ♖xh4 (or else ♖e4) 21 d4!, and in all cases White has a good ending.

2b) 16...♖h6 17 0-0-0 ♖g6 18 ♖he1! ♖xg2 (the lines 18...f6 19 d4 and 18...♔d6 19 d4 are also good for White) 19 ♖xe5+ (19 d4!? is interesting) 19...♔d6 (19...♔d8 20 ♖de1 ♗d7 21 d6 threatens ♖xh5) 20 d4 followed by ♘e4+ and again White has the advantage.

10   ♘xd5   ♕xe4+
11   ♗e3   ♘d4

This move, which is the only reasonable reply to the threat of ♘c7+, is the idea behind 9...d5!?.

12   ♘c7+   ♔e7

12...♔d8? allows White to take the a8-rook, while after 12...♔f8? White can either play 13 ♖c1 or take the exchange by means of 13 ♕d3 ♘xc2+ 14 ♔d2 ♕xd3+ 15 ♗xd3 ♘xe3 16 ♘xa8 ♘d5 17 ♖ac1 – a pleasant choice!

13   ♖c1!

Until this move was discovered Black had been doing rather well against 13 ♘xa8?! and 13 ♕d3.

13   ...   ♗g4

13...♖b8 14 c3 ♘f5 15 ♕d5! ♘f6 16 ♕xe4 ♘xe4 17 ♗a7 +– Gallagher-Verdier, Nîmes 1992.

14   ♕d3   ♕xd3
15   ♗xd3   ♖d8
16   h3 (D)

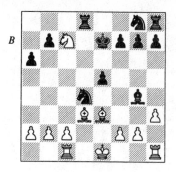

16 ... **♗c8**

The alternative is **16...♗h5 17 f4 f6 18 ♔f2 ♔d6 19 c3** and now:

1) **19...♔xc7** is bad due to 20 cxd4+ ♔b8 21 fxe5 fxe5 22 ♖c5.

2) **19...♘b3** 20 axb3 ♔xc7 21 ♗e4 ♘e7 22 ♖he1 ♘d5 23 fxe5 ♘xe3 24 ♔xe3 fxe5 25 ♖f1 ♖de8 26 ♖f5 ♗g6 27 ♖g5 ♗xe4 28 ♖xg7+ ♔c6 29 ♔xe4 with a winning position for White, Marjanović-Simić, Yugoslavia 1983.

3) **19...♘c6** 20 ♗b6 exf4 21 c4 ♘ge7 22 ♗e4 ♘c8 23 c5+ ♔d7 24 ♘d5 ♘xb6 25 cxb6 ♔d6 26 ♘xf4 ♗f7 27 ♖hd1+ ♔e5 28 ♔e3 with a clear plus for White, Winsnes-Hillarp, Rilton Cup 1988.

17 f4 **exf4**

17...♔d6 is met by 18 ♘a8!.

18 ♗xf4 **♘e6**

Otherwise White castles and Black is unable to develop his king's rook while e8 is covered.

19 ♘xe6 **♗xe6**

20 0-0

The outcome of the opening is very favourable for White. He has two active bishops supporting a queenside pawn majority and while so many pieces remain on the board Black's king is not well placed on e7.

20	...	♘f6
21	a3	♘d5
22	♗d2	♖d7
23	♖ce1	♖c8
24	♖f3	b5
25	b3	h6
26	c4	bxc4
27	♗xc4?!	

It was more important to drive away Black's centralised knight than to keep the queenside pawns intact. After 27 bxc4 ♘f6 28 ♗b4+ White has a passed pawn and an attack against Black's king.

27 ... **♖a8?! (D)**

A passive and nervous move. **27...♖c6** is better.

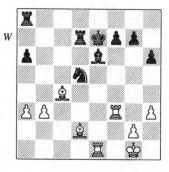

28 a4

Preparing both ♗c1-a3+ and b4-b5.

28 ... **♔d6**

An attempt to bring the king over to help in the fight against White's queenside majority, but two rooks and two bishops are a formidable attacking force and the king soon runs into trouble.

29	b4	♔c7
30	b5	axb5
31	♗xb5	♖d6
32	♖d1	

With the sneaky threat 33 ♗f4 ♘xf4 34 ♖c3+ winning the exchange.

32	...	♔b7
33	♗b4	♖dd8
34	♖fd3	♔c7

Trying to unpin the knight.

| 35 | ♖c1+ | ♔b6 |

35...♔b8 36 ♖c5 ♖a7 37 ♗c6 wins material.

36	♗c5+	♔a5
37	♖cd1	♖ac8
38	♗e7	♖e8
39	♗xe8	♖xe8
40	♖xd5+	1-0

Game 26
Chiburdanidze – Arakhamia
Tbilisi 1991

1	e4	c5
2	♘f3	♘c6
3	d4	cxd4
4	♘xd4	e5
5	♘b5	d6
6	c4	♗e7

6...♗e6 generally leads to a transposition.

7	♘1c3	a6
8	♘a3 *(D)*	
8	...	♗e6

Alternatives are:

1) **8...h6** (Black plans ...♗g5 but wants to recapture on g5 with a pawn; this turns out to be a rather dubious idea) 9 ♗e2 (or 9 ♘c2 ♗g5 10 ♗xg5 hxg5 11 ♕d2 ♖h6 12 0-0-0

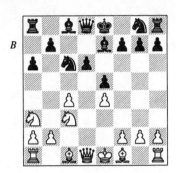

wsa good for White in Wedberg-Østenstad, Espoo Z 1989) 9...♗g5 10 ♘c2 ♘f6 (10...♗xc1 11 ♖xc1 ♘f6 12 0-0 0-0 13 ♕d2 ±) 11 ♗xg5 hxg5 12 ♕d2 ♖h6 13 ♕xg5 ♖g6 14 ♕e3 ♖xg2 15 0-0-0 with a clear plus for White, Hjartarson-Spraggett, Manila IZ 1990.

2) **8...♘f6** (abandoning the idea of exchanging dark-squared bishops is not really in the spirit of this line) 9 ♗e2 (9 ♗d3 also deserves attention) 9...0-0 10 ♗e3 ♗e6 11 0-0 ♖c8 12 ♕d2 ♘a5 (12...h6 13 ♖ac1 was slightly better for White in Dolmatov-Guseinov, Klaipeda 1988) 13 ♘d5 ♗xd5 14 exd5 b6 15 ♖ac1 ♘b7 16 f4 ♘d7 17 ♘c2 a5 18 ♘a3 with advantage to White, Dolmatov-Minasian, USSR 1988.

9 ♗d3 *(D)*

At the time of *BTS2* this line was very much in its infancy. It has now developed into one of the most solid lines in the Sicilian and plays a role in the repertoire of a number of strong grandmasters. Even so, no clear consensus has been reached on White's best line. Apart from the text, 9 ♗e2 and 9 ♘c2 are seen quite frequently and 9 ♗e3 and 9 ♘d5 appear from time to time. I have opted for 9 ♗d3, as opposed to ♗e2, firstly because it is safe from capture by a black knight on d4 and, secondly, because it feels more harmonious. The queen still has an open diagonal to the kingside and after the inevitable ♘d5, ...somethingxd5, exd5 will be a more tempting option. The only drawback of the move is that d6 is under less pressure, but it is quite rare for White to mount a serious attack against this pawn.

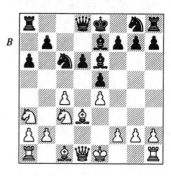

9 ... ♖c8

It is more common for Black to play an immediate **9...♗g5**. After **10 0-0** (10 ♘c2 can be played if White wishes to deny Black the opportunity of playing ...♘d4) **10...♗xc1** (10...h6 has been played but makes little sense as Black will soon have to capture on c1 anyway; e.g. Wang Zili-Arakhamia, Sydney 1991 was good for White after 11 ♘d5 ♘f6 12 ♘c2 ♗xc1 13 ♖xc1 ♗xd5 14 cxd5 ♘e7 15 ♘e3) **11 ♖xc1** we have:

1) **11...♘d4 12 f4!?** exf4 **13 ♗b1** ♘c6 14 ♔h1 ♘ge7 15 ♖xf4 0-0 16 ♖f2 ♘g6 17 ♖d2 ♕h4! was unclear in Conquest-Fossan, Gausdal 1991, but **13 ♘d5!?** looks like a possible improvement to me, whilst the aggressive 12 f4 is not the only way to treat the position, e.g. **12 ♗b1!?** or even **12 ♘c2**.

2) **11...♘f6 12 ♘c2 0-0 13 ♕d2** *(D)* (13 b4 ♖c8 14 ♘d5 is widely quoted as ±) with a further bifurcation:

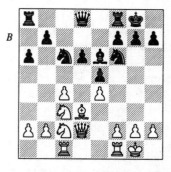

2a) **13...♕b6** 14 ♔h1 ♖ac8 15 b3 ♘d4? (15...♖fd8 was more solid) 16 ♘e3 ♕a5 17 f4! exf4, Fedorowicz-Salov, Wijk aan Zee 1991, 18 ♘ed5! and Black is in serious trouble after both **18...♗xd5** 19 exd5 and **18...♕d8** 19 ♕xf4, mainly because of the knight on d4 which is hanging in the middle of nowhere.

2b) **13...♖c8** 14 ♖fd1 ♕b6 15 ♗f1 ♖fd8 16 b3 ♕a7 17 h3 ♕b8 (Black has reached his optimum position, often not a good sign as it leaves you with nothing to do; White now builds up slowly, first tying Black down to the defence of d6 and then switching operations to the kingside) 18 ♕e3 ♕a7 19 ♕d2 ♕b8

20 罝e1 響a7 21 罝cd1 ②e7 22 罝e3
罝d7 23 罝d3 ②e8 24 ☖h2 罝dc7 25
g3 響c5 26 a4 (Black was actually
threatening to play ...b5) 26...響b6
27 罝b1 罝d7 28 ♗g2 罝dd8 29 f4 f6
30 f5 ♗f7 31 h4 with a clear advantage to White, Timoshenko-Kiselev,
Bucharest 1993. White can antici-
pate a successful pawn-storm as
Black lacks both counterplay and
space.

10	0-0	♗g5
11	②c2	♗xc1
12	罝xc1	②a5?

This move is too ambitious. Black
would do well to concentrate on her
development, after which the game
would resemble the lines in the note
to Black's 9th move.

| 13 | b3 | b5 |

This move cannot really be con-
demned, even if swallowing one's
pride and returning the knight to c6
is the lesser evil.

| 14 | ②e3 | bxc4 |
| 15 | ♗xc4! | |

It is the knights that are going to
cause the damage.

| 15 | ... | ②xc4 |
| 16 | bxc4 (D) | |

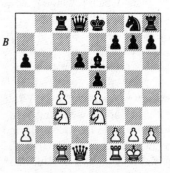

So Black has achieved her strategic aim of wrecking the white pawn
structure, but at a great cost. Her own
pawns on a6 and d6 are very weak,
and more significantly, her king is
still stuck in the middle and the
knight on g8 and rook on h8 are not
exactly playing a full part in the
struggle. The position can already be
assessed as '±'.

| 16 | ... | a5 |

Faced with the threat of 17 響a4+,
Black relinquishes control of b5. As
16...♕d7 would have been well met
by 17 ②cd5 響c6 (17...罝b8 18 c5) 18
c5! dxc5 19 ②c4, I think it was time
for Black to cut her losses and jetti-
son a pawn. After **16...②e7** 17 響a4+
②c6 18 響xa6 0-0 there is still some
hope.

| 17 | ②b5 | ☖e7 |
| 18 | 響f3 (D) | |

18 響a4 looks like a tempting alternative, but the main purpose behind moving the queen is to connect
the rooks and threaten 19 罝fd1 罝c6
20 c5!.

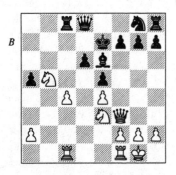

| 18 | ... | 響b6 |
| 19 | 罝fd1 | 罝c6 |

20 ♖b1   ♛c5
21 ♘c3!

After playing an important role in luring the black major pieces to unfavourable squares, the knight now clears the way for the rook and once again looks towards d5.

21 ...   ♘f6

And this knight finally develops itself, at least nine moves too late.

22 ♖b5   ♛a7

The queen must retreat as otherwise ♖b7+ would prove decisive.

23 ♘cd5+   ♗xd5
24 cxd5   ♖b6? *(D)*

A blunder, but 24...♖c5 25 ♘f5+ ♔d7 26 ♖xc5 ♛xc5 27 ♘xg7 is also pretty hopeless.

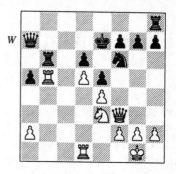

25 ♘f5+   ♔f8

The h8-rook never managed to move.

26 ♛e3   ♖a6
27 ♛xa7   ♖xa7
28 ♖b8+   ♘e8
29 ♘xd6   1-0

11 Pin Variation

There is no generally accepted name for this variation, which runs 1 e4 c5 2 ♘f3 e6 3 d4 cxd4 4 ♘xd4 ♘f6 5 ♘c3 ♗b4. There is certainly a pin involved, so 'Pin Variation' is a reasonable name. Up until about 15 years ago this was thought to be a very poor line for Black, but round about 1979 it suddenly reappeared with Black's play being based on a new idea involving an exchange sacrifice. After a few years, during which it was used in occasional grandmaster games, it entered a decline and is now very rarely seen. However it is worth studying because there are a lot of tricky tactics in the Pin Variation, and White players who do not know the correct antidote may well find themselves in trouble.

Game 27
Wagman – Barle
Biel 1981

1	e4	c5
2	♘f3	e6
3	d4	cxd4
4	♘xd4	♘f6
5	♘c3	♗b4
6	e5 *(D)*	

The only move to cause Black any difficulties.

| 6 | ... | ♘d5 |

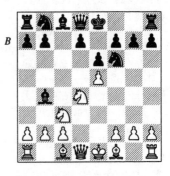

Black's two alternatives are close to losing by force:

1) **6...♕a5** 7 exf6 ♗xc3+ 8 bxc3 ♕xc3+ 9 ♕d2 ♕xa1 10 c3 (threatening 11 ♘b3 ♕b1 12 ♗d3) 10...♕b1 11 ♗d3 ♕b6 12 fxg7 ♖g8 13 ♕h6 and White wins.

2) **6...♘e4 7 ♕g4** and now:

2a) **7...♘xc3** 8 ♕xg7 ♖f8 9 a3 and now the lines 9...♗a5 10 ♗h6 ♕e7 11 ♘b3, 9...♗a5 10 ♘b3 ♕d5 11 ♗d3 and 9...♕b6 10 axb4 ♕xd4 11 ♗h6 ♕e4+ 12 ♔d2 ♕d4+ 13 ♗d3 ♘e4+ 14 ♔c1 are winning for White so Black must try 9...♘b5+ 10 axb4 ♘xd4 11 ♗g5 ♕b6 12 ♗h6 ♕xb4+ 13 c3 ♘f5 14 cxb4 ♘xg7 15 ♗xg7 ♖g8 16 ♗f6 but White's dark-square pressure gives him a very favourable ending.

2b) **7...♕a5** 8 ♕xe4 ♗xc3+ 9 bxc3 ♕xc3+ 10 ♔d1 ♕xa1 11 ♘b5 d5 12 ♕b4 ♘a6 (12...♕xe5 13 f4 ♘c6 14 fxe5 ♘xb4 15 ♘c7+ ♔d8 16

♘xa8 b6 17 ♗a3 is winning for White) 13 ♘d6+ ♔d7 14 ♗xa6 bxa6 15 ♘xf7 ♖g8 16 ♔d2 d4 (or else ♗a3) 17 ♗b2 ♕xa2 18 ♖a1 ♕d5 19 ♖a5 and White has a decisive attack (analysis by Euwe).

7   ♗d2

Originally theory gave **7 ♕g4** as best, but after 7...0-0 (the new idea mentioned above) 8 ♗h6 g6 9 ♗xf8 ♕xf8 Black has reasonable compensation for the exchange, with play against c3 and e5.

7   ...   ♘xc3

Or 7...♗xc3 8 bxc3 0-0 9 ♗d3 d6 10 ♕h5 (10 exd6 ♕xd6 11 0-0 is at least slightly better for White, Geller-Tseitlin, Moscow 1982, and 10 f4 dxe5 11 fxe5 ♘d7 12 ♕h5 g6 13 ♕e2 ♕c7 14 c4 ♕b6 15 ♘f3 ♘e7 16 ♗c3 ♘c5 17 ♕d2 proved favourable for White in Epishin-Ulybin, Tbilisi 1989) 10...g6 11 ♕e2 dxe5 12 ♕xe5 ♘d7 13 ♕d6 ♕f6 14 0-0 b6 15 ♘c6 ♘c5 16 c4 e5 17 ♕xe5 with a clear plus for White, Vogt-Ermenkov, Berlin 1982.

8   bxc3 *(D)*

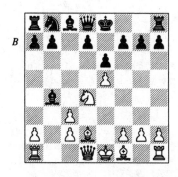

8   ...   ♗a5?!

A major decision point for Black. 8...♗a5 keeps the pressure against c3 but leaves the kingside dangerously bare.

Black should adopt the alternative possibility **8...♗e7 9 ♕g4** with four variations:

1) **9...g6** 10 h4 h5 11 ♕g3 ♘c6 12 ♘b5 was good for White in Rabar-Fuster, Munich 1942.

2) The remarkable idea **9...g5** 10 h4 h5 11 hxg5!? hxg4 12 ♖xh8+ ♗f8 was played in Grosar-De Waal, Sas van Gent 1986, and now 13 g6 fxg6 14 ♗h6 ♔f7 15 ♖xf8+ ♕xf8 16 ♗xf8 ♔xf8 17 ♗e2 is good for White.

3) **9...♔f8** also has to be taken into account, a recent example being Z.Varga-S.Horvath, Hungarian Cht 1991: 10 ♗d3 d6 11 f4 ♘d7 12 0-0 ♘c5 13 ♖ae1 ♘xd3 14 cxd3 h5 15 ♕f3 g6 16 ♖b1 d5 17 ♗e3 b6 18 c4 ♗b7 19 f5! gxf5 20 ♘xf5 exf5 21 ♕xf5 ♕e8 22 ♕g6! dxc4 23 e6 f6 24 ♖xf6+ ♗xf6 25 ♕xf6+ ♔g8 26 ♗d4 1-0.

4) **9...0-0 10 ♗h6 g6**, but even here the main line favours White after **11 h4!** *(D)*:

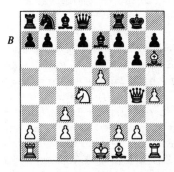

4a) 11...d6 12 h5 ♕a5 (12...dxe5 13 ♗d3! exd4 14 hxg6 fxg6 15 ♗xg6 wins) 13 0-0-0!? dxe5 (13...♕xc3 14 ♖h3 ♕a1+ 15 ♔d2 ♕xa2 16 ♗d3 ♕a5+ 17 c3 ♕xe5 18 hxg6 fxg6 19 ♗xg6 ♖xf2+ 20 ♔c1 and 13...♕xe5 14 hxg6 fxg6 15 ♗d3 ♖f6 16 ♖de1 ♕d5 17 ♗g5 ♖f7 18 ♗xe7 ♖xe7 19 ♗xg6 are winning for White) 14 ♘b5 a6 15 hxg6 fxg6 16 ♗xf8 ♗xf8 17 ♖xh7! ♔xh7 18 ♗d3 wins for White.

4b) 11...♕a5 12 ♕g3 ♖d8 (after 12...d6 13 exd6 Black may continue 13...♗xd6 14 ♕xd6 ♖d8 15 ♕b4 ♕xb4 16 cxb4 ♖xd4 17 c3 with the better ending for White, or 13...♗f6 14 0-0-0 ♕xa2 15 h5 ♘c6 16 ♘xc6 ♕a3+ 17 ♔d2 bxc6 18 ♗xf8 ♔xf8 19 hxg6 hxg6 20 ♗c4 and again White has the advantage) 13 h5 d6 14 hxg6 fxg6 15 ♗f4 dxe5 16 ♗xe5 ♖d5 17 f4 ♘d7 18 ♗c4 ♘xe5 (after 18...♖xe5+ 19 fxe5 ♕xe5+ 20 ♕xe5 ♘xe5 21 ♗b3 the e6-pawn is too weak) 19 ♗xd5 ♕xd5 20 fxe5 ♕e4+ 21 ♔d2 ♗d7 22 ♖ae1 ♕d5, as in Wedberg-Pokojowczyk, Copenhagen Open 1984, and now 23 ♖xh7! ♔xh7 24 ♖h1+ ♔g7 25 ♕h2 ♔f7 26 ♕h7+ ♔e8 27 ♕xg6+ ♔d8 28 ♖h8+ should win for White.

9 ♕g4

White can also use the move order **9 ♗d3** when after **9...d6** 10 ♕g4 Black has nothing better than to play 10...0-0 transposing into the main game. In Gallagher-Escott, London 1984 Black tried **9...♕c7** but suffered a horrible fate: 10 0-0!? ♕xe5 11 ♖e1 ♕f6 12 ♕h5 (threatening 13

♗g5) 12...♗d8 13 ♘f5! ♗c7 14 ♗g5 ♕xc3 15 ♖ad1 ♘c6 16 ♖e3 g6 17 ♕h6 gxf5 18 ♗f6 ♘e5 19 ♕g7!? ♖f8 20 ♖xe5! ♗xe5 21 ♗xe5 ♕c5 22 ♗b5! (threatening ♗d6; the b5-square was chosen as it pins the d-pawn) 22...♕xc2 23 ♖d4! ♕c1+ 24 ♗f1 f6 25 ♗d6! 1-0.

9 ...   0-0
10 ♗d3   d6

10...♘c6 is not much of an improvement, as can be seen from the game Pyhälä-Seppanen, Helsinki 1992: 11 ♘xc6 bxc6 12 ♕e4 g6+ 13 h4 f5 14 ♕f4 ♖f7 15 g4 fxg4 16 ♕xg4 ♕b6 17 h5! ♕xf2+ 18 ♔d1 ♕f3+ 19 ♕xf3 ♖xf3 20 hxg6 hxg6 21 ♔e2! ♖f5 22 ♗xf5 exf5 23 ♖ag1 ♔f7 24 ♖h7+ ♔e6 25 ♖xg6+ ♔xe5 26 ♖e7+ 1-0 (26...♔d5 27 c4+).

11 ♘f3

Byrne and Mednis suggest **11 ♗g5** with the variations **11...♗xc3+** 12 ♔f1 f5 13 exf6 ♖xf6 14 ♖d1 and **11...♕c7** 12 ♗f6 ♕xc3+ 13 ♔e2 ♕d2+ 14 ♔f1 g6 15 ♖d1. This has never been tried in practice but looks good to me.

11 ...   g6

Or else ♗xh7+ is crushing, for example **11...dxe5** 12 ♗xh7+ ♔xh7 13 ♕h5+ ♔g8 14 ♘g5 ♖e8 15 ♕xf7+ ♔h8 16 ♕h5+ followed by ♕h7+, ♕h8+, ♕xg7+ and ♘f7+ picking up the queen.

12 h4!

The strongest line – White just plays for mate. **12 ♘g5?!** h5! (but not 12...dxe5? 13 ♘xh7! ♔xh7 14 ♗g5 ♗xc3+ 15 ♔e2 ♕d4 16 ♕h3+ ♔g8 17 ♗f6) 13 ♕g3 dxe5 14 ♘e4

♘d7 15 0-0 ♔g7 enabled Black to defend in Peters-Arnason, New York 1980, while **12 0-0** dxe5 (Sigurjonsson mentions the attractive line 12...♘c6 13 ♗g5 ♕c7 14 ♗f6 ♗xc3 15 ♕h4 ♘xe5 16 ♘g5 h5 17 ♕xh5) 13 ♘xe5 followed by f4 only gave White an edge in Sigurjonsson-Arnason, Iceland 1980.

12 ... dxe5

12...h5 is met by 13 ♕g3 or 13 ♕f4.

13 h5 f5 (D)

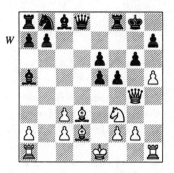

14 ♗xf5! exf5

14...♖xf5 15 hxg6 h5 16 ♖xh5 ♕f6 (16...♖xh5 17 ♕xh5 ♕c7 18 0-0-0 wins, while otherwise Black can hardly meet the threat of ♖h8+) 17 0-0-0 followed by ♖dh1 with a decisive attack.

15 ♕c4+ ♖f7

Or **15...♔g7** 16 hxg6 ♔xg6 17 ♘xe5+ winning for White.

16 hxg6 hxg6
17 ♘g5 ♕c7

If the queen defends the rook from any other square White wins by 18 ♘xf7 ♕xf7 19 ♖h8+.

18 ♕h4 ♔f8
19 ♘xf7?

Having conducted the attack so well up to here it is surprising that White should miss 19 ♕h8+ ♔e7 20 ♘xf7 when he is material up with a mating attack. Fortunately White is still winning even after 19 ♘xf7?.

19 ... ♔xf7
20 ♕h7+ ♔e6

The line 20...♔f6 21 ♗g5+ ♔e6 22 ♕xg6+ ♔d5 23 0-0-0+ ♔c5 24 ♗e3+ ♔b5 25 ♖d5+ is even worse.

21 ♕xg6+ ♔d5
22 ♖h6 ♘c6
23 ♕g8+ ♔c5
24 ♖b1!

White correctly adheres to the rule applying to king-hunts that it is more important to cut off the king's escape route than to give check.

24 ... b5
25 ♗e3+ ♘d4
26 ♗xd4+ exd4
27 ♕f8+

White misses it the first time round...

27 ... ♔c4
28 ♕g8+ ♔c5
29 ♖xb5+! .

...but spots it the second!

29 ... ♔xb5
30 ♕d5+ ♕c5
31 a4+ 1-0

12 Nimzowitsch Variation: 2...♘f6

Although this move surfaces from time to time, its appearances at the grandmaster level are very rare. White has a range of possible lines against 2...♘f6, which have all proved successful in practice. In this edition, as in *BTS2*, we are recommending 3 e5 ♘d5 4 ♘c3 e6 5 ♘xd5 exd5 6 d4, which is, incidentally, the most popular line as well. Play can become very sharp so it is certainly a good idea to familiarise yourself with the variations, as facing it over the board with no prior knowledge is a far from easy task. However, the well prepared player should be assured of gaining the advantage against 2...♘f6.

Game 28
Rhine – Sprenkle
USA 1981

1	e4	c5
2	♘f3	♘f6
3	e5	♘d5

3...♘g4 4 h3 ♘h6 may be met by 5 d4 or 5 c3, with advantage to White.

| 4 | ♘c3 | e6 |

Or 4...♘xc3 (4...♘b4 5 ♗c4 and 4...♘c7 5 d4 cxd4 6 ♕xd4 ♘c6 7 ♕e4 g6 8 ♗c4 ♗g7 9 0-0 0-0 10 ♖e1, Kindermann-Ostl, Bundesliga 1987, are good for White) **5 dxc3** *(D)* and now:

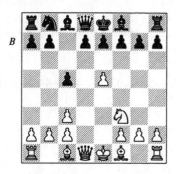

1) **5...d5** 6 exd6 ♕xd6 (6...exd6 7 ♗c4 ♗e7 8 ♗f4 0-0 9 ♕d2 followed by 0-0-0 puts severe pressure on the backward pawn) 7 ♕xd6 exd6 8 ♗f4 ♗g4 (8...d5 9 0-0-0 ♗e6 10 ♘g5 followed by g3 and either ♗g2 or ♘xe6 and ♗h3, when Black's central pawns will be fortunate to survive) 9 0-0-0 ♘d7 10 ♗c4 (even better than ♗xd6, since ...0-0-0 is prevented) followed by ♗xd6 winning a pawn.

2) **5...♘c6** 6 ♗f4 with the following examples:

2a) **6...e6** 7 ♕e2 ♕a5?! 8 ♘d2! ♕c7 9 ♘c4 f6 10 ♘d6+ ♗xd6 11 exd6 ♕a5 12 h4 with advantage to White, Van der Wiel-Bjelajac, Novi Sad 1982.

2b) **6...♕b6** 7 ♖b1 (7 b3!? would keep the right to castle long) 7...h6 8 ♗d3 g5?! 9 ♗e3 ♗g7 10 ♕e2 d6 11 exd6 ♗xc3+ 12 ♘d2 ♗xd2+ 13 ♕xd2 e5 14 ♗c4! ♗d7 15 h4 and the black position is a wreck, Totsky-Losev, St Petersburg 1994.

2c) **6...h6** 7 ♕e2 ♕c7 8 0-0-0 b6 9 ♕e3 e6 10 ♘d2 ♘e7 11 ♘c4 ♘f5 (but not 11...♘d5? 12 ♖xd5 exd5 13 ♘d6+ ♔d8 14 e6 wins) 12 ♕h3 ♗b7 13 ♖g1, intending g4, and White has some advantage, Van der Wiel-Murey, Moscow IZ 1982.

3) **5...g6** 6 ♗c4 ♗g7 7 ♗f4 0-0 8 ♕d2 followed by 0-0-0 and h4 gives White a strong attack.

4) **5...b6?** 6 e6! dxe6 (6...fxe6 and 6...f6 are both met by 7 ♘e5!) 7 ♕xd8+ ♔xd8 8 ♘e5 ♔e8 9 ♗b5+ ♗d7 10 ♘xd7 ♘xd7 11 ♗f4 and White is close to winning already.

    5 ♘xd5   exd5
    6 d4   ♘c6

If Black doesn't like to sacrifice a pawn he can try **6...d6**, but after **7 ♗b5+** *(D)* he cannot equalise, as the following analysis shows:

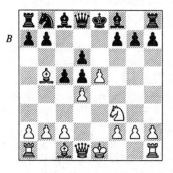

1) **7...♗d7** 8 ♗xd7+ ♕xd7 (not 8...♘xd7 9 dxc5) 9 0-0 ♘c6 10 exd6 ♗xd6 (10...♕xd6 11 dxc5 ♕xc5 12 ♗e3 is also good for White) 11 ♖e1+ ♘e7 12 dxc5 ♗xc5 13 ♗g5 0-0 14 ♕d3 f6 (or 14...h6 15 ♗xe7 ♗xe7

16 ♖ad1 ♖ad8 17 c4 ♗f6 18 cxd5 ♗xb2 19 d6 and White's passed pawn is very dangerous) 15 ♗e3 and Black has a poor isolated pawn position in which he has no active pieces to compensate for the static weakness.

2) **7...♘c6** 8 0-0 ♗e7 (8...♗e6 is also met by 9 c4 when Black has nothing better than to transpose by 9...♗e7) 9 c4 ♗e6 (9...dxc4 10 exd6 ♕xd6 11 d5 a6 12 ♗xc4 and 9...a6 10 ♗xc6+ bxc6 11 cxd5 cxd5 12 exd6 ♕xd6 13 dxc5 ♕xc5 14 ♗e3 are very good for White) 10 ♗e3 ♕b6 (White threatened exd6) 11 a4 a6 12 a5 ♕c7 13 exd6 ♕xd6 14 dxc5 ♕d8 15 ♗xc6+ bxc6 16 ♘e5 ♕c7 17 ♕a4 ± Unzicker-Pomar, Bad Aibling 1968.

    7 dxc5   ♗xc5
    8 ♕xd5   ♕b6

Here there is an important alternative: **8...d6 9 exd6 ♕b6** *(D)* (giving up another pawn to allow Black's pieces to come into play more rapidly) and now:

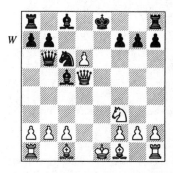

1) **10 ♗e3!?** (for brave players only) 10...♕xb2 (10...♗xe3 11 fxe3

♕xe3+ 12 ♗e2 ♗e6 13 ♕g5 is promising for White) 11 ♗b5!? and now **11...♕xa1+** 12 ♔e2 ♕c3 13 ♗xc6+ bxc6 (not 13...♔f8? 14 ♕xc5 nor 13...♔d8? 14 ♕xf7) 14 ♕xc6+ ♔f8 15 ♕xa8 ♕xc2+ 16 ♘d2 ♗xd6 17 ♖b1 leads to an advantage for White, **11...♕xb5** 12 ♕xc5 is depressing for Black, while **11...0-0** 12 0-0 ♗xe3 13 fxe3 ♗e6 14 ♕c5 was good for White in Boll-Lanz, Corr. 1982, so the best line is **11...♗b4+** 12 ♔e2 ♕xc2+ 13 ♘d2 ♗e6 with a total mess.

2) **10 ♕e4+ ♗e6** (10...♔d8 11 ♗g5+ f6 12 0-0-0! ♖e8 13 ♕h4 is good for White) **11 ♕h4!** *(D)* (11 ♗c4!? ♕b4+ 12 ♘d2 0-0 13 0-0 ♖ae8 14 c3 ♕b6 15 ♘f3 h6 16 b4 ♗xd6 17 ♗e3 ♕c7 18 ♗xe6 ♖xe6 19 ♕c4 and Black had insufficient compensation for the pawn, Short-Van der Wiel, Wijk aan Zee 1990) with the variations:

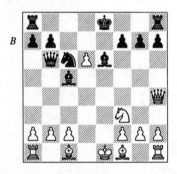

2a) **11...f6 12 ♗d3 0-0-0** (the line 12...♘b4 13 d7+! ♗xd7 14 ♕h5+ followed by 0-0 is good for White) **13 0-0** and now there is a further branch:

2a1) **13...♗xd6** 14 ♗e3 ♕xb2 15 ♖ab1 ♕a3 16 ♗c4 gives White good attacking chances for no sacrifice.

2a2) **13...♖xd6** 14 ♗e3 (I am not sure that it was necessary to return the pawn since Black has no immediate threats; 14 a3 intending b4 appears promising) 14...♗xe3 15 fxe3 ♕xe3+ 16 ♔h1 ♕c5? (16...♕b6 is just slightly better for White) 17 ♖ae1 ♗d7 18 ♕g3 g6 19 ♘d2! f5 20 ♘b3 ♕b4 21 a3 winning material, Chandler-Arnold, Bundesliga 1987.

2a3) **13...h5** 14 ♗e3 ♗xe3 15 fxe3 ♕xe3+ 16 ♔h1 ♗g4 (16...♖xd6 17 ♖ae1 ♕b6 18 ♖xe6 ♖xe6 19 ♗f5) 17 ♕g3 (17 ♖ae1 ♕c5 18 ♗e4 is good for White according to Gutman) 17...♕c5 18 ♖ad1 ♗b8 19 ♗e4 ♘e5 20 ♘xe5 ♗xd1, Hansson-Fernandes, London 1984, and although this game has appeared a number of times in print, nobody seems to have noticed that after 21 ♕xg7 Black can quite reasonably resign.

3) **11...♗xd6** 12 ♗e2 (even 12 ♗d3 ♘b4 13 0-0 ♘xd3 14 cxd3 0-0 15 ♕e4 h6 16 ♗e3 ♕xb2 17 ♖fb1 gave White a slight advantage in Hellers-Ivarsson, Sweden 1985) 12...♗e7 (12...♘b4 13 0-0 is good for White after 13...0-0 14 c3 or 13...♗e7 14 ♕e4 f5 15 ♕e5 ♘xc2 16 ♗g5) 13 ♕e4 0-0-0 14 0-0 ♗d5 (after 14...♘d4 15 ♘xd4 ♖xd4 16 ♕e3 ♗c5 17 ♕c3 White stands very well) 15 ♕g4+ ♔b8 (15...♗e6 16 ♕a4), Chandler-Bartsch, Bundesliga 1985, and now 16 c4! is good for White.

9 ♗c4   ♗xf2+

10 ♔e2   0-0
11 ♖f1   ♗c5

Black has regained the sacrificed pawn, but now f7 is exposed to attack.

12 ♘g5 *(D)*

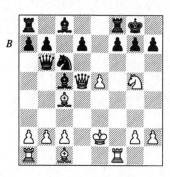

12 ...   ♘d4+

The best line; Black transfers the knight to e6 in order to shield f7. The alternative **12...♘xe5?** (12...d6? 13 ♖xf7! ♘d4+ 14 ♔d1 ♗g4+ 15 ♖f3+ ♔h8 16 ♕g8+ and mate) **13 ♕xe5 d5 14 ♕xd5** is inferior, e.g.:

1) **14...♗g4+** 15 ♖f3 ♗g1 16 ♔f1! ♖ad8 17 ♕e4 ♖d1+ 18 ♔e2 ♗xf3+ 19 gxf3 ♖fd8 20 ♗xf7+ ♔f8 21 ♘xh7+ ♔xf7 22 ♘g5+ ♔f8 23 ♕f5+ ♔e7 24 ♕f7+ ♔d6 25 ♗f4+ ♔c6 26 ♕c4+ ♔c5 27 ♕xc5+ ♗xc5 28 ♖xd1 ♖e8+ 29 ♘e4 1-0 Prokopchuk-Kuznetsov, USSR 1972.

2) **14...♖e8** 15 ♔f3 ♕f6+ 16 ♔g3 ♗d6+ 17 ♖f4! ♗e6 18 ♘xe6 ♖xe6 19 ♕xd6 ♕g6+ 20 ♖g4 ♖e3+ 21 ♗xe3 ♕xd6+ 22 ♔f2 ♖e8 23 ♖f4 ♖e7 24 ♗b3 ♕e5 25 ♖e1 g5 26 ♖f3 ♔g7 27 ♖d1 f6 28 ♔g1 g4 29 ♗d4 1-0 Spassky-Ciríc, Marianske Lazne 1962.

13 ♔d1   ♘e6
14 ♘e4

Here White has various possibilities, but this move, attacking c5 and restraining ...d6, looks best.

14 ...   d6

14...♗e7 is too passive and in Savkin-Tseitlin, Corr. 1972 White obtained a strong attack after 15 c3 (15 ♘d6 is also good) 15...d6 16 exd6 ♖d8 17 ♔c2 ♗xd6 18 ♖xf7! ♔xf7 19 ♘g5+ ♔e8 (19...♔g8 20 ♕e4 h6 21 ♗e3 ♕a5 22 ♗xe6+ ♗xe6 23 ♕h7+ and ♖f1+ wins) 20 ♘xe6 ♕f2+ 21 ♔b3 ♕b6+ 22 ♗b5+ ♗d7 23 ♘c7+! and Black resigned without waiting to see one of the lines 23...♕xc7 24 ♕g8+ ♗f8 25 ♗f4! or 23...♗xc7 24 ♕g8+ ♔e7 25 ♗g5+ ♔d6 26 ♖d1+.

15 exd6   ♖d8

15...♗xd6? is a miscombination which rebounds after 16 ♘xd6 ♖d8 17 ♗f4 ♘xf4 (Black saw the danger in Zaretdinov-Pugachevsky, USSR 1977 but still lost after 17...h6 18 ♗e5 ♘g5 19 ♖xf7, etc.) 18 ♕xf7+ ♔h8 19 ♕g8+ 1-0 Unzicker-Sarapu, Siegen 1970.

16 ♗d3   ♗xd6
17 ♕h5   f5
18 ♘xd6   ♕xd6

After **18...♖xd6** 19 ♕xf5, White's threats to f7 and h7 force Black to play 19...♖xd3+, but he does not gain enough compensation.

19 ♕xf5 *(D)*
19 ...   ♕xh2

Or **19...♘f8** (19...g6 20 ♕f7+ ♔h8 21 ♕f6+ ♔g8 22 ♗f4 liquidates to an ending in which White has a

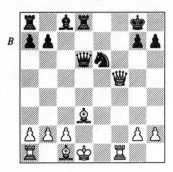

clear extra pawn) **20 ♕f7+ ♚h8 21 ♕f4** and now:

1) **21...♕c5** 22 ♗e3 ♕h5+ (after 22...♗g4+ 23 ♚d2 ♕a5+ 24 b4 ♕h5 25 ♕g5 White exchanges queens) 23 ♚d2 ♗e6 24 ♕g5 (24 ♗d4! looks very good to me since 24...♞g6 allows 25 ♗xg7+ ♚xg7 26 ♕f6+ and 24...♕d5 25 ♕e5! ♕xg2+ 26 ♖f2 ♕g4 27 h3! is a disaster) 24...♕e8, A.Rodriguez-Diaz, Cuban Ch 1983, and now 25 ♖f4 intending ♗d4 gives White a clear advantage.

2) **21...♕e7** 22 ♕g5 ♕e8, Short-Minić, Banja Luka 1985, and now Minić gives the line 23 ♗d2 ♗e6 (23...♕a4 24 ♗c3! ♖xd3+ 25 ♚c1 ♞g6 26 ♖f8+ mates) 24 ♗c3 ♞g6 25 ♚d2 ♖d5 26 ♕g3 ♕d7 27 ♖ae1, assessing the final position as being slightly better for White. I suspect that White's advantage is considerably greater than this; he is a pawn up with the two bishops, and if he consolidates with ♚c1 he must be winning. Therefore Black should play 27...♗f5, but after 28 ♖e3 followed by ♚c1 White is a pawn up for nothing.

20 ♕f7+ ♚h8

21 ♗g5 ♖g8
22 ♗e3! ♞d8

After this move White can gain a clear endgame advantage with no risk. The critical move is **22...♕xg2! 23 ♕h5!** *(D)* (I gave 23 ♖f2 in the first edition, but 23...♕g4+ 24 ♚d2 ♕b4+ 25 ♚d1 ♞g5! is good for Black) and now:

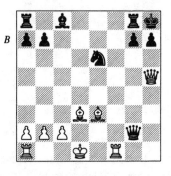

1) **23...♞f8?!** 24 ♖f4! (intending ♖h4 and mate on h7) 24...♕h3 (seemingly forced) 25 ♕xh3 ♗xh3, Odeev-Varlamov, Corr. 1987, and now 26 ♚d2 ♗g2 (26...♖d8 27 ♖h1 ♗g2 28 ♖h2 ♗c6 29 ♖fh4 h6 30 ♗d4 wins the exchange) 27 ♖g1 ♗c6 28 ♖h4 (intending ♖g3-h3) 28...♖d8 29 ♖g3 ♗d7 30 ♗d4 and White has a large advantage.

2) **23...g6** 24 ♕h4! (24 ♗d4+ ♞g7 25 ♗xg7+ ♚xg7 26 ♕e5+ ♚h6 is a draw) 24...♞g7 (24...♖d8 25 ♕f6+ ♚g8 26 ♕f7+ ♚h8 27 ♗d2! and 24...♗d7 25 ♖f7 ♖g7 26 ♗e4! are very good for White) 25 ♖g1 ♕f3+ (25...♕d5 26 ♖xg6 threatening 27 ♕xh7+ ♚xh7 28 ♖h6# is crushing) 26 ♚d2 ♗f5 reaching a position in which White has a very

strong attack for the pawn. I (JN) have not been able to find a forced win for White, but Black has a difficult defence in prospect, e.g. 27 ♖g3 ♕d5 28 ♖h1 h5 29 ♗d4 (29 ♕g5? ♖gd8!) 29...♗xd3 (the threat was 30 ♕xh5+) 30 cxd3 ♔h7 (to defend against both ♖xg6 and ♖g5 followed by ♖xh5+) 31 ♖g5 ♕e6 (31...♕f7? 32 ♕e4 ♘f5 33 ♖hxh5+ gxh5 34 ♖xf5 is winning) 32 ♖e5 ♕c6 33 ♖c1 ♕g2+ 34 ♔e2 ♕d5 (34...♕g4 35 ♕xg4 hxg4 36 ♖e7 wins) 35 ♖c5 ♕d6 36 ♖e7 ♖ad8 37 ♔c3 and Black is in big trouble since 38 ♖cc7 is threatened and 37...♖c8 fails to 38 ♖xg7+ while 37...♖d7 loses after 38 ♖xh5+.

23 ♕f2?!

As Rhine correctly points out, **23 ♕f4!** ♕xf4 (23...♕xg2 24 ♖g1 ♕d5 25 ♔d2 and ♖h1) 24 ♖xf4 would have given White a very favourable ending at no risk.

23 ...   ♘c6
24 ♔d2   ♕d6?

The bishop on d3 is the main enemy and Black should have tried to eliminate it by **24...♘e5**, when 25 ♗xh7 (25 ♖h1 ♘xd3) 25...♖d8+! (25...♘c4+ 26 ♔c3 ♕e5+ 27 ♗d4 ♕a5+ 28 ♔xc4 ♗e6+ 29 ♔d3 and White evades the checks) 26 ♗d3 ♘xd3 27 cxd3 ♕d6 28 ♕h4+ ♔g8 29 ♕e4 leaves White with some advantage, but in view of the opposite-coloured bishops it isn't clear how many winning chances he has.

25 ♖h1   h6

26 ♗c5! (D)

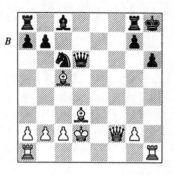

White's ambition is to gain f4 for his queen, when a sacrifice on h6 will be inevitable.

26 ...   ♕d5

26...♕c7 is spectacularly refuted by 27 ♕f6! and **26...♕e5** 27 ♖ae1 ♕g5+ 28 ♗e3 followed by ♗xh6 also loses quickly.

27 ♕f4   ♖d8

27...♕xg2+ 28 ♔c3 doesn't help to prevent ♖xh6+.

28	♖xh6+	♔g8
29	♖h8+!	♔xh8
30	♕h4+	♔g8
31	♕h7+	♔f7
32	♕g6+	♔g8
33	♕h7+	♔f7
34	♖f1+	♗f5

After **34...♔e6** or **34...♔e8**, 35 ♕g6+ ♔d7 36 ♖f7+ mates.

35	♖xf5+	♕xf5
36	♕xf5+	♔g8
37	♔c1	**1-0**

Quite apart from his material disadvantage there is no defence to the threat of ♗c4+.

13 O'Kelly Variation: 2...a6

This is generally called the O'Kelly Variation after the late Belgian grandmaster who played it with some regularity. I have to confess, though, that when I (JG) was about 12 years old I knew it as the 'Gallagher Variation'. Basically I used to play the Pelikan, with reasonable success except when my opponent replied to 5...e5 with 6 ♘b5, after which I was crushed. Therefore, I racked my brains and came up with the idea 2...a6 3 d4 cxd4 4 ♘xd4 ♘f6 5 ♘c3 e5 when the knight does not have b5 at his disposal. I was extremely proud of my brand-new idea, which brought me many points, until one day I won a copy of *ECO B*, and much to my amazement found several pages all devoted to the 'Gallagher Variation'. I gave it up soon afterwards.

In fact, 3 d4 is an error against the O'Kelly as it allows Black a favourable version of the Najdorf where he can develop his king's bishop actively at c5 or b4. 3 c3 is a sensible reply, which tends to lead to 2 c3 Sicilian positions in which Black has played the unusual move ...a6, which is perhaps not the best way to spend a tempo. However the strongest reply of all is 3 c4, which either leads to Maroczy Bind positions or to a sort of hedgehog.

In view of the rare occurrence of 2...a6 in practice, it perhaps does not rate a chapter of its own, but this did give me the excuse to include another of my own (JN) games in the book!

Game 29
Nunn – Surtees
Basingstoke Open 1977

1	e4	c5
2	♘f3	a6
3	c4 *(D)*	

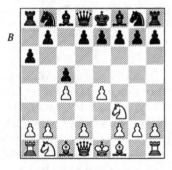

3	...	♘c6

Or:

1) **3...d6** (this may lead to a type of hedgehog) 4 d4 cxd4 (4...♗g4 is an interesting move, since 5 dxc5 ♗xf3 6 ♕xf3 dxc5 leaves Black with a grip on d4 to compensate for the two bishops; 6 gxf3! dxc5 7 ♕xd8+ ♔xd8 8 ♘c3 is possible, but

the simplest line is 5 d5 with a positional edge for White) **5 ♘xd4 ♘f6** (Black has also tried 5...g6, with similar play to Chapter 7. However, the early ...a6 can prove to be premature) **6 ♘c3 b6** (6...e6 7 ♗d3 leads to positions from Chapter 6, so we concentrate here on Black's attempt to develop early pressure against e4, which is unique to 2...a6) **7 ♗d3 ♗b7 8 0-0** (it is more accurate to play 8 ♕e2 ♘bd7 9 b3 – see the following note) **8...♘bd7 9 ♕e2 e6** *(D)* (9...♘e5 is interesting since 10 ♗c2 ♖c8 11 ♗a4+ ♘fd7 is unclear, so White would have to allow Black to take on d3) has occurred in three games between co-author Nunn and O'Kelly specialist Michael Franklin:

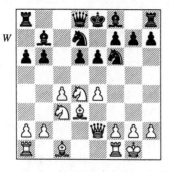

1a) **10 f4 ♕c7 11 ♔h1 ♗e7 12 ♗d2** is good, when Nunn-Franklin, London 1985 continued 12...h5 13 ♖ae1 h4 14 f5 ♘f8 15 fxe6 fxe6 16 ♘d5! ♕d8 17 e5 dxe5 18 ♕xe5 ♘xd5 19 ♘xe6 ♕d6 20 ♕xd6 ♗xd6 21 cxd5 1-0.

1b) **10 b3 ♕c7 11 ♗b2 ♕c5?!** (Black is playing too ambitiously with his king stuck in the centre –

11...♗e7 followed by ...0-0 is a better choice) **12 ♖ae1!** (exploiting the tactical point 12...♕xd4 13 ♘a4, White prepares a breakthrough by ♘d5) and now:

1b1) **12...♕h5** 13 ♕d2 g6 14 f4 ♗h6 15 ♕f2 g5 16 ♗e2 g4 17 ♕g3 ♖g8 18 ♗d1! also favoured White in Nunn-Franklin, London 1977 since e5 is imminent, while Franklin's later suggestion of 13...g5 allows 14 ♘d5! with added effect as the f5-square is now available.

1b2) **12...b5** 13 cxb5! ♕xd4 14 bxa6 ♗c6 15 ♘b5 ♕b6 16 ♗d4 ♕b8 17 ♖c1 ♘c5 18 a4! (this nullifies the threat of ...♘xd3 and prepares to break open the c-file by b4) 18...e5 19 ♗e3 ♗e7 20 b4 ♘xd3 21 ♖xc6 ♘xb4 22 a7 ♕b7 23 ♖b6 (heading for b8) 23...♕xe4 24 ♘c7+ ♔d7 25 ♕b5+! ♔xc7 26 ♖c1+ ♘c2 27 ♖xc2+ 1-0 Nunn-Franklin, Nottingham 1979, since 27...♕xc2 28 ♖b7+ ♔d8 29 ♖b8+ ♔c7 30 ♗b6 is mate.

2) **3...e6 4 ♘c3** and now:

2a) **4...♘c6 5 d4 cxd4 6 ♘xd4 ♗b4** (6...♘f6 7 ♘c2! is good for White) reaching an unusual position which does not seem to be considered by theory. 7 ♘c2 ♗xc3+ 8 bxc3 is one possibility, but I (JN) like **7 ♘xc6**. Then **7...bxc6 8 ♕d4** looks very awkward since 8...♘f6 and 8...♕f6 are both met by e5, so **7...dxc6 8 ♕xd8+ ♔xd8** is best. White will continue 9 ♗f4, intending 0-0-0+ and ♘a4 with good play against the weak dark squares at c5 and b6. If Black exchanges on c3

White has the dream square d6 for his bishop.

2b) **4...De7!?** 5 d4 cxd4 6 Dxd4 Dec6 7 ♗e2 Dxd4 8 ♕xd4 Dc6 9 ♕e3 ♗d6!? 10 0-0 0-0 11 b3 b5!? 12 cxb5 axb5 and now in Akopian-Rivas, Barcelona 1992 White accepted the pawn, but after **13 ♗xb5 ♗b7 14 ♗b2 ♕c7! 15 ♕h3 ♗e5!** Black had adequate compensation. Akopian suggests **13 ♗b2 b4 14 Db5** as an improvement which should give White an edge.

4	d4	cxd4
5	Dxd4	Df6

Or **5...e5** (5...e6 6 Dc2 is still good for White, and 5...g6 allows 6 Dxc6 and 7 ♕d4) 6 Df5 d5 (6...Df6 7 Dc3 transposes to Nunn-Surtees) 7 cxd5 ♗xf5 8 exf5 Dd4 9 Dc3 De7 (once again 9...Df6 transposes and 9...♗b4 10 ♗d3 ♕xd5 11 0-0 ♕d7 12 ♖e1 0-0-0 13 ♖xe5 was very good for White in Sherzer-Polovodin, Philadelphia 1991) 10 ♗d3 (10 f6 is also promising) 10...Dexf5 11 0-0 ♗d6 12 f4 with a dangerous initiative for White.

6	Dc3	e5
7	Df5	d5

After **7...d6** 8 ♗g5 (8 De3 controlling d5 is also good) 8...♗xf5 9 exf5 Dd4 10 ♗d3 White's control of e4 and d5 gives him a clear plus.

8	cxd5	♗xf5
9	exf5	Dd4
10	♗d3	Dxd5
11	0-0 *(D)*	
11	...	♗b4

Black has tried a variety of moves in this position, but without coming

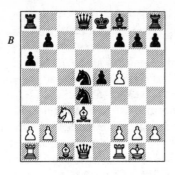

close to equality, e.g. **11...Dxc3** 12 bxc3 Dc6 (once the knight has to move from d4 the only asset of Black's position vanishes) 13 ♖b1 ♖b8 14 ♕f3 ♕c7 15 ♗e4, Ravinsky-Kliashchitsky, USSR 1966, **11...Df6** 12 ♖e1 Dc6 13 ♕b3 ♗b4 14 ♖d1 ♕e7 15 ♗g5, Rogatsovsky-Konovalov, Corr. 1972 or **11...♗e7** 12 ♗e4 Dxc3 13 bxc3 Dc6 14 ♖b1 ♕c8 15 ♕g4, Matanović-Perez, Belgrade 1961 with a clear advantage for White in every case.

12	♗e4!	Dxc3
13	bxc3	♗xc3
14	♖b1	0-0

In the game Altshuler-Fink, Corr. 1960 Black tried to hold on to the pawn but after **14...♖b8** 15 ♕g4 g6 16 ♗g5 gxf5 17 ♗xf5 f6 18 ♕h5+ White had a winning position.

15 ♖xb7

This simple move was suggested by Gligorić and Sokolov as an improvement over the unclear continuation 15 ♕g4 ♕d6 16 ♖d1 ♖ac8 (but not 16...♖ad8? 17 ♖d3 ♗b4 18 f6!) 17 ♖d3 ♖c4 in which White lacks a knock-out blow.

15	...	♕d6 *(D)*

White's main threat was 16 ♗a3, driving the rook away from the defence of f7, followed by ♕h5 and if Black manages to defend f7 White still has the crushing blow f6 in reserve. Black's ...♕d6 is of course designed to prevent ♗a3, but alas the move loses by force. He had to try **15...♖b8** although 16 ♖xb8 ♕xb8 17 f6 gives White a strong attack with no material investment.

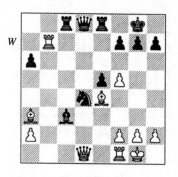

A piece of rather unnecessary flashiness since 19 ♕h5 ♕f6 (or 19...♖c7 20 f6) 20 ♗d5 wins quite easily.

| 19 | ... | ♕g5 |

19...♔xf7 20 ♕h5+ ♔g8 (20...♔f6 21 ♕xh7 ♔f7 22 ♕h5+ forces the king to g8 in any case) 21 f6 g6 22 ♗xg6 ♕d7 23 f7+ wins, but Black can hardly hope to survive long after losing the vital f7-pawn.

| 20 | ♗d5 | ♔h8 |
| 21 | f6 | g6 |

21...gxf6 22 ♗e7 costs material.

| 22 | ♕a4 | e4 |

Losing at once, but Black's king would have succumbed soon in any case.

| 23 | ♖xh7+ | 1-0 |

After 23...♔xh7 24 ♕d7+ ♔h6 25 ♕g7+ ♔h5 26 ♕h7+ ♔g4 (26...♕h6 27 g4+ ♔g5 28 f4+ exf3 29 ♗c1+) 27 ♕h3+ ♔f4 28 ♗d6+ ♖e5 29 ♕xc8 the position speaks for itself.

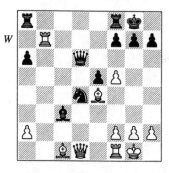

16 ♖b3!
White utilises the undefended queen to threaten ♗xa8, ♖xc3 and ♗a3. Black's reply is forced.

| 16 | ... | ♖ac8 |
| 17 | ♗a3 | ♕d8 |

If the queen moves anywhere else, 18 ♗xf8 ♘xb3 19 ♗xg7 wins a pawn and demolishes Black's kingside.

| 18 | ♖b7 | ♖e8 *(D)* |
| 19 | ♖xf7 | |

14 Unusual Lines

The material in the first thirteen chapters will be sufficient to prepare the reader for the vast majority of the games he will have as White against the Sicilian, but there remain a substantial number of unusual lines which Black might adopt. Only a few have any pretensions to respectability and we concentrate on these few in this chapter. Wilder eccentricities are usually best dealt with by an application of common sense and straightforward development. The following breakdown of lines considered in this chapter will aid the reader in locating the variation he is looking for.

A) The pseudo-Dragon 1 e4 c5 2 ♘f3 ♘c6 3 d4 cxd4 4 ♘xd4 ♘f6 5 ♘c3 g6.

B) Unusual lines with 2...♘c6 apart from the pseudo-Dragon: 1 e4 c5 2 ♘f3 ♘c6 3 d4 cxd4 (3...d5) 4 ♘xd4 ♘f6 (4...a6, 4...d5, 4...♕c7, 4...♕b6) 5 ♘c3 ♕b6.

C) Unusual lines with 2...d6: 1 e4 c5 2 ♘f3 d6 3 d4 cxd4 (3...♘f6) 4 ♘xd4 ♘f6 5 ♘c3 e5 (5...♘bd7, 5...♗d7) 6 ♗b5+.

D) Unusual lines with 2...e6: 1 e4 c5 2 ♘f3 e6 3 d4 cxd4 (3...d5) 4 ♘xd4 ♗c5 (4...♗b4+, 4...♕b6).

E) Unusual Black second moves: 1 e4 c5 2 ♘f3 g6 (2...♕c7, 2...b6) 3 d4 ♗g7.

A:

1	e4	c5
2	♘f3	♘c6
3	d4	cxd4
4	♘xd4	♘f6
5	♘c3	g6 *(D)*

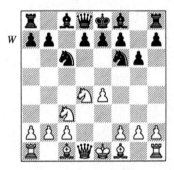

This is an attempt by Black to reach Accelerated Dragon positions without allowing White the option of playing the Maroczy Bind. It has been played a few times in grandmaster chess, but White can obtain a clear advantage with accurate play.

6 ♘xc6   bxc6

Or **6...dxc6 7 ♕xd8+ ♔xd8 8 ♗c4 ♔e8** (not 8...b5? 9 ♗xf7 e6 10 ♗g5 ♗e7 11 0-0-0+ winning, while 8...♗g7 9 ♗f4 ♔e8 10 0-0-0 ♘d7 11 ♗c7! is good for White since Black is not allowed to castle) **9 e5** and now:

1) **9...♘g4** 10 f4 h5 (if Black plays 10...♗f5 11 h3 ♘h6 12 g4, the

bishop has to go back as 12...♗xc2 13 ♖h2 ♗a4 14 ♘xa4 b5 15 ♗b3 bxa4 16 ♗xa4 ♖c8 17 ♖c2 ♔d7 18 ♗e3 is winning for White) 11 ♗d2 h4 (or 11...♗f5 12 h3 ♘h6 13 0-0-0 ♗g7 14 ♖he1 with advantage to White) 12 ♘e4 ♘h6 13 ♗c3 h3 14 e6 ♖g8 15 exf7+ ♘xf7 16 0-0-0! with a clear plus for White, Maus-Schlick, Bundesliga 1987.

2) **9...♘d7** 10 f4 (10 e6 fxe6 11 ♗xe6 ♗g7 12 ♗e3 b6 13 0-0-0 ♗xc3 14 bxc3 ♘c5 15 ♗xc5 bxc5 16 ♗xc8 ♖xc8 17 ♖he1 ♖f8 18 f3 ♖f4 19 ♖e5 only gave White a slightly superior rook endgame in Shirov-Ljubojević, Buenos Aires 1994) 10...♘c5 11 ♗e3 (11 ♗e2!?) 11...♗e6 12 ♗xe6 ♘xe6 13 0-0-0 ♗g7 14 g3 b6 15 ♖d3 ♖d8 16 ♖hd1 ♖xd3 17 ♖xd3 f6 18 exf6 exf6 19 ♘e4 f5 20 ♘d2 ♗f8 (20...♔e7 21 ♖a3 is good for White) 21 ♘c4 ♖g8 22 ♘e5 with a clearly advantageous ending for White, Hellers-Karlsson, Östersund Z 1992.

7 e5   ♘g8

After **7...♘d5** 8 ♘xd5 cxd5 9 ♕xd5 ♖b8 10 e6! (with ♕e5 if the pawn is taken) 10...f6 (10...♗g7 11 exf7+ ♔f8 12 ♗h6! ♗xh6 13 ♕e5, as in A.Sokolov-Lutskan, Latvian Ch 1994, is certainly not an improvement) 11 ♗f4 ♖b4 12 ♗d2 (12 0-0-0!? ♖xf4 13 ♗b5 was also very good for White in Varga-Barletta, Budapest 1991) 12...♖b6 13 ♗b5 ♖d6 14 ♕c4 White has a winning position.

8 ♗c4 *(D)*

8 ...   ♗g7

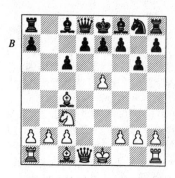

Other moves are no better for Black:

1) **8...d5** 9 exd6 ♕xd6 (9...exd6 10 ♕f3 d5 11 ♘xd5 cxd5 12 ♗xd5 ♕e7+ 13 ♗e3 ♖b8 14 0-0 ♗g7 15 ♗f4 with a decisive attack) 10 0-0 ♕xd1 11 ♖xd1 ♗h6 12 ♗xh6 ♘xh6 13 ♖d2 ♘f5 14 ♘e4 is very pleasant for White, Geller-Stein, USSR Ch 1966/7.

2) **8...♕a5 9 0-0** and now:

2a) **9...♕xe5** 10 ♖e1 ♕a5 (or 10...♕b8 11 ♕d4 f6 12 ♘e4 ♗g7 13 ♗f4 ♕b6 14 ♘d6+ ♔f8 15 ♕d3 ♗b7 16 ♗xg8 ♖xg8 17 ♕c4 1-0 Tiviakov-Mugerman, Pinsk 1989) 11 b4 ♕d8 leaves Black in a dreadful mess. In Karaklajić-Ivanović, Yugoslavia 1974 White won Black's queen by 12 ♘e4 e6 13 ♗b2 f6 14 ♗xe6 dxe6 15 ♘xf6+ ♕xf6 16 ♗xf6 ♘xf6, which proved sufficient in the end, but I would not be surprised if White had an even stronger continuation.

2b) **9...♗g7** 10 ♕f3 f5 (10...e6 11 ♗f4 and 10...f6 11 ♖e1 are also good for White) 11 ♗f4 leads into the note to Black's 10th move on the following page.

9 ♕f3   f5

Relatively best, e.g. **9...e6** 10 ♗f4 ♕a5 11 0-0! ♗xe5 12 b4 ♕c7 13 ♘b5 ♕b8 14 ♗xe5 ♕xe5 15 ♖ad1 d5 16 ♖fe1 ♕b8 17 ♗xd5 cxd5 18 ♕xd5 ♔f8 19 ♕c5+ (even stronger than 19 ♕d8+) 19...♔g7 20 ♖d8 ♕b7 (20...♘f6 21 ♖xh8 ♔xh8 22 ♕f8+ ♘g8 23 ♘d6 h6 24 ♘e8) 21 ♕f8+ ♔f6 22 ♘d6 ♕e7 23 ♘e4+ ♔f5 24 ♕xe7 1-0 Geenen-Miranda, Novi Sad OL 1990.

10 ♗f4   e6 *(D)*

10...♖b8 (10...♕a5 11 0-0 ♗xe5 12 b4 ♕c7 13 ♘b5 ♕b8 14 ♗xe5 ♕xe5 15 ♖fe1 ♕b8 16 ♕c3 is now immediately decisive) 11 0-0 e6 12 ♖ad1 followed by ♖fe1 and just as in the main line White has an unpleasant bind, Andersson-Bilek, Teesside 1972. Black has no way to solve the problem of his backward d-pawn and the g7-bishop is inactive. White players must be on the lookout for the exchange sacrifice ...♖b4xf4, which can be good for Black if he can get the e5-pawn, but provided White keeps his bind on Black's position he can be optimistic about the future.

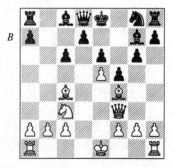

11 0-0

The correct choice; in some other games White played 0-0-0, but this gives Black counterplay down the b-file.

11 ...   ♘h6

We give the rest of the game Short-Sosonko, Wijk aan Zee 1986, which is a model example of how to play such positions. Black is never allowed to free himself and is finally overcome by the problems resulting from the backward d-pawn:

12 ♖ad1 ♕c7 13 ♖fe1 ♘f7 14 ♕g3 0-0 15 h4 ♔h8 16 ♘a4 a5 17 b3 ♖e8 18 ♕e3 h6 19 g4! ♖g8 20 ♗g3 ♗f8 21 ♕b6 ♖a7 22 f3 ♕xb6+ 23 ♘xb6 ♗c5+ 24 ♗f2 ♗xf2+ 25 ♔xf2 fxg4 26 fxg4 ♔g7 27 ♘a4 g5 28 h5 ♖f8 29 ♔g3 ♘d8 30 ♘c5 ♖f4 31 a4 ♔f8 32 ♗d3 ♔e7 33 ♗g6 ♖a8 34 ♖e3 ♖b8 35 ♖ed3 ♖bb4 36 ♖xd7+ ♗xd7 37 ♖xd7+ 1-0.

B:

1	e4	c5
2	♘f3	♘c6
3	d4	cxd4

3...d5 (highly dubious) 4 exd5 ♕xd5 5 ♘c3 ♕e6+ (or 5...♕h5 6 d5) 6 ♗e3 cxd4 7 ♘xd4 ♕d7 8 ♘db5 ♖b8 9 ♕e2 and White is probably winning already, Boleslavsky-Gurgenidze, USSR 1960.

4 ♘xd4   ♘f6

4...a6 5 c4 transposes to Chapter 13, **4...♕c7** 5 ♘c3 e6 transposes to Chapter 8, **4...♕b6** 5 ♘b3 ♘f6 6 ♘c3 transposes back into the main line and **4...d5** 5 ♘c3 dxe4 6 ♘xc6 ♕xd1+ 7 ♔xd1 bxc6 8 ♘xe4 ♗f5 9

♗d3 0-0-0 10 ♔e2 e6 11 ♗f4 ♔b7 12 ♖ad1 is just good for White.

5	♘c3	♛b6
6	♘b3	e6
7	♗e3	♛c7
8	♗d3 (D)	

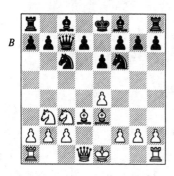

8	...	♗e7

Or:

1) **8...♗b4** (at one time White players regularly spent a tempo on a3 to prevent this, but now it's not thought to be good for Black to give up his dark-squared bishop) 9 f4 (9 0-0 0-0 10 ♘b5 ♛b8 11 f4 was good for White in Gheorghiu-Forintos, Monte Carlo 1968, but Black can also play 9...♗xc3) 9...♗xc3+ 10 bxc3 d6 11 0-0 e5 12 ♔h1 h6 13 ♛e1 b6 14 fxe5 dxe5 15 ♛g3 ♔f8 16 ♘d4! ♘h5? (16...♘e7 was more solid, although after 17 ♘f3 ♘g6 18 ♘h4! ♘xh4 19 ♛xh4 White's chances are still to be preferred) 17 ♛g6! exd4 18 cxd4 ♘f6 19 ♖xf6! gxf6 20 ♛xf6 ♖g8 (or 20...♔g8 21 ♖f1 ♛e7 22 ♛xc6 and White is clearly better) 21 ♗f4 ♛d7 22 ♗d6+ ♔e8 23 ♗b5 ♗b7 24 d5 ♖c8 (24...♛d8 loses to 25 dxc6) 25 ♖d1 a6 26 dxc6 ♗xc6 27

♖d5! 1-0 Vouldis-Grivas, Greek Ch 1993.

2) **8...a6** 9 f4 d6 10 ♛f3 (White may also start his kingside pawn advance immediately, for example 10 g4 b5 11 g5 ♘d7 12 ♛d2 {12 ♛f3} 12...♗b7 13 0-0-0 ♘c5 14 ♛f2! with some advantage to White, Beliavsky-Gufeld, Sukhumi 1972) 10...b5 (if Black plays ...♗e7 we transpose to the main line below) 11 0-0-0 (11 g4 is again possible) 11...♗b7 12 ♔b1 ♘a5 13 ♘xa5 ♛xa5 14 g4 0-0-0 15 g5 ♘d7 16 a3 ♔b8 17 ♛f2 ♗e7 18 ♗d4 e5 19 fxe5 dxe5 20 ♗a7+ ♔a8 21 ♘d5 with a clear plus for White, King-Wirthensohn, Bern 1988.

9	f4	d6
10	♛f3	

This is the most popular choice as White keeps open the option of castling on either side. However, if he is certain he wants to castle kingside there is an argument for doing so at once as he may be able to dispense with ♛f3. For example **10 0-0 0-0?!** (it's better to play 10...a6, transposing to the main line) **11 g4!?** (D) with a couple of examples:

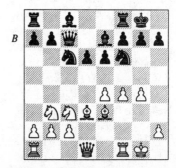

1) **11...♘d7** 12 g5 ♖e8 13 ♖f3 a6 14 ♖h3 gave White a very strong attack in Wedberg-Benko, New York Open 1989; the finish was 14...♘f8 15 ♕h5 ♘b4 16 ♖f1 ♗d8 17 a3 ♘xd3 18 cxd3 b5 19 f5 exf5 20 ♘d5 ♕d7 21 ♗d4 fxe4 22 ♖h4 e3 23 ♘xe3 ♖e6 24 ♖hf4 ♖g6 25 ♖xf7 ♕xf7 26 ♖xf7 ♖xg5+ 27 ♕xg5 ♗xg5 28 ♖xg7+ 1-0.

2) **11...d5** 12 e5 ♘d7 13 ♕f3 (13 ♖f3!?) 13...♖d8 14 ♘b5 ♕b8 15 c3 b6 16 ♘5d4 ♗b7 17 ♘xc6 ♗xc6 18 ♕h3 g6 19 ♘d4 ♗b7, Gallagher-Efimov, Paris 1992, and now 20 f5! is extremely strong because after 20...♘xe5 21 fxe6 fxe6 (Black has to play the ugly 21...f6) 22 ♘xe6 ♘xd3 23 ♕h6, **23...♗f8** loses to 24 ♖xf8+ and **23...♕e5** to 24 ♗d4 ♗g5 25 ♘xg5.

10 ...	a6 *(D)*

Black also delays castling since **10...0-0** 11 g4 ♖e8 12 g5 ♘d7 13 h4 ♘b4 14 h5 ♗f8 15 0-0-0 a6 16 g6 gave White an immense attack in Jansa-Martinović, Vrnjačka Banja 1982.

Another try is **10...♘b4**; Leko-Anastasian, Moscow OL 1994 continued 11 0-0-0!? ♗d7 12 ♔b1 a5 13 ♘d4 0-0 14 g4 a4 15 a3! ♘xd3 16 cxd3 b5 (16...♗c6 17 f5 is good for White) 17 ♘a2! b4 (Black invests some material as he wants to steer clear of lines such as 17...♖fc8 18 g5 ♘e8 19 f5) 18 ♘xb4 d5 19 g5 dxe4 20 dxe4 ♗xb4 21 axb4 a3 (21...♘e8 22 e5 is also good for White) 22 gxf6 axb2 23 ♕g2! g6 24 ♕xb2 ♕b7 25 ♖he1! and Black had nowhere near

sufficient compensation for the sacrificed piece.

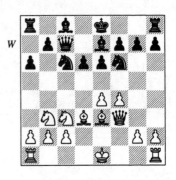

11   0-0

White has a choice of good lines.

11 g4 and now:

1) **11...b6** (this rather odd move is designed to support c5 in anticipation of the manoeuvre ...♘d7-c5) 12 g5 ♘d7 13 0-0-0 ♘c5 14 ♔b1 (to answer ...♘xd3 by cxd3) 14...♗d7 15 h4 ♕b7 16 ♗e2! (now the c5-knight isn't doing much) 16...♘a7 17 f5 ♘b5 18 ♗d4 ♗c6 19 fxe6 ♘xc3+ 20 ♗xc3 ♘xe6 21 ♖hf1 0-0 22 ♗d3 b5 23 a3 ♘c5 24 ♘xc5! dxc5 25 ♕f5 ♖ae8 (or 25...c4 26 ♕e5 f6 27 gxf6 ♗xf6 28 ♕e6+ ♖f7 29 ♖xf6!) 26 ♗xg7! ♗d7 (26...♔xg7 27 e5) 27 ♕e5 ♗d8 28 ♕d6 ♔xg7 29 ♕h6+ ♔h8 30 e5 f5 31 exf6 ♗e6 32 ♖de1 c4 33 ♗g6 ♖f7 34 ♗xf7 ♕xf7 35 g6 ♕xg6 37 f7 1-0 Kavalek-Hübner, Buenos Aires OL 1978.

2) **11...h6** 12 0-0-0 b5 13 ♖hg1 ♘d7 14 ♕f2! (this possibility explains Black's preference for ...b6 in line '1', since once he has played ...b5 the knight on d7 is hard to redeploy) 14...♗b7 15 ♔b1 ♗f6? (Black's

...h6 renders the kingside too dangerous for ...0-0 – he should have played 15...♘b4) 16 e5! dxe5 17 ♗xb5 0-0 18 g5 hxg5 19 fxg5 ♗e7, Estrin-Kopylov, USSR 1973, and now 20 ♕h4! axb5 21 ♖g3 would have given White a decisive attack according to Estrin.

3) **11...b5 12 g5 ♘d7 13 0-0-0** and now:

3a) **13...♘c5** (13...♗b7 is well met by 14 ♕h3!) 14 ♘xc5 dxc5 15 e5 ♗b7 16 ♗e4 ♖d8 17 h4 with an edge for White, Tiviakov-Anastasian, USSR 1989.

3b) **13...♘b4** 14 ♔b1 ♗b7 15 ♕h3 0-0 16 ♖hf1 ♖fe8 17 f5 exf5 18 exf5 ♘xd3 19 ♖xd3 ♘f8 20 f6 ♗d8 21 ♘d4 with a great position for White, Sax-Urday, Manila OL 1992. The game finished 21...♗c8 22 ♕f3 ♖b8 23 fxg7 ♔xg7 24 ♘d5 ♕b7 25 ♘c7 1-0.

11 ... 0-0 *(D)*

Not **11...b5** 12 e5, but perhaps Black can consider 11...♗d7.

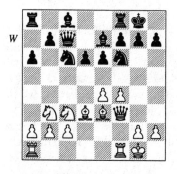

12 ♖ae1

White can also start the pawn-storm, with **12 g4**:

1) **12...♖e8?!** 13 g5 ♘d7 14 ♕h5 g6 15 ♕h6 ♗f8 16 ♕h4 ♗g7 17 ♖f3 b5 18 ♖h3 ♘f8 19 f5 ♗xc3 20 f6 ♗xf6 21 gxf6 h5 22 ♕f4 e5 23 ♕h6 ♘e6 24 ♔h1! (now nothing can stop ♖xh5) 24...♕d8 25 ♖f1! 1-0 Akopian-Prakash, Mamaia Wch jr 1991. A model game; every one of White's moves was geared towards his kingside attack.

2) **12...b5** 13 g5 ♘d7 14 ♕h5 ♘b4!? (14...g6 15 ♕h6 f6 16 ♘d4! ♘xd4 17 ♗xd4 ♖f7 18 f5 ♗f8 19 ♕h3 was good for White in Ulybin-Akopian, USSR 1988) 15 ♖f3 (15 f5 deserves consideration) 15...g6 16 ♕h6 f5! 17 gxf6 (17 exf5 exf5 18 ♖h3 ♖f7 19 ♗d4 ♘f8 is unclear according to Grivas) 17...♖xf6 18 ♖g3 (18 ♘d4 g5!) 18...♘f8 19 ♘d4 ♘xd3 20 cxd3 ♗d7 with a tense struggle ahead, Bellia-Grivas, Vinkovci 1989. Unless 15 f5 is very strong this looks like Black's best defensive set-up. The knight goes to b4, covering d5 in some lines and in others allowing him to remove the potentially dangerous bishop on d3, while leaving the rook on f8 so that a timely ...f5 and ...♖f7 can be played to defend h7.

12 ... b5?! *(D)*

Played on countless occasions but it now appears suspect. Perhaps Black should play **12...♘d7** and if White plays 13 g4 then 13...b5 14 g5 ♗b7 transposes into Nunn-Grivas, Athens (1) 1991, which continued 15 ♕h5 ♘b4 16 ♖f3 ♘xd3!? (with the bishop on b7 the defence with ...g6 and ...f5 doesn't work, e.g.

16...g6 17 ♕h6 f5 18 exf5 exf5 19 ♖h3 ♖f7 20 ♗d4 ♘f8 21 ♗xf5!) 17 cxd3 (17 ♖h3 is an interesting alternative) 17...♖fe8 and now White should have played 18 ♗d4! when **18...g6??** allows 19 ♕xh7+ and **18...♘f8** 19 f5! exf5 20 ♖xf5 g6 21 ♕h6 ♘e6 22 ♖xf7! is completely crushing. **18...♖ac8** is best, even though White's game is still to be preferred.

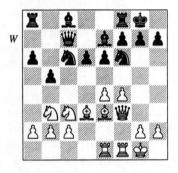

13 e5! dxe5

Maybe Black should settle for **13...♘d7**, but White does have a number of dangerous-looking continuations, such as 14 exd6 ♕xd6 (14...♗xd6 15 ♗xb5!) 15 ♗e4 (15 ♘e4, 15 ♕h3 and 15 ♖d1 also come into consideration) 15...♗b7 16 f5.

14 fxe5 ♘xe5?

Black had to play **14...♘d7** after which White should play 15 ♗f4! before getting on with the attack.

15 ♕xa8 ♘eg4

15...♗b7 16 ♕a7 doesn't help.

16 g3!

This position was analysed in *Informator 33* by Matulović, who attached a '?' to 13 e5, but he only gave

16 ♗f4 which loses to 16...♕b6+ 17 ♔h1 ♗b7.

16 ... ♗b7
17 ♕a7 ♕c6

Perhaps everyone had thought this was the end of the road for White. But...

18 ♗e4! ♘xe4
19 ♘a5!

...and in fact it's the end of the road for Black. Lücke-Grivas, Dortmund 1992 finished 19...♕c5 20 ♗xc5 ♗xc5+ 21 ♕xc5 ♘xc5 22 b4 1-0.

C:

1 e4 c5
2 ♘f3 d6
3 d4 cxd4

Black quite often plays **3...♘f6** in order to avoid the line 3...cxd4 4 ♕xd4. White should reply 4 ♘c3 when Black is obliged to play 4...cxd4 5 ♘xd4 transposing to normal lines.

4 ♘xd4 ♘f6
5 ♘c3 e5 (D)

Or:

1) **5...♘bd7** 6 ♗c4 ♘b6 (Black's development is not easy because ...e6 and ...♗e7 will allow a ♗xe6 sacrifice, while 6...g6 7 f3 ♗g7 8 ♗e3 0-0 9 ♕d2 is a Dragon in which Black has developed his knight to the inferior square d7) 7 ♗b3 e5 8 ♘de2 ♗e6 9 ♗g5 ♗e7 10 ♗xf6 ♗xf6 11 ♘d5 ♘xd5 12 ♗xd5 ♕b6 13 ♗b3 0-0 14 ♘c3 and White's control of d5 gives him a clear advantage, R.Byrne-Cuellar, Siegen OL 1970.

2) **5...♗d7 6 ♗g5 e6** and now:

2a) **7 ♘db5 ♗c6 8 ♗xf6 gxf6 9 ♕h5** looks tempting, but Kupreichik has done well with Black from this position. For example 9...a6 10 ♘d4 ♗d7 11 0-0-0 ♘c6 12 ♘xc6 (12 ♗c4 ♕a5!) 12...bxc6 13 ♗c4 ♕b6 14 ♖hf1 ♖b8 15 ♗b3 c5 16 ♕e2 ♗b5 with good attacking chances for Black, Spasov-Kupreichik, Moscow OL 1994.

2b) **7 ♕d2** may be best, with a probable transposition to Chapter 3 after 7...a6 8 0-0-0 ♘c6.

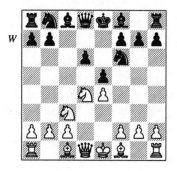

6 ♗b5+

One of the points behind 5...a6 is to prepare ...e5 by preventing this move, so it is the only logical reply to 5...e5.

6 ... ♘bd7

After **6...♗d7 7 ♗xd7+ ♕xd7 8 ♘f3** (8 ♘f5 allows Black to complicate the issue by 8...♘xe4) the exchange of light-squared bishops enhances the weakness of d5.

7 ♘f5 a6

8 ♗xd7+ ♕xd7 *(D)*

This is the critical moment. White has a number of possible plans, but

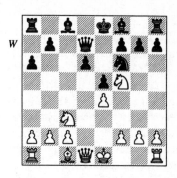

it is absolutely unclear which one is best:

1) **9 ♗g5 ♘xe4 10 ♘xg7+ ♗xg7 11 ♘xe4** and now:

1a) **11...d5?!** 12 ♘f6+ ♗xf6 13 ♗xf6 0-0 (13...♖g8 14 0-0 is also very bad) 14 ♕d3 e4 15 ♕d4 ♖e8 16 g4! ♕d6 17 0-0-0 ♕f4+ 18 ♔b1 ♖e6 19 g5 ♖e8 20 ♗h8 f6 21 gxf6 ♕f5 22 ♖hg1+ ♔f7 23 ♖g7+ ♔e6 24 ♕b6+ 1-0 Camacho-Cruz Lima, Cuba 1986.

1b) **11...0-0** (this pawn sacrifice is the point of the variation, but it may not be correct) 12 ♕xd6 f6 (12...♕f5 13 ♘f6+ ♗xf6 14 ♕xf6 ♕e4+ 15 ♔f1 ♗h3 16 f3 ♕c4+ 17 ♔e1 ♕b4+ 18 ♗d2 favours White) and I doubt if Black has enough compensation for the pawn. After 13 ♗e3 (13 ♕xd7 ♗xd7 14 ♗d2 f5 15 ♘c5 ♗c6 did allow Black fair compensation in Am.Rodriguez-Nijboer, Amsterdam 1989) 13...♕g4 14 ♘c3! ♗f5 15 ♕d5+ ♖f7 16 h3 ♕g6 17 0-0-0! ♖c8 (17...♗xc2 18 ♖d2 ♗f5 19 g4 is good for White) 18 ♖d2 h5 19 g4! White had a clear advantage in Klovan-Mochalov, USSR 1981.

2) **9 ♘e3 ♛c6** and now:

2a) **10 ♛d3** (this gives White a small but safe advantage) 10...♗e6 11 0-0 ♖c8 12 ♗d2 (12 a4 ♗e7 13 ♘cd5 ♗xd5 14 exd5 ♛c7 15 a5 g6 16 b3 0-0 17 ♘c4 ♖fe8 18 ♗e3 ♗f8 with equality in Popović-Rajković, Vršac 1987) 12...♗e7 (12...g6 is a possibility, but White retains a slight plus) 13 ♘cd5 ♗d8 (now 13...♗xd5 14 exd5 ♛c7 15 ♘f5 is good for White; ♗d2 is much more useful than a4) 14 c4 0-0 15 ♖ac1 ♖e8 16 b3 ♘d7 17 ♘b4 with advantage for White, Ehlvest-Kupreichik, Moscow TV 1987.

2b) **10 ♘ed5 ♘xd5 11 ♘xd5 ♗e6** 12 0-0 ♖c8 13 c4!? ♛xc4 14 ♘b6 ♛xe4 15 ♘xc8 ♗xc8 16 ♖e1 ♛g4 17 f3 with a small advantage for White, Krnić-Jovanović, Yugoslavia 1982.

2c) **10 0-0 ♘xe4** (10...♗e6 is probably better, when White may have nothing better than 11 ♛d3 transposing to line 2a) 11 ♘xe4 ♛xe4 12 ♘d5 ♖b8 13 b3 ♗f5 14 c4 f6 15 ♗a3 ♔f7 16 ♛d2 ♖d8 17 ♖fe1 ♛g4 18 ♘e3 ♛g5 19 ♛d5+ with advantage to White, L.Schneider-Bator, Sweden Ch 1986.

2d) **10 ♛f3!?** b5 11 0-0 ♗b7 12 ♘cd5 ♘xd5 13 ♘xd5 ♛xc2 14 ♗g5 ♗xd5 15 exd5 f6 16 ♖ac1 ♛g6 17 ♗d2 ♗e7 18 ♖c7 with good compensation for the pawn, Kudrin-Conquest, London 1986.

D:

1	e4	c5
2	♘f3	e6

3	d4	cxd4

3...d5 4 exd5 exd5 5 ♗b5+ ♘c6 gives Black an uncomfortable isolated pawn position after 6 ♘c3 or 6 0-0.

4	♘xd4	♗c5

The idea behind this move is to reach a position similar to that after 1 e4 c5 2 ♘f3 e6 3 d4 cxd4 4 ♘xd4 a6 5 ♗d3 ♗c5 (see Game 18), but without wasting a tempo on ...a6. Naturally this exposes Black to the possibility of ♘b5 at some point, but attempts to exploit this directly don't work. White has to be a bit more careful to gain the advantage against 4...♗c5.

Other moves are:

1) **4...♗b4+**, and now White can transpose to Chapter 11 by 5 ♘c3 ♘f6, but it is also possible to play 5 c3 ♗e7 6 c4, with a Maroczy Bind position.

2) **4...♛b6 5 ♘b3 ♛c7** *(D)* and now:

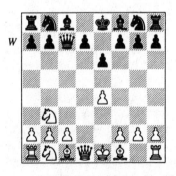

2a) **6 ♘c3 a6** 7 ♗d3 b5 8 ♗g5!? ♗b7 9 0-0 ♘f6 10 f4 b4 11 e5 bxc3 12 exf6 cxb2 13 ♖b1 g6 14 ♖xb2 with advantage to White, Hellers-

Kveinys, Oslo 1992, but Black's play can probably be improved.

2b) **6 ♗d3 ♘f6 7 ♘c3** (7 0-0 d5 8 ♘c3 dxe4 9 ♘xe4 is completely harmless; both 9...♘xe4 10 ♗xe4 ♘d7 11 ♕d4 ♗d6, Torok-Kveinys, Budapest Spring 1992 and 9...♘bd7 10 ♘xf6+ ♘xf6 11 ♗b5+ ♗d7 12 ♗xd7+ ♘xd7 13 ♘d4 a6, Luther-Kveinys, Bonn 1993, were satisfactory for Black) a6 8 f4 d6 9 0-0 ♘bd7 10 a4 b6 11 ♕e2 ♗b7 12 ♗d2 ♗e7, Umanaliev-Kveinys, Manila OL 1992, shows Black's plan in action; he has reached a normal position, but with the knight on b3 instead of d4.

2c) **6 c4 ♘f6 7 ♘c3** and now:

2c1) Black could continue with normal development by **7...a6**, intending to adopt a hedgehog set-up; however, the position of the knight on b3 introduces some slight differences, for example White might try to meet ...d6 by ♗f4, ♕d2 and ♖d1 aiming for a quick attack on d6.

2c2) **7...♗b4** was Nunn-J.Polgar, Hastings 1992/3. The game continued **8 ♗d2**, but **8 ♗d3** is probably better since 8...d5 9 exd5 exd5 10 ♕e2+! is good for White after both 10...♗e6 11 ♘d4 and 10...♕e7 11 ♕xe7+ ♔xe7 12 0-0. In view of this, Black would do better to meet 8 ♗d3 with the quiet 8...♘c6.

5   **♘b3**   **♗b6** (D)
6   **♘c3**

Simple development guarantees at least a slight advantage. The ambitious **6 c4** is also promising, for example 6...♘e7 7 ♘c3 (White must

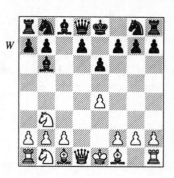

prevent ...d5) 7...0-0 (or 7...♘bc6 8 ♗f4 e5 9 ♗g5 f6 10 ♗d2 d6 11 ♕h5+ ♔f8 12 ♗d3 ♗e6 13 0-0 and White is better, Howell-S.Arkell, London Lloyds Bank 1986) 8 ♗f4 (it is essential to reach d6 with the bishop before Black prevents it with ...f5, e.g. 8 ♗e2?! f5 and ♗f4 is impossible) 8...f5 9 ♗d6 ♘bc6 10 ♗e2 and now if Black plays **10...fxe4** 11 c5 ♗c7 12 ♘xe4 White's hold on d6 cannot be broken, while after **10...f4** aiming to play ...♘g6-e5 (after a rook move, of course) White might even consider 11 ♗h5!?.

6   ...   **♘e7**
7   **♗d3**

Or 7 ♗g5!? f6 8 ♗h4 0-0 9 ♕h5 ♘bc6 10 0-0-0 ♘e5 11 ♗g3 ♘7g6 12 ♔b1 f5 13 f4 ♘c6 14 ♗c4 ♕f6 15 e5 ♕e7 16 ♘b5 a6 17 ♘d6 ♔h8 18 h4 ♘a5 19 ♘xa5 1-0 Šibarević-G.Welling, Lugano 1989. Weak play by Black, but this direct plan could be dangerous.

7   ...   **0-0**

8 0-0 ♘bc6 9 ♗f4 f5 (9...d5 10 exd5 ♘xd5 11 ♘xd5 ♕xd5 12 c4 ♕d8 13 ♗d6!) 10 ♗d6 f4 11 ♕h5 f3 12 g3 ♗c7 13 e5 g6 14 ♕g5 ♗xd6

15 exd6 ♘f5 16 ♕xd8 ♘xd8 was played in Wedberg-Nunn, Helsinki 1983, and now the continuation 17 ♗xf5 ♖xf5 18 ♘d4 ♖f8 19 a4! a5 20 ♖a3 would have favoured White.

E:

1	e4	c5
2	♘f3	g6

One of the most important lines in this chapter, since it has occurred many times in grandmaster chess and White can probably only secure an edge against it. Other second moves are very unusual and can be met by normal development, e.g. **2...b6** 3 d4 cxd4 4 ♘xd4 ♗b7 5 ♘c3 ♘c6 (or 5...a6 6 ♗d3 g6 7 f4 ♗g7 8 ♘f3 d6 9 0-0 followed by ♕e1-h4 with attacking chances) 6 ♗f4 ♖c8 7 ♘xc6 dxc6 8 ♕f3 ♕d4 9 ♖d1 ♕c5 10 e5 ♖d8 11 ♖xd8+ ♔xd8 12 ♗e2 ♔e8 13 0-0 f5 14 e6 ♘f6 15 ♖d1 ♘d5 16 ♗e5 1-0 Beliavsky-Quinteros, Vienna 1986, or **2...♕c7** 3 c3 (it is probably not a good idea to play 3 d4 since 3...cxd4 4 ♘xd4 ♘f6 5 ♘c3 a6 followed by ...e5 gives Black a type of Najdorf position in which his king's bishop can still be developed actively at c5 or b4) 3...♘f6 4 e5 ♘d5 5 d4 cxd4 6 cxd4 d6 7 ♘a3 a6 8 ♗d3 e6 9 ♘c4 dxe5 10 dxe5 b5 11 ♘e3 ♗b7 12 0-0 followed by a4 when Black's queenside pawn structure will be weakened.

3   d4

The attempt to reach a Maroczy Bind position by **3 c4** ♗g7 4 d4 can be met by 4...♕a5+, when it is not at all easy for White to maintain any advantage.

3	...	♗g7

3...cxd4 4 ♘xd4 transposes to lines examined earlier, for example **4...♘c6** 5 c4 and **4...♗g7** 5 c4 end up in Chapter 7, **4...♘f6** 5 ♘c3 d6 is Chapter 5, and **4...♘f6** 5 ♘c3 ♘c6 leads to line A in this chapter.

4	dxc5	♕a5+ *(D)*

4...♘a6 5 ♗xa6 ♕a5+ 6 c3 ♕xa6 7 ♕e2 ♕c6 8 ♗e3 ♕xe4 9 ♘bd2 ♕c6 10 0-0 ♘f6 11 ♘d4 ♕c7 12 ♘b5 ♕d8 13 ♗f4 was good for White in Rajna-Nagy, Hungary 1960.

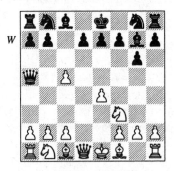

5   ♘c3 *(D)*

Natural, but **5 c3** may be stronger, for example 5...♕xc5 6 ♗e3 ♕c7 7 ♗d4 and now:

1) **7...e5?** 8 ♗e3 ♘f6 9 ♘a3! 0-0 10 ♘b5 ♕c6 11 ♘xe5 ♕xe4 12 ♘xf7! with a large plus for White, Marić-Tringov, Bar 1977.

2) **7...♘f6** 8 e5 ♘g8 (8...♘g4 9 ♘a3! is also better for White) 9 e6 f6 10 exd7+ bxd7 11 ♘a3 ♘c6 12 ♗c4 ♘h6 13 0-0 ♘f7 14 ♖e1 0-0 15 ♗c5 ♗g4 16 ♘b5 ♕c8 17 ♗e2 with a clear plus for White, Nunn-E.Sakhatova, Port Erin 1994.

3) **7...f6** 8 ♘a3 ♘h6 9 ♗c4 a6 10 0-0 e6, Nunn-Kotsur, Moscow OL 1994, and now 11 ♗b3 (threat ♘c4) 11...b5 12 ♕d2 (threatening ♗xf6) 12...♘f7 13 c4 with some advantage for White.

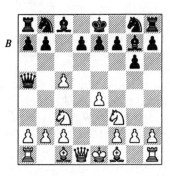

5 ...   ♘f6

Or:

1) **5...♕xc5** 6 ♘d5 e6 7 b4 ♕f8 8 ♘c7+ ♔d8 9 ♘xa8 ♗xa1 10 ♗g5+ ♗f6 11 ♗xf6+ ♘xf6 12 ♕d4 ♕e7?! 13 ♗b5 b6 14 ♘xb6! axb6 15 ♕xb6+ ♔e8 16 0-0 was very good for White in the game Mohrlok-Breazu, Corr. 1987.

2) **5...♗xc3+** 6 bxc3 ♕xc3+ 7 ♗d2 ♕xc5 8 ♗d3 (8 ♗e2 ♘f6 9 e5 ♘g4 10 0-0 ♘xe5 11 ♗e3 ♘xf3+ 12 ♗xf3 ♕c7 13 ♕d4 was also promising in the game Petrov-Limonikov, Corr. 1974) 8...♘f6 (8...d6 9 0-0 ♗g4 10 ♖b1 ♕c7 11 ♖b3 ♘d7 12 ♖c3 ♘c5 13 h3, Ambrož-Petran, Czechoslovakia 1979 gave White more than enough for the pawn) 9 0-0 0-0 10 e5 ♘g4 11 ♖b1 ♘xe5 12 ♖b5 ♘xf3+ 13 ♕xf3 ♕c7 14 ♗h6 ♖e8 15 ♗f5 ♖f8 (*New in Chess* gave 15...f6 as unclear, but 16 ♖e1! appears crushing after 16...♕c3 17 ♗c4+! ♕xc4 18 ♖xf6) 16 ♗xf8 gxf5 17 ♗xe7 d5 18 ♖e1 ♗e6 19 ♗f6 ♘d7 20 ♗d4 ♕d6 21 ♗xf5 ♗xf5 22 ♕xf5 ♘f8 23 ♕g5+ ♘g6 24 h4 ♖f8 25 h5 1-0 Frivaldszky-Monostori, Corr. 1986.

6 ♗d3   ♕xc5
7 ♗e3   ♕a5

7...♕h5 is possible, but I cannot find any practical examples of it.

8 ♕d2   ♘c6

9 0-0 0-0 10 h3 d6 11 a3 ♗e6 12 ♘g5 d5 (12...♗d7 13 f4) 13 exd5 ♗xd5 14 b4 ♕d8 15 ♖ad1 and White has a slight advantage, Sveshnikov-Romanishin, USSR Ch 1977.

Index of Variations